Holy Food

How Cults, Communes, and Religious
Movements Influenced What We Eat
≺ An American History ≻
by Christina Ward

Holy Food: How Cults, Communes, and Religious Movements Influenced What We Eat

ISBN: 978-1934170946

Process Media
1240 W Sims Way #124
Port Townsend WA 98368
www.processmediainc.com

Designed by Ron Kretsch

PROCESS

CONTENTS

Whoever needs,
come and eat.

—Babylonian Talmud. Ta'anit 20b

INTRODUCTION

HERE'S THE QUESTION I'VE BEEN ASKED MANY TIMES: WHY DEDICATE THE PAST five years to researching and writing about American spirituality and food? My answer is this: It's an interesting and far more complex topic than one may think.

Americans are fascinated by identity. We define ourselves by geography, politics, gender, sexuality, religion and so on to create a self that reflects who we believe ourselves to be. The quest for individual expression of identity can often conflict with mainstream society. Yet it is the outliers in mainstream society who have outsized influence on the future. The influencers and trendsetters—whether intentional or accidental—are reacting to and reflecting the various ideas that influenced them. The elements of identity whether inherited, accepted, or constructed become the ingredients that make up who we are. We rarely recognize the subtle forces that have influenced us.

Thinkers, from Plato onward, have contemplated the moral relationship between the desire to eat and the food we actually eat. The idea of "appetites" that reside in us and must be controlled preoccupied all early philosophers. The Greeks, in describing the triumvirate parts of the soul, placed Desire firmly in the stomach. (Reason, of course, was in the head, while Courage was in the chest.) Balancing the three parts of the soul resulted in eudemonia, the good life. The Bhagavad Gita tells stories of ascetic monks who attain spiritual revelations by controlling their appetites for sex, human companionship, and food. While *Holy Food* focuses on American religious and food history, understanding the evolution of those beliefs from its far-flung roots helps make sense of the entire story. Like the nation itself, American food and religious traditions reflect the melting pot of our shared ancestors.

Yet how Americans construct their personal stories and the all-encompassing story of America itself is messy. I believe that history is never static and gains more relevance when we know the personal stories of those who left their mark on our shared culture. Few of us have learned about the history of obscure and forgotten religious movements that held our great-grandparents enthralled. We're unaware of the food trends and fads of the previous centuries. We feel nostalgia for the food of our childhood without understanding what brought those recipes to the table.

As I write in the second decade of the twenty-first century, America seems at war with itself. And in many ways, it is. But, I think, more importantly, that America has always fought cultural battles of identity. You may also be asking, "What the heck do religious identity and culture wars have to do with food?" In *Holy Food*, I try to tell a different history of America. A story that explores how we eat and what we believe, and of the spiritual, legal, and political ideas that have shaped who we are and what we eat.

At first glance, religion and food may seem unlikely partners, but this book is an attempt to show how both are inextricably twined together. To understand the twists and turns of how religious and utopian movements changed how we eat, we need to understand what followers believed and how these beliefs evolved as the United States grew. It may seem that connecting a few rarified facts and long-forgotten people are a diversion from food history, but it's the experiences and ideas of these early thinkers and leaders that lead us to strawberry shortcake and Little Debbies. This intertwined history reveals the lineage of a group's beliefs as each revelation is added to the ones that came before. These lineages say something about our American obsession with authenticity. A people descended from the Lost Tribes of Israel. A preacher trained at the feet of a revered teacher. A cook apprenticed to a Michelin-starred chef. We are more inclined to trust a fisherman and his sole meunière if we can see an indicator of knowledge and authority. Lineages for prophets and chefs serve as that authority. American food history has religious ideas thoroughly mixed into the batter.

Spiritual ideas and food are further muddled with politics and economics, and are defiantly non-linear. A modern group finds the kernel of its truth in a text written hundreds of years ago. A long-forgotten law made to protect or encourage a specific industry in the early 1800s becomes relevant when reinterpreted and challenged. As the saying goes, everything old is new again. The relationship between all these competing interests extends to communes and utopian ideas, which were born out of the notion that people can create a society (a Garden of Eden) that sustains mind, body, and spirit, sometimes with God but often without. Non-religious communal and utopian living experiments posit the question of whether humanity can thrive without religious hierarchies or control. The history of fringe-to-mainstream movements also speaks to the pervasive tension in American culture about who is allowed to write history and what is lost in the silence.

A term gaining academic currency that I use throughout *Holy Food* for this fusion of diverse beliefs recast in new ways is "polyculturism." Polyculturism recognizes the wide-ranging inputs of a fluid spirituality. The word easily applies to foodways as well. To embrace the idea that the United States is a polycultural country recognizes that claims to both purity and authenticity—whether it be claimed in religion or food—are fundamentally flawed. The notion of who owns a story, recipe, and cuisine is fraught with emotional and political subtext. A person growing up in a defined food tradition has a legitimate claim toward authenticity for a specific recipe or cuisine, but what of families with a complex heritage? Dishes and recipes naturally morph and change for all the reasons *Holy Food* explores.[1] Polyculturism also recognizes that previous generations of white historians and food writers have made the grievous error (as some still do today) of thinking that Black and brown people in the Americas are a monolithic body with a singular identity.

---

1   I stand firm: recipes that claim to be an elevated version of a culturally traditional dish "created" by a white (usually male) culinary-school-trained chef are inherently problematic.

I also attempt to acknowledge our entangled feelings surrounding eating rules. Eating disorders are a manifestation of psychological illness when an individual exerts control over the timing, circumstances, quantity, and types of food eaten. Food rules can be coercive and unhealthy. Food rules can be silly. Even the food eaten in relation to spiritual traditions can trigger extreme reactions from joyful nostalgia to dark memories of trauma. We make cultural judgments about the tastes and smells of cuisines unfamiliar to us. We make so-called moral judgments on every type of food, calling it good, bad, or junk. We often take satisfaction in judging people we perceive as enjoying too much food. It's all too easy to mock someone else's rituals and traditions. In *Holy Food*, I detail how we Americans have a history of selecting spiritual and culinary ideas from an overflowing buffet to create something vaguely new. In religious studies, it's called syncretism; in culinary terms, it's called fusion; in practice, it creates the intriguing and convoluted polycultural history of prophets, cooks, gurus, health nuts, and a couple of outright con men.

In my explorations of religious belief, I've concluded that for me, God is man's creation who, when deployed in benign situations, can bring comfort but, when weaponized, is a force for destruction. Yet, I genuinely want to understand why and what people believe and how those beliefs impact our lives. The believers I've met have faith that something better is available to them if they believe hard enough. I envy their certainty.

I've spoken with both the saved and the damned. I've listened to personal accounts from people who lived in high-control groups. I've read scholarly journals and academic research—about food, utopias, and religious movements. I am thankful to every single person who devoted time to tell their truth. I am incredibly grateful for scholars in the exponentially growing field of food studies for their research. I have had the pleasure of speaking to and tangling with brilliant women studying and teaching at colleges and universities across North America.

My goal with *Holy Food* is twofold: to tell the uniquely American story of how New Religious Movements and utopian ideas influenced our food culture, and to bring forward recipes that are historically resonant and affiliated with a specific group. For me, religion and food have been the prevailing obsessions of my life; I hope I did a good job sharing some of the ecstatic highs and somber lows in this delicious history of the United States.

NOTES ON SUBSTANCE AND STYLE

Many of the pre-1920s recipes are updated for modern cooking techniques, as the Shakers and Rappites assumed anyone reading a recipe already knew how to cook on a wood stove.[2] Pre-1950s recipes were more of a guide to ingredients and notes on specific techniques than the step-by-step instructions of modern recipes.

---

2   Many modern cooks are baffled by old recipes that call for a "moderate oven" or "slow oven." Wood-burning or coal-burning ovens didn't have a temperature regulator nor did most homes have an oven-proof thermometer (it wasn't invented yet), so baking instructions weren't given at a precise Fahrenheit measurement. It was the skill of the cook to know her oven. A cook would hold their hand over the hot oven and count, using that as a basis for estimating the temperature; a longer time equated to a lower temperature. In using a wood-burning stove, one would add wood and stoke the fire in the morning. Items requiring a "hot oven" would be cooked when the fire was most robust; items needing a "moderate oven" would be baked later, when the oven had cooled. Depending on the needs of the household, the fire might be extinguished overnight, or the embers banked until morning, so a tired cook need only to add fuel to the fire and not start a new one. Another thing: many old bread recipes call for the dough to set and rise overnight on the stove because the residual warmth would help the yeast expand. Here are the Fahrenheit temperature equivalents: Very slow oven: 200 to 250°F. Slow oven: 300 to 325°F. Moderate oven: 350 to 375°F. Hot oven: 400 to 450°F. Fast oven: 450 to 500°F.

It would be an easy task to find the most illogical and bad-tasting examples that I discovered and include them so we can laugh and mock what this group or that group ate. In researching cookbooks, archives, and interviews with believers, there are more than enough examples of what modern cooks would consider unpalatable. Instead, I take a different path and present recipes that give a sense of a group's traditions and might actually taste good. A small group of friends and neighbors spent their pandemic days testing recipes, and provided notes. Each recipe was tested twice by different cooks of varying skill levels to ensure no recipe was beyond the range of an average cook. A few recipes that looked good on paper were rejected during testing and tasting. (Looking at you, True Light Beavers; the Mock Chopped Liver was vile.) As all taste is subjective, I know there may be a few misses for some readers.

Some of the recipes are taken from cookbooks published by a religious group or commune. This is America, where everything can be monetized. I lightly touch on the purely American phenomenon of the "church cookbook," but for communal-living societies, developing revenue streams like restaurants, preserved foods, and cookbooks were all part and parcel of keeping the enclave financially solvent. The cookbooks also served as a tool to help new converts acclimate to a prescribed diet. Sometimes the cookbooks are another method of proselytizing to potential recruits. And because of our shared and universal culture of hospitality, people are likelier to listen to your message if they had just shared a tasty meal. Man does not live on bread alone.

Readers may notice that there aren't many "meaty" recipes. That is not my personal choice, as it reflects a prevailing trend of vegetarianism in a community's foodways. Religious groups have found words in holy books and experienced divine revelations leading them to vegetarianism. Meat was also the most expensive protein to serve. A commune that struggled for cash ate a lot of cheap beans. The included recipes also reflect the era of their creation. It takes a few decades of groats for Americans raised with meat-filled diets to figure out how to get the most flavor from vegetables. I've omitted recipes and sections of recipes that instruct the maker on how to create "gluten loaf" (seitan) and homemade tofu. These instructions would have been critically important to newly converted believers unfamiliar with the diet and before the widespread availability of commercially produced meat substitutes, but less needed now. The recipes are, with very few modifications, as the group conceived them. Some recipes, specifically those created during the later decades of the twentieth century, reflect global influences but are not authentic to the region or culture. What the recipes do reflect is polyculturalism in a group's religious practices—cherry-picking elements without fully understanding the whole.

And a few words about hermeneutics: nonfiction writing about obscure topics is a labor of obsessive love. The facts here have been checked to the best of my ability, and the conclusions are solely my own and based on my lengthy and wide-ranging research. I borrow an attitude from the legendary chronicler of early American New Religious Movements, Gilbert Seldes (*The Stammering Century*, 1928). He eschewed multiple academic-style citations in a text as a superfluous curlicue. There are far too many footnotes in *Holy Food*, but they intend to provide deeper context. At the end of the book, you'll find a bibliography of books, journals, and scholarly papers that have been indispensable to my research, but in the spirit of Seldes, academic-style citations are few and only when I feel they benefit the reader.

I am atheist. I have no belief in a God (or gods), but I exist in an American culture that has been informed, mainly, by Christianity. I make no judgment on the nature of any religious belief, only on the actions of maleficent believers. There are occasions when lines from various sacred texts are referenced, and for clarity's sake, I've footnoted the exact quote and from which holy book it's taken.

I've also worked to bring forward the role of Black Americans in the development of American religious beliefs and food culture. As a white American with European immigrant grandparents on my maternal side and Puritans going back to the 1600s on my paternal side, critics could dismiss my attempts to tell Black stories as "wokeness" or malign them as pandering. In answer, I invoke the spirit of public-school teacher and Black Panther Mrs. Underwood, and the memory of our fourth-grade classroom filled with white and Black kids making and wearing dashikis as we learned about Malcolm X. I would rather embrace the contributions of Black Americans to religion and food culture than omit them based on the ongoing debates about who can tell what story of America. I choose to include the stories, recipes, and ideas from many sources, not just white Americans. I'm exceedingly grateful for the many Black scholars and independent researchers working to document and preserve Black American history. I want to read more about food and religion written by Black people. Learning more about the lives and work of Black Americans has given me a richer, more nuanced understanding of American history. And it is the personal narratives of Black writers throughout the past four hundred years that have helped me reckon with my own family stories. Black history is American history.

I am grateful to have met so many generous people who shared meals and stories. If anything, what I've learned and what I hope you take from *Holy Food* is that our personal histories are an essential part of "official" history. Please keep telling your family stories around the dinner table, so they are remembered and written into books like this one.

In a nod to the most common complaint about modern recipes and cookbooks weighed down by notes and anecdotes, *Holy Food* is organized into sections that place recipes after the history of that era. Can readers skip the history and go directly to the recipes? Of course, you can! It's a fundamental American character trait to use what we like and reject the rest. Yet I do hope that while the Mazdaznan Dough Gods are baking or the Hare Krishnas' version of burfi is simmering, you explore the fascinating stories of just how outré religious ideas and American cuisine have shaped our bodies and beliefs.

One
IN THE BEGINNING...

AS WITH ALL THINGS, WE BEGIN IN THE BEGINNING. AN APERITIF, IF YOU WILL. THIS overview of the earliest documented history of how food and religion are enmeshed serves as the mother sauce for every rule and recipe that follows for the next few millennia. And again, we uncover that no recipe or belief is as straightforward as it may seem.

Humans have always had rules about eating. Sometimes the rules are about what can and cannot be eaten. Sometimes the rules are about when you can eat and, of course, when you shouldn't eat. Having rules helped humans differentiate edible plants from poisonous ones. Our brains evolved to give us a happy jolt when we eat foods containing vital nutrients—these are the sweet, salty, and fatty foods—once rare in hunter-gatherer communities. As humankind evolved, so did our palates. We developed taste preferences and began to cultivate plants and animals for our delectation.

At the same time, humans were inventing agrarian society and discovering the limits of the world around them. Early people were challenged to explain the unknowns of the universe, and in response, our spectacularly versatile brains came to know God. Or gods, as the case may be. We are storytellers, mythmakers, creators, inventors, liars, seekers, sinners, and believers. We see divinity in the planet's gifts and, during our thousands of years of existence, have tried mightily to find a truth. Over time, rules about food became a way of identifying members of a tribe and bringing them together in familiar ritual. Many of our gods have incredibly detailed and specific ideas about how we should eat. There are millennia-old traditions that, when followed, not only honor a god but ensure a high level of cleanliness that would bring tears of joy to a food-safety scientist. Are we so contrary that we need God to tell us to wash our hands? It seems like we did and still do.

Feasting in thanks and celebration is universal. Fasting is less so in modern America. We offer up our pleasure and pain to God in hope of desired results. For an awfully long portion of human history, our gods were bound by geography and governments. Religion and ruler twined together, often in opposition, with believers at the mercy of not their god but their king, who, in many cultures, was also a god. These ancient rituals become essential to us as they are the root of our modern religious systems.

The pervasive influence of all sorts of religious beliefs on food is uniquely American. Yes, spiritual practices meld with culture and geography to create a regional-specific cuisine, but only in the United States in a relatively short time did a people transform (and destroy) one way of living and invent an entirely new way of living. It was through the will of man that the land we know as the United States was colonized by people with new thoughts about God and how best to serve Him (mostly Him, rarely Her). These settlers[1] brought the food traditions of their homelands, then learned to adapt recipes to suit the grains, meats, and vegetables at hand while they remade the territory with their vision of how best to live in God's perpetual grace.

Many of the earliest colonizers came to the United States as part of separatist religious movements outlawed by their home countries. These sects were considered unorthodox and even blasphemous to European state-sponsored religions. These groups were actively encouraged by their home countries to colonize the New World to ease the tension these religious-minded groups caused for the ruling government and act as a non-militarized occupying force. It was a win-win scenario for the European powers of the 1600s. Without rehashing all American history, the occupying settlers (in a historical instance of cognitive dissonance) did not enjoy being ruled by a faraway government . . . even as they subjugated Indigenous residents and engaged in slaveholding. After nearly two centuries of steady immigration from Europe to North America, the descendants of the early religious settlers decided to strike out on their own and declare independence.

It is for this reason, and this reason alone, that the United States encoded 'freedom of religion' in its founding documents.[2] This first of the five freedoms prevents the government from establishing a state-sponsored religion and prevents the government from favoring either by law or by decree any single religion over another. The framers—a mix of Deists[3] and mainstream Protestants—of the Constitution were wary of the new country becoming a theocracy, and rightly so, as much of Europe was under the dual sovereigns of king and Christ. It is the second clause of the sentence that makes us the country we are today: "prohibiting the free exercise thereof." Those five words ensured that America is a fantastical chaos machine churning through the half-baked notions of prophets and madmen.

We may personally disagree on who exactly is a prophet of God, but the ideas these prophets explored—and how they approached feeding themselves and their flocks—resonate with us today. We become American through our stomachs, and many a new believer has found God over the dinner plate at a church, temple, or dining hall. Is there an easier way to feed ourselves? Surely, yes. But can we both feed ourselves and save our souls? Our American experiment is peppered with fascinating characters, each trying to carve out a version of their idealized vision. It is only in the flawed soil of the United States that a prophet can attempt such an audacious concept. A plan for living. A recipe for life.

---

1   I use the word "settlers" which can also be read as "invaders." The challenge of telling an American story is getting the language correct. I recognize that Europeans coming to the North American continent actively worked to eliminate Native people who existed on the land for millennia. I attempt to introduce the people who populate this book where they are in history—not to excuse their thinking and behavior but to better understand how our strange country came into being.
2   "Congress shall make no law respecting an establishment of religion, or prohibiting the free exercise thereof; or abridging the freedom of speech, or of the press; or the right of the people peaceably to assemble, and to petition the Government for a redress of grievances."
3   Deism is a philosophical belief that rejects revelation as a source of religious knowledge and asserts that reason and observation of the natural world are sufficient to establish the existence of a God.

The Landing of the Pilgrims, 1620. **Engraving by Nathaniel Currier, courtesy of the Library of Congress.**

MAN'S CONTEMPLATION OF THE NATURE OF EXISTENCE AND RELEVANCE TO THE universe at large begins to solidify into something we recognize as modern around 500 BCE. Not to say that humans hadn't previously engaged in navel-gazing, but that our modern concepts of belief took shape during the three-hundred-year period from approximately 500 BCE to 200 BCE. Religion and philosophy become concepts that we still reference today. Travel influenced the burgeoning growth in ideas as empires grew. Trading routes collectively known as "the silk road" brought merchandise, food, and ideas 5,000 miles overland from Athens to Chengdu. One can imagine a traveling merchant coming to the Agora to learn a bit about Greek philosophy and share ideas from his homeland.

In contrast, sea routes took travelers around the Arabian Peninsula and Indian subcontinent and through the Indonesian archipelago (the Spice Islands) to reach the Chinese port of Guangzhou. It is an interesting thought exercise to imagine, as some have, that Pythagoras, Gautama Buddha, Mahavira, and Confucius were contemporaries and knew of each other's work. The notion is possible when we consider the multitude of new ideas promulgated during this three-hundred-year cultural zeitgeist of ancient civilizations.

It was during this era that Confucius' concepts of personal responsibility and morality were written. His philosophical writings use parables and examples of correct living but are absent from any food admonishments. Confucius is conscientious about following the tradition of feasting to honor ancestors and the ritual planting and harvest celebrations, but no single food item is forbidden. Yet, Confucius' idea that people are inherently good but flawed and need to be taught the rules of correct behavior fits neatly into modern belief systems.

Pythagoras is remembered as a mathematician, but he was also a philosopher who defined the Greek concept of *metempsychosis* or the "transmigration of souls." This concept—that a human is more than their physical carcass and contains an ineffable essence which travels throughout all realms of existence to temporarily reside in a human body—later becomes a theological tenet for many New Religious Movements. His ideas are similar to Vedic and later Buddhist concepts of reincarnation. Pythagoras was on shakier ground when explaining where that essence—or soul—goes when one's body is deceased. He suggested that spirit could be reborn in any living thing and theorized that one's soul could be transferred to a cow or dog. Or a bean.

"A fabis abstineto" (Abstain from beans). A woodcut engraving of Pythagoras from a Parisian book, c. 1515.

Pythagorean disciples were vegetarians who shunned beans to avoid consuming a potential soul. No one is sure why beans and not other plants, but scholars suggest that because beans resemble the human fetus, shunning them would have been a symbolic gesture. Fava beans are associated with Hades and Egyptian death myths, with which Pythagoras would have been quite familiar, so that's another possibility. Other philosophical wags have made the simple conclusion that Pythagoras was prone to flatulence and avoided eating them out of an abundance of caution. When building a religion, sometimes a teacher, prophet, or guru imposes personal preferences.

East of Athens, the Persian "greats" ruled from the eastern Mediterranean Sea to the banks of the Indus River. The Persian rulers found it wise political policy to allow inhabitants of conquered lands to worship their existing gods. The Persian kings would claim to either be that god or his high priest, whichever was the most efficient to ensure peace. As long as a god didn't agitate against the Persian government, believers were free to pursue their worship practices. Under the Achaemenids' occupation of the Levant, the people of Abraham and Moses codified the Book of Leviticus. As a result, the twenty-four books of Jewish scripture—properly called *Tanakh*, an acronym comprised of the first syllable of the Hebrew name of the three major sections considered the "Jewish Bible," *Torah* (the instructions or laws), *Nevi'im* (prophets), and *Ketuvim* (writings)—now have a recognizable form. This is a significant development as many religious food rules are sourced from the *Tanakh*, which was later reorganized and recast as the Old Testament of the Christian Bible. While in Babylon, thousands of distinct gods with particular tastes needed regular sexual appeasement and food sacrifices.

In the highlands of now-western Iran, Zarathustra (Zoroaster) might have heard (or hallucinated under the haze of the sacred plant-based drink *haoma*)[4] God's voice via fire. He revealed to Zarathustra the dual nature of a single God—a being that encompasses all that is good but created evil to test mankind. This concept originated the complicated thesis of multiple Godheads like the Christian trinitarian concept of God the Father, God the Son, and God the Holy Spirit. Or like the Process Church of the 1960s, which believed in triumvirate gods.

Siddhartha Gautama received and began sharing his vision of enlightenment in the northern plains of the Ganges. He does not refute the timeless Vedic gods but offers a new pathway to spiritual awakening. His rules include an ascetic lifestyle that forgoes mundane human pleasures to focus on honing the physical self into a wholly spiritual being. To become the Buddha—the one who has gone and come—Gautama renounced the world of men and allowed others to join him in his monastic pursuit of nirvana, the end of suffering.

The Indian subcontinent had a robust system of hierarchical gods representing facets of humanity. English colonizers coined the colloquialism "Hindu" in the early 1800s to describe the vast, decentralized pantheon of gods and traditions. German-born British scholar Max Müller founded a new field of research, Religious Studies, to better understand Indian spiritual practices. Müller's work rejected Indian matriarchal traditions and elevated gods that he saw as having a Christian equivalency. Today, we find "comparative" studies unsupported by objective research, yet because the past two hundred years of religious study have been informed by Müller and his successors' work, we must acknowledge that many New Religious Movements stand on crumbling feet of theological clay. This is quite true when looking at Hindu-based movements. Müller was an "orientalist" whose work connected the ancient Aryan people of central and north Asia to nineteenth-century definitions of whiteness. At the time, Müller's view of the complex Indian belief system was considered blasphemous, as mainstream religious leaders were outraged that he compared Christian deities to lesser foreign gods.

Hinduism has many denominations, and within those denominations are sects and a variety of traditions. Of particular interest is the concept of "Sant Mat," which emerged in the thirteenth century. Sant Mat is the veneration of holy men, devotional teachers, and gurus. Sikhism is of the Sant Mat tradition, as are many yogic-influenced teachers who began visiting the United States in the 1920s. The concept of an anointed spiritual teacher is firmly within traditional Hindu and Sant Mat beliefs, but essential to the development of American New Religious Movements is how self-appointed Sants came to dominate twentieth-century consciousness.

The Mahavira is credited with solidifying the belief system of the Jains of the Indian subcontinent. The Jains have no creator god and believe all living things are eternal and vital. The death of any creature harms the soul. We'll see the idea of "ahimsa," the avoidance of killing living things, resurface many times in the beliefs of New Religious Movements. Jains follow a strict vegetarian diet to reduce what they believe is the wanton killing of animals for food. Americans use the word "karma" as a cosmic shorthand to mean balance, yet for

---

4   *Haoma*, or soma, or *hum* is mentioned in the Avesta and the Vedas. Haoma is a beverage made from hallucinogenic mushrooms and the ephedra plant. (Ephedra is the source of the stimulant ephedrine.)

devoted Jains, Hindus, and Buddhists, it is a sophisticated ideological and religious tenet that takes multiple lifetimes to completely understand.

The Islamic phrase "People of the Book" describes Jews, Christians, and Muslims whose holy scripture narrative overlaps. All three traditions affirm (to some degree) the teachings in the Old Testament and Tanakh. The Book does not include the Gospel, or New Testament, as that is a wholly Christian document. Though Islam recognizes Jesus as *a* Messiah and the harbinger for Muhammad, the Quran is clear that Jesus is not God incarnate. The Hadith is a secondary text filled with Muhammad's history and wisdom and is often used to guide laws and behavior. In Judaism, scholars dismiss the Gospel as not a holy book and consider Jesus a bit of a high-stepper and definitely not the Messiah. These and every other sacred document mentioned have inspired a New Religious Movement.

Buddhism too has a version of a messiah-like figure, the Maitreya,[5] who is expected to be the future Buddha. The Islamic tradition of the Mahdi, the righteous one who will lead the faithful during the end times, isn't quite a messianic figure yet still a revered and holy one. Many have claimed to be the Maitreya or the Messiah but have not provided definitive proof. Regardless of the religious affiliation, proving oneself to be a god-like being is challenging at best. Yet, waiting on, predicting, and sometimes acting like a (the) Messiah/Maitreya—the human incarnation of God sent to redeem the world—is the focus of many belief systems.

The Book is the fulcrum on which many of the earliest American religious movements teeter. In its multiple translations and interpretations, there is no singular and universal revealed truth, though many have claimed to have received a divine message. Every variety of Christian church rejected the Old Testament's strict food prohibitions and rules as no longer necessary because God had given them a new covenant through Jesus, who essentially rewrote the rules with the Gospel or New Testament. The Catholic church consolidated the stories and testimonies contained within the Book for the past two millennia and has, for the most part, succeeded in keeping its faith dogmatically intact. That orthodoxy, and the fact that until the 1960s implementation of Vatican II reforms, Catholic Mass was in Latin and under the control of a priest caste, meant there was little room for freelance preachers and prophets to lure away the faithful.

Schisms in practice and interpretation of any belief system, of every religious belief, are the genesis of every New Religious Movements, many that have become accepted and mainstream. The most popular American religions today began as schismatic offshoots of an established religion. The early Catholic Church dramatically split in 1054 due to bishopric political and theological differences to become the Roman Catholic Church and the Orthodox Catholic Church. The sixteenth-century Protestant movement broke from Catholicism, creating a new direction in Christianity that allowed believers to speak directly to God without a priestly intermediary. Hinduism was also subject to regional and priestly influences, giving rise to

---

5   The word *Maitreya* is often translated, especially in American usage, as World Teacher. The concept of the Maitreya is Buddhist in origins, and refers to the future Buddha who is to come. According to Buddhist tradition, Maitreya is a pure seeker who will appear on Earth in the future, achieve complete enlightenment, and teach the pure dharma. Maitreya has taken on apocalyptic meaning since the twentieth century as Eastern religious traditions have been adopted and often misunderstood by Westerners. Many American cults and New Religious Movement leaders have proclaimed themselves the Maitreya.

Holy Food

elevating the worship of one god over another. Islam also has distinct sects that have each produced smaller sects. Americans often make the mistake of thinking of Islam as a monolithic religious body, when in fact it is a diverse practice influenced by geography and charismatic thinkers from its founding to today. Sunni, Shi'a, Sufi, and Ahmadiyya are the main branches of Islam, but within those are dozens of schismatic groups, sects, and heretics (depending on perspective). Many heretical and schismatic Islamic sects revolve around deciding who is the Mahdi, just as Christian-inspired groups debate who is the reborn Jesus Christ.

Jewish faithful have an additional religious text, the Talmud, which is a compendium of teaching, philosophy, folklore, and history. Jewish cultural tradition has long encouraged the study of the Talmud to better understand the meaning of the text, ensuring that different readers will interpret the words differently. Finally, there is also a collection of "mystical" Judaic texts that gained popularity with rabbinical scholars during the Middle Ages, collectively called Kabbalah. The Kabbalah, once the purview of devoted rabbis, came to prominence in the United States during the early 2000s when it was co-opted by a polycultural New Age group that attracted famous devotees.

A section of the Torah has an outsized influence on religious food culture: Leviticus. The third "book" of The Book outlines God's words to Moses to be shared with the Israelites. It also includes what are commonly called "the rules," especially Leviticus 11, the kashrut, or food laws. This section details what believers can and cannot eat, and specific rituals and rules about food preparation. The prohibition against pork and shrimp is well-known and is also followed by Muslims. Many American Protestant sects follow variants of the rules as laid out in Leviticus 11 as well as verses in Exodus and Genesis.

These food rules were elaborated upon in the seventeenth century by conservative rabbis who felt that the anti-Semitic pogroms sweeping across Eastern Europe were G-d's punishment for not following His laws closely enough. The Hasidic, or Piety, movement bore similarity to Christian piety movements of the same era. The Jewish orthodox movement also gave rise to one of the largest sects—the Lubavitchers. They emerged from Ukraine in 1775 from the Hasidic tradition of a patriarchal lineage of rabbis or anointed rabbinical teachers. Lubavitchers came to the United States in the 1930s and are a fundamentalist Jewish sect who seek to carve out a separate existence in modern society just as the Puritans did hundreds of years earlier.

T HE EDENIC COVENANT[6] IS COMPRISED OF THE VERSES IN GENESIS THAT PROMISE man dominion over the Earth and every living creature on it. Again, interpretation is key, as many people have taken the verses to mean that God wants us to be vegetarians, while others claim it means that everything is edible. Can all this scriptural text analysis become overwhelming? Absolutely! The difficulty in understanding various readings of The Book is why prophets and preachers have success in recruiting new adherents: having it spelled out with clear rules of behavior is much easier for an average believer to follow. And, if one's entire family and village have signed on to a system of belief, a person is more likely to follow the

6   Genesis 1, 28–30 (NIV): "Behold, I have given you every plant yielding seed that is on the surface of all the earth, and every tree which has fruit yielding seed; it shall be food for you; and to every beast of the earth and to every bird of the sky and to every thing that moves on the earth which has life, I have given every green plant for food."

edicts due to social and cultural pressures.

Scholars (and heretics) cite even more obscure lines taken from every section of the Old and New Testament as inspiration for a diet.[7] The Manicheans are an interesting example of early Christian schismatic thinking. The Manicheans were followers of the prophet Mani, who lived in the Persian highlands circa 215–274 CE and was an early polycultural thinker who blended all the prevailing regional beliefs into a single neo-Christian movement. As with many obscure belief systems, the details are complicated. Manicheans believed that Jesus was a being of light comprised of holy Light particles and had an equal opposite in the Devil, who of course, was composed of evil Dark particles. People were also comprised of a combination of Light and Dark particles which affected their

Chart showing "Clean and Unclean Foods" developed by followers of the British-Israelites in the 1880s based on Jewish food laws. This chart has been modified and reused by other fringe nationalist and Christian groups.

behavior and relationship with God. Manicheans also believed, like Pythagoras and those following the Vedic gods, in reincarnation with the possibility of a soul reborn into a plant or animal. Foods were categorized as either Light or Dark.[8] For a Manichean, the goal was to consume Light foods and avoid Dark ones. Even the act of harvesting and preparing a Light food brought potential pain to the Light particles within the food item, which then continued a cycle of atonement for perpetuating evil.

The Manichean movement spread westward along the Mediterranean until the Manichean faithful tried the patience of St. Augustine of Hippo. He makes note of and mocks their Light and Dark eating system in *Against Faustus the Manichean*, written approximately in the year 400 CE. As Augustine said, "Christ never taught you that you should not pluck a vegetable for fear of committing homicide." The Manichean Heresy was popular for about two centuries and bedeviled the early Church so much that the Pope finally sent Augustine to debate

---

7   Keep in mind that there are as many translations of the Bible as there are recipes for tuna fish casserole. These many and often discordant translations and iterations are cause for both scholarly discussion and schismatic practices.
8   "Light foods" are plants and vegetables that grow above ground. Dark foods are anything grown below the earth and animal products. One may also wonder how the Light particles and souls trapped within the food are released. The answer, to the delight of eight-year-olds everywhere, is through excrement. Yes, to the Manichean, every bowel movement was an act of creation.

Mani, Persian prophet, founder of Manichaeism, scene, his beheaded body is displayed at the gates of Gundeshapur, miniature painting, Baghdad, 1307–1308.

Manichean priests in an attempt to stamp out the movement. Manicheaism also spread eastward and challenged the state-sponsored ancestor/nature worship-based religion of the Chinese Dynasties, who referred to the Manicheans as "vegetarian demon worshippers." Both Western and Eastern powers legislatively banned the religion and then escalated persecution of believers with a series of genocidal exterminations. The Manichean Heresy is important to note because variations of their original syncretism of Jewish, Christian, Jain, Buddhist, and Zoroastrian ideas about food resurface in the twentieth century, in many of the writings by New Religious Movements that claim Jesus Christ as a space alien or as one of many harbingers from another dimension.[9]

---

9   Readers may also recognize the Manichean concepts of dueling good and evil gods within us as part of the core beliefs of the 1960s–70s-era Process Church of the Final Judgment.

FEASTS & FASTING

I DO NEED TO MAKE NOTE OF THE CANNIBALISTIC RITUAL OF EATING THE FLESH OF the dead as part of religious ceremony. Rarely seen in the twenty-first century, but once prevalent in nomadic and small-band tribal cultures, the consumption of human flesh was more than symbolic, it was a tangible transference of the wisdom and power of the deceased to the next generation. Cannibalistic impulses and traditions are still with us in symbolic forms. The Roman and Orthodox Catholic transubstantiation ritual of investing bread with the spirit of God and then consuming it is a direct link to the idea that God is *within* us. The words of the Roman Catholic consecration ritual are quite clear:

"Therefore, O Lord, we pray: may this same Holy Spirit graciously sanctify these offerings, that they may become the Body and Blood of our Lord Jesus Christ for the celebration of this great mystery, which he himself left us as an eternal covenant.

For when the hour had come for him to be glorified by you, Father most holy, having loved his own who were in the world, he loved them to the end: and while they were at supper he took bread, blessed and broke it, and gave it to his disciples, saying: TAKE THIS, ALL OF YOU, AND EAT OF IT, FOR THIS IS MY BODY, WHICH WILL BE GIVEN UP FOR YOU. In a similar way, taking the chalice filled with the fruit of the vine, he gave thanks, and gave the chalice to his disciples, saying:

TAKE THIS, ALL OF YOU, AND DRINK FROM IT, FOR THIS IS THE CHALICE OF MY BLOOD, THE BLOOD OF THE NEW AND ETERNAL COVENANT, WHICH WILL BE POURED OUT FOR YOU AND FOR MANY FOR THE FORGIVENESS OF SINS. DO THIS IN MEMORY OF ME."[10]

The Protestant Reformation rejected transubstantiation. Martin Luther took an intellectualized approach to Holy Communion as a symbolic ritual of the faithful. Holy Supper remains the focal point of Protestant church services and open to everyone. Catholic teaching restricts taking the Eucharist only to those who have gone through the canonical rites of passage

---

10   There are variations of the Eucharistic prayer as written by saints and doctors of the Catholic church, but the version cited above is the common, post-Vatican II iteration as used in most American Catholic churches.

of Sacraments of Penance and First Holy Communion and have been recently Confessed. (Readers should rest assured that all veterans of Catholic schooling can share at least one anecdote of nuns and lay teachers punishing the most egregious of "I'm eating Jesus" jokes.)

Aside from Holy Supper, Christian tradition also requires believers to fast as an act of penance, supplication, or ascetic purity. Food restriction in the name of penance, the belief that offering one's suffering to God earns His favor, returns to American consciousness in the most restrictive of high-control religious groups. Groups that are defined as cults usually have extensive rules about eating and other activities. We know from stories told by former cult members that food deprivation is used to control people—sometimes to the point of severe illness. Fasting later morphs into a dietary fad during the 1920s when a small group of German expatriates in California engage in the practice. Studies by health researchers have found that adhering to a low-calorie diet that includes fasting can be a viable method to increase longevity. Though Christianity has an outsized influence in the United States, every modern mainstream religion has designated fast days, like the prohibition of eating during daylight hours during the month of Ramadan in Islam. Most are short fasts that end with a feast.

The Catholic church has relaxed its fasting rules since the modernization movement resulting in the Vatican II Council edicts. Where once believers had to refrain from eating meat every Friday, the practice is now reserved for Lenten Holy Friday. Traditions take precedent over papal decrees in the Great Lakes region of the United States. Immigrant Catholics took advantage of the readily available fresh-caught perch and began serving fried fish dinners to parishioners in church basements from Buffalo to Sheboygan. During the Prohibition era, bars adopted the Friday Fish Fry to generate income. The Fish Fry has passed into American food culture and is enjoyed by everyone, and inspired McDonald's Filet-o-Fish sandwich.

The Christian Lenten season—the forty days leading to Easter Sunday—is considered the holiest of the liturgical calendar and calls for fasting. Though as we see throughout the evolution of traditional and newer religions, the rules are malleable. Those with Catholic backgrounds may remember childhood days of "giving up" something for Lent: sometimes a morally transgressive behavior like swearing, but most commonly a food. Giving up candy, sweets, soda pop, chocolate, desserts, and the like were the go-to items for many a pious kid, though nuns and parents alike were vigilant against the sassy among us who "gave up" vegetables and other disliked foods.

Those committed to a religious life in a sequestered community endured a rigorous Lenten fast to remind them of the suffering of Jesus Christ and offer their own discomfort as penance for sins. A fundamental belief of Catholicism is that through the act of confessing and the consequent atonement, one can reduce one's personal sin burden, and avoid having the judgment of St. Peter (keeper of the gates of heaven) be the proverbial thumbs-down resulting in a trip to hell, or maybe that in-between place of purgatory. Fasting was meted out by confessors as penance for specific sins. But penance wasn't doled out arbitrarily. Penitentials were guides for priests and abbots hearing confessions that prescribed acts of atonement for a host of sinful doings. The English penitential associated with Archbishop of Canterbury Theodore, circa 700 CE, is an example of the use of fasting as punishment.

"If he defiles himself, he is to abstain from meat for four days. He who desires to fornicate himself and is not able to do so, he must fast for 40 days or 20 days. If he is a boy and does it often, either he is to fast 20 days or one is to whip him."

Much of Anglo-Saxon law is based on the early penitentials, and one can see the relationship between priests prescribing a seven-year bread and water fast for confessed sins and a prison serving inmates unpalatable food, or in the worst instances, bread and water.

Yet not everyone received the same punishment for the same sins. During the Medieval period the disparity between the wealthy ruling class and the disempowered laity was so vast that the Catholic church allowed penances for the wealthy to be subcontracted out to others. The Medici and their compatriots could sin without remorse as they would hire poor people to take on the penance of fasting. Churches offered the penitents-for-hire extra indulgences—a reduction on their karmic balance sheet, to mix religious metaphors.

"Sin eaters" took on a ritualized performance in Protestant Wales and western England. When someone died, the family called upon an impoverished man from the community to consume specially prepared bread and beer over the body of the deceased. It was believed that the act would transfer any unconfessed sins from the dead person to the sin eater, who would be paid for this service.

The practice has survived as a symbolic rather than actual transference of sin in the United States and is influenced by the culture of origin. People with Bavarian ancestors may remember hearing about a "corpse cake" placed on the chest of the deceased, then eaten by the closest relative. Dutch *doed-koecks* (dead-cakes)[11] were brought to New York by early colonists in the seventeenth century. Dead-cakes were given to mourners as a ritualized form of sin eating whose original meaning had passed into homey tradition. We would recognize dead-cakes today as a large sugar cookie flavored with caraway and marked with the initials of the deceased. The practice of sin eating faded in the late nineteenth century, but surely our traditions of eating and drinking after the funeral of a loved one are born from many cultural food rituals associated with death.

Entangled in our funerary customs are foods associated with mourning rituals as prepared by American religious groups. Unlike dead-cakes, these foods do not convey symbolic or ritualistic purpose as they are specific to specific to a time, people, and tradition; examples include the infamous "funeral potatoes"[12] favored by Latter-Day Saints providing food to assembled mourners and the "funeral pie" prepared by the Pennsylvania Dutch. (The misnomer "Pennsylvania Dutch" refers to German Anabaptists—Amish and Mennonites—that settled in southeastern Pennsylvania who described themselves as *Deutsch*, the German word for, well, German.) Funeral pie is made with a single lard-pastry crust filled with sweetened raisin filling. Today, it may not seem like an extravagant delicacy, but raisins were an expensive and difficult-to-create ingredient. To make raisins, one must harvest grapes, then remove the seeds of each grape one at a time by hand, then dehydrate and store. In Anabaptist communities, the raisin pie was made for grieving neighbors as an expression of their respect for the deceased and their

11   Recipe for New York dead-cakes as published in *Colonial Days in Old New York* by Alice Morse Earle (1896): "Fourteen pounds of flour, six pounds of sugar, five pounds of butter, one quart of water, two teaspoonfuls of pearlash, two teaspoonfuls of salt, one ounce of caraway seed. Cut in thick slices four inches in diameter."
12   See page 88 for the recipe for "Heavenly Funeral Potatoes."

Holy Food

A Welsh funeral of 1814, showing the custom of passing food across the body of the deceased. Hand-colored engraving by I. Havell for *The Cambrian Popular Antiquities*.

family. It came to symbolize death and mourning. By the early 1900s, raisin pie was *only* served at funerals. To bring a raisin pie to any other gathering was considered, at best, bad manners, and at worst, to wish death upon another.

Pennsylvania Dutch funerary feasts grew into conspicuous displays of wealth that were seemingly out of step with a religious culture that in every other circumstance was conservative. German Anabaptists embraced hearty and simple fare, but a funeral became the event where cooks trotted out their best recipes and luxurious foods. While mourners brought foods for the family and to be added to the heaving tables, the host family was expected to provide substantial repast for those who traveled great distance to pay their respects. Preferred foods were long-lasting and didn't require cold storage. The feast would feature multiple breads made from expensive fine white flours instead of heavier whole-grain breads. Families would bring hard cheeses, preserved fruits, and cured meats. Newspapers covering large funerals of prominent residents would note the growing issue of "funeral crashers" who attended services to gain access to the feast. An early twentieth-century joke makes light of the tradition by declaring that a man should save his best ham for his funeral.

Funeral feasts are still a large part of how Americans ritualize death. Multi-day feasts of the last century have given way to banquet halls and restaurants where friends and family gather to remember a loved one and eat well in their name. Jewish families bring deli trays laden with pickled vegetables, cured fish, and pastrami to families observing *shiva*—the traditional seven-day period of mourning after the burial of a loved one. Church basements are filled with the potluck of casseroles made to feed mourners and sustain a grieving family. In all the infinite ways to be human, the sharing of food with people during times of struggle has transcended any single religious tradition and become a wholly American practice. It is a reminder from our earliest forays into building tribes and community that caring for another at their weakest moment—when they are unable to gather food—bonds us to others. We are, after all, as strong as our last meal.

Catholics have instituted intricate rules for those in religious communities. Monasteries follow food and prayer rules as set by their respective founders. Many require monks and nuns to eat in silence while contemplating the gifts of the Lord and their personal unworthiness to receive them. Other orders are less dour. The Benedictines have a liberally interpreted rule that allows for one pound of bread per person per day, in addition to two cooked and one raw dish, and wine. In the spirit of self-sufficiency and commerce, monasteries have also been the source of specialty food items: beer, liqueurs, cheeses, jams, and fruitcakes are produced and, in a full embrace of our modern era, sold online.

Directly opposite a jolly monk hoisting an oversized mug of beer is the saintly teenage nun wasting away to nothingness. During the thirteenth through nineteenth centuries, young women were treated as a commodity to be brokered in marriage for financial and/or social gain.[13] Often, and this option was only available to wealthy girls, a plea could be made for a holy calling, resulting in life as a nun in a cloistered convent community. An accepted way to show godly devotion was fasting, so much so that it produced the phenomenon called "holy anorexia." Psychologists differentiate between the anorexia of psychological distress (anorexia nervosa) and the anorexia of religious excitation and devotion (anorexia mirabilis). Women and girls experiencing limited autonomy would find a small measure of control by restricting food intake and, if accepted as a novitiate, could change the course of their life. That these extreme fasters were held up as a model of female perfection has influenced social judgments still foisted on women's bodies.

Christian extreme fasting is traced back to Biblical stories of Jesus abstaining from food for forty days while meditating in the desert to discern his religious calling. Starvation is a proven method to generate hallucinations and dissociative states that can be interpreted as religious visions. Fasting and holiness is further defined in the writings of St. Thomas Aquinas on the sin of gluttony, where fatness equated to moral weakness, while thinness and the denial of food showed a divinely inspired moral strength.[14] It was said that St. Catherine of Sienna survived for decades on the Eucharist alone. Lest we think this practice is a remnant of the past, in 2004 the Vatican beatified Alexandrina Maria da Costa, citing her thirteen-year Eucharist-only fast as one of the signs of her holiness. Da Costa died in 1955 weighing seventy-three pounds, and had been subject to inconclusive medical investigations during her fasting years (1942–1955) carried out by skeptical doctors and bishops. She has a devoted following in her homeland of Portugal and in Ireland.

As mentioned, most religions have both scheduled and punitive fasting observances. Jain, Hindu, and Buddhist followers follow a regimented eating schedule with one difference: they hold two standards of adherence, one for citizens and one for monks and priests. Buddhist monks from most traditions are prohibited from eating any food after noon. In the more ascetic Jain and Buddhist monasteries, monks may only eat what they have begged for that day and

---

13   I pause, as Virginia Woolf did, to ponder the centuries of lost genius because women were denied autonomy and liberty.
14   Aquinas constructs his treatise on deadly sins from the moral philosophies of Aristotle.

Holy Food

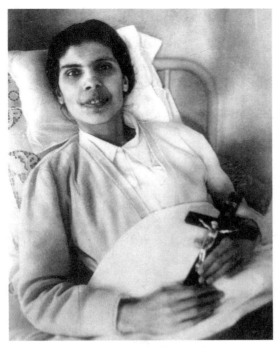

Blessed Alexandrina da Costa of Balasar (1904–1955).

must eat all they are given. Outside of Holy Days, individuals can choose to fast to generate less karma in the world and to offset negative actions they may have committed. All Jains and some Hindu (depending on sect) ban certain foods altogether. Root vegetables cannot be eaten, as doing so would kill the plant. The Jain diet closely resembles a fruitarian regimen, with the addition of leafy greens that can be harvested without causing too much harm to the plant.

Jewish fasting also varies by tradition and personal piety. The holiday of Yom Kippur is the holiest in the religious calendar and begins with a fast to purify the body from sin before asking God's forgiveness for personal transgressions. Personal fasting is restricted to newlyweds on the day of their marriage, and to adults on the anniversary of a parent's death. Unique to Jews is that fasting days are used to mark important dates from their lived history, with fasts to commemorate the destruction of the Temple in Jerusalem and Queen Esther's fast to dissuade her husband, the Persian king, from allowing one of his factotums, Haman, to slaughter the Israelites. Esther's brilliance and the defeat of Haman is celebrated with the feast of Purim, featuring pastries called Hamantaschen.[15]

Protestants gave up prescribed calendar-driven fasting with the Reformation, save for some of the more extreme fundamentalist groups. It is noted in diaries of the Plymouth colonists that leaders would call for fasts to atone for presumed sins that caused God to make life in the new colony difficult. The Pilgrims also called for feasts to thank God for his benefice. Most famously, the feast held to thank God for a decent harvest in 1621 is celebrated as Thanksgiving to this day. The colonist diaries also note that the newcomers received assistance from local Indigenous tribes who brought them food and taught them about native food plants.

The inspiration for Protestant fasting is derived from the Old Testament/Tanakh story of Daniel, who was held hostage by King Nebuchadnezzar after the first siege of Jerusalem. He refused to eat the King's food, including meats and wine, as it was not prepared according to Jewish dietary rules. Daniel demanded and ate only vegetables and water. As Daniel was a member of Jewish nobility and held hostage for political gain, King Nebuchadnezzar was

---

15 Hamantasch is a single pastry, hamantaschen is the plural. The pastries have a triangular shape that is said to represent Haman's tri-cornered hat or Haman's ears, or the Three Patriarchs of Judaism (Abraham, Isaac, and Jacob) or, controversially, the female reproductive system. Hamantaschen can be sweet or savory, but Americans prefer sweet hamantaschen filled with a poppyseed paste, or prune or apricot jam.

Pieter Brueghel the Elder, *Gula* (Gluttony), 1556–57, in the collection of the British Museum.

concerned about Daniel's health. After ten days of nothing but water and vegetables, Daniel and his comrades proved to be in fine fettle and continued their proto-vegan diet for the three years they remained in Babylon.

The Daniel Fast was adopted as a Lenten fast by early Methodists and Baptists but has enjoyed renewed popularity as a practice by fundamentalist non-denominational megachurches, as well as other groups that trace their lineage back to Wesleyanism. The Daniel Fast also has been recommended as a "biblical" weight loss program in some Christian churches. At the most extreme, the Daniel Fast was a central aspect of Christian weight-loss author Gwen Shamblin Lara, whose work paired scripture with dietary advice. Shamblin Lara's program was often criticized as not nutritionally sound, as it advocated extreme calorie restriction along with other prohibitions. In twenty-first-century America, we tend to enjoy the bounty of feasting more than the rigor of fasting.

Though one might think that a prohibition on gluttony appears in the Book, it does not. Greek philosopher Aristotle, much admired by early Christian thinkers, developed a list of virtues a "good" person should aspire to have. His list included "temperance," and noted that for every virtue there was an attendant vice. The first generations of Christians adopted Aristotle's vices as hurdles one must conquer to become a good Christian. That list became known as the Seven Deadly Sins (down from Aristotle's original list of eight)[16] and was codified in 590 CE by Pope Gregory. As noted earlier, gluttony made the cut, and was further defined

16   Despair was removed from Aristotle's list of Vices. Though in the apocryphal books of the Gospel, Jesus is said to have told Judas that his sin wasn't the betrayal of the Christ to the Sanhedrin, but that he despaired of God and did not seek forgiveness.

Holy Food

by Thomas Aquinas in the 1200s by detailing the five ways one can commit the sin of gluttony.[17] Even after the Protestant schism, the Deadlies remain as a touchpoint for Christian believers regardless of denomination.

These ancient religious rules against eating scavengers or dining with menstruating women and eating dinner with too much joy may seem archaic. Still, these ideas are the basis of our modern American food culture. Even people who have a casual relationship with religious teachings are quick to judge a fat person as gluttonous and intemperate. Our beliefs about food are never quite as straightforward as we think.

---

17   Thomas Aquinas' definition of Gluttony: Eating too expensively, eating too daintily, eating too much, eating too soon, eating too eagerly.

Three
UTOPIAN DREAMS

ONE COULD EASILY MAKE THE CASE THAT THE GARDEN OF EDEN, AS DESCRIBED IN Genesis, is in fact a utopia. And its failure is directly linked to a violation of God's prohibition against eating an apple, or maybe a quince, from a restricted tree.[18] For believers, the implication is clear: if God says 'don't eat it,' then don't eat it! But to some, the story of the Fall of Man is a sign that there is the possibility of a perfect place on Earth, and following the Word is the best method of creating it. Of course, in discussing utopias, it becomes clear that man's vision of Eden is always subject to the foibles of the visionary. But utopias as a designed community allow for its creator and subsequent communards to put into practice ideas about how and what people should eat.

Human preoccupation with the ideal location and conditions for living a happy and carefree existence shows up in various ways throughout Western culture. Medieval French serfs used the word "cockaigne" to name this imagined land of plenty. Cockaigne was so universally understood during the fourteenth century that an infamous and ribald poetry collection by one Michael of Kildare describes "Cokaygne" as a delightful world of sexual liberty, freedom from work, and endless food including a sky that rains cheese. In Ireland, a "cocaigne" was a small sweet cake for children. The French poem "The Land of Cocaigne" from 1350 riffs on Michael of Kildare's food and sex fantasy to include houses made of barley sugar candy, streets paved with pastry, and walking pork roasts that carved themselves.

The notion of Cockaigne spread throughout Europe, as evidenced by the linguistic and geographic words that sprang up during the fourteenth and fifteenth centuries. The Dutch used *Luilekkerland* (luscious-delicious land). In German it became *Schlaraffenland*, an unsurprising compound word meaning lazy fool. Swedes too took a dour perspective on the anti-work fantasy land and called it *Lubberland—Lubber* meaning fat and lazy then, which has gentled to only mean clumsy. Cockaigne falls out of usage after a few hundred years, but shadows of it remain in our food culture. One only need look at *The Joy of Cooking* by the Rombauer family. The seminal cookbook has been in print since 1936 and uses the word "Cockaigne" to describe delicious, home-style recipes that were the Rombauers' personal favorites.

---

18   NIV, Genesis 16–17. And the LORD God commanded the man, "You are free to eat from any tree in the garden; but you must not eat from the tree of the knowledge of good and evil, for when you eat from it you will certainly die."

Map of the island of Utopia, woodcut by Ambrosius Holbein. From the 1518 edition of Sir Thomas More's *Utopia*.

Utopia, a word coined by Sir Thomas More in 1516, is a neologism from Greek words meaning "good place." Utopia is also a play on words, as the Greek words for "good" and "no" sound alike. So, in the beginning, More lets us know that the Good Place might, in fact, be No Place at all. Imagining and describing Good Places goes back to Plato's description of an ideal of government in *The Republic*. Plato also takes on man's nature by ascribing happiness to those who are "just" and follow a philosophy for living. Plato's utopia—Kalliopolis—is ruled by a wise philosopher-king. Like the utopian thinkers who follow, Plato is wary of pure democracy, and distrusts ordinary people to make informed decisions based on facts for the good of the entire community. The residents of Plato's utopia have souls that exist outside of time and place but are attached to individual people and affected by the moral choices of their human host.

Scholars now accept More's *Utopia* as a fictionalized satire of England in the 1600s. Yet, throughout the centuries, people have taken More's work, as they have Plato's, as a blueprint for building the ideal society. More's book is still debated in academic circles, but suffice to say that his vision, whether satirical or empirical, would be an ideal for white men. Women are subjugated to their husbands, though widows have the option of becoming priests, and each household is guaranteed at least two slaves, either purchased or captured.

The Enlightenment Era of the seventeenth and eighteenth centuries is when philosophical atheism in the West enjoys, if not a vogue, at least a tolerance. At least for the upper classes. Catholic priests in Europe held political power insomuch as they spoke directly to people on behalf of a deity, which created a de facto balance of power between rulers and gods. That is not to say that *outré* thinkers and philosophers of Europe had invented anything new by questioning the existence of God. Throughout history, there are examples of both tolerance and persecution of atheist inclinations. Greek leaders of the ancient world would be prosecuted and executed for apostasy, but only when a rival political faction could not indict them on anything else. Ancestor worship is considered atheistic as there isn't a godhead or creator, and millions of people living outside the Levant and western Asia practiced a form of nontheistic ancestor worship without any notice from God.

The Protestant Reformation movement that began in sixteenth-century Europe fueled a nearly constant state of war between rival factions for the next 150 or so years. Jumping back to the Constitution's First Amendment and the Establishment Clause (as the "freedom of religion" guarantee is officially noted), in the writing of that sentence, the framers left open the option for citizens to not believe in any god. As trite as it may sound, the freedom of religion also means freedom *from* religion. It must be stressed that in the late 1700s, to have atheism enshrined in a governmental document was indeed revolutionary. It is one thing to question the existence of deity privately but quite another to publicly proclaim that God is dead. From a historical perspective, even today, our societal discourse is not that far from witch trials and calls for the execution of heretics and apostates.

So, what of utopias? Is it possible for a people—any people—to live together in harmony? Utopia scholar Lyman Sargent said that "all utopias will fail because society itself is not homogeneous." This truth has never dissuaded a budding utopianist. Having an organizing ideology and principles was a critical element to the most successful of the failed experiments. The United States has examples of all sorts of utopian communities based on affinities like economic, religious, sexual orientation, racist, feminist, ecological interests, and combinations of interests like Christian nudists. Beyond the organizing ideal that brought people together, a utopian society needs an operations plan.

FOOD SECURITY ISN'T SOMETHING MODERN WESTERNERS THINK ABOUT DURING their day-to-day lives, unless, of course, war or natural disasters trigger a breakdown of supply chains. Yet building reliable and plentiful food systems was a paramount concern for utopianists. Few twenty-first-century Americans have experienced starvation or even true hunger, yet we are not that far from the 1930s when drought decimated the breadbasket of the Great Plains and starved out millions from their homes. We have cultural memory of recent ancestors standing in breadlines during the Great Depression or leaving their homeland because of war and famine. When you're without income or escaping war it's nearly impossible to carry enough food to survive more than a few weeks. A straightforward reading of the Book of Genesis clearly says that the Garden of Eden is a food paradise lost to humankind due to sin. And since the Fall, each and every utopian thinker has incorporated a sustainable food model that detailed the growing, harvesting, and cooking of food because it represented the perfect ideal: a place where no one would ever go hungry. A new Garden of Eden.

The utopianist and part-time traveling salesman Charles Fourier conceived of a deist, proto-socialist, and self-sufficient commune where the promise of humanity's potential could finally be realized. His first manifesto, published in France in 1808, found few readers until a patron helped fund and disseminate his writing. By the time of Fourier's death in 1837, his ideas had spread throughout the Western world, and intersected with other philosophers considering the plight of humanity after the twin cataclysms of the Industrial Revolution and the French Revolution of 1789. The Industrial Revolution separated peasants from the land and the rule of the bourgeois landowners, while the French Revolution went further and separated the bourgeois from their collective heads.

'Human Happiness—food for the asking in the Fourierist utopia.' Grandville, 1844.

The theoretical ideal of a citizen with upward mobility was a social threat to the aristocracy; an empowered and armed working class was a legitimate threat to the way of life privileged classes enjoyed for centuries. Curiously, it was thinkers and activists from the recently enriched middle classes that devoted their philosophical thoughts to trying to solve the problem of the poor laboring classes.[19] Fourier was rich enough to look askance at excesses of the French Republic yet not wealthy enough to fund his experimental ideas.

Fourier was not an outlier of his time. His utopia, named Harmonie, was criticized by Karl Marx as being too outlandish and anti-industrial, while being praised by Friedrich Engels for his ideas regarding women's rights and less oppressive social class structures. Fourier's contemporary, Robert Owen, believed in action instead of treatises and put *his* ideas to the test by purchasing a controlling portion of a wool mill in New Lanark, Scotland. With a workforce of 2,000 adults and 500 children, he brought his version of socialist communalism to life in New Lanark. Not all the implemented changes were successful, but they informed his future work as a reform campaigner and urban planner as he advocated for mandatory education for children, living wages, and most enduringly, the slogan: "Eight hours labor, Eight hours recreation, Eight hours rest." Owen believed that people were a product of their environment, and communities that shared work, meals, and child-raising would become happy and productive workers.

The knock against Owen and Fourier is that both of their utopian visions rely on a social caste system where the lowliest members would remain in place as low-status communards. They would be better fed and no longer living in squalor, but still very much under the sufferance of their social betters. Fourier goes as far as to allocate food according to class, where the most aristocratic residents live on the top floors of his multi-story "phalansteries" and eat thirty-course meals while the lowest-ranked live on the ground floor and make do with ten-course meals. In Fourier's vision, the plebeian ranks will be ecstatic with their ten-course meals because, before that, they only had one paltry meal per day, let alone the glory of gourmet food.

---

19   Class struggle is always about access and use of power. In the modern world, money secures power, and the struggle for the upper and middle classes is how to allow the working classes *enough* money to sate them but not so much that they too attain power.

Still, modern readers would find much to approve in Fourier's vision. He views women as near equal to men (he is credited with coining the term feminism), values physical and intellectual labor equally, and proposes that the least enjoyable jobs should come with the most reward. Aside from his absurd food allocation formula, his food philosophy would find welcome in today's culinary literature. Fourier was quite detailed when discussing food in Harmonie;[20] it would be fresh, delicious, and consumed with a passion because it was grown with love and prepared with the highest degree of care. Very akin to locavore and Slow Food movements of today.

Fourier coined the word "gastrosophy" in direct opposition to the gross excesses of the gastronome who ate without consideration, like those in the recently deposed court of Louis XVI. Nor did he embrace the performative austerity favored by ardent French Republicans who subsisted on turnips and black bread and mocked coffee as a childish obsession. In Fourier's utopia, food—the growing, preparation, and consumption—was a sensual pleasure second only to sex.

Like Owen and other socialistic thinkers, Fourier paid particular attention to children's education and relationship with food. He emphasized that children from the age of two onward be introduced to eating foods prepared to the highest standards. No barley mush or pablum for utopia tots! Only the most exquisitely prepared dishes for the children of the phalansteries, so as to train their palates to recognize quality and learn to revel in the pleasure of eating. Children should also assist in the preparation of food, to learn to respect and revere every iota of work that goes into a meal. This was not a punishment in Fourier's utopia, because of the sensuous nature of food: to experience it from growing leaf to bountiful harvest was a gift to children.

Fourier's system of food growth, preparation, and consumption is far more complex than described here, but his general theme is that eating is the first and last pleasure known to man, which makes it essential to a good life.[21] Fourier's vision of Harmonie also includes a delightfully Rabelaisian alternative to warfare. Instead of the wholesale slaughter of youth, armies of chefs representing warring parties would meet at the banquet table, preparing delicacies for all combatants, with the winner decided over successive meals and agreed upon by all. That is a butcher's bill anyone would be happy to pay.

As Fourier and Owen were designing conceptual utopias, German Lutheranism experienced multiple schismatic breaks from orthodoxy by a growing number of renegade clergy espousing new ideas of Pietism.[22] George Rapp was the leader of a separatist Lutheran group in the Wurttemberg region of Bavaria who felt the state-run churches were far too liberal and straying from the rigorous word of the Lord. Rapp's followers grew to about 10,000 strong as he defied local Bavarian officials by his continued preaching and critique of the government. Persecution

---

20   Fourier refers to his utopia as "Harmonie," using the French spelling. Owen and George Rapp—in a nod to Fourier—use the English spelling of "Harmony" in naming their utopian settlements.

21   Fourier, *Le Nouveau monde amoureux*, 126.

22   Pietists, derived from the word piety, were part of a movement within Lutheranism that embraced individual responsibility to Biblical doctrine and a muscular form of Christianity. Believers strive toward the rigorous command to live a holy life with a goal of sanctification. The movement began in Germany in the early 1700s and spread throughout German-speaking lands and into Scandinavia. Many of the early American communal settlers were Pietists who moved entire villages and congregations en masse in the face of legal and physical threats. The various Pietist sects influenced Protestant denominations throughout the United States, leading to evangelicalism as a core tenet of both American Lutheranism and other Protestant denominations. Pietism evolved in later Protestant sects as the "Holiness Movement" and then later into "Pentecostalism."

increased until he announced a mass immigration scheme to move his followers to the United States. They arrived in 1803 to build their American Eden, called—in reference to Fourier's theoretical utopia—Harmony.

The Harmonists first settled in Pennsylvania where they could provide a valuable commodity to the growing country: wine. Father Rapp had a background in Rhenish winemaking and decided that it was to be the primary income source for his followers. Experiments with native grapes produced a poor-quality wine, but after research and further

Two residents of the Rappite commune of Economy, Pennsylvania, c. 1900.

experimentation, the Harmonists were making quality wine from Catawba grapes. They later expanded the communal settlement to 7,000 acres along the Wabash River in southwestern Indiana with the intent to expand their vineyards. Indiana proved to be a poor climate for grapes, and after ten years of crop failures and violent threats from pro-slavery advocates in nearby Kentucky, Rapp moved the entire colony back to Pennsylvania.

Father Rapp absorbed new ideas from, as he claimed, divine revelation, yet his proclamations regarding Millennial prophecy as promised in Revelation was becoming a standard tenet of Pietist Protestant groups of the era. He told followers to prepare for the second coming of Christ and organized the communities on the model of New Testament discipleship. Property was held in common. They dressed alike: women in plain dresses and a shawl, bonnet, and apron, while men wore simple blue pants and jackets, and high-crowned hats. Men could request work that fit their interests and skills, but all hands came together for planting and harvesting. The Rappites did not actively engage in recruiting new followers. To join, one had to sign over any assets to the community and undergo a one-year trial period. Many left due to the strict religious edicts and embrace of celibacy. Father Rapp and his adopted son, Johan, who led the group after Father Rapp died, changed the rules to allow for marriage, but sex was only to be engaged in with the express purpose of conceiving a child.

The Harmony settlements were insular, which preserved their Bavarian dialect and recipes, yet the Harmonists were just one group among the many other German Anabaptist groups that immigrated to the region. So much so that the swath of land from western Pennsylvania east to central Iowa still has thriving "Amish" communities. Their century of success can be ascribed to the homogeneous makeup of the group as well as their relative economic prosperity. Like other Anabaptists, the Rappites banned tobacco but enjoyed wines, beers, and ciders. Their recipes reflect a hearty fare that maximizes caloric intake (needed to fuel the long days of manual labor), and frugal use of ingredients. The spartan living conditions

Owen's proposed design for New Harmony, Indiana.

combined with insularity and celibacy reduced community numbers until only a few families were remaining in 1905. The last of the Rappites agreed to dissolve the association and sell the remaining assets in 1906.

Robert Owen and his son, Robert Dale Owen, came to America in 1824 to test his New Lanark style of social reform. He discovered Father Rapp's colony in Harmony, Indiana, and the Rappites' desire to go back to Pennsylvania. Owen bought the charter to Harmony, Indiana, lock, stock, and barrel. He recruited colonists from Scotland, England, France and beyond by promising a state-of-the-art cooperative community that encouraged scientific experimentation and progressive policies. He succeeded in recruiting migrants who were, as his son and communal-living activist in his own right, Robert Dale Owen, described them, "a heterogeneous collection of Radicals, enthusiastic devotees to principle, honest latitudinarians,[23] and lazy theorists, with a sprinkling of unprincipled sharpers thrown in."[24]

Owen's collection of Radicals and sharpers failed to keep Harmony economically viable, and the commune ceded its charter in 1827. The experience taught Owen that social reform on a nationwide scale must occur before any utopian community can exist. It was the age-old problem of how to convince people to contribute their fair share to benefit the collective. He returned to England to champion workers' rights and suffrage for all men.[25]

---

23 A term to describe moderate Anglicans (Episcopalians).

24 Attributed to Robert Dale Owen, in *Robert Owen: Pioneer of Social Reforms* by Joseph Clayton (A.C. Fifield, London, 1908).

25 Voting in England was restricted to an elite few. At various times throughout the 1800s the voting franchise had only been extended to those who have owned land, received a university degree, or somehow qualified to pay tax directly to the government. "One man, one vote" was not fully established in the United Kingdom until 1950. It could be argued that the United States still has not fully embraced universal suffrage as it enacts laws about the criteria of voter eligibility.

Holy Food

NOTHER INFLUENTIAL IMMIGRANT WAS MOTHER ANN LEE OF THE SHAKERS. Mother Ann Lee had established a radical new belief system born of the Industrial Revolution in northwest England: the Shakers. The name was at first an insult that, over time, became one of many nicknames of The United Society of Believers in Christ's Second Appearing. The Shakers were formed in 1747 as a breakaway Quaker group and were, no doubt about it, radical. They believed in a physical manifestation of the spirit that took the form of uncontrollable body jerks, speaking in tongues, and frenetic dancing. But more than the outward appearances, it was their evolving beliefs in celibacy, women as equal spiritual leaders and vessels for holy messages, communal living, and technological enterprise that were far more radical.

Mother Ann Lee

Mother Ann led a small group of Shakers from England to settle in rural Watervliet, New York, in what is now suburban Albany. The Shakers were originally millennialists who believed that Christ would be born again but in the form of a woman.[26] While Ann Lee was instrumental in building the theology of Shaker belief, it is Joseph Meacham and Lucy Wright, two early converts, who implemented communal living. Meacham died in 1794, leaving Mother Lucy Wright as leader of the group. She carried on the proselytizing mission of Mother Ann Lee into the new century. As the nineteenth century begins, the Shakers and Wesley-influenced spiritual practices gain more followers and imitators.

Shaker culture to many Americans is focused on the industrious craftsmanship and spare, proto-modern design aesthetic. Yet the Shakers' beliefs scandalized Americans in the early 1800s. Mother Lee's revelations of the future coming of Jesus—as a woman—and her denial of the trinitarian God, as well as the demand that Believers remain celibate, marked the religion as a threat. Early Shakers were physically attacked, prompting their move to the then-rural area outside of Albany, New York. Converts were required to sign a binding covenant that gave over any assets and bound their souls to the Believers forever.

Mother Wright received a vision that the Believers should send missionaries west to Ohio. Two intrepid Shakers walked throughout the Ohio River Valley and found people receptive to the Believers' cosmology. Many of the new converts had recently attended brimstone-filled camp revivals and were open to new ideas about God. They had already broken away from the staid old ways, and what the Shakers were saying wasn't too different. Unsurprisingly, women saw the benefit of equal treatment, shared burdens, and celibacy.[27]

26 To better understand what many of the New Religious Movements believed, we must take a moment to define "millennialism" (also called "millenarianism" or "chiliasm"). It is the belief that before Judgment Day when God ends the world, the righteous (or "saints") will live with Christ as ruler on Earth in bounteous peace for a thousand years. This notion is based on interpretations of the writing in the New Testament chapter the Book of Revelation.

27 In 1850 (the first census year with complete statistics), the maternal death rate was 1 in 100 women. The death rate for children 0–3 was 216 deaths per 1,000. The average number of children a white woman birthed during her average thirty-nine-and-a-half-year lifespan was 5.62. For Black women, that number is eight, though they died much younger at an average of twenty-three years old. And 340 per 1,000 of their babies died.

Cheese Room at Canterbury Shaker Village, Concord, New Hampshire, c. 1870s.

After the success in Ohio, more Shaker missionaries traveled the new country and established communal villages. The missionaries brought along the recipes used to feed their brothers and sisters back east. Two missionary sisters working in Ohio lightly complained about the food in a letter to Mother Wright, stating that they feared the other missionaries might be malnourished as the fare was so different than in the East. Indeed, the "westerners" lived on wild game, cornbread, and milk, with few vegetables or variety.

The Shaker communes in New York and Maine honed their farming skills and developed not only a good revenue from selling fresh and preserved produce, but from selling vegetable seeds. The Believers began planting pear and apple orchards in the early 1820s, experimenting with hybridization to perfect the fruit. They also developed extensive herbariums for both medicinal and culinary needs. Herbs would be dried and sold in local mercantiles, and later via mail order. Traveling missionaries would share seed stock, knowledge, and scions with other Shaker villages so all would benefit.

The Mount Lebanon Shaker family began experimenting with vegetarianism. It was proposed by two Elders to experiment with "bloodless meals" as a method to improve overall health as well as speak to the Believers' ideas about simplicity and nonviolence. In correspondence between different communes, the vegetarian idea spread, but it was left to the Elders of each village to decide whether to embrace vegetarianism. There was pushback from the Elders in charge of teaching children[28] as it was believed that they needed meats to thrive.

Over time, the Shaker cooks came to a varied menu of near-vegetarian cooking. Seafood dishes were typical in communes near the Atlantic Ocean, while chicken and beef recipes began appearing more and more after 1890. Sister Frances Carr (1927–2017), who embraced Shaker vegetarianism, writes in her cookbook *Shaker Your Plate* of uneasiness in preparing meat dishes but did so when they were on the menu.

---

28   In the era before state-run social services, churches took responsibility for those in need. Many of the Shaker communes took in abandoned and orphaned children, who either chose to leave or join the Believers when they became adults. The Shakers also took in impoverished widows and, to the rancor of many, women escaping abusive husbands and formerly enslaved people.

Holy Food

Amana women preparing food in Ruedy House communal kitchen. Courtesy of the Amana Heritage Society.

MIDWESTERNERS MAY BE FAMILIAR WITH AMANA AS A QUAINT HISTORICAL tourist attraction in eastern Iowa featuring artisan craftwork and German culture. Others may hear the name and immediately think of refrigerators. Both are correct. But before the Amana Colonies became a tourist destination, it was a successful religious commune.

In the early 1700s, radical pietism was spreading from France into Germany and beyond.[29] Many itinerant Pietist preachers found their way to the city of Halle (near Leipzig), where they were tolerated by the local government and Lutheran church. Three brothers by the name of Pott experienced a profoundly more evangelical inspiration of the divine in 1714. Like the Shakers, the Potts were given over to physical manifestations during prayer and eschewed violence of any kind, which included the mandatory military service required from most German princes. They incurred the wrath of other Pietists and adopted the name Inspirationalists. They were often at odds with other Pietist movements, like the Anabaptists (better known by their American offshoots: the Amish, Mennonites, and Hutterites).

A key element to the Inspirationalist practice was the revelation of a *Werkzeug,* who was the person chosen as the instrument—or as the German word means, tool—that would communicate God's word to the believers. The *Werkzeug* is considered the spiritual leader of the group until the Divine Spirit moves to another. The *Werkzeug* makes the proclamations decreed by God, then a council of elders either agrees, modifies, or rejects them. Too many rejected inspirations were a sign that the Spirit is no longer present with the *Werkzeug.* Barbara Heinemann became the *Werkzeug* at age twenty-three in 1818 and remained so for five years. Many Inspirationalist elders refused to recognize her because she was a woman and her outspoken pronouncements attracted notice from the government. She was arrested yet continued to claim that God was speaking through her. Only Christian Metz recognized her divine ordination.

In Inspirationalist culture, married people could not contain the Spirit nor be a *Werkzeug.* Heinemann chose to marry George Landmann in 1823 and gave up leadership to Christian

---

29   Germany, as we know it today, did not come into being as a nation-state until 1871 under the first Kaiser, William of Prussia. Prior to that, it was a loose confederation of thirty-nine bickering states, each with its own prince.

Metz. The group was still at odds with other Inspirationalists, and faced increasing pressure from the local government. The remedy for Metz's group was to emigrate en masse to the United States. Christian Metz as the *Werkzeug* undertook the founding of the first colony on land purchased from the Seneca people near Buffalo, New York, in the early 1840s. As the believers built and grew their settlement in the next decade, Metz was convinced that they needed more room to expand, and wanted to get away from the corrupting influence of the port city of Buffalo. The group moved to the Iowa River valley and founded the Amana Colonies, which grew to seven separate but intertwined villages. Barbara Heinemann, now Landmann, came to Amana with her husband and lived a quiet life as a member of the community. In 1849, Barbara Landmann, by now a widow, once again received the gift of Inspiration. Metz recognized the Spirit in her and they led the Amana Colony together as co-*Werkzeuge*. The Colony continued to thrive after Metz's death in 1867 with Landmann as sole *Werkzeug*. Testimonials of residents note that Landmann alone was much stricter in her decrees. She banned photographs and Christmas presents, and admonished against reading anything but the Bible. Her death in 1887 brought a relaxation of the rules and, consequently, the eventual demise of the Colony.

The Amana Inspirationalists, like many other religiously motivated communal groups, took their organizing principle from a passage in the New Testament: "And all that believed were together, and had all things in common; and sold their possessions and goods, and parted them to all men as every man had need."[30] They organized themselves as they had begun at the Ebenezer Colony in New York: family units consisting of partnered couples, extended and adopted relatives, and sometimes children living in a house. Marriage could only occur with the blessing of the Elders and the *Werkzeug*. Each family had assigned chores but was also responsible for specialized work in the village. The villages were self-sufficient enterprises that featured a wool mill, farming, wood and metal shops, and of course, a community bakehouse and kitchen. The Inspirationalists shared breakfast and dinner together in their communal dining rooms. Many of the oldest houses in the Colony did not have kitchens.

The communal kitchens or *Küchbaase* served thirty to forty people. Men and women sat separately. Food was considered necessary but never celebrated. Meals were eaten in near silence. Though the menus in each *Küchbaase* varied slightly, all adhered to a uniform diet to ensure no members were favored over others. The cuisine is Rhenish with German and Alsatian influences. By 1900 the practice of communal dining faded away as modernization crept in, and families wanted to eat together.

At its peak in 1908, Amana was home to 1,800 people in the seven villages, with assets of $1.8 million dollars. After Landmann's death the community was without a *Werkzeug* for the remainder of its existence. In 1932, the members of the Colony decided to end the communal experiment and revert ownership of the assets as a for-profit corporation held equally by remaining members. An interesting outcome for descendants came about due to how the collective holdings were split: the Electrical Equipment Company founded in 1934 was partially owned by the community. It grew to become the Amana Refrigeration Company and was sold

---

30 Acts 2:44–45.

Holy Food

for a substantial profit a decade later, making the Amana Colonies one of the more financially successful communal experiments in American history.

A sadder fate awaited the Swedish Pietists who followed Erik Jansson to Illinois. Pietism was, as can be seen by the sheer number of sects and breakaway groups, a popular movement in German-speaking areas of Europe and in Scandinavia. Erik Jansson was born in 1808 outside of Uppsala, Sweden, when the Lutheran Church was part of the Swedish government, and both were ruled by the Swedish royal family.[31] The state-sanctioned religion had no place for visionaries or any practice outside accepted dogma. In 1830 Jansson had a heavenly vision and declared himself cured of the rheumatism that had plagued him as an adolescent. He turned to Bible study and reading the writings of other visionary seers, and experienced more prophetic episodes. He began preaching to neighbors about his visions, and was tolerated until he called on people to burn their Luther catechisms. That was the limit for the Swedish church and government.

Jansson was arrested and released multiple times until death threats prompted his escape to Norway in 1845. He had been telling his thousands of followers to prepare for an exodus and to build a new Jerusalem. A loyal follower scouted and acquired land in western Illinois near the Mississippi River. Jansson made the journey with four hundred loyalists, with others to come on later voyages. The Janssonites were besieged by bad luck. One of the ships sank. People became sick with cholera during the overland journey from the New York docks to Illinois. When they arrived at what was to become Bishop's Hill, it was too late in the season to plant crops or even build shelter. They dug crude sod houses to get them through the winter. Nearly one hundred people died.

Life was hardly idyllic. Jansson was adamant that followers be loyal to God first, and instituted regimented prayer schedules. Some became overwrought and tried to leave but Jansson posted armed guards to keep anyone from escaping. The group survived on boiled corn mash. By the spring of 1847, more arrivals from Sweden rejuvenated the Janssonites and they began to build. Bishop's Hill grew to seven hundred residents, and while acclimated to the harsh winter climate, they still experienced winter food shortages. The following year, two hundred members left to join area Methodist congregations.

Still, faced with food shortages and financial insolvency, Jansson and his followers persevered. He called for celibacy and renewed faith. In 1848 they sowed enough crops to sustain the community and sell for profit, and built a carpet factory that did quite well. But luck was never with Jansson. Successive years brought more cholera outbreaks that continued to kill residents, including his wife. He paid for a doctor to come from the Mormon settlement of Nauvoo with the promise of payment for services. The doctor was a quack and land speculator who foreclosed on several of the Janssonite properties when residents could not pay his exorbitant bills.

The sad end of Erik Jansson comes about in 1850. His cousin and ward married a violent man who was not part of the community. He agreed to join the Janssonites as a condition of marriage

---

31 At least until 1810. After the Russo-Swedish war, King Gustav Adolf was replaced by his uncle, who had dementia and named his nephew as King. He died. The Swedish aristocracy appealed to Napoleon to name a king and the job was given to Jean-Baptiste Jules Bernadotte in 1818. The Bernadottes are the reigning family to this day.

Erik Jansson surrounded by some of his disciples. Oil painting by Olof Krans.

but could not bear the strict regimen. He kidnapped his wife and young child and took them one hundred miles east to Chicago. Jansson followed to mount a successful rescue and bring her and the child back to the commune. A few months later, the estranged husband walked up to Jansson near his home in Bishop's Hill and shot him. Jansson died on May 2, 1850.

The Bishop's Hill community tried to stay together as Jansson intended, but no clear leader emerged. Members of the council had taken on speculative investments that were wiped out in the financial crash of 1857. The charter was dissolved in 1862, with members each receiving an equal value of the communally held property. The buildings of Bishop's Hill are now a historic landmark and tourist attraction. Many of the original settlers stayed in the area, and their descendants keep the Swedish food traditions of their pioneer forefathers alive with reunions and celebrations.

Fourier never saw his plans put into practice. Still, hundreds of influential thinkers used his and Owen's ideas and theories to build their version of utopian communities in the United States. Each experiment in living had unique challenges and failed in its own specific way. It was a naïve hope that brought these experiments, dissenters, believers, charlatans, and prophets to America. Communal living, whether organized around a shared religious belief or political ideology, could only hope to bear fruit in the United States, where the freedom of and from religion allowed these pioneers to flourish or fail. It is only in the United States where anyone could deny God, or be a God, or have a conviction that their will IS God's will. It is in this over-stirred pot of liberation, revolution, and mysticism that we discover that God cares a lot about what you put in your mouth.

 # SHAKERS

(The United Society of Believers in Christ's Second Appearing, Shaking Quakers)
Years active: 1747 to present day
Affiliation: Protestant / Restorationist / Spiritualist
Founder / Leader: Mother Ann Lee, then Father John Meacham and Mother Lucy Wright

The recipes included here are from both the early founding days and the height of the movement in the mid-1800s when approximately 5,000 people had signed a covenant with God to live as a Believer.

SHAKER FISH & EGG

(Serves 6. Gluten-free.)
Tools: 9x12 casserole dish
Oven temperature: 325°F

Notes from Sister Frances Carr's *Shaker Your Plate* cookbook: "This recipe has been included in every Shaker cookbook ever published. It was considered an economical dish when we had our own dairy herd, and we bought salted cod for 39 cents a pound."

Ingredients:
2 cups half & half
1 Tablespoon butter
3 boiled potatoes (sliced thin after cooling)
1 cup cod, boiled and shredded
6 hard-boiled eggs
¼ teaspoon salt
Dash of pepper
½ teaspoon mix of dried basil, marjoram, parsley, tarragon, and thyme (Shaker Fines Herbes blend)
This recipe requires pre-cooking the eggs and potatoes and pre-soaking of the salted cod. Plan ahead or use leftovers.
The night before: Place cod in bowl filled with ice-cold water. After 1 hour, replace water, then place bowl in refrigerator to soak overnight.
Steps:
1. Preheat oven to 325°F.
2. Wash potatoes, then boil until tender but still firm. Remove potatoes and set aside to cool.

3. Hard-boil 6 eggs. Set aside to cool.

4. Boil cod in quart-sized pan. Cool, then shred and set aside.

5. Scald milk, then add tablespoon of butter. Set aside to cool until warm.

6. Butter casserole dish. Thinly slice cooled potatoes and hard-boiled eggs.

7. Beginning with sliced potatoes, place a layer in buttered dish, then add layer of shredded cod, then layer of hard-boiled eggs. Repeat until dish is filled.

8. Sprinkle salt, pepper, and herbs on top.

9. Pour warm cream mixture over casserole. Gently poke with butter knife, so mixture seeps through.

10. Place into oven and bake for 45 to 50 minutes until all the cream mixture is absorbed.

11. Remove from oven and garnish with a sprinkle of parsley.

Sister Frances Ann Carr in Sabbathday Lake kitchen in 1967.

Holy Food

SHAKER APPLE PIE

(Vegetarian. Serves 8.)
Tools: One 9-inch pie plate
Oven temperature: 350°F

Notes from Sister Frances Carr's *Shaker Your Plate* cookbook: "In 1912, Brother Delmar expanded our orchards at Sabbathday Lake to over 2,500 trees. The main crop consists of MacIntosh, Cortland, and Red and Yellow Delicious varieties, but we also have many nineteenth-century varieties, including the Yellow Transparencies, Ben Davis, Winter Banana, Strawberry, Northern Spy, and Baldwin."

Ingredients for pie crust:
1 cup vegetable shortening
2½ cups flour
1 teaspoon salt
4–5 Tablespoons cold water

Steps:
1. Sift flour and salt together into bowl.
2. Mix in shortening using a pastry cutter or large fork until the mixture is the size of peas (about ¼-inch round).
3. Gradually add cold water 1 tablespoon at a time until dough comes together. Don't overmix.
4. Separate dough into two sections. On flat, lightly floured surface, roll out to fit pie plate.
5. Place 1 crust in pie plate. Set other aside.

Ingredients for pie filling:
3 cups cored, peeled, and sliced apples (use a mix of tart and sweet apples)
⅔ cup sugar
2 Tablespoons cream
2 Tablespoons rosewater

Steps:
1. Preheat oven to 350°F.
2. Wash, peel, core, and slice apples to measure 3 cups and place in large bowl.
3. Add sugar, 1 tablespoon each of cream and rosewater, and mix thoroughly, so all ingredients are evenly distributed.
4. Fill lined pie plate with apple mixture, then cover with top crust.
5. With a sharp paring knife, trim any extra overhanging crust. Pinch top and bottom crusts together with thumb and forefinger. Slit top crust with four 1-inch vent holes.
6. Mix remaining cream and rosewater together. Brush top crust with a mixture.
7. Place in oven and bake for 50 minutes.
8. Remove when done and cool.

MOTHER ANN'S BIRTHDAY CAKE

(Vegetarian. Serves 12.)

Tools: Three 8-inch round cake pans

Oven temperature: 325°F

Ingredients for cake:

1 cup butter

2 cups sugar

3 cups all-purpose flour

½ cup corn starch

3 teaspoons baking powder

1 cup whole milk

2 teaspoons rosewater

12 egg whites, beaten

1 teaspoon salt

Steps:

1. Preheat oven to 325°F.
2. Beat butter and sugar together until smooth and color is pale yellow. Add rosewater and mix.
3. In a separate bowl, sift flour, corn starch, and baking powder together.
4. Add flour mixture in small amounts alternating with milk into the butter mixture, beating after each addition.
5. In a separate bowl, add the egg whites and salt. Beat until stiff.
6. Lightly fold the stiffened egg whites into the batter.
7. Using butter, lightly grease and flour the 3 cake pans.
8. Pour the batter equally into the pans.
9. Bake for 25 minutes. Remove from oven and cool.

Ingredients for frosting:

4 cups confectioner's sugar, sifted

2 Tablespoons butter

¼ cup half & half

1 Tablespoon rosewater

Steps:

1. In medium-sized bowl, combine all the ingredients.
2. Mix until smooth.
3. To finish cake: Fill between the cakes with a layer of peach jelly. (Or use your favorite flavor of jelly.) Cover cake with Rosewater Frosting.

SHAKER STEWED TOMATOES

(Vegetarian. Serves 4 to 6.)

Tools: 2-quart saucepan or small stockpot

Ingredients:

1 quart tomatoes (either home-canned or commercial canned whole tomatoes)

½ cup whole milk

1 Tablespoon sugar

¼ teaspoon baking soda

¼ teaspoon Bouquet Garni herb blend (thyme, bay leaf, and parsley)

¼ cup saltine cracker crumbs

1 Tablespoon butter

Steps:

1. In large saucepan or stockpot, add tomatoes and heat through on medium burner.

2. Add milk and baking soda. Simmer for 5 minutes.

3. Add the cracker crumbs. Simmer until cracker crumbs have swelled in size.

4. Add the sugar, salt, and herbs. Mix all together then remove from heat.

5. Add the butter and allow to melt.

6. Serve.

Dining Room at Canterbury Shaker Village, Concord, New Hampshire, c.1870s.

AMANA COLONY

(Community of True Inspiration, True Inspiration Congregations, Inspirationalists, Amana Church Society)

Years active: 1842–1932

Affiliation: Pietism, Anabaptist

Founders / Leaders: Christian Metz and Barbara Heinemann Landmann

TRAUBEN PASTETE (TWO-CRUST GRAPE PIE)

(Makes one 9-inch pie. Vegetarian.)

Tools: Conical sieve or sturdy mesh sieve and one 9-inch pie plate

Ingredients:

4 cups grapes (Note: The grapes traditionally used are Concord, or a tart-tasting, dark purple, wild grape. If using commercial grapes, purchase the least-sweet purple grapes available.)

Dash of salt

¾ cup sugar

2 teaspoons lemon juice

3 Tablespoons flour

1 Tablespoon melted butter

(Two prepared 9-inch pie crusts*)

Steps:

1. Wash grapes, separate skins from pulp and cook pulp until soft. Set the grape skins aside.
2. Place grape pulp into sieve and press through to remove seeds. Place pulp in bowl and add reserved grape skins.
3. Mix sugar, flour, and salt together in small bowl, then combine with grape pulp. Add lemon juice and butter and gently mix together.
4. Pour into 9-inch pastry-lined pie plate. Place top crust, adjust and slit top crust and flute edge.
5. Bake 10 minutes in hot oven, 450°F. Then reduce heat to 350°F and bake until top crust is nicely browned (approximately 30 minutes).
6. Remove from oven and let cool a minimum of 8 hours (to allow the filling to set) before serving.

*The Shaker pie crust recipe would work well for this pie.

HEFENKLÖSSE MIT ZIMMETSOSZE
(YEAST DUMPLINGS WITH CINNAMON SAUCE)

(Vegetarian. Serves 4 to 6.)

Tools: Covered cast iron skillet, or heavy stainless steel skillet pan. Double boiler (or improvise with larger, sturdy metal bowl placed over saucepan filled with boiling water). Large, covered casserole baking dish.

Ingredients:

1 cup whole milk

2 eggs, beaten

½ cup lard (butter can be used as a substitute)

½ cake compressed yeast (This is 1 ounce of cake yeast and can be substituted with 4 teaspoons or 2½ packages of dry active yeast.)

1 Tablespoon sugar

1 teaspoon salt

¼ cup warm water

4 cups sifted all-purpose flour

For cooking:

1 Tablespoon lard (butter can be used as a substitute)

1 cup boiling water

1 teaspoon salt

Steps::

1. Dissolve yeast in ¼ cup of warmed water. Set aside and check that yeast is good and active.

2. Heat milk to body-temperature warmth in pan or microwave oven. In stoneware bowl, pour the warmed milk and add the lard, sugar, salt and beaten eggs. Add dissolved yeast mixture. Mix.

3. Add flour and mix until all ingredients are blended. Cover bowl with cotton dish towel and place on warm area of counter or on the back of stove. Let rise overnight, or for a total of 8 hours.

4. When ready to make, form dough into dumplings about 2 inches across and place on cloth covered cutting board and let rise again until each has doubled in size.

5. Using pan or microwave, bring the 1 cup of cooking water to boil. Pour the water into the heavy skillet and add lard and salt.

6. Place dumplings into skillet, side by side, cover pan with lid and simmer 15 minutes without removing lid.

7. When dumplings are done cooking (test by gently pushing the center of one dumpling—it should feel firm), place into covered casserole baking dish.

While the dumplings are cooking, begin making Cinnamon Sauce. (You can also make the sauce in advance and re-warm for serving.)

Cinnamon Sauce Ingredients:

¾ cup sugar

¾ cup flour

2 teaspoons cinnamon

½ cup cold whole milk

2½ cups scalded whole milk

Steps:

1. Whisk sugar, flour, and cinnamon together in a bowl. Set aside.

2. Scald 2½ cups milk in microwave or in saucepan on stovetop. Remove from heat.

3. Add cold ½ cup milk to dry ingredients, mix roughly until moistened then transfer to top section of heated of double boiler.

4. Add scaled milk to mixture. Whisk together as you continue cooking for approximately 20 minutes, until sauce is slightly reduced and thickens. Stir occasionally to prevent lumps or burning.

5. Remove from heat and pour over dumplings. Cover until served.

SCHINKEN SALAT (HAM SALAD)

(Makes approximately 1½ quarts.)

Tools: Food processor

Note: Ham salad is a common way to use up leftover ham in Central and Eastern European food traditions. Midwesterners will not be surprised to see this grocery store deli-counter staple, but for those unfamiliar or disdainful of the commercial version, try the Amana version.

Ingredients:

4 cups boiled ham (1⅓ pound), cut in smaller pieces for food processing

1 large pickle (or a few smaller-sized, approximately ½ cup in total)

2 hard-boiled eggs

½ cup celery (approximately 2 stalks of celery)

¼ cup carrot (about 1 medium carrot, peeled)

1 cup heavy cream

¼ cup vinegar

Salt and pepper to taste

¼ teaspoon dry mustard powder

2 eggs

1 Tablespoon butter

Steps:

1. Place ham, pickle, hard-boiled eggs, celery, and carrots into food processor set to "chop" (or hand mince). Place into bowl and set aside.

2. In a saucepan, add heavy cream, vinegar, eggs, and butter. Begin heating while stirring constantly.

3. Add in mustard powder and salt and pepper. Keep stirring.

4. Bring to boil, then turn down heat to simmer for 1 minute. Stir. (The mixture should be thickened.) Set aside to cool.

5. When cooled, add to ham mixture and hand-mix together. Chill in refrigerator.

6. Use as a sandwich filling, or in summer, to stuff into fresh tomatoes.

HEISZER KARTOFFEL SALAT (HOT POTATO SALAD)

A recipe note from the original Amana cooks: "Best if made ahead of time and reheated."

Ingredients:

1 quart boiled, sliced potatoes (boiled in jackets/skins). Use Yukon or red salad potatoes.

1 medium-sized onion, minced

2 Tablespoons lard (butter or vegetable shortening can be used as a substitute)

2 Tablespoons flour

½ Tablespoon salt

3 Tablespoons vinegar

Dash of pepper

2 cups water

Steps:

1. In small stockpot, boil approximately 2 quarts of water.

2. Wash potatoes. Cut into ¼-inch-thick slices. Add potato slices to boiling water. Cook until potatoes are soft, yet still hold their shape, about 10 to 15 minutes.

3. Remove from heat, drain, and rinse with cool water. Set aside.

4. Mince onion.

5. In a large skillet, add lard and onion until onions are soft.

6. Stir in flour and blend well. Add in salt, vinegar, and pepper and blend again. Stir in water, mix, and cook until thickened. Remove from heat.

7. Pour mixture over potatoes and gently fold together.

8. Serve immediately or refrigerate overnight and reheat before serving.

RAPPITES

(Harmony Society, Harmonists, Harmonites)
Years active: 1805–1905
Affiliation: Pietism-Anabaptist
Founder / Leader: George Rapp

APPLES & BACON

(Serves 4 to 6.)
Tools: Cast iron skillet with lid

Note from the *Rappite Cookbook*:
"A good breakfast dish—or
supper on a cold night."

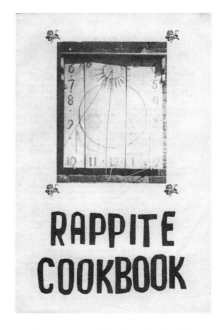

Front cover of the *Rappite Cookbook*,
printed by the Evansville, Indiana,
Gas & Electric Company, 1971.
Author's collection.

Ingredients:

Tart apples* (about ½ medium-sized apple per person)

Thick-cut bacon (about 2 slices per apple)

Brown sugar

Steps:

Peel apples. Remove core and slice into 2-inch sections. (Hold apples in cold water acidified with 1 tablespoon of lemon juice to prevent oxidation browning.)

Fry bacon in skillet. Remove from pan and hold in warm oven.

Drain all but ¼ cup of the bacon fat from the pan.

Add apple sections to skillet. Sprinkle with 1 to 2 tablespoons of brown sugar. Place lid on pan and cook over low heat for approximately 15 minutes until apples are tender.

Remove lid from skillet and carefully turn apple sections over with a flat spatula. (Some sections may break, it's okay.) Continue cooking in open skillet until lightly browned.

On a platter, lay bacon slices. Using flat spatula, lift apple slices out of skillet and lay on top of the bacon.

Tart apple varieties include: Granny Smith, Braeburn, Jonathan, Empire, and Cortland.

Holy Food

MOLASSES COOKIES

(Vegetarian. Makes about 5–6 dozen cookies.)

Oven temperature: 375°F

Note from the *Rappite Cookbook*: "These cookies are made in fall, stored in tubs under the bed and served as part of the winter sweets."

Ingredients:

¾ cup unsalted butter, melted (can substitute with shortening)

2 cups flour

2 teaspoons baking soda

1 teaspoon ground cinnamon

1 teaspoon ground ginger

¾ teaspoon salt

½ teaspoon ground cloves

1½ cups sugar

¼ cup dark molasses (sorghum and blackstrap molasses can be substituted)

1 large egg

Optional ingredients: 1 cup chopped nuts and 2 cups raisins. (Soak raisins in ½ cup hot water for 30 minutes then drain off liquid prior to use.)

Steps:

Preheat oven to 375°F.

Mix brown sugar, melted shortening, and molasses together in large bowl.

Add baking soda, ginger, and cinnamon; mix until equally blended.

In a small bowl, beat eggs. Fold beaten eggs into mixture until thoroughly blended.

Add flour; stir until thoroughly mixed.

Separate dough into 4 sections. On a large working surface, roll out a section of dough to approximately ¼-inch thickness. With a medium-sized cookie cutter,* cut out. Repeat until dough is gone. Extra dough after cutting should be rolled into the next section of dough.

Place cut circles onto parchment-lined cookie sheet with 1-inch space between cookies.

Bake for 8 to 10 minutes. Remove from oven and allow to cool on pan for 10 minutes, then transfer to cooling rack.

*For a proper Rappite-style cookie, use the rim of a juice glass or a scalloped-edge biscuit cutter to make the shapes.

JANSSONITES

(Bishop Hill Community)
Years active: 1846–1858
Affiliation: Pietism
Founder / Leader: Erik Jansson

SVAG DRIKA (SMALL BEER)

(Vegetarian. Makes 4 gallons.)
Tools: 5-gallon carboy and fitted airlock

Ingredients:

3½ pounds malted barley syrup (available at brewing supply stores and online)

16 ounces unsulphured molasses or sorghum

1 package active dry yeast

4 gallons distilled (or boiled) water

Steps:

Warm water to approximately 100°F, then pour into carboy.

Pour malt syrup and 8 ounces of molasses into water.

Add package of yeast.

Swish to mix. Place airlock into neck of carboy.

Wrap carboy with a towel and place in dark corner.

Let ferment for 3 to 4 days. Add remaining 8 ounces of molasses.

Ferment for 3 more days, then it's ready to drink.

BOMMULS KAKA WITH KRAM (COTTON CAKE WITH JAM)

(Vegetarian. Makes 1 skillet.)
Tools: Cast iron skillet

Ingredients:

2 cups whole milk

1½ cups all-purpose flour

2 eggs

2 teaspoons sugar

¼ teaspoon salt

½ cup butter

Steps:

1. Preheat oven to 400°F.
2. In a medium-sized bowl, add all the ingredients and mix. Set aside.
3. Coat skillet in butter.
4. Pour batter into skillet and place into oven.
5. Bake for approximately 20 minutes, until set.
6. Remove from oven. Serve warm with butter and jam.

NOTE: This pancake is like a "Dutch baby" and bakes unevenly.

CARDAMOM HORNS

(Vegetarian. Makes 2 dozen.)
Tools: Pastry brush
Oven temperature: 375°F

Ingredients for dough:

3 Tablespoons butter
3 Tablespoons sugar
1 package active dry yeast
2 Tablespoons lukewarm water
¾ Tablespoon salt
¾ cup lukewarm whole milk
1 teaspoon ground cardamom
3 cups all-purpose flour
Brown sugar (for sprinkling)
½ cup butter

Steps:

1. Preheat oven to 375°F.
2. Cream butter and sugar together in medium-sized bowl, then beat in egg.
3. Add yeast and then lukewarm water and stir gently.
4. Mix in salt and cardamom powder, then mix in lukewarm milk.
5. Mix in flour, then cover bowl with clean, cotton towel. Set in a warm place to rise.
6. When the dough has doubled in size, divide into quarters.
7. On a lightly floured surface, roll out each quarter section into approximately 9 inches round.
8. Melt butter in a small bowl. Using brush, lightly cover dough with butter. Sprinkle 1 tablespoon of brown sugar on dough.
9. Cut into 8 triangular pieces.
10. Beginning at the wide end, roll each section toward the point. Bend ends toward each other and pinch together.
11. Place horns onto parchment-lined jelly roll pan. Cover with light cotton dishcloth and let rest until doubled in size.

12. Place into oven and bake for 10–12 minutes.

13. Remove when done and brush with more butter. When cool, drizzle with icing.

Ingredients for Icing:

1½ cups confectioner's sugar, sifted

4 Tablespoons whole milk

Steps:

1. In medium-sized bowl, combine all the ingredients.

2. Mix until smooth.

SWEDISH MEATBALLS

(Makes 30 meatballs.)

Tools: Cast iron skillet

Ingredients:

1½ cups breadcrumbs or saltine crackers

1 cup half & half

½ cup chopped onion

1 Tablespoon butter

¾ pound ground beef

½ pound ground veal

¼ pound ground pork

1 egg

¼ cup finely minced parsley

1¼ teaspoons salt

Dash of black pepper, ginger, and ground nutmeg

3 Tablespoons butter

Ingredients for gravy:

2 Tablespoons of butter

2 Tablespoons of flour

1 Tablespoon beef flavor Better Than Bouillon concentrated stock

1¼ cups boiling water

½ teaspoon instant coffee powder

Steps:

In a frying pan, add 1 tablespoon of butter and onions and cook under medium heat until "sweated."

In a small bowl, add the half & half and breadcrumbs and soak for 5 minutes.

In a medium-sized bowl, mix the meats, cooked onions, soaked breadcrumbs, egg, parsley, salt, and spices. Mix by hand until thoroughly combined.

Place in refrigerator for 1 hour to chill. (Mixture is soft, and chilling makes it easier to work with.)

Using a scoop or hands, shape into 1½ inch-diameter balls.

Add the remaining 2 tablespoons of butter to frying pan, then the shaped balls, and brown under medium heat.

Remove meatballs from frying pan and set aside.

Add 2 more tablespoons of butter. Under medium heat, melt butter and add flour. Stir until lumps are gone.

Add bouillon and boiling water, stir. Add instant coffee and stir together.

Stir until gravy thickens and bubbles. Add meatballs and cover pan. Reduce heat to low.

Simmer for approximately 30 minutes, basting occasionally.

Serve over cooked egg noodles or mashed potatoes.

The Bishop Hill Steeple Building, c. 1900. Photo courtesy of the Bishop Hill Heritage Association.

Chapter Three: Utopian Dreams

Four
THE GREAT AWAKENING

"Elijah is coming. Washed in the blood of the lamb. Come on, you winefizzling, ginsizzling, boozeguzzling existences! Come on, you dog-gone, bullnecked, beetlebrowed, hogjowled, peanutbrained, weaseleyed fourflushers, false alarms, and excess baggage! Come on, you triple extract of infamy! Alexander J. Christ Dowie, that's yanked to glory most half this planet from Frisco Beach to Vladivostok. The Deity ain't no nickel dime bumshow. I put it to you that he's on the square and a corking fine business proposition. He's the grandest thing yet and don't you forget it. Shout salvation in King Jesus!"

—From Chapter 12, *Ulysses* by James Joyce (1922), talking about
the founder of Zion City, Illinois, faith healer and reincarnation
of the Prophet Elijah, J. Alexander Dowie (1847–1907).

RELIGION IN THE UNITED STATES UNDERWENT A STARTLING SHIFT DURING THE 1800S. Before the fire and brimstone of the Great Awakening, there were little fires erupting across the landscape that threatened established religions and redefined what *is* religion. Over the course of 250 years, as the American experiment continued (and continues), our collective ideas about worship and spirituality have grown to absorb many new ideas. If Americans are anything, we are unorthodox in our beliefs.

It is often observed that the fiery passion of revolution dissipates over time, and especially if the revolutionaries have gained a position of power. When religion is added to a political or cultural movement, the situation becomes murkier—is this leader someone genuinely hearing the voice of God? The corrosive influence of ego and absolute authority over people and money has led many a well-intentioned preacher down a dark pathway. Is that the devil exerting his power of temptation? The current diagnostic criterion of mental illness considers extreme religiosity and direct communication with God and his/her minions as delusional behaviors. Yet modern American Protestant religions and New Age movements are rooted in having a direct relationship with a godhead. It becomes difficult for anyone, let alone believers, to sort the wheat of divine inspiration from the chaff of opportunistic con.

Prophet Elijah J. Alexander Dowie (1847–1907).

The post-colonial revival of religious fervor is referred to as the Great Awakening and roughly covers the growth of New Religious Movements and schisms within mainline and established religions from about 1790 to 1860. It was the era when the "western United States" was Ohio and the lands of the Great Lakes, and across the Mississippi River was the unmapped home to Indigenous peoples leery of restless Americans trampling that home. The Louisiana Purchase under the Jefferson Administration in 1803 tripled the legal territory of the United States. Yet to "own" the land on paper, when the reality was that these lands were defended by the Native Americans that had lived there for millennia, was problematic for the young United States government, to say the least. Jefferson and successive presidents chose to wage war by sending both armies of soldiers and settlers to forcibly claim the Indigenous lands.

Though the Calvinist separatist Congregationalists[32] had been outcasts when they came to the shores of what is now Massachusetts in 1620, they, along with Episcopalians, were known as Mainline Protestants or the "Old Lights" by 1800. In the East, churches followed the English tradition of having religious leaders attend college or an approved divinity school where a man could study and ultimately gain an accredited license to preach. Sermons of the time were cerebral, intended to explain—through scripture—man's relationship to God and Christ. They were filled with references to other pastoral thinkers and pursued what was considered a noble path of an intellectual understanding of Christianity. Long gone were the Puritans who burned witches and banished fallen women with a scarlet "A." The God of the East was a benign entity interested in the finer points of Christian philosophy and doctrine. A newly ordained minister would use his family connections to gain an existing parsonage, or he could attempt to establish a new congregation. Many of these ministers traveled west in search of lost souls and new parishioners.

32 Congregationalism is the catch-all phrase used to describe the reformed Protestant churches that began first in England and later grew out of the separatists and Puritans that emigrated to America. The churches are self-governing by the congregation—therefore, Congregationalist. At the risk of oversimplifying, Presbyterians are the opposite of Congregationalists as they organize churches in a hierarchical fashion with each church ruled by a council of elders, a region or presbytery is ruled by more senior elders, and so on. Presbyterians do not have a bishop or leader but rely on a council and general assembly of councils to decide issues of policy and scripture. Theologically, Congregationalists and Presbyterians share a near-identical conservative Calvinist doctrine.

Oh, there were whiffs of smoke before the conflagration of the Great Awakening took hold of the land. One important figure was Jonathan Edwards (grandfather of Aaron Burr), who shook the staid Congregationalists of Connecticut and beyond with his fiery sermons during the 1720s–50s. Where later preachers would ease the pathway to Heaven, Edwards erected hurdles. It was not enough to sit in the family pew and pay a tithe; one must fear God and subjugate one's individual will until one becomes a vessel for God's will.[33] As a formally ordained and licensed minister, he traveled throughout New England, spreading his fevered message. Other theologians and pastors criticized Edwards as creating religious fanatics by his exhortations. Edwards also broke ranks by advocating for a presbytery and consolidation of churches under a central authority. Though Edwards lived and preached decades before the Great Awakening, it was his model of preaching and sermon writing that became a blueprint for those who followed.

I F ONE LEARNED AMERICAN HISTORY FROM MOVIES AND FROM TELEVISION, IT WOULD be easy to think that every American was devotedly religious. In fact, the opposite is true. In 1800, according to the census, the population of the United States was 5,308,483 people (of which 893,602 were enslaved Africans and their children). Only 14% of that total non-enslaved population were religious adherents.[34] Broken down into hard numbers, this means a total of 618,084 church members across all denominations of Protestants and Roman Catholics. In contrast, the census of 1890 notes the percentage of believers increased to 45% of the overall increased population of 62,979,766 people.

How did the United States change from a nation of diverse, multicultural, free-thinking, individuals to a Christian-centric, culturally restrictive, capitalistic society? It was the unfettered growth of the country itself that fueled the coming religious revival. Earlier generations of settlers were now settled. They had land and power and saw new immigrants and Black freemen as a threat to their way of life. The poor, recent immigrants, pioneers, and Black people were not welcomed in the Old Light churches or society. More ministers took up Jonathan Edwards' "angry god" style, but others found a new message and messenger.

John Wesley was the antithesis of the Episcopal (Anglican) church in which he was raised and ordained in England during the 1720s. He was significantly impressed by a group of Moravian Christians he met on their way to the United States from German Bohemia. Like many of the German Lutheran separatists, they were Pietists[35] who believed in the idea of Perfectionism,

---

33   A small sample of Jonathan Edwards' most famous sermon rhetoric: "The God that holds you over the pit of hell, much in the same way as one holds a spider, or some loathsome insect, over the fire, abhors you, and is dreadfully provoked; His wrath towards you burns like fire; He looks upon you as worthy of nothing else but to be cast into the fire; He is of purer eyes than to bear to have you in His sight; you are ten thousand times more abominable in His eyes than the most hateful venomous serpent is in ours. You have offended Him infinitely more than ever a stubborn rebel did his prince: and yet, it is nothing but His hand that holds you from falling into the fire every moment. It is to be ascribed to nothing else, that you did not go to hell last night; that you were suffered to awake again in the world, after you closed your eyes to sleep; and there is no other reason to be given . . . But His mercy; yea, no other reason can be given why you do not this very moment drop down into hell."

34   Religious historians Roger Finke and Rodney Starke have devoted their careers to studying American religious movements. Their 1986 paper on creating a mathematical formula to enumerate church members, and the later 2005 book *The Churching of America, 1776–2005: Winners and Losers in Our Religious Economy,* are considered the platinum standard of both research and statistics. I rely on their data here and elsewhere throughout *Holy Food*.

35   This paints Pietism with a broad brush. The German and Scandinavian Pietist thinkers each brought a slightly different interpretation of the Book to believers, many of whom formed sects to preserve those teachings. We will continue to meet many more Pietists in the coming pages.

which means that through the grace of Christ, God forgives sins, and if one lives according to His Word, that one remains blessed and in God's good stead. Most importantly, a person can, through that grace, have a personal relationship with God. Wesley, influenced by the Pietists, refined his beliefs and practices, which came to be known as Methodism.

Wesley was, arguably, the most significant influence on modern American Protestantism and, ultimately, on American-style Christianity. Prior to Wesley, ministers and church leaders had authority over determining who was or was not saved. What Wesley took from the German Pietists was the idea that ultimate salvation is achieved through a personal relationship with God and Jesus. This idea of a direct relationship with God is a tenet of belief that connects all American Protestant religions. Wesley taught that a person can be "reborn" through faith in Christ, and is assured a righteousness imparted to them from God through that belief in Christ and the practice of piety or pious deeds. The definition of pious deeds is not what we think of as garden-variety good deeds like helping our neighbors, but specific acts: prayer, searching the Scriptures (often called "sacred time" or "sacred meditation" by modern churches), holy communion/supper, fasting, Christian community, and healthy living. The seven pious deeds become, under the interpretation of successive generations of pastors, another source of schisms that birth numerous sects, religiously imposed diets, and communes.

F RENCH ENGINEER MICHEL CHEVALIER, VISITING THE UNITED STATES IN THE EARLY 1800s, made this observation about Americans: "No one assimilates a new method more rapidly; he is always ready to change his tools, his system, or his profession. He is a mechanic in his soul."[36] During this era, Eli Whitney not only invented the cotton gin, but also the machines to create standardized uniform-sized gun parts for quick assembly and repair. Robert Fulton built steamboats to move crops and soldiers as canals were dug at a furious pace. American invention and inventors did not compartmentalize their engineering advances as only scientific inspiration. These men saw their inventions as divinely inspired by God to help the American people, and by doing so, He showed His favor to America and those who believed. We may recognize this idea today in modern "prosperity gospel" preachers who proclaim that monetary success and public acclaim are God's reward for their brand of fealty. Americans in the early 1800s began to take the Calvinist notion of being the "chosen" or "selected" people to more radical ends as new interpretations of that concept now incorporated unorthodox beliefs and became both religious and political ideologies.

The United States government offered incentives—free land but claim it at your own risk—under a variety of laws and schemes to colonize the North American landmass. Large families were rewarded with hundreds of acres of land, while entire European villages were recruited to come to America with the promise of wealth and prosperity. Just like the British did in the 1600s, the American government encouraged persecuted religious sects to emigrate to the United States. Internal and external migrants recognized that the opportunity to own land was a singular way to build wealth. Cheap access to reliable transportation made it possible

---

36 Quoted by Seldes in *The Stammering Century*, yet I could find no other reference within the vast expanse of the internet. I suspect the quote is a liberal translation of Chevalier's 1836 collection of letters published as *Letters on North America*.

for nearly anyone to forge their way to the far West. The newly designed Conestoga wagon could carry a family and all their worldly possessions thirty miles in a single day. Yet it was a difficult life. Food was scarce and the terrain needed to be radically altered to grow crops the European way. These settlers rejected wisdom from Indigenous

Gaspar River Revival.

peoples on working with the land, and sought to subjugate both Native people and the land until both bent to their will. The Edenic Covenant had become the inspiration of the governmental and personal policy of Manifest Destiny. God was on the side of the occupying settlers.

It was not uncommon for a family homesteading on a remote piece of land to go months without seeing another human being outside of their immediate kin. It was in these wildlands of Kentucky and throughout the rolling hills of Ohio, and into southern Indiana and Illinois, that we see the first flames of the burning fires of the spirit ignited. In the west, away from the established Congregationalists, Episcopalians, and Catholics, and away from the civilized cities of the Atlantic seaboard, men focused on making money and taming the land. The trappers, loggers, farmers, and rivermen put God low on their priority list. Religious leaders felt that God was absent from these wild western regions. The people, both settlers and native, must be brought into God's grace before it was too late, and the entire country loses God's favor. It was time for a revival.

Along the Gaspar River near present-day Bowling Green, Kentucky, where Scots and Protestant Irish immigrants settled the mountainous land and built small villages, itinerant preachers came to find new souls. Visiting each farmstead was near impossible, so the minister would find a clearing on the river, near enough to a town but far enough away to accommodate the hundreds, maybe thousands, of people they hoped would arrive. Advertisements in newspapers throughout the region announced the date and place. The word would spread along the river outposts and through the back country that there was to be a camp meeting.

Thousands did come. Sometimes tens of thousands. A revival could last for days, maybe weeks. Souls were saved in gaudy fashion. Jerking like the Shakers, but wild and unruly. The Holy Spirit would invade a body, throwing the sinning wretch to the ground with the power of the Word. The saved would begin speaking a guttural gibberish deemed to be a spiritual gift from God as foretold in Corinthians, that those touched by Jesus would speak in foreign tongues. The preaching continued. The beseeching continued. As one minister fell over from exhaustion, another stood up on a makeshift pulpit rigged up from a pony cart.

It continued for days. Attendees slept on the ground. Families stayed close together and ate their simple provisions. Farther away from the preaching, vendors sold a variety of food and drink (non-alcoholic, of course) to fuel the saving. Young women flush with the frantic energy of

Cartoon mocking revivals.

the pulsating crowd wandered off into the woods where the devil in the form of a good-looking young man often found them. Sinners of the worst sort, the deniers and mockers who came to gawp at the spectacle, were seized by the Lord. Men, women, children all came forward to testify that they were but lowly worms before the love of Jesus Christ sanctified them.

The preaching was not the brimstone of Edwards nor the considered quiet faith of Wesley, but it is of them. Absent Oxford and Yale educations, these new men of God are the muscular Christians who are wresting souls from Satan's maw. These pastors saw themselves as soldiers in God's army, and throughout the Ohio River Valley and beyond, they traveled calling to everyone: Repent! Christ is coming.

The ferocity of large-scale camp meetings lasted for a scant few decades, but their influence was immeasurable. People were awakened to a new way to consider who exactly God was to them and what was His function in their lives. As evangelists traveled the country, they spoke to people and published their interpretations of scripture and, more controversially, what God had personally told them. So taken was the western frontier with religious fervor that the Shakers sent missionaries from their New York Mother House to spread Mother Ann Lee's message. Other preachers with nascent ideas of how to worship and how to live in accordance to God's will flooded the Ohio River Valley.

NEW YORK, FROM ALBANY TO THE LAKE ERIE SHORES, WAS ALSO CONSUMED BY THE flame of the Holy Spirit. The man holding the match was Charles G. Finney. He too, was a man of his time, a spiritual seeker who as a young man attended Baptist services with his family, then went on to study law. He was baptized in the Holy Spirit[37] after seeing a vision of Jesus Christ while he was contemplating scripture in a forest glade. He renounced both the law and his membership in the Masonic brotherhood[38] and studied to become a minister. He became renowned for his mesmerizing preaching.

He also embraced the new ideas of other religious reformers and prophets. Like the Shakers, he voiced equal rights for women and the abolition of slavery. He took Wesleyan Methodism further by eroding even more barriers that stood between God and man. New converts were immediately welcomed as full members of his Free Church.[39] He believed in a God of love, not of fury, who was angry at the sin, never at the sinner. The movement he began is often referred to as the "Holiness Movement."[40] Though the camp meeting had given way to the smaller and less combustible tent revival, Finney saved souls and—according to critics whose predecessors hurled the same invective about Jonathan Edwards a century earlier—drove people to insanity.

Finney traveled throughout New York and Connecticut, preaching the word of God to hungry listeners. Among those hearers were Church of Latter-Day Saints founder Joseph Smith and end-times preacher William Miller. Smith mentions Finney's writing and was familiar with the story of the evangelist's conversion in a wooded glade. Miller had met Finney as they crossed paths during their missionary travels throughout New York state. Another person influential to the next wave of religious visionaries who met and received a blessing from Finney was Robert Matthews, a.k.a. Matthias, a.k.a. Matthias the Jew, a.k.a. Jesus Christ. The story of Matthias would be a lurid footnote to this and every American history except for the fact that he was a harbinger of future religiously inspired and divinely deranged cultic leaders.

Robert Matthews was born in western New York, orphaned at a young age and raised by neighbors. His family was known in the Washington County area to be eccentric. Matthews was born again in the Holy Spirit at a Finney revival and left behind a wife and a failing business to become Matthias. His early travels are scattered and erratic. We know he traveled through the South and into western areas still fully occupied by Native Americans to preach the gospel, then returned to New York City. As Matthias, he built a small coterie of devoted wealthy followers who gave him money and free access to their houses. As time passed, he became increasingly demanding, masking his requests to sprinkle his bath water on virgins and sleep with the wives of his benefactors as vision-driven commands from God.

A Black, formerly enslaved servant from the home of one of Matthias' followers, named Isabelle, believed in the truth of his preaching and became his assistant and servant during those years. As he grew more demanding, his benefactors abandoned him for another pastor and balked at giving him more money. In retaliation, Matthias (allegedly) poisoned them and

---

37   In Methodist tradition that was later shared with Pentecostal and Holiness movements, "baptism by the Holy Spirit" is not a benign nor organized church ritual; for believers, it is the moment that the spirit of God enters your body and redeems your soul. As proof, believers will display "gifts," or physical "signs" like falling faint, speaking in tongues, and aggressive physical contortions.

38   It was common for middle- and upper-class men to join fraternal organizations for comradery and networking.

39   Literally, a free church. Prior to Finney, a member of a Protestant church had to pay a tithe and a rental fee for their family's pew, which excluded poor people from attending or relegated them to standing areas in the back of a church.

40   "Holiness" was a descriptor given to the offshoot Methodists who, like the Perfectionists, believed that once a believer had been reborn through the sanctifying grace of Jesus Christ, that they were forgiven from not only past but future sin. In the begats of American Protestantism, the Holiness Movement is a direct parent of the Pentecostal Movement.

Holy Food

L: Robert "Matthias" Matthews.
R: Portrait of Sojourner Truth, c. 1864. Courtesy of the National Portrait Gallery/Smithsonian.

claimed their illnesses and the death of an unfortunate former follower as punishment from God. He fled from the law to rural New York, taking Isabelle with him.

Matthias and Isabelle traveled to visit other preachers, trying to convince them that *he* was ordained by God as the voice of the Lord. They spent a week at Joseph Smith's first Mormon communal living experiment in New York around 1830. Smith notes in his diary that "Joshua the Jew" (as Matthias was calling his disguised self) had many good points to make but seemed mentally unstable. Matthias was eventually arrested and tried. He was acquitted. The family who accused Matthias then published an attack on Isabelle, claiming that it was she who poisoned the unfortunate Mr. Pierson with tainted blackberries. She more than denied this accusation. She sued for slander and won.

Robert Matthews traveled west and is lost to history. Isabelle, who prior to meeting Matthias was a member of the African Methodist church (Mother Zion in New York City), and in 1843 was reborn in the Holy Spirit, changed her name to Sojourner Truth. As Sojourner Truth she found fame in publishing her life story and was hailed as a magnetizing public speaker.

But before Sojourner Truth found her calling, and after her acquittal in New York City, she followed the ministry of William Miller, founder of the Millerism movement. Miller, a Baptist, then Deist, then recommitted Baptist, was a student of scripture. He rejected the mainline Protestant belief that the Second Coming was far off in the unknown future. In 1840, he began publicizing his belief that he had uncovered—using complicated mathematical formulas and scriptural clues—that Jesus Christ was coming back to Earth on October 22, 1844. Researchers estimate that Miller printed and distributed over a half-million tracts detailing his beliefs throughout the English-speaking world. Thousands of worshipers and many other ministers subscribed to Miller's prediction that the end of the world was nigh, and with Christ's return, the Biblical prophecies in the Book of Revelation would be made real. Believers would be saved, live with Jesus in a thousand-year paradise, then be brought directly up to heaven to sit at the feet of God.

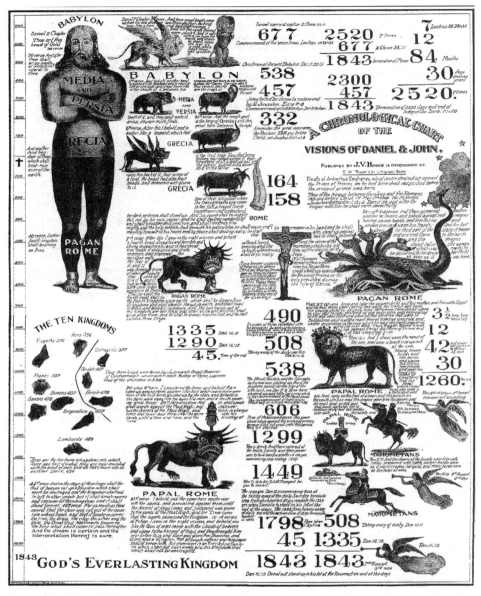

Chart explaining William Miller's methods and formulas used to calculate the second coming of Christ (1843–1844) resulting in the Great Disappointment, and ultimately, the Seventh-Day Adventist movement.

This did not happen.

After what in Seventh-Day Adventist history is called the Great Disappointment, most Millerites abandoned Miller and his Bible-based predictions. Many rejoined Methodist or Baptist congregations, and a healthy number joined Shaker communities. A few remained loyal to Miller's work and visions, and embraced his belief that the Jewish Sabbath of Saturday was the holy day to honor the Lord, not the Catholic and Protestant worship day of

Sunday. And that the Second Coming of Jesus Christ was an event in the near future and not a theoretical abstraction. Miller's popularity gave rise to the general boom in eschatology during the 1850s. Between 1845 and Miller's death in 1849, remaining followers began to refine the details of Miller's proclamations. Believers came from different Protestant denominations, so there was little agreement about a cohesive theology at these meetings. But the popularity of his ideas about the Bible and end-of-the-world studies fractured mainstream Protestantism.

A small group of Millerites published his ideas along with their own about thoughts about Biblical revelations during the ensuing decades. It wasn't until the Civil War, when Ellen G. White revealed her own visions of the Bible, that a new denomination was born. It was Ellen G. White who picked up Miller's mantle and further refined Miller's idea into a cohesive theology and way of life. Officially, Seventh-Day Adventism was incorporated in 1863 in Battle Creek, Michigan. One of the ten tenets of Adventism is the belief that the body, soul, and spirit are all one, and that keeping the body healthy is just as important as keeping the soul healthy. Adventists embraced vegetarianism. They also followed the rules outlined in Leviticus and additionally forbade alcohol and caffeine. White was a proponent of missionary work, and under her leadership, the Adventists grew exponentially in the last half of the nineteenth century.

The Seventh-Day Adventists embraced nutritional science and built sanitariums where people could rejuvenate both the flesh and the soul. Ellen White wrote extensively on "scientific" food pairing for optimum health, the timing of when to consume meals, as well as the amount of food eaten. Much attention was paid to regular bowel movements as a signal that the human machine was functioning correctly. Adventists of the late 1800s believed that foods should be neither too hot nor too cold and be relatively bland in taste. Excessive amounts of spiced foods caused sexual excitation and led to masturbation. The notion that spicy foods stimulate passion is linked to pseudo-science and anti-Catholic bigotry, as spicy foods were equated with cuisines from countries with large Catholic populations. The popularization of morning breakfast cereals is directly linked to Adventism's healthy-eating proselytizing. As Ellen White said in her influential book *The Ministry of Healing*, "Our bodies are Christ's purchased possession, and we are not at liberty to do with them as we please."

In Battle Creek, Michigan, a recent convert to Adventism, John Harvey Kellogg, developed what were considered "health" foods. Bland flaked corn. Simple pottages. And the first meat substitute that was a mix of gluten, soy, and peanuts. Called Protose, it was a protein-packed hybrid of peanutted seitan and tofu. Years later, a group of Adventists settled in Loma Linda, California, and continued their research into nutrition and human health. The Loma Linda brand of meat substitutes, which evolved from Kellogg's Protose and other ready-made products, including the Morningstar brand of frozen meat substitutes, was owned by the church-associated Worthington Company. The company was sold in the past decade and is now owned by the small Atlantic Natural Products company. (After a few years of being held by the conglomerate Kellogg's, begun by brother and rival of John Harvey, William Keith.) McKee Foods, makers of the Little Debbie brand of snack cakes, is owned by an Adventist church affiliate. Little Debbie cakes are for many eaters their introduction to carob as a chocolate substitute.

Yet for any criticism of the most fantastical claims about nutrition, the Adventists were essentially modernists using the science of the day mixed with scripture to find a path to God. Their work goes on at Loma Linda University, and Adventist-run health care facilities and hospitals in California, Florida, Maryland, and Ohio. Modern human-biology researchers have declared Adventists the healthiest population group, with the longest lifespan in the United States due to their vegetarian and often vegan diets.

J OSEPH SMITH WAS ALSO SPEAKING WITH GOD. HE WAS FIFTEEN YEARS OLD WHEN he had his first vision of God and Jesus as two separate beings. He also attended Charles Finney revivals. Three years later, an angel visited to tell him where to find an important book. It was the Book of Mormon. As described, it was written on gold plates and buried near Smith's home in Palmyra, New York. It took him several years of divine assistance to translate the testimony of Semitic Christians written in "reformed Egyptian" on gold plates into English. When the project was finally completed, he published his "translation" as The Book of Mormon. He was twenty-four.

Smith quickly converted his family and then neighbors to his revelations that Christians had lived in the Americas since ancient times and were descended from the Lost Tribes of Israel. Without going into too much detail about the Book of Mormon, Smith considered his new religion as a restoration of early Christianity. Smith was also influenced by social philosophers describing the ideals of communal living. Smith was a charismatic missionary who drew a small group of men to his new religion. He sent them west to share this "new message of Jesus Christ." Though often met with hostility and sometimes violence, Smith and his missionaries built a substantial number of followers. Smith was driven from New York and went to Ohio intending to build his new communal city, New Jerusalem.

Ohio was a logical choice for Smith. The region had been the scene of many camp meetings and revivals and was already home to several religious communes like the Shakers and others sprouted during the Awakening. He and his missionaries would convert entire congregations to Mormonism. But northeastern Ohio was not as open to the idea of thousands of Mormon converts moving to the town of Kirtland. It wasn't just that the religious beliefs were suspect, but that a monolithic voting bloc would be created and give Smith and his followers too much political and economic power. The Latter-Day Saints were scouting for other locations to build their new city, with Missouri and Illinois both under consideration. Smith dispatched small settler groups to test the areas for agricultural viability and societal tolerance.

In the years between 1831 and 1840, Smith stayed in Kirtland, Ohio, and suffered beatings and a literal tar-and-feathering that left him nearly dead. He was also receiving visions and new proclamations on how to build and organize the new religion. Smith finally left Ohio to visit the outpost settlements in Missouri and Illinois. Animosity toward the Mormons grew during the decade. The settlers in Missouri were repeatedly burned off their farms until the skirmishes grew into armed standoffs in 1838. The Missouri governor declared that any Mormons were to be either exterminated or driven from the state.

The Mormons surrendered, and Smith and other leaders were taken into custody. One of the earliest converts, Brigham Young, assumed leadership and led the remaining thousands of believers to settle and build the city of Nauvoo in western Illinois, on the eastern bank of the Mississippi River across from Fort Madison, Iowa. Smith escaped from the Missouri jail and resumed leadership of the Saints in Illinois. Though tarnished as a prophet, Smith continued to reveal new doctrines to his closest supporters. The most controversial was, of course, "plural marriage."

The Mormons took an increasingly isolationist stance in the face of personal and governmental animosity to the group. They began to build more ways to be self-sufficient. The Relief Society was founded in 1842 as a Mutual Aid group that put women in charge of ensuring individual members of the faith would be assisted when faced with difficulty. The Relief Society developed a rigid social structure that included all girls and women who would make clothing, harvest and preserve food, and tend to each other's households when the need struck.

By 1844, Smith's personal excesses—including the spiritual marriage to other women while unbeknownst to his first and legal wife—caused a rift within his close circle of priests. There was also increasing pressure from the Illinois governor and the federal government, who felt that Smith and the Mormons were treasonous as they declared their loyalty first to the Latter-Day Saints and secondarily to the United States. Smith and his brother Hyrum were again taken to jail, but this time an angry mob stormed the jailhouse and shot both Smith brothers. After a brief power struggle within the Mormon council, Brigham Young was elected as the new leader. Young led the thousands in the journey across the Western Plains to settle in Utah in 1846, fifty years before the territory became a state. The lack of state and federal government officials allowed the Mormons to settle and build cities and infrastructure to sustain them through any kind of attack or privation.

While the official history of the LDS is centered on the male founders and subsequent leaders, what is often overlooked is that within Mormonism there are schismatic sects and denominations who saw differing visions for the faith and remained in the previous settlements in Missouri and Ohio. Those groups are on a spectrum from the Fundamentalist Church of Latter-Day Saints, who espouse plural marriage and a rigid patriarchal control of extended families, to the much more liberal Reorganized Church of Jesus Christ of Latter-Day Saints (or Community of Christ) that ordains women as priests.

Several of the sects were founded in the wake of the death of Joseph Smith and claim legitimacy through blood lineage: the Community of Christ was founded in 1860 by Smith's son in Independence, Missouri. James Strang began his group (who embraced polygamy) in Voree, Wisconsin, and later moved to Beaver Island in northern Lake Michigan, where the entire colony built a small shipping—some say pirating—empire for nearly a decade. Others were begun in the early twentieth century because of notions of doctrinal purity, like the breakaway polygamy groups who claim that church elders betrayed the original vision of the church by renouncing plural marriage in 1890 as a condition of Utah joining the United States.

Young re-established the Relief Society, which in the following years helped homogenize the expected duties of a Mormon woman. To this day, women do not take official leadership

Mormon charity group canning food. Hansel Mieth for *LIFE Magazine*, September 1937.

roles in the largest and most recognizable form of the LDS church based in Salt Lake City, but they are the organizing engine that ensures social cohesion within the group. Women maintain the home and family, which is the backbone of Mormon culture. The Relief Society is one of the oldest women-led organizations in the United States. With its focus on education and alleviating suffering of families during large and small crises, it established a template for self-sufficiency and Mutual Aid. The Relief Society follows a similar hierarchical organization system as the church does, usually with the wife of the Ward (congregation) leader running the branch group. They report up to the Stake (district), who in turn report to the General Office which is run by a trio of women leaders appointed by Stake leaders. For context, as of 2012, there are 30,000 LDS Wards and 3,000 Stakes in the United States.

Brigham Young encouraged women to pursue education and work outside the home in the earliest days of the Utah colony's founding. Lesser known to non-LDS members is that Mormons established a woman's right to divorce during its days governing the Utah territory. Women who objected to polygamy often divorced their husbands. The divorce rate in the late 1800s was nearly 30%. Women operated businesses, became doctors and lawyers, and even ran for governmental office. The church grew more conservative and patriarchal post-World War II, curtailing individual women's rights just as the nationwide women's rights movement gained momentum.

A girl growing up in an LDS community will attend Young Women, a youth group that teaches girls LDS history, personal growth, and homemaking skills. At the age of eighteen, or younger

Holy Food

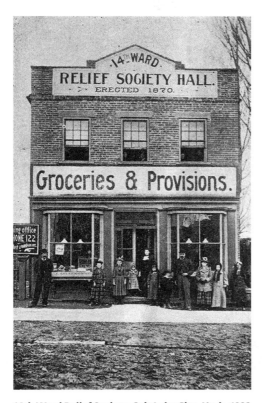

14th Ward Relief Society, Salt Lake City, Utah, 1893.

if she has a child, she automatically becomes a member of the Relief Society. The group is a boon to young mothers who often rely on older members for parental wisdom and occasional child-minding. Single mothers are rarely abandoned and are supported by the community. At the Ward level, the Relief Society meets twice a month and spends time with scripture or the latest bulletin from the president of the church. The other time is spent on classes focused on self-improvement and homemaking skills. Even women with full-time jobs outside the home are expected to attend and participate.

The homemaking aspect of the Relief Society has created an oral tradition of sharing recipes and cooking techniques. This tradition has led to a relatively homogeneous food culture. But with the growth of the LDS church through its missionary work around the world, young missionaries brought home favorite dishes from the countries they visited. In what can be lightly called a reverse colonization, the once-mocked "white people" food of the Mormons now reflects the cuisines of Saints from every country. The Relief Society and the *Deseret News* (owned by the LDS) has published cookbooks for over one hundred years that, when studied, reflect the changing cuisine and diversifying palate of the Mormon faithful.

It is also worth noting that the women of the LDS Relief Society are skilled food preservationists. Their mandate to keep at least a year's food supply on hand at all times has influenced the cuisine. Many of the favored recipes are ones that utilize home-canned vegetables and meats, with a focus on soups, casseroles, and stews. The recipes included here are taken from historic twentieth-century LDS cookbooks and are stalwart recipes used by millions of Mormon cooks.

The LDS church refers to food and other restrictions in the Words of Wisdom and often updates those guidelines. The Mormon faithful are to resist stimulants, including coffee and tea. A 2012 update allowed for the consumption of soda pop—yes, even caffeinated soda. The lifting of the soda pop ban gave rise to the Mountain West Mormon corridor phenomenon of specialty soda cafés that sell unique flavor combinations of soda pop, often referred to as "dirty" soda. These shops take up the same social-communal space that coffee shops do in other areas of the country. The most successful soda pop shops are expanding throughout the

United States. The curious should seek out Swig, Fiiz, Sodalicious, or Twisted Sugar locations to check out this rising religious-influenced food trend. Yet a 2019 message aimed directly to younger LDS members doubled down on the "no coffee, no tea" rule. It seems that in our Starbucks era, young Mormons were indulging in overly fancy drinks with Italianesque names without realizing they contained coffee.

IN THIS GREAT AWAKENING OF SPIRIT, AND THE WORRY THAT THE SECOND COMING was imminent, grew the idea that Christ had already returned and redeemed all sinners for eternity. This meant that God's promise of a heavenly kingdom could be built on Earth right now. Perfectionism in various iterations is also a part of the belief system of other newer Protestant religions, but none took the concept further than John Humphrey Noyes and his Oneida Community. Oneida is now known for its silverware, but before the knives and forks, the communards were thought to be a sex cult.

Noyes, like William Miller, Joseph Smith, and even the renegade Matthias, had heard Charles Finney preach and was moved to convert. He latched onto the idea of Perfectionism, stretching it to include the idea that since God is perfect and created man in His image, then a God-believing man can attain perfection through correct beliefs and actions. And all ideas coming from man would also be perfect and divinely inspired. This notion got him kicked out of Yale. Noyes went back to his Putney, Vermont, home to marry and further develop his ideas about the ideal living situation for every man, woman, and child to live without sinning. In his vision of Perfectionism, Noyes believed that social constructs were man-made and that he was no longer bound by them. Noyes was also influenced by his marital experiences. He and his wife lived together for five years and during that time she endured five miscarriages. Noyes was horrified by his wife's suffering, which inspired his practice of "male continence."[41]

Noyes and his wife then decided to live apart. He founded the Putney Bible School in 1836, where students could reside and study the Bible and learn about Noyes' new theories. In 1844, the school became a commune that embraced all of Noyes' concepts, including "Free Love." In his thinking, "Free Love" meant that traditional, lifelong marriages were incompatible with happiness. He felt, using "male continence," people could live together in a "complex marriage" where partners choose each other as desired for a non-defined period of time. The state of Vermont was not a partner in this arrangement. Noyes was arrested for adultery in 1847. While awaiting trial, he and other members of the Putney Bible School (many of whom now also had outstanding arrest warrants) moved en masse to Oneida, New York. There, sympathetic followers gave Noyes a home and land on which to build a newer version of his communal living vision. The Oneida Community was officially formed in 1848 and was founded as a Christian commune Noyes described as "Bible communism." Though founder Noyes was on the periphery of orthodoxy with his idea of Perfectionism and embrace of women's rights, abolition, and eugenics, he maintained that Oneida members professed the same faith. Not all did. In the weekly "criticism circles" many were accused of atheism. Some recalcitrant members were subjected to physical punishment for their lack of belief and other offenses against the order.

---

41   Noyes used the term "male continence" which is a euphemism to describe any method of sexual congress that prevented a man from ejaculating inside a woman's vagina.

Visitors eating strawberry shortcake in quadrangle, c. 1880. Courtesy of the Oneida Community Collection, Special Collections Research Center, Syracuse University Libraries.

Another core practice at Oneida, besides complex marriage, was "mutual criticism." When reading the diaries of Oneida members, it is obvious that mutual criticism is the one practice no one enjoyed. It is as it sounds: during the weekly meetings, each member had to hear a critique about their personality or an observed offense against the rules.[42] As much as everyone was striving toward perfection, there were many failings along the way.

Noyes considered himself a socialist and attempted to develop Oneida as a place of equality. Every person was required to work and allowed to choose their jobs, but the reality was that women were relegated to domestic work. He wanted the Community to be independent and self-sufficient, which gave rise to the many industries begun by the Community, including leatherwork and the silverware factory. The Oneida Community embraced a Fourierist organizational structure and formed numerous committees and administration sections—a far larger bureaucracy than needed to sustain its members. Yet the industriousness and organizational skills proved useful when the Community began multiple businesses. They built animal traps, a preserved food business, and of course, the metalworks producing dinnerware that bears the Oneida name. These businesses became so successful that over two hundred non-Community members were employed in manufacturing jobs.

While outwardly successful, the Community struggled with gender equality in practice. Women were granted absolute autonomy over their own bodies, which was rare at the time. Critics predicted an increase in "godlessness" as a natural outcome of the Community's embrace of women's rights. Work was assigned by capability and desire, not by gender.[43] The women of Oneida embraced "bloomers" and were active correspondents with other activists like Fanny Wright and Elizabeth Cady Stanton. Yet there were limits to what women could

---

42   Interestingly, the practice of public, mutual criticism has been adopted by countless groups labeled as cults.
43   It was still the late 1800s; most of the domestic labor was performed by women.

achieve within the commune. The much-lauded "free love" and "complex marriage" did mean that women were free to reject, accept, and make sexual advances to the men of their choosing, but they were pressured to accept the advances of higher-status men, including Noyes himself. Legal marriages and conception also had to be approved by Noyes.

In the complex marriage system, women were allowed to refuse sexual overtures. Women also had the choice of becoming pregnant. Even with the practice of male continence, there were unplanned children. Noyes wanted children living the Oneida lifestyle, but they had to be the correct type of children. Noyes was a proponent of an early iteration of eugenics called "stirpiculture" and wanted Oneida children to be ideal. To become a parent, Noyes subjected the man and woman to an extensive interview and examination to ensure they were spiritually and physically sound. Then, and only then, would procreation be allowed. A fact that will surprise very few: from 1869 to 1880, of the fifty-eight children born at Oneida, Noyes fathered nine of them. Children were highly valued by the Community and treated with kindness and indulgence, which was contrary to the prevailing "spare the rod, spoil the child" theories of the day. Children did not live with their birth parents but in a separate kids' wing of the main building. The Oneida did not seek to entirely erase the parental bond, but to temper it with a uniform nurturing from all members. All children were educated, and most were sent to prestigious universities—girls too—with the idea that the next generation would bring wisdom and new ideas back to the Community.

At the zenith of the Community, there were about three hundred members at five different locations. Noyes was sensitive to the bad press after the failure of the Putney experiment, and on Sunday afternoons invited visitors to observe the community and hear about their practices. There were already mumbles in the surrounding towns about Oneida being a sex cult and people were delighted to visit and see for themselves. Unfortunately, there wasn't much to see—only a group of modestly clad men and women giving tours of the main house and gardens. Visitors would get a bit of a lecture and dessert, including Oneida's most popular creation, the strawberry shortcake. Yet the "open house" events became so popular during the 1870s that Oneida began charging for the tour.

Free love is rarely easy in practice. After 1875, debates about sexual education and the age of consent bedeviled the group. Younger members felt no inclination to have sex with older members. The country, too, was becoming more conservative as the decades of proselytizing and missionary work had doubled the number of churchgoers in the United States. Noyes was arrested for statutory rape in 1879 and then fled across the border to Niagara Falls, Ontario. He wrote a letter to the Community telling them to renounce "complex marriage" and placed his son Theodore in charge of the commune. He never returned to the United States.

Theodore was agnostic and soon dismissed the religious aspects of the commune. Noyes' other son, Pierrepoint, an atheist, led the communards to disband and created a joint-stock company to oversee the group's businesses. The Oneida experiment was over by 1881, yet its influence is still felt today because of the voluminous writing by Community members about their theories, practices, and experiences. Regardless of the failings of the Oneida Community, the next generation of communards see it as a model of Perfection.

Settlemant at Nashoba, 1932.

A N ARGUMENT CAN BE MADE THAT THE GREAT AWAKENING SPURRED THE American Progressive movement. Abolitionist politics and an inclination to embrace new ideas led to the first instances of the modern concept of "intersectionality." Latter-Day Saint Joseph Smith had met Charles Finney and Matthias. John Noyes at Oneida knew of Smith's revelations, met Finney, and participated in lengthy correspondence with Bronson Alcott at his Fruitlands commune. Noyes was also an abolitionist and proto-feminist who read activist Fanny Wright's work and supported Frederick Douglass. From the 1830s to the 1880s, the men and women (mostly men) involved in what would become called progressive politics, communal experiments, and New Religious Movements, knew of each other. They visited each other's communes and homes. They shared ideas at Chautauquas and in newspapers. And while these visionaries pursued their religious and social ideals, the looming and all-important issue of slavery brought progressive thinkers of diverse backgrounds together. With the abolition of slavery their ultimate goal, many looked to communal living as the answer. But as for how abolition could and should be brought about led to disasters.

Fanny Wright stands out as an early radically-minded reformer. She was a wealthy Scots orphan raised by a progressive aunt who encouraged her exploration of French philosophy and politics. At sixteen, she moved to Glasgow to live with her great-uncle, the philosopher and professor James Mylne. Wright read widely under her uncle's tutelage and became familiar with the economic theories of Adam Smith (a family friend) as well as new ideas from revolutionary France. She traveled through the United States at age twenty-three and published her observations about the country in 1821.

The Marquis de Lafayette became infatuated with the young idealist and invited her to travel to the United States with him in 1824. The General introduced her to Thomas Jefferson, James

Madison, and other living Founders. She met the red-haired, dark-skinned enslaved people at Monticello who were so obviously Jefferson's kin, and was enraged. Wright was wholly disappointed in what she saw as the wide chasm between what the United States was in practice and its purported ideals.

She left Lafayette at Monticello to visit the Harmony colony in Butler County, Indiana. She arrived as Robert Owen and his son Robert Dale Owen were completing the purchase of the land and buildings to establish the New Harmony commune. Wright thought Owen's ideas were more aligned to how she saw the potential of the United States, with equality as its founding principle. She then decided to establish her own Owen/Fourier utopian planned community comprised of formerly enslaved people. Wright was a "gradualist"[44] and published *A Plan for the Gradual Abolition of Slavery in the United States Without Danger of Loss to the Citizens of the South* in 1825 that detailed her scheme. In a nutshell, her plan was that enslaved people could earn their freedom and become fully vested stockholders of the commune.

In practice, her commune, Nashoba, was an abject failure. It was established on 320 acres of swampy land on the banks of the Wolf River in western Tennessee. The land was barely arable and prone to mosquito-borne diseases like malaria and encephalitis. Wright hired a white man to oversee the property and purchased enslaved people (with the promise of eventual freedom) to move to Nashoba. The conditions were grim as the settlers had to clear the land by hand without proper housing or food supplies due to Wright's poor planning.

Illness ravaged the settlement. Wright suffered from a bout of malaria and traveled back to Owen's New Harmony to recover and write. In addition to her abolitionist views, she was a proponent of women's rights and an early voice of the anti-marriage movement. Her writing and public speaking appearances made her a notorious figure in both the English and American press. Upon returning to Nashoba a year later, it became glaringly apparent that her experiment was a failure. The white overseer had abused the Black settlers while the surrounding communities flung accusations that it was a Free Love commune that encouraged "miscegenation." Wright was despondent about the outcome and escorted the remaining settlers to Haiti, where they could truly live as free people.

BEING BLACK IN AMERICA HAS BEEN AND REMAINS A CONSTANT BATTLE FOR DUE recognition of what were called at the time "natural rights," which would now be recognized as human and civil rights. There were as many free Black people in America in the period from the 1820s to the 1840s as there were enslaved. As the abolition movement gained support, the slaveholding powers fought to retain their property. Federal laws enacted during this period made it a crime to assist a Black person escaping slavery. White Northerners were complicit in accepting these anti-Black laws and did not embrace free Black people as equal partners in the American experiment. Many free Black people moved to the frontier areas to develop Black-only communities. These towns and settlements were not considered communal by current definitions. They were, however, successful and vibrant

---

44 "Gradualists" were people who believed in the abolition of slavery but also held racist beliefs. Most of the gradualists argued that Black people were not intelligent enough to manage freedom and would have to be taught how to be citizens. Sadly, this paternalistic notion that a "white savior" is required to rescue Black Americans is still pervasive today.

Holy Food

James Forten.

self-sufficient enclaves that built schools, churches, government, and a culture that was uniquely theirs. Many of these communities remained intact until the post-Reconstruction Jim Crow era and resurgent racist groups like the KKK purposefully destroyed Black spaces both in Black-only towns and in larger cities.

Philadelphia was home to a growing free Black population and its leaders began to explore ideas for protecting free Black people from white violence. The growth of the African Methodist Church played a role in coalescing around the idea that Black people in America *are* Americans. James Forten, a wealthy sailmaker whose grandfather had "freed himself" in the early 1700s, proclaimed in 1817 to the 3,000 attendees at Mother Bethel Church: "We never will separate ourselves voluntarily from the slave population of this country; they are our brethren by the ties of consanguinity, of suffering, and of wrongs." Forten understood that, like his grandfather, he would have to free himself.

Religious leaders in the North tended to hold a progressive ideology with a conservative application regarding abolition. Many supported manumission and sought to convince slave owners to release enslaved persons through a change in conscience and revelation of the Spirit. Others looked to the federal government to change the laws that allowed for slavery. White people would write letters of outrage, but few took active steps to demand a definitive end to slavery and the myriad state and federal laws that allowed and supported it. White Bostonian William Lloyd Garrison founded the Anti-Slavery Society in 1833. His stance was considered more radical than the gradual emancipation favored by most abolitionists. There grew a factionalism within the abolitionist movement, with "Come Outers" putting forward the idea that the "silent majority" must become vocal oppositionists and actively anti-slavery. They joined the "non-resistants" who advocated an early form of civil disobedience and pledged not to follow any laws that violated their abolitionist beliefs.

James Forten felt the work of the Anti-Slavery Society effective and respected Garrison. Forten funded Garrison's concept for a newspaper dedicated to abolition. The first issue of *The Liberator* was published in 1839. Forten realized that for true abolition to happen in the United States, it would take a majority of the white people in the country to finally denounce slavery and white supremacism. *The Liberator* was the tool to speak to those white people and help bring the issue of abolition forward. Its subscribership of 3,000 people read the writings and ideas of hundreds of diverse activists. It became the leading newspaper publishing on anti-slavery and but also on women's rights and communal living ideas.

Frederick Douglass, a leading intellectual advocating for Black emancipation, also supported women's rights and suffrage and wrote movingly about universal rights in *The Liberator*'s pages. Women's rights leaders Elizabeth Cady Stanton, the Grimke Sisters,[45] and transcendentalists Ralph Waldo Emerson and Bronson Alcott, along with communard socialists John Humphrey Noyes and Robert Dale Owen and even radical free-love advocate Fanny Wright, were all subscribers and contributors to *The Liberator*. The newspaper was the organ that brought together influential thinkers and activists who coalesced around the abolition movement and believed that communal living (in many forms) was the answer to how both Black and white people can thrive in America.

NOTHING OCCURS IN A VACUUM. THIS, OF COURSE, IS AS TRUE OF HISTORY AS IT IS OF religious movements. They absorb and reflect the prevailing social and political beliefs of the day like dumplings in soup. While spiritual-minded folks considered the end of the world, science-minded seekers were looking for less cosmological answers. Darwin's theories on the origin of mankind, which spoke about evolution and the vast diversity of life, also inspired a century of pseudo-science. There were an alarming number of theories which fall under the umbrella of Social Darwinism that viewed humans like prize hogs at the State Fair to be bred and judged. As despicable as it is from today's perspective, more religious thinkers than John Humphrey Noyes embraced eugenics as a legitimate methodology to improve humankind.

The Civil War paused many of the most outlandish communal practices of the day—the fruitarians of Bronson Alcott's Fruitlands come to mind.[46] Whether in good faith or bad, spiritual leaders looked to science to explain the mysteries of God and came up with astonishing ideas. The scientific breakthroughs in identifying the individual components of food (fats, proteins, sugars) led to further crackpot theories about how best to build the ideal human being.

---

45   Sarah and Angelina Grimke were born to a wealthy, slaveholding plantation-owning father in South Carolina. After his death, both sisters moved north to Philadelphia to join the Quaker Church and become active in the abolition movement. Angelina married but Sarah did not. The sisters remained close, and both moved to a large farm in New Jersey to teach in a boarding school that taught progressive principles, started by Marcus Spring in the Fourierist manner. The group incorporated as the Raritan Bay Union commune in 1853 and lasted seven years.
46   Louisa May Alcott's diaries and auto-fictional stories of Fruitlands make for grim between-the-lines reading. Her mother bore the brunt of all the domestic labor of the male-led, labor-shy residents. The food restrictions combined with the lack of skill and knowledge of farming led to near-starvation during the winter and spring months. It was an unhappy experience for her.

Holy Food

SEVENTH-DAY ADVENTISTS

(SDA, Adventists)

Years active: 1863 to present day

Founded in: Battle Creek, Michigan

Affiliation: Protestant Christian

Founder: Ellen G. White

ARABIC BREAD (PITA)

(Vegan. Makes 12 small loaves.)

Tools: Pizza or baking stone (if you have one)

Oven temperature: 475°F

Ingredients:

1 teaspoon sugar

2 cups lukewarm water

1 package active dry yeast (1 Tablespoon)

2 teaspoons salt

3 cups stirred whole-wheat flour

3 cups enriched all-purpose flour

Steps:

(Note: Step-by-step instructions are exactly as written in the Seventh-Day Adventist cookbook.)

1. DISSOLVE sugar in water in bowl; sprinkle yeast over; let stand 10 minutes.

2. COMBINE all ingredients; work into a medium-stiff ball.

3. KNEAD until smooth and elastic (about 8 minutes).

4. COVER; let rise in warm place until doubled.

5. FORM dough into a long roll; cut in 12 equal pieces. Form each into a ball.

6. COVER and let rise 30 minutes.

7. ROLL each ball into ¼-inch-thick circle.

8. COVER; let rise again 30 minutes.

9. HEAT oven to 475°F; place circles of dough *directly on racks*. As soon as dough puffs up (2 to 5 minutes), place under broiler for a few seconds until lightly browned.

10. COOL and store or freeze.

NOTE: These small round loaves are hollow in the center. In testing this recipe, we've found that using a pizza or baking stone instead of placing the dough directly on the rack controls for over-browning. But they still turn out great when cooked on the rack.

POWWOW PORRIDGE

(Vegetarian. Can be made vegan if using plant-based milk. Serves 6.)
Tools: Medium-sized bowl and saucepan

From the *It's Your World* cookbook on the origins of this recipe: "Corn is a native grain that was grown by the American Indians. It was roasted, boiled, dried, ground, and made into flat cakes that sustained them and the Pilgrims during the winter when other food was scarce."

Ingredients:

¾ cup yellow cornmeal

3 cups water

¼ teaspoon salt

⅓ cup chopped dates

¼ cup slivered almonds, lightly toasted

¼ cup coconut

2 Tablespoons raisins (can be omitted or substituted with dried cranberries)

¾ cup evaporated milk

½ teaspoon coconut flavoring or vanilla (optional)

¼ teaspoon ground coriander and/or 2 drops of anise flavoring (optional)

Steps:

1. In a medium-sized bowl, moisten cornmeal with ½ cup of the water.

2. In a medium saucepan, bring the rest of the water to a boil. Add salt.

3. Add in the cornmeal, stirring constantly until smooth and somewhat thickened.

4. Continuing cooking at low heat for approximately 15 minutes while stirring frequently.

5. Add the remaining ingredients and stir well. Remove from heat and serve immediately.

The ideal Seventh-Day Adventist lifestyle c. 1910 as depicted in advertisement for the SDA-endorsed coffee and tea substitute, Postum.

CRUNCHY CHIC SALAD

(Vegan. Makes 8 servings.)
Tools: Small bowl

Ingredients:

2 cups cubed Meatless Chicken*
½ cup coarsely chopped salted peanuts
1 cup diced celery
⅓ cup Soyannaise* (use your
    favorite brand of vegan mayo)
1 Tablespoon lemon juice
⅛ teaspoon tarragon
¼ teaspoon salt
1 cup croutons (homemade
    or commercially made
    croutons are acceptable)

Front cover of 1983 edition of *It's Your World Vegetarian Cookbook.* Author's collection.

Steps:

1. Chop the Meatless Chicken,
   celery, and peanuts.
   Combine in large bowl.
2. In a small bowl, mix the Soyannaise, lemon juice, tarragon, and salt together, then fold into
   Meatless Chicken mixture.
3. Add in the croutons and toss just before serving.
4. To serve, mound on an individual lettuce leaf or stuff into a cored tomato. Garnish with
   watercress or parsley.

In the early 1970s when the Loma Linda-based Adventists created this recipe, commercial meat substitutes and soy-based mayonnaise replacements were just being introduced to the market. Before that, cooks would create their own gluten-based seitan-style "meat" and whipped soy-based vegan sauces. For this recipe, use your favorite brand of fake chicken and remember that the Heritage Health Foods company, maker of the Worthington brand of meat substitutes, is still affiliated with the Adventist Church.

PEAS AND MINT

(Vegan. Makes 8 servings.)
Tools: Steam basket or rack for saucepan or stockpot

Ingredients:

2 pounds freshly shucked peas
2 Tablespoons coconut or light vegetable oil

2 Tablespoons chopped fresh mint leaves

2 Tablespoons chopped fresh parsley

1 teaspoon kosher salt

Steps:

1. Shuck fresh peas and place into a small bowl. Rinse with cold water then place into steam basket or steam rack. Steam until just tender, approximately 5 minutes.

2. Chop mint and parsley leaves and place into medium-sized bowl. Add salt and oil and mix together.

3. Remove peas from steamer and add to mixture. Lightly toss together and serve.

POTATO-KALE BAKE

(Vegan. Makes 8 servings.)

Tools: 9x12 baking dish, steam basket or rack for stockpot

Oven temperature: 325°F

Ingredients:

3 pounds white potatoes (Yukon Gold or other thin-skinned varieties)

½ cup white or yellow onion

1 pound kale (any variety or mixed)

2 Tablespoons olive or light vegetable oil

2 teaspoons kosher salt

Steps:

1. Preheat oven to 325°F.

2. Wash and scrub potatoes. Place into steamer or on steam rack in a stockpot filled with approximately 3 inches of water. Place lid on pot and over medium-high heat, bring to low boil to generate steam. Steam until potatoes are tender. Time will vary based on size of potatoes but will take approximately 15 minutes.

3. Chop onion into small pieces then sauté in 1 tablespoon of oil until tender but not browned.

4. Wash kale leaves, cut away tough end of stem. Place the kale leaves on top of the onions and cover pan. Continue to cook until kale is tender. Remove onions and kale from pan and chop again until cut fine. Set aside.

5. Remove potatoes from steam and place into large bowl. Coarsely mash potatoes and add remaining tablespoon of oil and the salt. Add the chopped onion and kale.

6. Place potato mixture into baking dish then place in oven to warm through. (Approximately 15 minutes.) Serve.

THE CHURCH OF JESUS CHRIST OF LATTER-DAY SAINTS

(Mormon, LDS)
Years active: 1830 to current day
Affiliation: Protestant and Lost Tribes
Founder / Leader: Joseph Smith

OLD-FASHIONED WHEAT BREAD

(Vegetarian. Makes 2 loaves.)
Tools: Bread loaf pans
Oven temperature: 375°F

Ingredients:

1 package (2 Tablespoons) active dry yeast

⅓ cup warm water (ideal temperature of water is 115°F)

1 Tablespoon shortening

1 Tablespoon honey

1 Tablespoon molasses

2 teaspoons salt

3 cups whole milk, scalded and cooled

6 cups whole-wheat flour, stirred and measured

Steps:

1. In a glass measuring container, activate yeast in warm water.

2. In a medium-sized bowl, melt shortening. Into the melted shortening, add and combine the honey, molasses, and scalded milk. Set aside to cool to lukewarm temperature.

3. When cooled, add in yeast, and stir mixture.

4. In a large bowl, add wheat flour and salt. Then pour in liquids and mix enough to make soft dough. Knead thoroughly.

5. Shape dough into 2 loaves. Place in greased 8½ x 4 ½ x 2½-inch loaf pans.

6. Cover bread pans with lightweight cotton towel. Allow to rise until not quite double in bulk (about 1½ to 2 hours). Preheat oven to 375° when dough has been rising for approximately 1 hour.

7. Bake for 45 minutes or until done. (Note: It's done when its top is golden brown, and the bottom of the loaf sounds hollow when "thunked" with the back of your finger.)

DEVILED EGG CASSEROLE

(Makes 12 servings.)

Tools: Small saucepan, 7½ x 11½ casserole dish

Oven temperature: 350°F

Substitutions: In place of ham, 1 can (12 ounces) corned beef, cubed, or 1 can (12 ounces) luncheon meat, cubed, may be used.

Recipe Notes from *Mormon Country Cooking*: "Liquid drained from canned mushrooms may be frozen and used in soup, white sauce or as substitute for dry red or white wine in cooking."

For Deviled Eggs:

Makes 12 servings (enough for casserole recipe).

Ingredients

6 eggs

3 Tablespoons mayonnaise

¼ teaspoon onion salt

1 teaspoon Dijon mustard

½ teaspoon vinegar

Dash white pepper

Dash Tabasco sauce

Dash paprika

Salt and pepper

Steps:

1. In a medium saucepan, arrange 6 eggs. Add cold water to cover eggs by 1 inch.
2. Bring to boil. Cover saucepan and then remove from heat. Let stand for 20 minutes then plunge eggs into cold water until cooled.
3. Crack and remove shells. Cut cooled eggs in half lengthwise.
4. Carefully remove yolks and place into a small mixing bowl.
5. Mash eggs with mayonnaise, mustard, vinegar, white pepper, salt, and black pepper. (Add spices to taste.)
6. Pile mixture back into egg halves. Sprinkle with paprika.

For Casserole:

Ingredients:

6 hard-cooked eggs, deviled (see above)

¼ cup (½ stick) butter or margarine

¼ cup flour

2 cups milk

1 can (10½ ounces) cream of mushroom soup

1 Tablespoon lemon juice

2 cups (⅔ pound) diced cooked ham (can use leftover, tinned, or deli ham)

¼ pound fresh mushrooms, sliced and browned lightly in butter (canned mushrooms can be used instead)

Chopped parsley

Optional: 1 cup shredded cheddar cheese and 1 cup smashed potato chips

Steps:

1. Preheat oven to 350°F.
2. In casserole dish, arrange the deviled egg halves, filled side up.
3. Clean and slice mushrooms. Lightly brown in a small sauté pan with butter. Set aside.
4. Dice ham into small pieces. Set aside.
5. In a medium saucepan over medium heat, melt butter. Then stir in flour until blended. Add milk. Cook until sauce thickens and is smooth.
6. Add can of soup and mix together. Stir in lemon juice. Add browned mushrooms and ham pieces and mix.
7. Pour mixture over deviled eggs in casserole dish. (If using shredded cheese and potato chips, add them.) Sprinkle chopped parsley on top.
8. Bake for 20 minutes (or until top bubbles). Remove from oven and serve hot.

Recipe testers universally agreed that the Deviled Eggs recipe is a keeper without making the entire casserole. Testers also suggest serving over cooked egg noodles for dinner or fried potatoes/hash browns for breakfast.

FROG EYE SALAD

(Vegetarian. Makes 8–10 servings.)

Tools: Stockpot, large bowl

Ingredients:

Kosher salt (for pasta water)

Two 8-ounce cans crushed pineapple, drained (save the juice)

Two 8-ounce cans pineapple tidbits, drained (save the juice)

½ cup granulated sugar

2 Tablespoons all-purpose flour

¾ teaspoon salt

2 large eggs

1 cup acini di pepe pasta

One 16-ounce can mandarin oranges, drained

1 cup unsweetened shredded coconut, plus a large pinch for garnish

1 cup mini marshmallows

8 ounces frozen whipped topping, thawed

Steps:

1. Bring a large pot of salted water to a boil.

2. While the water is coming up to boil, open cans of fruit and drain the crushed pineapple and pineapple tidbits over a bowl, pressing lightly to squeeze out the juice (reserve the juice).

3. In a medium saucepan, combine the sugar, flour, and salt. Whisk in the saved pineapple juice. Then whisk in the eggs. Bring mixture to simmer over medium heat while stirring constantly until thickened. Strain this custard mixture into a large bowl, cover with plastic wrap and refrigerate until cooled.

4. Now cook the pasta according to the package directions. Drain and run under cold water until pasta has cooled.

5. Open can of mandarin oranges and set aside a few slices for garnish. Remove custard from refrigerator and add cooked pasta, pineapple, oranges, coconut, and marshmallows and stir until coated. Add the whipped topping and stir until well mixed.

6. Transfer to decorative serving bowl. Place saved orange slices and on top with a pinch of coconut flakes. Cover with plastic wrap and refrigerate at least 2 hours before serving.

HEAVENLY FUNERAL POTATOES

(Vegetarian. Makes 12 servings.)
Tools: 11x13 casserole dish
Oven temperature: 350°F

Recipe Notes from *Mormon Country Cooking*: "Funeral potatoes are an easy-to-make and even easier-to-love comfort food casserole that is totally heaven sent."

Ingredients:

1 30-ounce bag frozen Southern-style hash brown diced potatoes (you can substitute shredded hash browns)
8 Tablespoons butter, divided
½ cup yellow onion, diced
1 pint sour cream
1 can (15 ounces) cream of chicken soup (2 smaller cans of soup will work too)
1 teaspoon kosher salt
¾ teaspoon freshly ground black pepper
2 cups shredded Colby & Monterey Jack cheese blend or cheddar cheese
2 cups corn flakes (plain, not sweetened)

Steps:

1. Preheat the oven to 350°F.

2. Thaw the hash browns completely and set aside.

3. Melt 1 tablespoon butter in a large nonstick skillet over medium heat. Add the chopped onion and a pinch of kosher salt and cook for 3–5 minutes or until the onion is just soft.

4. While the onion is cooking, melt the rest of the butter in a medium-size bowl and set aside.

5. In a large mixing bowl whisk together the sour cream and cream of chicken soup with 5 tablespoons of the melted butter, kosher salt, and black pepper.

6. Add the thawed potatoes and the cooked onion to the mixture then stir to combine. Add the shredded cheese until mixed well.

7. Transfer the mixture to 11x13-inch baking dish and top with more cheese if desired.

8. Add the cornflakes to the remaining melted butter and toss lightly to coat. Spread evenly over the potato mixture.

9. Bake for 1 hour 30 minutes. (Check the casserole at about 1 hour 10 minutes and if the corn flakes are getting too browned, tent the pan with aluminum foil.)

Rest for 5 minutes before serving. This casserole is great for serving hot or warm.

Front cover of the 1983 edition of *Mormon Country Cooking*. **Author's collection.**

ONEIDA COMMUNITY

Years active: 1848–1881
Affiliation: Protestant Perfectionist / Fourierist
Founder / Leader: John Humphrey Noyes

In keeping with the Fourierist philosophy, the Oneida embraced food as a sensual joy. The community-supported farmland and generated income ensured access to fresh and quality ingredients. The food culture was shaped by Noyes' younger sister, Harriet Skinner, who joined the Community at its founding. She oversaw the kitchens as well as the preserved food business. The Oneida embraced vegetarianism. It was believed that eating meat that required killing was not aligned to generating peace in a perfect world. Skinner oversaw the weekly feasts laid out for visitors, including serving the famous Strawberry Shortcake. Skinner also authored a cookbook that featured favorite recipes and her wise cooking and kitchen management tips in 1873.

GREEN CORN (OR CREAMED CORN)

(Vegetarian. Serves 4 to 6.)
Tools: Covered casserole dish, steam rack insert for stockpot

"Green corn" is an older name for sweet corn. It's also Amish slang for marijuana. The Oneida cooks give this note about Green Corn: "Nice as this dish is, we are vulgar enough at our family table to sometimes prefer the corn on the ear. It is the old Puritanic blood pre-dominating in the Community which appears in this taste perhaps. It is something quite abhorred by the present Englishman."

Ingredients:
Fresh ears of corn
Butter
Heavy cream

Amounts of butter and cream needed are based on how much shucked and cut corn kernels you have. The ratio is as follows: 4 cups of corn to 1 tablespoon of butter to 5 ounces of heavy cream.
Steps:
1. Choose fresh ears of sweet corn. Remove outer leaves and fibers. Rinse.

2. Using a sharp knife (or a corn cutter), carefully and as "close to the cob as you can and not take a particle of the hull" cut off the kernels into a bowl.
3. Place steam rack into stockpot. Fill with a few inches of water. Place corn kernels on the steam rack and place lid on pot. Turn on heat and steam for 15 minutes. Turn off heat and remove lid.
4. In the casserole dish, add the butter and cream. Then pour hot corn into dish. Gently mix until butter is melted. Place lid on casserole dish. Serve immediately.

STRAWBERRY SHORTCAKE

(Vegetarian. Makes 1 dozen.)
Tools: Pastry cutter, large bowl
Oven temperature: 400°F

Notes from the bakers who shared the recipe in their 1873 cookbook, *Oneida Community Cooking*: "It is a good rule to sugar your strawberries before you begin to make your cake, and if they are large, or not very ripe, it is best to cut them in two or mash them a little. Don't calculate for these cakes standing on the stove hearth a minute. They should be served like griddle-cakes—no time lost between the oven and the table. Observe these rules and you will have a dish as dainty as Izaak Walton's[47] Baked Fish, of which he said, 'It is too good for any but very honest people.' When strawberries are gone, red raspberries are very nice in their place. White currants are also very much liked as a substitute, and peach shortcake is hardly surpassed by the strawberry itself, if the peaches are first-rate. All these fruits should be prepared by sweetening an hour or two before wanted."

Ingredients:
4 cups all-purpose flour
3 Tablespoons baking powder
1 teaspoon salt
2 Tablespoons butter
16 ounces heavy cream
Steps:
1. Preheat oven to 400°F.
2. In a large bowl, sift flour, baking powder and salt together until thoroughly blended.
3. Using a pastry cutter (or food processor), rub the butter into the flour mixture until "pebbly."
4. Add heavy cream. Mix with large spoon or hands. Work the dough until it is combined, but do not overwork. (It is a soft, somewhat sticky dough.)
5. Take about ¼ cup of dough and shape into a rough ball with hands. Place on jelly roll pans lined with parchment paper approximately 2 inches apart. Pat down until about an inch in height. (Note to modern bakers: This method is different from sweet biscuits that are rolled and cut.)

---

47   Izaak Walton (1593–1683) was an English writer most famous for his book *The Compleat Angler*.

6. Cover pan with cotton cloth and set on top of hot stove to rise for about 15 minutes.

7. Remove towel and place into oven. Bake for about 20 minutes. (Check them at 15 minutes. If you have "hot spots" in your oven, swap the pan positions halfway through baking.)

8. Remove from oven and serve immediately.

For a true Oneida strawberry shortcake, split the biscuit in half with a fork and liberally spread both halves with butter. Ladle on freshly cut and sweetened strawberries. (Ideally, your strawberries should have been cut and macerating in a bowl with a bit of sugar while you were making your biscuits.) Cover with top half of biscuit.

The Oneida version does not specifically mention whipped cream. But according to the sample Bill of Fare published in the *Oneida Community Cookbook*, they served both ice cream and "sweet cream," which is freshly skimmed heavy cream. Eater's choice when you take your plate and consider the benefits of complex marriage.

Dinner at the Oneida Community c. 1860s.

Holy Food

HEARING VOICES

THE TANAKH AND THE OLD TESTAMENT HAVE SIMILAR VERSIONS OF JEREMIAH, Chapter 23, that warn against prophets and believers delivering "messages" from God, as God is perfectly capable of communicating with his believers, thank you very much. Yet there are entire belief systems that have been constructed out of interpreting the Word versus comprehending the meaning of the words ascribed to God. For many believers, the Book gives clear examples of God speaking to specific people, confirming for them that God *can* choose to speak to whomever, whenever. But is He speaking to you?

We must also accept and consider that there may be other voices from the cosmos speaking to Americans. Depending on the hearer, the speaker could be anyone from the angelic hosts to an Ascended Master dwelling in other dimensional realms of the universe. Moses heard the Lord Jehovah. Catholic saints were visited by angels and other saints. Signs and wonders seen in the mundane seemed to foretell God's will. Humans have a long history of hearing voices.

For the evolving belief systems in America, deciding who legitimately heard God's message took on significant importance as a mark of authenticity. In our modern world, hearing the voice of (a) God[48] is sadly often a symptom of psychological illness. While incongruent with American ideas about mental health, in many cultures hearing voices was a mark of favor by the gods. In Hindu and Indigenous cultures, a person hearing voices or sounds from within would be supported by elders and initiated into their spiritual tradition. Americans today are objectively more open-minded about how individuals experience the divine, yet claiming to have a message or new revelation from God is as controversial now as it was a few hundred years ago. But because so many American religious movements owe their start to an encounter with a disembodied voice transmitting knowledge, the phenomenon deserves our attention.

We know that the American version of Protestantism originating in New England was separatist and fundamentalist. It had earlier distinguished itself in Europe by drawing a firm

---

48   There are many respected, mainstream religious and spiritual leaders who share basic guidelines for discerning if the voice you're hearing is God speaking directly to you, created by mental illness, or a manifestation of your own ego. Some religious leaders attribute unsavory ideas and messages to a demonic influence and not godly. Here are five indicators shared by Evangelical Protestant pastors who use these criteria to assist people in determining if the voice they're hearing is godly: 1. God doesn't address *your* individual problems. 2. God doesn't gossip or point out the moral failings of others, or let you in on his judgment of others. 3. God will speak to your heart only about you, never about what others should do. 4. God doesn't give you direct answers. 5. God never contradicts Scripture.

boundary between the Catholic veneration of Saints, who could be called on to intercede with God in spiritual matters. Church leaders could not stop people from finding ways to communicate with dead souls and other residents of the ethereal plane when seeking divine guidance. Religious leaders and scholars in the 1600s were willing to accept that spirits, ghosts, and demons existed as much as God did, and went to great lengths to prove it. This was not a rarified pursuit. It is not an overstatement to say everyone in England and the British colonies during this era was a bit ghost-crazy.

Newspapers of the day thrilled readers with ghost stories purported to be taken from witness accounts. Serious-minded scientists spent time trying to verify any and every manifestation while searching for physical evidence of the afterlife. The craze was partially born out of the Cromwellian hatred of Catholicism, which denied the many Catholic saints who once enjoyed an elevated status as pagan or household gods. And partially born from the Enlightenment-era philosophers who asked the age-old question: what happens when we die?

The notion of death, absent the now theologically banned Catholic waiting room of Purgatory, left Calvinists with a doctrinal problem. If one is not saved and of the elect, are those poor souls consigned to Hell? In many modern iterations of Protestantism, the answer is still yes, a soul is hell-bound. This tenet is the motivating fervor of the evangelical work to bring new believers to the fold. Those proselytizers sincerely believe they are saving a soul from eternal damnation. But is there a third way? This isn't to say that ghosts were invented during the Protestant schisms in Europe during the sixteenth century—the concept of ghosts has hovered around the periphery of human existence for a very long time—but Protestant Christians, without a transactional pathway to heaven as described by the Catholic church, were left in the lurch.[49] Ghosts and spirits grew to fill that need to communicate with those who died and intercede with Heaven.

By the late 1600s, in Calvinist New England there was debate amongst intellectuals and clergy as to whether ghosts and specters were godly or demonic manifestations. Puritan Cotton Mather was the son of Massachusetts church and political leader Increase Mather. He received his ordination after graduating from Harvard (where his father was president of the college), and embarked on his religious career as his father's assistant at Boston's North Church around 1680. Cotton Mather's main interest was investigating ghosts, specters, and other demonic hauntings.

Cotton Mather devoted much of his study to proving that souls exist outside of the corporeal body. He believed that in addition to the Devil and his minions, there were also "immortal souls" and that witches control them. In 1688, Mather investigated a case of "hysterical fits" occurring in the Goodwin children of Boston. To Mather's reasoning, there was no organic or physical reason for the children to suffer from "fits," and therefore it was the work of malevolent spirits under the control of someone. That someone was determined to be a witch who also was a Catholic washerwoman from Ireland working for the Goodwin

---

49 The Catholic church, as evidenced by numerous hagiographies, accepted that God and any number of holy messengers could and did communicate with common believers. Receiving such a gift would be investigated by the local parish, then further investigated by clergy in the chain of hierarchical governance. Once confirmed to the satisfaction of the ecclesiastical investigators, the hearer would be revered in their community and oftentimes join the church as a priest, nun, or monk. For women, experiencing ecstatic visions was a pathway to power within their community.

Trial of Ann Glover, Boston, 1688.

family, Ann Glover. It is a sad case. Ann was convicted of witchcraft mostly due to her inability to speak English as the judge and jury thought her native Gaelic was a demonic language. She eventually confessed to Mather that she consorted with the Devil after suffering deprivation and mistreatment in jail. She was hanged in Boston in 1688.

Misogyny was also a factor in how women outside the closed, Calvinist society were viewed. The othering of anyone outside the homogeneous community was couched in religious terms. In the cultural hierarchy, white male landowners and church pew owners were at the top of the pyramid, while white male nonbelievers were next, Puritan women came below that, and non-Puritan women and enslaved Black men and women were at the bottom. Women who worked in the homes of the wealthier Puritans were treated as less than full members of the community, and subject to sexual and physical violence at the hands of their masters. These women worked in households as domestic laborers and found the tools of their work—various food items, brooms, and cooking pots—recast as tools of nefarious and demonic workings. Mather was also involved in the 1692 witch trials in Salem, Massachusetts. There are many theories about the origins and motivations behind the Salem Witch Trials, but suffice to say that the Puritan belief in ghosts, witches, and demonic influences made it easy for people to engage in misogynistic and racist beliefs under the guise of witch hunting.

What is often missing from the stories of witch trials and the growth of spiritualist-inflected versions of Christianity is Black people. Missing is the long tradition of ancestral communication and a nature-inspired spirituality that is central to African and Indigenous belief systems. Black people are mostly absent from mainstream narratives of American Christianity and New Religious Movements even though many of the defining elements are informed by African American tradition.

An enslaved Black woman, Tituba, lived in Salem, Massachusetts, as property of the Parris family and was implicated as a corrupting force during the infamous 1692 witch trials. The

Parrises' daughter Elizabeth and her friend Abigail Williams accused Tituba of teaching them magic, setting into motion the madness of Salem witch fever. Tituba was originally from Barbados, descended from enslaved Africans whose religious-spiritual practice was rooted in the complex traditions of West Africa and indigenous Carib people sometimes described as *Obeah* or *Obi*. In Longfellow's 1868 play about the trials, he specifically said Tituba was of the "Obeah people."

Tituba and children.

Looking at Tituba's story from her perspective changes the narrative. She was a human being purchased by the Parris family and brought to Massachusetts far away from her Black Atlantic home. She was an outsider to the white Puritan culture and entirely devalued as a person. The one element of her life she could control was her interior, spiritual, and intellectual life. It is through her Obeah practice she could transcend her lived experience and exist as more than a commoditized Black body.

Tituba was accused of teaching the Salem girls how to kill a love rival and ensnare a man via a potion drunk from a "special" cup and eating a "witch cake."[50] Obeah practices and many Black spiritual practices are signified by plants—worn and consumed. A conjurer, or root worker, mixes a blend of medicinal (and sometimes hallucinogenic) plants into a drink or cake to empower the seeker in manifesting a desire or protecting them from danger. Tituba was sharing her spiritual practice with the girls who, in this early documented instance of cultural appropriation, claimed the performative part of the ritual absent the deep understanding of the meaning.

Tituba was accused of witchcraft and consorting with demons by the white men who ruled Salem. Parris beat a confession out of her then abandoned her to jail, refusing to pay the jailer's fee. The town of Salem turned her over to another white man who paid the outstanding fees in lieu of purchase price, and the rest of her story is sadly lost to time.

Much of early American Black spiritual practice was held in secret as a protection against those who would criticize or, worse, try to outlaw it. The Black experience in early America was an existential war of survival to carve out an identity while fighting against the white suppression of personhood. To share something as intimate and complicated as a belief system that was outside of what was acceptable to white people brought scrutiny and a very real threat of physical violence. Research into esoteric African American spiritual practices is growing, adding much to our understanding of American religions. Because as cultural and literary critic Harold Bloom suggested in 2006, to properly understand the growth of American religious movements we need to look at the influence of Black people *on* the church, and not of the church on Black people.

---

50   The term "witch cake" is noted in the Salem documents held at the University of Rochester. In John Parris' testimony, he claims to have asked Tituba to make a "witch cake" to cure the symptoms of the girls. Other cure books from the era note a recipe of a cake made with barley and "child's water" (urine) and fed to a dog can relieve a child of "ague" symptoms. Other researchers have claimed that the "witch cake" is a diagnostic used to discover a witch.

Holy Food

Bethel African Methodist Episcopal Church, Philadelphia, c. 1830. Courtesy of the Library of Congress.

Enslaved Africans did not convert to Christianity in large numbers until the early 1800s.[51] In fact, they were forbidden from becoming Christians because of the prevailing idea from the 1600s to early 1800s that Protestant supremacy was ordained by God. This supremacist concept was subsequently enacted into law, especially in the English-ruled Southern Atlantic colonies. Prior to the American Revolution, it was English law that decided voting rights, and in the colonies those rights were granted only to free white Protestant men over the age of twenty-one.

Slaveholders feared that with Christianity would come knowledge of equality as written in the King James Bible. It is during the late 1700s and the severing of the colonial relationship with England that American slaveholding regions changed voting laws from requiring Protestant church membership to just being "white." The white churches forbade converting Black people, free or enslaved. Early Black converts took to heart both the intellectual challenge of Bible study and the power it gave them within white spaces. Many early Black Christians paid special attention to Acts 8, where the apostle Philip seeks out an enslaved Ethiopian and baptizes him in the name of Jesus so that he too can enter the kingdom of heaven, as a special message to them. For future generations, this spiritual connection to Ethiopia as noted in Acts 8 sets in motion a religious narrative that spurs New Religious Movements within Black American and Caribbean communities.

Free Blacks who had settled in the Northern colonies embraced Protestant Christianity as a pathway to power. Many of the leading thinkers in the Black community formed strong, independent congregations in the late 1700s because though the North did not engage in

---

51   It should also be noted that there were a small number of enslaved African Muslims brought to the United States.

direct enslavement, many white people wouldn't allow Black parishioners to be equal members of a church. Richard Allen founded the Bethel Church of Philadelphia in 1794 after being beaten by white church members for praying in the "whites only" sacristy. His single congregation grew to become the African Methodist Episcopal (AME) church in 1821. The values Allen and the founding members (all members of the Free African Society[52]) espoused of Mutual Aid, literacy, education, and economic advancement for Black people are still part of the core mission of the AME Church to this day.

Many kidnapped African people were faithful to and passed along their traditional belief systems. These beliefs varied widely depending on where on the African continent they were from, but most western and central African religions revered multiple gods that oversaw the cycles of nature and life, while often incorporating aspects of the thousand-year influence of Islam on the continent. Beliefs were based on having direct communication with gods and spirits. As families were torn apart and people from different regions were forced to live together for hundreds of years, regional beliefs were lost or mixed with other traditional practices.

Sixteenth- to eighteenth-century religious movements and sects are usually labeled as syncretic, as their influences and genealogies were, for the most part, easily traceable— one could see the exact divergent pathway that resulted in a distinct belief and/or practice. But the untrammeled growth in the United States during the nineteenth century that unhomogenized the dominant white populations is when the word "syncretic" begins to fail us. As noted earlier, polycultural is a better word to describe the scattered political, economic, spiritual, geographic, and esoteric influences on American religions. More than that, when recognizing the spiritual beliefs of Black people in the Americas, we need to include the Caribbean islands and parts of Central and South America. Increasingly, scholars recognize that area of the Gulf and Atlantic coasts as the socially and culturally connected Black Atlantic region.

When discussing Black American New Religious Movements, it is important to refocus away from whiteness and Christianity. While it is true that by the 1800s[53] enslaved Black people began to embrace Christianity as both a sincere expression of belief and a powerful tool for emancipation, we know that Black American religion is also informed by so much more than the Book. From this history grows a new style of Christianity, incorporating remnant African traditions with Protestantism, that continues to morph into new sects and New Religious Movements while subtly transforming the white church.

Looking back again on the early life of Sojourner Truth, we can now view her spiritual journey as a seeker looking for a religion that aligned with her core doctrine that Paradise once existed on Earth and could again if only the wicked could be driven into the sky,[54] and not an uneducated

52 The Free African Society (FAS) was founded in Philadelphia in 1787 by Richard Allen and Absalom Jones to provide Methodist services to Black people barred from white churches, and Mutual Aid for newly escaped and manumitted people. The members of the FAS provided instrumental nursing care to ALL the people of Philadelphia during the Yellow Fever epidemic of 1793. It should be noted that while wealthy white people fled the city, Black residents remained, only to be later accused of taking economic advantage of and stealing from white residents.
53 Though bringing kidnapped African people to be enslaved was banned in the United States in 1807, there was a steady illegal trade in human trafficking. The last known group of trafficked Africans were Yoruba people from Dahomey forcibly brought to the United States in 1859.
54 Sojourner Truth explains her beliefs in her dictated autobiography *The Narrative of Sojourner Truth* (1850), published by *The Liberator*'s Lloyd Garrison.

George Washington Carver in a field by Frances Benjamin Johnston, c. 1906. Courtesy of the Library of Congress.

woman who followed charlatans. She spent the years 1843 to 1845 at the Northampton Association of Education and Industry (NEI), a fully integrated communal living experiment in Florence, Massachusetts.[55] The community was supported by a silk mill that only used 100% free and fairly paid workers. Frederick Douglass visited and lectured. It is where Sojourner Truth collaborated with a fellow communard to dictate and publish her life story.

The relationship of Black Americans to food and spirituality is interconnected. Plants were imbued with sacred qualities, and plants could be food. Enslavement limited Black people's access to the plants that fed their spirits and bodies. Access to reliable and abundant food sources begins to be woven into Black spirituality in the 1800s. The foods described as "soul food" take on a larger social, spiritual, and political meaning when we rightfully connect these foods to their history.

Many enslaved people carried precious seeds for okra, cowpeas (black-eyed peas), watermelon, and peppers with them on their horrific journey across the Atlantic Ocean. Their captors, in search of a cheap way to feed enslaved people and develop a new agriculture in the Carolinas, brought West African rice to the Americas. As rice cultivation in the American lowlands grew lucrative, slavers captured people exclusively from the rice-growing regions of Africa (modern-day Sierra Leone, Liberia, and the countries along the northern coast of the Gulf of Guinea). The current chef-favored rice variety, Carolina Gold, is genetically related to Ghanaian rice.[56] Other enslaved cooks were forced to find native-grown substitutes for familiar African foods, and developed American versions of recipes made with scraps and wild-harvested items. The persistent threat of starvation to enslaved people created a movement toward self-sufficiency.[57]

George Washington Carver, hailed as the "peanut man," exemplified the idiosyncratic beliefs that entwine faith and food together. He was born enslaved in Missouri but was a sickly child. After experiencing a harrowing kidnapping as an infant where he and his mother were brought south, the Carver family, of whom it is said felt a bond with their enslaved laborers, found and brought baby George back to Missouri. Carver's mother was never found. George learned

---

55 The NEI closed in 1846 after failing to remain economically viable but the town of Florence remained a center of Black industrial entrepreneurship.

56 Do read culinary historian Michael Twitty's book *Rice* (University of North Carolina Press, 2021) for an in-depth history of the grain that includes historic recipes.

57 I do hope that epigenetic researchers begin looking at the connection between the starvation trauma and nutritional deficiencies experienced by enslaved people and the obesity epidemic among Black Americans today. We know that obesity is a complex disease that has very little to do with gluttony and much to do with genetics.

to read and showed an affinity toward plants and animals. In his own telling, when he was about nine years old, "God just came into my heart one afternoon while I was alone in the loft of our big barn, shelling corn to carry to the mill to be ground into meal."

After the Civil War, he left the white Carver homestead and was taken in by a free Black couple in Neosho, Missouri, Andrew and Mariah Watkins, who encouraged his pursuit of education. Mariah Watkins was a midwife who taught Carver about the medicinal herbs used in caring for women and children. He worked as a cook in hotel kitchens in Winterset, Iowa, to earn college tuition. He went on to earn bachelor's and master's degrees in science from Iowa State by 1896. Carver then moved to Alabama to work and teach at the Tuskegee Institute as the head of the agriculture department under college president Booker T. Washington.

Carver wrote that he saw himself as an instrument of God to bring plant knowledge to Black farmers. The clear-cutting of forests, along with monoculture growing of cotton and other cash crops employed by plantations, had left the once-rich soil depleted. His mission was to discover and give Black people the means to become self-

Help for the Hard Times

Important to Farmers Take Note

Published and Distributed under the auspices of the Extension Department of the Tuskegee Normal and Industrial Institute, Tuskegee Institute, Alabama

191-

Tuskegee Institute Experimental Agriculture Bulletin written by G.W. Carver, c. 1905. From the foreword by Booker T. Washington: "If the farmers will follow the advice given by Prof. Carver, instead of the present low price of cotton proving a drawback it is going to prove a permanent blessing..." Courtesy of the Library of Congress.

sufficient. His research brought him to legumes and specifically the cowpea earlier generations of Africans secretly carried with them. (Legumes have nitrogen-fixing properties that replace minerals and nutrients depleted by other crops.) His great achievement was creating Tuskegee's Extension office that worked directly with Black farmers, teaching them how to gain the most from their land without destroying it. How to grow their own food. How to become self-reliant with little need to interact with the white world.

Most people associate Carver with peanuts, and yes, Carver worked with peanut plants that had been brought to the United States by conquistadors on the march north from South America. While he did not invent peanut butter, he developed approximately 300 uses for the peanut plant. He also worked with hybrid sweet potato varietals to improve cultivars, and developed more uses for the tuber. He advocated for wild-harvesting native fruits and greens. His Extension bulletins contained more than scientific findings; they contained recipes, meal plans, and nutritional advice. The bulletins included delicate drawings by Carver to not just illustrate, but to make beautiful the knowledge he shared. Carver's philosophy (and Tuskegee's) was often at odds with other Black leaders who argued that higher education in and of itself was the key to equal rights. Carver felt that education was important, but self-sufficiency was critical to prevent dependency on processed and purchased foods which was a dependency on white people. During the forty-seven years Carver was at the Tuskegee Institute he authored forty-four agricultural bulletins and a syndicated newspaper column, "Professor Carver's Advice."

Carver's religious practice also gained him notice and fame. He was a self-proclaimed Presbyterian but throughout his life had attended Baptist, Methodist, and other Protestant services. He was a vegetarian, a decision informed by his scriptural interpretations. He confided to his Sunday school students that God spoke to him about plants. Contemporaries describe him as a quiet man with a very high-pitched voice who nonetheless enthralled listeners when Carver spoke of his simple version of Christianity. Since his death in 1943, religious groups of all stripes claim Carver as one of their own.[58]

Carver's forty years of work teaching Black farmers how to grow, cook, and preserve food played a significant role in what is understood to be Southern food, Black food. The other influence is, of course, the foods enslaved people ate and adapted from generations in bondage. How a person views these foods would later become an identifying practice for Black New Religious Movements and an antithetical rejection for others.

B
Y THE MIDDLE OF THE 1700S, AMERICAN GHOSTS ARE RELEGATED TO SPOOKY STORIES and folk tales. Few are possessed by the devil or compelled by his minions. Educated people dismissed ghosts and specters as the realm of the poor and unlettered. But the religious revivals of the early 1800s drive a renewed interest in having meaningful conversations with God and departed loved ones. Mother Ann Lee of the Shakers heard both the voice of God and communicated with spirits. Barbara Heinemann of the Amana Colony claimed the mantle of leadership via ethereal communications with God. Burning bushes aside, Charles Finney caught the spirit in a forested glade, while Joseph Smith was visited by the Angel Moroni who told him where to find the golden plates.

Scientists (a word coined in 1834) made discoveries, or at the least put forward theories, at a rapid pace with little understanding of how to discern the real from the hokum. In 1760, German physician Anton Mesmer developed a theory that the human body contains unseen elements that can be controlled by an external practitioner and used to heal the body, or worse, control another. It was thought that this invisible force might be a magnetic field or something quite new. European physicians studied it and declared it bunk many times over, yet the idea persisted.[59]

Anton Mesmer was not alone in searching for scientific meaning in the inexplicable. It is the inspiration of scientists everywhere to bring order to chaos. Unlike Mesmer, mathematician-philosopher Emanuel Swedenborg experienced direct visions of God through his dreams that he claimed gave him powers to see the future and communicate with the ethereal plane. His

---

58 Including the International Spiritual Experience group, an American stew of so-called ancient Incan spiritual practices of crystal skull consultation, reiki, hallucinogenic plants, and "sound healing." The ISE has proclaimed George Washington Carver a mystic who had divinely accessed secret plant knowledge.
59 Mesmer's "God particles" have similarities to the Manichean Light and Dark elements that live within plants and animals.

early anatomical work in mapping the human brain and correctly postulating that each system was connected by nerves and neurons that controlled the body confirmed (for him) his belief, like Pythagoras, that the human soul was made of *something*. He devoted the last decades of his life to the research of ethereal communications and published his conversations with God.

Swedenborg's conception of God's creation was not limited to the Earth; it encompassed the entire universe. He believed that there were beings who lived on the other planets who were part of God's creation and that humans could communicate with them as well. He claimed that Christ's second coming had happened in 1757, but it was a spiritual returning and not a physical manifestation on Earth—still, Christ judged man lacking. Swedenborg rejected the Trinitarian concept of a God in three parts (the Father, Son, and Holy Ghost) and said that Jesus was God. He was said to be psychic. He believed that each and every word in the Bible was prophecy if interpreted with the correct spiritual attunement. He also wrote that God told him to be a vegetarian.

As outlandish as any or all of this may sound to modern ears, Swedenborg was a respected scientist and member of the Swedish aristocracy. There were a few clerical and scientific critics who looked askance at his religious pronouncements, but it was also a time when every thinker worth his quill was questioning accepted beliefs. If the man who successfully invented a way to smelt copper claims that beings live on other planets and that dreams manifest visions of God, who is to say otherwise? Swedenborg published his dream journals and visions and sought to speak to other religious thinkers, but he never broke away from the Protestant Swedish State church nor did he start a new religion.

His writings made their way to England where they were studied by the intelligentsia and interested spiritual thinkers. Fifteen years after Swedenborg's death, the New Church, based on Swedenborg's interpretation of Christianity, established itself in London in 1789. As the New Church grew, it incorporated more of Swedenborg's mystical revelations as it sought to thin the veil between the material and spiritual plane. One American convert has a special place in American food history—Johnny Appleseed.

John Chapman was an apprentice orchardist who traveled westward from his Massachusetts home in the early 1800s. He built orchards for farmsteads and towns, and preached the gospel of charity and communicating directly with God throughout the Ohio River Valley. He was known to have a special bond with animals and is said to have gentled a wolf who became his traveling companion. He was the opposite of the fire-and-brimstone Revivalists promising damnation if people did not immediately convert. Chapman told stories of a kind and benevolent God who loved his people best when they did good for others. It was this peaceable New Church that struck many as a better way to know God. And like Swedenborg, Chapman was a vegetarian. People have long wondered, what kind of apples did John Chapman cultivate? Cider apples, not eating apples. Johnny Appleseed was, in the words of Michael Pollan, the American Dionysus bringing alcohol and the means to make it to the western frontier.[60] Until the latter part of the 1800s, potable water was hard to come by on the frontier. Brewing and distilling fruits or grains into alcohol rendered it pathogen-free and safe to drink. During the 1800s, on average,

---

60 See also the Small Beer recipe from the Bishop's Hill Commune on page 56.

Holy Food

John "Johnny Appleseed" Chapman.

each man, woman, and child consumed approximately 10.5 ounces of hard cider per day.

Vegetarianism wasn't encoded into the New Church's doctrine but most of its followers did not eat meat in emulation of Swedenborg. The New Church was unique in that it didn't establish behavioral rules, as it valued God's gift of free will. Swedenborgians believed that with faith and by example people would make choices that please God. Even Chapman's method of orcharding—starting apple trees from seed rather than grafting—was part of his Swedenborgian beliefs. It was thought that each living thing, even trees, have a life force that can be harmed, and that grafting limbs of one tree onto another caused the tree great pain.[61]

Swedenborg's reputation as the mystic seer grew as readers like Ralph Waldo Emerson and Carl Jung cited his influence on their own work. Swedenborg was like so many religious thinkers throughout history working to understand what or who was God; he didn't have answers but questions. The question of faith was just that: was faith enough? Could God be proven real? Was there a way to reveal the invisible realm of the spirits to humans? It was the question many seekers were asking during the 1840s.

Call it Mesmerism, magnetism, galvanism, animal magnetism, or finally, as coined by Scots physician and translator James Braid in 1841, hypnotism. The notion that the human body has an invisible energy that can be controlled, subjugated, and tamed has never completely gone away. Braid's English translation of Anton Mesmer's then nearly hundred-year-old book and émigré practitioners of hypnotism made their way to the United States. The Marquis de Lafayette even demonstrated Mesmerism techniques to the faithful Shakers at the Niskayuna Village commune during his 1824 visit with Fanny Wright.

At first introduction, Americans considered hypnotism a parlor trick, a magician's sleight of hand, but to a few, it seemed like a revealed secret to a new way of seeing the universe. Out of the millions who embraced the hypnotism fad, there were those that blended hypnotism with religion. Their experiences had tremendous influence the development of New Religious Movements during the second half of the 1800s.

---

61   Readers may have an "aha" moment in seeing a similar belief—ahimsa—in the religious systems originating from the Indian subcontinent. It is unknown if Swedenborg had read or was influenced by "Eastern thought."

Andrew Jackson Davis was known as the Poughkeepsie Seer, and parlayed his gift for clairvoyance and medical diagnosis into setting up a lucrative practice in New York City in 1845. He gained the notice of Horace Greeley's *New York Tribune* and with the subsequent good press, people clamored for appointments. Davis soon left the diagnosis business behind and held exclusive salons with the New York elite, billing himself as a Seer and visionary who communicated with the great beyond. He enjoyed the support of the Swedenborgian New Church and growing Universalist movement that preached a kinder, gentler bootstrap Christian capitalism. The emergent Universalists were a hybrid of Swedenborgians and transcendentalists and decidedly non-denominational. They sought to bring progressive social reforms *through* religion. The Universalists were also open to the idea that, yes, spirits from the netherworld could communicate with more than simple "yes" and "no" answers but hold well-developed ideas about current-day events.

Davis incorporated spirit communication into his clairvoyance sessions and was quite in demand. Davis attracted a young follower, Thomas Lake Harris, who was a charismatic preacher from the newly established and socially progressive Fourth Universalist Society in New York City. Harris was also a romantic poet. Harris was a loyal student and promoter of Davis' work, but after a few long and intense months Davis grew concerned by Harris' fawning devotion to him. Harris was a bit too earnest for Davis the charlatan. He wanted to keep the money flowing but wasn't as interested in becoming a godhead, and sent Harris off to evangelize in the Midwest. Davis hoped the adoration had cooled when Harris returned to New York in 1848. It did. Harris became more convinced of his *own* spiritualist abilities that confirmed that Davis was a fraud. Harris exacted revenge on his former mentor by exposing a sexual liaison Davis enjoyed with one of his married supporters. Hell hath no fury like a disillusioned acolyte. Harris took over Davis' newspaper columns in the Universalist newspapers.

During Harris' travels west through the Pennsylvania wildlands and the Ohio River Valley, he saw both the brimstone camp meetings and the Fourierist-informed religious communes. Harris believed, like many religious and social reformers of the Second Great Awakening era, that the world, and mainly the United States, was falling into an abyss of sin. Harris took the social progressive stances of women's rights, abolition of slavery, and fair labor practices, and melded them with the esoteric religious practices he saw in the Shaker and Ephrata communes. We cannot confirm if Davis taught Harris his specific hypnotism techniques, but we do know that Harris began channeling spirits who gave him unique revelations about the world.

But it wasn't just Reverend Thomas Lake Harris speaking to the dead. "Spirit-knocking," as made infamous by the Fox Sisters in 1848, became all the rage in American society. No single group owned spiritualism, and many practitioners engaged in religious and secular communications. Mediums set up séances to speak to dead relatives. Other channelers specialized in communicating with the Founding Fathers, who expressed regret over their support of slavery. Mediums were often women, of whom it was said had the correct electrical alignment to channel spirits. But it was Harris who incorporated spiritualism, socialism, and Christianity into a singular new religious practice.

Kanaye Nagasawa and members of the Brotherhood of New Life celebrating at the winery at Fountaingrove, c. 1900. Courtesy of History Museum of Sonoma County.

In Harris' version of Christian Spiritualism, the ethereal road went in both directions. Not only could spirits find outlet through him, but he could also project himself into the celestial realm. Harris reached his peak in 1859 and tumbled from grace with his increasingly outlandish proclamations. He claimed, while channeling Socrates, that other mediums were false and only his visions were true. Then, after relating a story of battling demons in the form of poets Shelley and Wordsworth, his supporters in the Church of the Good Shepherd had had enough of his outrageous spirit conversations. Harris scuttled off to England where he remained until after the Civil War.

But Harris was not to be denied his utopia. His ideas about building a Christian Spiritualist commune crystallized while in England, and upon his return to the States he brought along a wealthy aristocratic widow, her son, and fifteen young Japanese men from the Satsuma province who had been studying in England under the sponsorship of the Emperor. Harris began a religious commune in the Hudson Valley, then later moved everyone to western New York before finally settling in Santa Rosa, California, in 1875 as The Brotherhood of New Life at Fountain Grove. While in Santa Rosa, he continued the successful experiments in grape-growing and winemaking begun in New York. That success was due to the work and talents of follower Kanaye Nagasawa.

It is the wine that makes the Fountain Grove community an example of the intermingling of food and religion. Of course, wine holds religious symbolism for Christians as the embodiment of Christ's blood. As mentioned earlier, the Christian belief in transubstantiation, where the invocation to God during Mass transforms wine into the blood of Christ and bread into his body, was inspiration for many religious groups to embrace winemaking as a blessed endeavor.

Nagasawa studied agriculture at Cornell for a year and then rejoined Harris' commune. He was a gifted vintner. The wines Nagasawa created at Fountain Grove earned international renown. Harris and Nagasawa claimed that the wine was spiritually imbued. Harris also developed a series of breathing techniques that, if done correctly, allowed a person to become possessed by Christ and attain immortality. Harris left Fountain Grove in 1891 to pursue a new spiritual mission and escape prosecution for bilking followers out of their fortunes, and placed Nagasawa in charge of The Brotherhood and the winery. Harris died in 1906 and Nagasawa in 1934.[62] Harris

---

62 Sadly, due to anti-Japanese racism, Nagasawa's will bequeathing the land and winery to his American-born nephews was ignored. The State of California instead sold the estate at auction. In 2008, thirty acres of the original Brotherhood settlement and winery was designated a park named in honor of Kanaye Nagasawa. In 2017, the site of the former Brotherhood and winery burned in a wildfire.

and Nagasawa's Brotherhood is a harbinger of the emerging twentieth-century New Religious Movements that blended many ideas while establishing an economic engine to keep the group viable. Harris and Nagasawa were the new American religious leaders—wholly syncretic and polycultural as they absorbed new ideas while reaching back to the successful-ish model of Father George Rapp's wine-making Harmony communes.

Spiritualism remained popular as both a religious practice and secular exploration. In the early 1890s practitioners in England organized as the National Federation of Spiritualists to help fight against legal prosecutions of fortune-telling and other archaic laws. Women took the leadership roles of many of the organizations and churches. They mixed Spiritualism with politics as

***Leaves of Healing* Spiritualist Magazine, Volume 1, Number 3, September 14, 1894.**

they advocated for voting rights and alcohol prohibition. Like Harris channeling Wordsworth and Socrates, Spiritualists would channel the spirits of respected thinkers and—depending on your beliefs here—transmit, or attribute positions and manifestos to them. English Spiritualist church leader Emma Britten channeled the spirt of utopian Robert Owen who transmitted ideas that became their Seven Principles.[63]

Women had long-lasting impact on what became a more organized leadership of Spiritualist churches. Philadelphian and later Chicagoan Mercy Cadwallader became the leader of the American-based National Spiritualist Association (NSA). She brought a rigor and respectability to the craft of mediumship. Through the NSA, an interested party could join a church and then learn accredited techniques for channeling spirit guides. Cadwallader also served as expert witness in criminal proceedings against fraudulent mediums. Joining an NSA-affiliated Spiritualist church protected a practitioner from accusations of fortune-telling, which was and still is illegal in many states.

American Spiritualist churches have an area designated as the Lyceum that is dedicated to learning about the craft of mediumship and history as seen from the Spiritualist viewpoint. A key innovation to American Spiritualism was the construction of rural Spiritualist Camps. These were summer camps advertised to church members and the general public as a place

---

63   1. The Fatherhood of God. 2. The Brotherhood of Man. 3. The Communion of Spirits and the Ministry of Angels. 4. The Continuous Existence of the human soul. 5. Personal Responsibility. 6. Compensation and Retribution hereafter for all the good and evil deeds done on earth. 7. Eternal Progress open to every human soul.

to retreat from urban gloom while communing with fellow seekers. They were modeled on the then-popular Methodist-founded Chautauqua[64] assemblies that featured lectures and entertainment. The camps included outdoor recreation in addition to classes and guest lecturers. The camp at Lily Dale, New York (near the home of the infamous Fox Sisters), has a lyceum named after Andrew Jackson Davis. The Spiritualist church today remains a loose collection of independent congregations which are still quite active.

Black Americans were full members of the integrated Spiritualist church until the 1920s, after Jim Crow laws enforcing race-based separation were enacted at state and federal levels. Black members were expelled from the National Spiritualist Association of Churches in 1922 and formed their own non-affiliated churches. Spiritualism appealed to many Black Christians as a natural way to practice both Christianity and esoteric worship. Black spiritualist churches combine spirit channeling and healing with an ecstatic and vocal worship style. This is in contrast with the more sedate white spiritualist churches that wrapped connections to the Other Side in scientific explanations.

Another common thread the Spiritualists share with other emerging religious movements is faith and spiritual healing. There is a theological difference between faith healing and spirit healing, and a long history of both. Faith healing is when the God you worship cures a malady; spiritual healing is when the undefined "energies" and gods of the universe heal. To a non-believer, the difference may sound inconsequential, and the intertwined beliefs that slalom in and out of these faith traditions make this a convoluted history at best. Yet, faith healing is an accepted belief and practice in most Christian religions. A simplistic way to say this is: faith healing is every prayer, offering, and plea to your god for relief from physical or mental disease. Spiritual healing is another person harnessing divine energies to bring about relief from a malady.

Protestant religions cite the stories of Jesus curing the lepers, healing a boy of blindness, stopping the bleeding disease of a woman, and of course, in one infamous story—if you don't count Jesus himself—of bringing a dead man, Lazarus, back to life as evidence that God heals people. Each book of the New Testament has versions of healing acts by prophetic Jesus. But it is the apostle Paul who sets forth the idea that healing is not the Lord's business alone. Paul says in Corinthians 12,[65] and I paraphrase, that it is the spirit of the Lord that heals, and that true believers may be favored and chosen to be an instrument of the Lord.

---

64   Chautauqua's were not vaudeville, minstrel, or medicine shows but cousin to them. Their intended audience was the growing middle classes and those working classes who wanted to improve themselves. Popular lecturers included Progressive Wisconsin Senator Fightin' Bob LaFollette, Eugene Debs, Jane Addams, and William Jennings Bryant. Music and lighter comic monologues were also presented. Religion was never explicitly a topic, but it was assumed that attendees were fine, upstanding Christians. If anything, Chautauqua's most modern equivalent would be the now-defunct Public Radio program *Prairie Home Companion*.

65   Here is the passage from Corinthians 12 speaking about spiritual healing: "Now concerning spiritual gifts, brothers and sisters, I do not want you to be uninformed. You know that when you were pagans, you were enticed and led astray to idols that could not speak. Therefore I want you to understand that no one speaking by the Spirit of God ever says 'Let Jesus be cursed!' and no one can say 'Jesus is Lord' except by the Holy Spirit. Now there are varieties of gifts, but the same Spirit; and there are varieties of services, but the same Lord; and there are varieties of activities, but it is the same God who activates all of them in everyone. To each is given the manifestation of the Spirit for the common good. To one is given through the Spirit the utterance of wisdom, and to another the utterance of knowledge according to the same Spirit, to another faith by the same Spirit, to another gifts of healing by the one Spirit, to another the working of miracles, to another prophecy, to another the discernment of spirits, to another various kinds of tongues, to another the interpretation of tongues. All these are activated by one and the same Spirit, who allots to each one individually just as the Spirit chooses."

Catholics also believe in the power of faith as an instrument of healing. Beyond the laying on of hands—which is a method to transmit a healing—one can make a pilgrimage to an approved holy site where a venerated saint has proven to bestow healings. A criterion for becoming a Catholic saint is to have at least three Vatican-verified miracles under your belt, and one of the more

Mary Baker Eddy Christian Science healing, 1897.

provable miracles is medical healing. There are also gurus of the Sant Mat Hindu tradition that lay claim to faith healing, as do some Islamic sects and even Scientologists.

Spiritual healing, on the other hand, does not imply a direct power from God. A spiritual healer is working to channel the divine energy of the universe, the *shakti* or the *qi*, to heal an ailment. The now popular practice of reiki, derived from a regional Japanese shamanistic practice based in Buddhist and Shinto traditions, gained traction in Japan and the United States in the early 1910s–20s. Spiritual healing, while from the tradition of faith healing, is part of the next wave of religious movements that nearly brings us to the twentieth century.

An influential mystic scientist and spiritual healer of note to this history was Phineas Quimby. A clockmaker in Maine by trade, he was privy to a demonstration of Mesmerism in 1836. He was so impressed that he apprenticed himself to the French hypnotist for a few years to learn the secrets. By 1840, he embarked on his own tour with a partner who was highly susceptible to hypnotic trance. Like Andrew Jackson Davis, he began a hypnotic healing business and began to cure patients.

Quimby's methods of mind-healing were considered scientific and not religiously inspired, though he felt that they were akin to the methods used by Jesus. He explained that diseases were a manifestation of wrong or bad thoughts, and that healing was brought about by discovering and replacing the detrimental thoughts with one's personal truth. More than curing a disease, Quimby felt that a person could be made whole and successful by transforming their thoughts. Illness was, indeed, mind over matter.

Quimby left a trove of writing expounding on his ideas about how to manifest health and prosperity from within and by one's will. His students and patients carried his ideas further. One student, Mary Baker Eddy, founded what became Christian Science partly based on Quimby's work but also influenced by her interpretation of Protestant Christianity. Eddy blended the two into a new religion that declared evil was caused by bad thoughts, heaven and hell were only states of mind, and that God was an all-encompassing being, not a triangulated being of God/Son/Holy Ghost. Christian Science embraces prayer not as a supplication to a divine being but as an affirmation of the god within mankind. In the manner of Quimby's teaching, she wrote that "right thinking" prevented disease and illness was rooted in incorrect thoughts, specifically referencing Corinthians 3:16 (KJV):

Don't you know that you yourselves are God's temple and that God's Spirit dwells in your midst? If anyone destroys God's temple, God will destroy that person; for God's temple is sacred, and you together are that temple.

THEOSOPHY AS TERM OF DESCRIPTION HAS BEEN USED SINCE THE EARLY 1500s regarding beliefs that embrace a study of the mystical workings of God. The word is a Greek neologism of the word *theos*, meaning God, and *sophia*, meaning wisdom.

Madame Blavatsky, c. 1880s.

The early Pietists were considered theosophers. But upper-case Theosophy was the word chosen by Madame Helena Blavatsky as the name of her group of men and women searching for a way to understand the modern world. The staid Christian stories of creation were scrutinized in the light of science. How could one sustain a simplistic belief such as God creating Adam and Eve when archeological finds, Mendel's experiments in early genetics, and Darwin's theory of evolution controverted those stories?

Blavatsky and her Theosophists looked to the ancient past and to Eastern traditions. Theosophy is a complex blend of Westernized Hindu and Buddhist philosophies combined with Spiritualism. Though it never claimed to be a religion, those who embraced the tenets of Theosophy believed in reincarnation and direct communication with beings from other times and dimensions who hold secret information about the workings of the world. The information is said to be powerful and can only be given to those who embark on a long course of study. From Theosophy, the term "Ascended Masters" and a reductive understanding of karma and chakras enter the Western lexicon.

Theosophy embraced an intellectual openness that sought to reconcile Christianity to the modernization of the United States. It was thought that just as science develops, so too could the souls and intellect of humans be developed. And that instead of channeling the voice of a deity, or a long-dead politician, one could—with the correct training and initiation—channel an Ascended Master from a different plane of existence who would share the knowledge of the universe. Theosophy also adopted the Buddhist concept of the Maitreya, the reborn redeemer of the world signaling the end of the current timeline. In our modern world, the Maitreya has been separated from its Buddhist origins and adopted by many other polycultural religions as their end-times savior. Finally, Theosophists believed in human Free Will. It was a stark change from merely one hundred years ago when crusading preachers proclaimed that submission to God's will alone is the only way to avoid the depths of hell. American notions of identity and selfhood had grown malleable. The influence of stories of the "self-made man" fired the collective imagination of Americans to believe that there were no limits on what an individual person could achieve. One could harness the power of the mind and connect to the energy of the universe.

Madame Blavatsky claimed that the Ascended Masters lived in the high mountains of Tibet, and moved the headquarters of the Theosophists to a town outside Chennai, India, in 1880. Upon her death in 1891, the group split into factions. Annie Besant headed up the international group based in Chennai, and the American branch was led by Katherine Tingley (after a short stint by William Judge). Tingley founded the Theosophist community, Lomaland, outside of San Diego in 1900. The Theosophists joined the Seventh-Day Adventists, Thomas Lake Harris and Kanaye Nagasawa's Brotherhood, and other New Religious Movements in establishing a home in California.

Theosophists also adopted Buddhist and Hindu ideas about eating meat and taking stimulants. William Judge wrote in the December 1888 issue of *The Path* magazine about what was Theosophist cuisine. The article combines Eastern thought with Western pseudoscience to allow for a vegetarian diet while never calling for a complete prohibition against eating meat. He says:

> It must make much difference in the conclusion whether one is speaking of a man belonging to the western nations or of one who, like the Hindu, comes of a race which for ages has taken no animal food. It is held by many physiologists that the stomach is an organ for the digesting of animal food only, and that in a vegetarian the pyloric valve leading from the stomach is so paralyzed from want of use that the food passes directly into the intestines. It must therefore follow that the western man may be placing himself in danger of fatal derangement of his system when he leaves meat eating and takes up vegetarianism. This has, indeed, been proved in many cases to be a real danger. I have before me the reports of several theosophists who found that it was not possible for them to make the change; at the same time others have made it with perfect safety. The trouble did not arise from weakness following lack of meat, but from imperfect digestion causing disease. This is due to the retention in the stomach of vegetable matter for so long a time that yeast and other growths were thrown into the circulation; these are sufficient to bring on tuberculosis, nervous diseases, and other manifold derangements. It is well known that a man who has melancholia due to systenemia cannot expect to reach a high development in occultism.

Of course, Judge was writing during a time when less was known about how the human body functions, but one can see how Theosophists, much like Tibetan Buddhists, wrestled with the issue. Vegetarian Theosophist leaders made the correlation to enlightened vegetarian Indian gurus and determined that the negative energy one generated by killing an animal for food was an impediment to mystic knowledge. Judge argues back that the prohibition is against killing anything oneself, and not eating meat killed by others is an act of selfishness by blindly following a rule. He mixes in a bit of Christian theology to make the point:

> It is plain, if this rule be the correct one—and I think it is—that a person who stops the eating of meat in order that he may by complying with that condition attain to a development he has set before him misses the mark, and has acquired a selfish motive for

the line thus adopted. It is an old and true saying that the kingdom of God cometh not from taking or refraining from meat, nor from the refraining from anything whatever, but that it is within us.

This is a critical insight into Theosophist thought. Ultimately, it was the immanence of God within mankind and an individual's free will choices that determined their success at ascending to higher planes of existence. Judge reinforces this idea in his conclusion:

What, then, is the true theosophic diet? It is that which best agrees with you, taken in moderation, neither too much nor too little. If your constitution and temperament will permit vegetarianism, then that will give less heat to the blood; and, if it is practiced from the sincere conviction that it is not true brotherhood to destroy living creatures so highly organized as animals, then so much the better. But if you refrain from meat in order to develop your psychic powers and senses, and continue the same sort of thoughts you have always had, neither cultivating nor practicing the highest altruism, the vegetarianism is in vain.

The inner nature has a diet out of our thoughts and motives. If those are low or gross or selfish, it is equivalent to feeding that nature upon gross food. True theosophic diet is therefore not of either meat or wine; it is unselfish thoughts and deeds, untiring devotion to the welfare of "the great orphan Humanity," absolute abnegation of self, unutterable aspiration to the Divine—the Supreme Soul. This only is what we can grow upon. And vain are the hopes of those who pin their faith on any other doctrine.

Judge makes note that "black magicians" ate meat and attained high levels of power. He concluded, "that power over nature's forces is not solely in the hands of the vegetarian."

There were other Theosophists who explored darker pathways. Paschal Beverly Randolph was—by American one-drop laws—a Black man. He was, like so many Americans, an embodiment of his immigrant, Native, and enslaved ancestors. Randolph was born in New York City in 1825. He claimed to be related to the wealthy and influential Randolph family of Virginia but the circumstances of his birth to an impoverished barmaid belied the fact that his Randolph relatives didn't acknowledge him. His mother died when he was five years old. He was taken in by an older sister and then joined the merchant navy at age twelve. There was no doubting his profound intelligence. During his travels, he taught himself French, Turkish, and Arabic. He was interested in and pursued study of the "mystery schools" in Egypt and India. When he returned to land for good in 1845 at age twenty, he was well versed in esoteric studies.

Upon his return, he discovered that New Yorkers were in thrall to Swedenborgian spiritualism, mesmerism, and other esoteric pursuits. He fashioned himself as a seer in the Spiritualist sense, but his exploration and education soon surpassed spirit-knocking and speaking with the dead. He was an excellent writer who communicated what were highly complex ideas with accessible text. His writings gained him fame, which he used to further his study of Western magic and spiritualism. He eventually rejected communicating with spirits, claiming it took a toll on his body and mind, but not before impressing Napoleon III with his skills. It was Napoleon III in his role as the head of the Rosicrucian Order who inducted Randolph into the Order and charged him to start Rosicrucian chapters in the United States.[66]

Randolph opened numerous Rosicrucian Reading Rooms along the East Coast. He continued his private study of all mystical traditions. He enjoyed entrée to the White House, and according to his autobiography was considered a friend by Abraham Lincoln, who was interested in spiritualism. He conducted a lengthy and entirely telepathic relationship with Madame Blavatsky. He corresponded with European practitioners of the darker arts and expanded his

Paschal Beverly Randolph, c. 1874.

understanding of human nature. Randolph saw sex as a powerful energy that could be controlled and sublimated into magical works. As he explored sex magic and the power of the Will, he came to odds with Madame Blavatsky who, as others have testified, tried to kill him with her mind.

Randolph's iteration of Rosicrucianism grew independently from what is understood as international Rosicrucianism. Rosicrucians groups have turned up in multiple places and in many forms since the first publications promising access to secret and esoteric knowledge appeared in Europe in the early 1600s. The belief embraces Christian and Jewish mysticism, alchemy, and esoteric magic. The name is derived from an image first noted in a tenth-century Byzantine altar carving of a cross with a rose at the center. Early adepts claimed that The Order of the Rosy Cross was as old as the tenth century and possibly older, but alas, as with many secret and secretive groups, that claim cannot be proven. A 1614 narrative tells the story of Christian Rosenkreuz, who traveled throughout the East absorbing Sufi and other esoteric thought from various masters. The writing was considered allegorical by followers, but those outside the Brotherhood read the book with alarm. Other manifestos and writings appeared that reflected interests in magic, science, medicine, governance, and religion. Over their long history, the Rosicrucians have influenced everyone from Freemasons to pulp author Dan Brown.[67]

There are few groups active today that claim to be the sole repository of Rosicrucian knowledge. The Rosicrucian Fellowship was founded in 1909 by Max Heindel in Buffalo, New York, and focused on the Christian mystic aspects of Rosicrucianism. The goal of Heindel's group was to uncover the mysteries of the Bible to help bring about the Age of Aquarius, commonly called the Second Coming. Rosicrucians also believe that the Christian God is master of this

---

66   Randolph wrote autobiographical sketches and later Grand Master R.S. Clymer wrote an extensive biography of Randolph, but Clymer was interested in creating a hagiography that linked all notable European and American "occultists" to Randolph. Some of what is known about Randolph, such as his friendships with Napoleon and Abraham Lincoln, is thought to have been embellished by Clymer.

67   The Rosicrucians are either related to or begat the Illuminati. Sometime in the early nineteenth century, the lineage of Jesus Christ and the Albigensian Heresy was incorporated into the legend. At the risk of veering too far off course, if any of this reminds you of Dan Brown's awful novel *The Da Vinci Code*, then you're recognizing the origins of a tangential theory made famous in the 1986 best-seller *Holy Blood Holy Grail*, which posits that in addition to accepting that the descendants of the Lost Tribes are "hidden" in aristocratic families of Europe, also theorizes that Jesus' wife was pregnant at the time of the crucifixion, and with the assistance of Joseph of Arimathea escaped across the Mediterranean Sea to her (Lost Tribe) relatives in France. And contrary to Indiana Jones, the Grail is not the cup of a poor carpenter but the actual son of Jesus.

Holy Food

solar system and that there are many gods ruling other systems under a supreme deity who oversees them all. Astrology plays an important role in understanding the behaviors of the other solar systems and gods. To be an adept is to refine the three components of man—body, mind, soul—so that one can know all the gods.

Randolph cited both Christian Gospels and Hermetic Law[68] as the genesis of Rosicrucian dietary laws. The diet was 100% vegetarian with 50% of total consumption coming from vegetables. He believed that the spirit is held back by a poor diet. Randolph used Biblical verses and magical law to shape the Rosicrucian diet. He, like other groups, cites Corinthians 3 where Paul tells readers that the body is a temple of God, belonging to God, and to treat it properly. Randolph also said that an acolyte cannot grow spiritually if the physical body is neglected. Mind and body are united, and both must be treated with respect. Rosicrucians practice spiritual healing and astrology, which they believe is based on ancient science. They believe in a direct relationship between individual malevolent actions and bodily consequences. Someone who has cancer is suffering for a wretched action taken against God. Caring for the physical body is important, as it carries the astral body. Seekers are admitted for a course of study as a Regular Student that offers introductory material, but to enter the order as a Probationer, the adept must give up alcohol, tobacco, drugs, and any animal-derived foods. Cookbooks published by the Rosicrucians were important to early vegetarian cuisine as they taught recruits how to adopt to a new way of eating.

Randolph died under suspicious circumstances in 1875. Local authorities claimed it was suicide; others suspect he was shot by someone else. Randolph's death did not end the Rosicrucians in America, and set the stage for dueling Rosicrucian groups. His successor, Freeman Dowd, continued teaching Randolph's writings and Rosicrucian writings and, notably, incorporated some of Randolph's early teaching on sexual magic. Influential Grand Master Reuben Swinburne Clymer, who was Grand Master from 1922 to 1966, incorporated naturopathic healing and chiropractory to the health regimen advocated by the group. Clymer's long reign as Grand Master shaped Randolph's East Coast Rosicrucian group so much that it is now much different from its West Coast rival, the Rosicrucian Fellowship (An International Association of Christian Mystics). The Rosicrucian Fellowship found a receptive home in 1911 Los Angeles, where they built a permanent home in Oceanside, California, on Mount Ecclesia. While the group is currently active, they no longer enjoy the robust membership of a hundred years ago; however, astute observers will still see advertisements for the group's literature in the back pages and classifieds of esoteric publications. Yet, adherence to a vegetarian diet is a core tenet for both groups.

Randolph's writings on Theosophy, spiritual growth, and sex magic served as inspiration for the Ordo Templi Orientis and Aleister Crowley. Some Rosicrucian terms will sound familiar to those with a passing interest in twentieth-century esotericism. Akashic records, astral projection, and angels (who are considered the next evolutionary step after humans) all begin to appear in the American spiritual lexicon at this time. Randolph's work has often been overlooked by historians because Theosophists wrote him out of their history after his falling-

---

68   Hermetic law: As above, so below; as below, so above.

out with Blavatsky. Randolph's life and work are another instance of Black esoteric spiritual pursuits marginalized by historians.

An emerging through line in American food and religious history is that for every religious belief existing in the world, there is a 99% chance that a schismatic break occurred that spawned a breakaway sect. And in the case of Mazdaznan, founder Ha'nish took his inspiration from Mazdakism, a lesser-known sect of

Mazdaznan spiritual image, from the 1893 edition of the *Mazdaznan Cookbook*. Author's collection.

Zoroastrianism, and married it with New Thought and Theosophist practices. Zoroastrianism is considered the oldest continuously practiced religion in the world, with its earliest history traced back to approximately 2000 BCE. It began in the Persian highlands of what is now Iran by the prophet Zoroaster, who rejected a pantheon of gods in favor of a supreme being, Ahura Mazda, creator of the world. Humans are given free will to follow the Truth as laid out by Ahura Mazda or give in to lies or the spirit of negative thoughts, the Angra Mainyu. The notion of "bad spirit" is later personified and elevated as Ahriman, an evil but still lesser than Ahura Mazda figure. Followers study Zoroaster's writings or Gathas.

While the rituals and practices have evolved over time, a few main tenets are intact to modern-day believers. For one, the command to hold good thoughts, do good deeds, and speak good words and live this credo because it *is* good, and not for the expectation of an earthly or spiritual reward. Mazdak was a priest in the Sassanian era of rulers (c. 200–535 CE) who embraced the teaching of Zoroaster but was defiantly anti-clerical. He encouraged people to treat each other as equals and reject the social caste system. He also preached equality for women and benevolence for animals, rejecting both animal sacrifices and the eating of meat. Mazdak was thought to be a contemporary of the Christian heretic Mani (namesake of Manicheaism), who taught duality of man and god as well as a highly restrictive food system that avoided evil and darkness.

It goes without saying that neo-communist Mazdak and his followers, even with support of King Kavadh, were bound to fail. The hereditary priests, whose living was made from the tithe (to use the Christian term) paid to keep Ahura Mazda's fires burning, joined forces with wealthier citizens to depose the king. Mazdak and his followers were brutally tortured and killed. History books littered with references to Mazdak's beliefs were disseminated through the highlands and beyond. Researchers claim that a few Shi'a sects have incorporated Mazdakian thought. Orthodox Zoroastrians still consider Mazdak and his egalitarian ideas heretical.

Mazdakism was truly a blip of a sect of a small religion forgotten by everyone except specialized scholars until 1890, when either of these things occurred—there are two versions of this story. Version one: Otoman Zar-Adusht Ha'nish, son of the Russian diplomat in Teheran, suffered from a heart ailment and was sent to a monastery high in the Persian mountains, run by a secret society of Zoroastrians who taught him secret breathing techniques to cure his hypoxia, and other secrets of the universe. Or version two: Otto Haenisch was born in 1856 to German immigrant parents in Milwaukee, Wisconsin. Young Otto moved to Mendota, Illinois, to try his hand as a shepherd, then a typesetter, before training as a mesmerist. He embraced spiritualism and joined the Mormon Church, then quit to join Alexander Dowie's commune city of Zion, Illinois.

By 1890, Ha'nish met up with German refugee and devotee of New Thought studies, David Ammann. They moved their headquarters to Chicago in 1900 and quickly gained followers with their combination of food-based cures, breatharian exercises, and, as revealed in Ha'nish's book *Inner Studies*, advanced sexual techniques for spiritual growth. More books followed, including *The Science of Dietetics*, and a magazine named *Mazdaznan* begun in 1908 for German followers. As a religious practice, Mazdaznanism is quite convoluted to modern eyes.

Followers nominally worshipped Ahura Mazda, but in truth the group was more aligned with other New Thought groups that promoted self-control as a pathway to success on the earthly and heavenly plains. Mazdaznan books prescribe a rigid calendar of eating, declaring certain foods can only be consumed at specific times of the year. They paid great attention, like many of the health faddists of the day, to bowel movements as an indicator of overall health. The Mazdaznans also embraced a combination of physical postures combined with breathing techniques that are not yoga but claim to allow the practitioner to achieve a higher mental state.

Ha'nish made several appearances in front of the Chicago circuit courts. He was sued a few times as a party to child abuse (children living in the Mazdaznan temple were treated as mini-adults and expected to follow the same diet), and as party to several divorce proceedings where it was claimed he ensorcelled fragile housewives to join his cult. He and Ammann moved to Los Angeles in 1917, where climate and culture were more open to New Thought groups.

Ha'nish died in Los Angeles in 1936 at the age of eighty-five. David Ammann and his wife Frieda and successive followers kept the Mazdaznan movement alive in various forms over the ensuing years. The headquarters was moved from Los Angeles to Encinitas in 1980, before closing for good in 2001 when the last Mazdaznan in the area stopped attending to business. But the outreach done by the Ammanns in Germany kept the movement thriving through both World Wars, even surviving a ban by the Nazis. As of today, there are approximately 20,000 Mazdaznans in the world. And in 2007, a Canadian follower built a website devoted to the writings and teachings of Ha'nish.

I N 1879, MARY BAKER EDDY'S CHRISTIAN SCIENCE WAS CONSIDERED A CULT, YET gained mainstream acceptance by the early 1900s during the unregulated era of medicine and doctoring. Students of Phineas Quimby, Annie Besant, and Helena Blavatsky built upon their foundations of thought-science and harnessing the energy power of the universe, and are now considered a larger part of the New Thought Movement. The ideas splintered and were reinterpreted through numerous messengers throughout the nineteenth and twentieth centuries, spawning further practitioners and movements. The New Thought Movement doesn't have a centralized, overseeing officiate, and can be as simple as someone proclaiming the power of "Positive Mental Attitude," to the "prosperity gospel" favored by preachers wearing $5,000 sneakers, to the truly nefarious practices that take advantage of a person's ill health and desperation.

The wide-ranging field of faith and spiritual healing was and still is fraught with con men and fakers in the face of genuine spontaneous and unexplained cures. Suffering patients seek to gain comfort from the prayers of friends, family, and strangers. But the despair of suffering leaves too many opportunities for bad actors. So too have many New Thought Movements cherry-picked elements of what was once a considered and rigorous exploration of belief to become multi-level marketing schemes that fleece believers while laying the guilt of failure at their feet.

One may be thinking at this point, "What does any of this have to do with food?" I assure readers that Spiritualism, mediumship, channeling, faith healing, and hearing voices influence the next wave of religiously inspired food practices. Science is conflated with belief while verifiable discoveries are made. On the horizon is a new mania for controlling and restricting what we eat. No longer are food rules solely informed by scripture and inspired visions; they are wrapped in the latest science or pseudo-science. It is from these ideas that daffy yet benign groups emerge to influence twentieth-century food. But it is also from these ideas that the darker and more sinister movements use food as a cudgel against their believers and sometimes the entire culture.

FRATERNITAS ROSAE CRUCIS

(Rosicrucian Brotherhood, Fraternity of the Rosy Cross, RSC, Paschal Beverly Randolph)
Years active: 1858 to present day
Affiliation: Gnostic-Mysticism
Founder / Leader: Paschal Beverly Randolph

DILLY BREAD

(Vegetarian. Makes 1 loaf.)
Tools: Bread pan
Oven temperature: 350°F

Ingredients:

1 package dry yeast
1 cup cottage cheese
1 Tablespoon minced onion
2 teaspoons crushed dill seed
½ teaspoon baking soda
2¼ – 2½ cups whole-wheat flour
¼ cup water
2 Tablespoons honey
1 Tablespoon butter
1 teaspoon sea salt
1 egg

Steps:

1. Preheat oven to 350°F.
2. Soften yeast in warm water (105°–115°). Set aside.
3. Warm cottage cheese to room temperature.
4. In a large bowl, combine warmed cottage cheese, honey, onion, butter, dill, salt, soda, and egg.
5. Add flour to form a stiff dough. Beat well.
6. Place a light cotton cloth over a cutting board. Sprinkle with flour then knead for about 5 minutes.
7. Place dough in an oiled bowl, cover with a light cotton cloth and let rise in a warm place until doubled in size.
8. Punch the dough down then knead a little. Place in pan and let rise again until indentation with finger stays.
9. Bake at 350°F for 40 minutes.

THE ROSICRUCIAN FELLOWSHIP

(An International Association of Christian Mystics)
Years active: 1909 to present day
Headquarters: Oceanside, California
Affiliation: Gnostic-Mysticism
Founder / Leader: Max Heindel

POTASSIUM BROTH

(Vegan. Makes about 6 cups.)
Tools: Stockpot

Note: Vegetarians at the dawning of the food science era became obsessed with creating dishes that supplied nutrition that eaters would normally get from meat. The Rosicrucians and Mazdaznans both developed variations on Potassium Broths that were later adopted by the Seventh-Day Adventists. Modern "wellness" advocates have been touting Potassium Broth to maintain vital nutrients during cleanses and fasts. The less scrupulous make claims that Potassium Broth "blasts fat cells." Stripped of religious meaning, Potassium Broth is akin to a homemade version of V8 Juice, which was created by New England Products Company in 1933 as Vege-min 8. All in all, Potassium Broth is a healthy vegetable beverage.

Ingredients:
1 cup finely shredded celery (leaves and stalk)
1 cup finely shredded carrots
1 cup shredded spinach
1 quart distilled water
1 teaspoon vegetable salt
1 cup tomato juice
1 Tablespoon shredded parsley
Steps:
1. In a medium stockpot, add the shredded vegetables and distilled water.
2. Tightly cover and simmer for 30 minutes.
3. Add tomato juice and vegetable salt. Simmer a few minutes longer.
4. Strain and serve.
Use as a drink throughout the day.

VEGETABLE ROAST

(Vegetarian. Makes 8 to 10 servings.)
Tools: Jelly roll pan or baking dish

Note: This recipe begins with an assumption that you have cooked beans in reserve. This may sound odd today, but many cooks who followed the Rosicrucian and other vegetarian diets of the late 1800s kept cooked beans at the ready as they were used in many recipes.

Ingredients:

2 cups cooked beans, ground (use a ricer or food mill to grind/mash cooked beans)

1 cup chopped parsley

1 cup steamed onions

¾ cup beets, shredded fine

2 carrots, grated fine

2 cloves garlic, mashed

1 cup whole-wheat breadcrumbs

1 cup diced celery

1 teaspoon sweet basil

½ cup wheat germ

1 raw onion, cut fine

2 egg yolks

Vegetable salt*, if desired

3 Tablespoons vegetable oil

Front cover of the 1930 edition of the *Rosicrucian Cookbook.* Author's collection.

*Vegetable salt was introduced as a vegetarian-specific spice. It's usually made of a mixture of mineral salt, paprika, celery, onion, carrot, parsley, spinach, kelp, beet root, hydrolyzed soy protein, molasses, and dill seed. Lower in sodium than iodized salt, vegetable salt was recommended for people following a vegetarian diet. Popular brands still on the market today are Spike Vege-Sal and Aromat Seasoning.

Steps:

1. Preheat oven to 400°F.
2. Using a steaming rack insert for a saucepan, fill with 2 inches of water. Place quartered, peeled onion on rack and steam for about 10 minutes, until soft.
3. In a large mixing bowl, combine all ingredients. Mix until thoroughly blended.
4. Form mixture into loaf or individual patties.
5. Place on jelly roll pan lined with parchment paper and lightly oiled with olive oil.
6. Bake about 20 minutes. Remove from oven when lightly browned.
7. Serve alone or with a complementary gravy or sauce.

MAZDAZNAN

Years active: 1890 to current day
Founded in: Chicago, with outposts in New York, Los Angeles, and throughout Germany
Affiliation: Zoroastrianism (Mazdakism sect)
Founder: Otoman Zar-Adusht Ha'nish (*né* Otto Haenisch)

DOUGH GODS

(Vegetarian. Makes approximately a dozen.)
Tools: Paper grocery bag and jelly roll pan

Recipe Notes from *The Science of Dietetics*: "The reason we call them Dough Gods is because the ancients realized that the Sun with its radiations is the God unto life, the life-giver the creator, and that which perpetuates form manifestation is a Dough God. These Dough Gods can be made in the frying pan."

Note that this recipe does not contain any salt; as the Mazdaznan cooks say, "You are not to eat any salt this season. This will allow Nature an opportunity to adjust herself, especially the blood."

Ingredients:
2 cups whole-wheat flour
1 cup warm water
2 Tablespoons dry active yeast
Cinnamon sugar and/or brown sugar
For frying, 2 Tablespoons peanut oil or other lighter vegetable oil
Steps:
1. Fill a glass or plastic measuring cup with 1 cup of warm water (ideal temperature is 115°F). Add and mix the yeast.
2. In a medium-sized bowl, add the whole-wheat flour.
3. Add the yeasted water to the whole-wheat flour and mix together.
4. Knead dough for about 10 minutes. Texture of dough should be "like cold molasses."
5. Set a thin cotton towel over top of bowl and let dough rise about 30 minutes.
6. In a medium frying pan, add oil, cover with fitted lid, and set burner to medium-high.
7. While oil is heating, prepare paper grocery bag by splitting down seam, fold in half, and flatten. Lay paper on jelly roll pan.

8. Into the whole-wheat flour, put cold water and mix, making a paste the thickness of cold molasses. In a small dish, add cinnamon sugar blend. (Or, if using brown sugar, add the brown sugar.)
9. Being careful of the hot oil, drop tablespoon-sized pieces of dough into pan until dough is gone. Cover with lid.
10. Cook for 10 minutes, then remove lid and using tongs, turn over. Replace lid and cook for another 10 minutes. Or until dark brown.
11. Using tongs, remove each Dough God from hot oil and place onto paper bag to drain for approximately 2 minutes.
12. Roll Dough Gods in cinnamon sugar blend then set onto plate. Or split in half and fill with brown sugar. Serve hot.

More from the Mazdaznans: "This bread or Dough God will do you a lot of good eaten regularly even though it looks heavy. If you feel out of sorts, bake a Dough God and eat it."

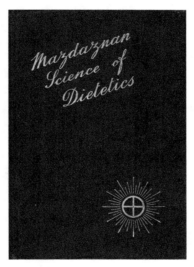

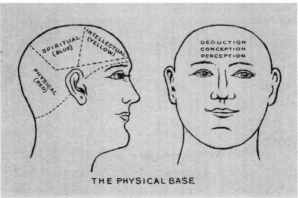

Front cover and interior illustration from 1950 edition of _Mazdaznan Science of Dietetics_. Author's collection.

Six
THE LOST TRIBES

ELIGIOUS TEXTS READ AS AN ACCURATE HISTORICAL RECORD OF EVENTS HAVE LED many a would-be prophet into perilous theology. While religious texts often contain actual people and moments in history, so much of what we understand as The Book is a compendium of highly edited stories and parables intended to illustrate moral precepts. We know this. Still, there is the temptation to find the kernels of plausibility and build an entire religion from What If? Specific passages have inspired styles of worship, and of course dietary traditions, yet a few sparse references in II Chronicles and I Kings from the Old Testament and Tanakh have fueled nearly a thousand years of identity crisis and thriving food cultures. These are the passages that reference the Lost Tribes of Israel.

A quick summary of Chronicles and Kings: According to the narrative in the Tanakh, the sons of Jacob (grandson of Abraham) were allocated land in the Levant. Each son had an inclination toward a specific job or holy responsibility. Their descendants are Members of the Tribe. In approximately 722 BCE, the Assyrians conquered the Kingdom of Israel. The Assyrians deported and depopulated the conquered region. Some Jews were enslaved and sent to the Mesopotamian homelands, and some fled to . . . well, where the Jewish tribes fled is our story. Historian Josephus, writing in the century after the Romans conquered Jerusalem in c. 60 ACE, backs up the claims that there were only two tribes remaining in the Levant during his lifetime but unknown numbers from the Ten Tribes living east of the Euphrates River.

The two Levantine tribes (whom modern Jews claim as ancestors) were Judah and Benjamin; they were loyal to King Rehoboam, the son of Solomon. The Ten Tribes' land holdings were to the north of the Dead Sea and west of the Jordan River. (Most scholars note that the number twelve is symbolic as it retains spiritual and mystical meanings in the Kabbalah.) Enumeration aside, the Ten Tribes were led by Reuben, Simeon, Dan, Naphtali, Gad, Asher, Issachar, Zebulun, Manasseh, and Ephraim.[69] The tribe of Levi were hereditarily a priestly caste and did not have direct land holdings, but did have responsibility for maintaining the Temple in Jerusalem. It is a long-held belief in some Jewish and many Christian traditions that when the Twelve Tribes are reunited to worship in the Temple in Jerusalem that the promised Messiah will appear. For

---

69 Manasseh and Ephraim were the sons of Joseph who received a double inheritance when his brother Reuben ticked off their father Jacob for either sleeping with his concubine Billah (mother of Dan and Naphtali), or throwing her out of the patriarch's tent. Biblical genealogies and family practices are often convoluted. But any of the modern religious groups who practice polygamy cite these early families as proof that God wants men to have many wives and concubines.

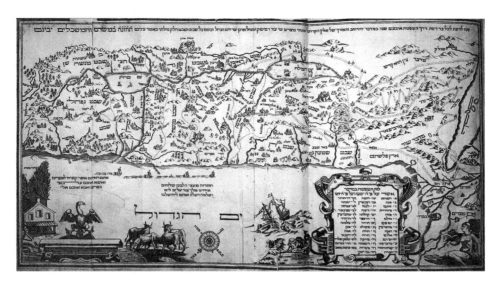

1695 Eretz Israel map in Amsterdam Haggada by Abraham Bar-Jacob.

Christians, it would be the Second Coming and the restoration of God's heaven on Earth. This is the very minimum of Biblical history required to help understand what happens next.

The Quran mentions the Lost Tribes, as do passages scattered throughout the Tanakh, but it isn't until the seventeenth century that the notion appears that European Christians might just be part of the Lost Tribes too. And if Europeans might be, then so too could people from Africa and the Indian subcontinent. And then why not include Indigenous Americans? Soon, a cottage industry of theoretical genealogies and specious proofs claiming descendance from a Lost Tribe appeared in print. The first to gain popularity in the English language was Rabbi, philosopher, diplomat, and Kabbalist, Menasseh ben Israel, who ran a Jewish printing press in Amsterdam after his family's expulsion from Spain during the Inquisition. Seventeenth-century Amsterdam was a center of intellectual thought and refuge for a wide swath of persecuted religious peoples, including the Protestant fundamentalists, Puritans, and Pietists who were making their way to the United States. Ben Israel printed Hebrew texts translated into Portuguese, Dutch, and English. He was a respected scholar and teacher intrigued by explorers and conquistadors returning from the "new world" with tales of Indigenous peoples. There was a speculative theory amongst the intelligentsia that these Native peoples were descended from the Lost Tribes. Ben Israel saw the Lost Tribes idea as a catalyst for gaining sociopolitical acceptance for Jewish people in Europe, especially in England.

Beginning in 1215, the Vatican decreed that all Jews living in Catholic-led nations (most of Europe) must wear distinct clothing and a badge identifying them as Jews. And Jews were expelled from European countries and principalities with regularity. England banished all Jews from the island in 1290. Jews enjoyed relative autonomy in Eastern Europe under the four hundred years of Polish-Lithuanian reign, only to suffer brutal massacres under the Cossack-led regime during the 1600s. During the 1700s Jews were further restricted by the Catholic church and European monarchy as to where they could live and what jobs they could hold. Jews were forbidden from owning land and relegated to designated neighborhoods, called *ghettos*. They could not join artisan guilds nor take on apprentices. Many found work in academia and banking—mainly in financial lending, which was a job forbidden to Catholics. Priestly scholars in the Middle Ages had begun promulgating the logic-defying "blood libel" lies that persist today.[70] Even the Protestant revolution of Martin Luther left Jews with less freedom than under Catholic rule. Luther's anti-Semitic screed *On the Jews and Their Lies* (1543) set the tone for increasing violence against Jewish people.

For ben Israel, the possibility that the "new world" was populated by Lost Tribes of Jews was revolutionary. In his work *The Hope of Israel* (1650), directed toward English readers and specifically Oliver Cromwell, ben Israel appeals to Christian theology and posits that reuniting the Lost Tribes will bring about the awaited Messiah. It was an important distinction because Cromwellian Protestants were fundamentalists and millenarians invested in the apocalyptic significance of the year 1666. Ben Israel used the Lost Tribes argument to appeal to Cromwell to reverse the four-hundred-plus-year law and allow Jews to live in England once again. In 1655, Parliament decided that the ban was a royal decree and not law, so Jews could return at will. Later scholars have argued whether ben Israel truly subscribed to the Lost Tribes theory of scattered Jews populating the Earth, or if he cannily used it to convince the English government to set aside the 1290 decree. Convincing arguments have been made by both sides, yet the long-term effect is one ben Israel would have never imagined—the Lost Tribes of Israel narrative has been claimed by many American New Religious Movements as a legitimate heritage and revelation.

As of this writing, there is a growing phenomenon of fundamentalist Christian sects adopting the Jewish holiday of Passover as a Christian holy day. The holiday is celebrated with a Seder dinner that mimics and reimagines the traditional rite as symbolic deliverance from perceived persecution by mainstream society. Lost Tribes thinking also appears in Jewish- and Muslim-influenced New Religious Movements. The degree and extent to which any group recognizes themselves as members of a Lost Tribe varies from "It's part of our early history but we've evolved" to "We are working to bring about our triumphant return to the Jerusalem Temple." It should be noted that a common element among extremist New Religious Groups and sects is that they believe they are a persecuted minority, and followers are part of an unrecognized and suppressed group with access to secreted knowledge. Scholars warn that religious groups that teach believers that they are oppressed when combined with other high control demands, like unhealthy fasting and severe food restrictions, are cults.

Eighteenth-century believers in the Lost Tribes narrative began to theorize that the Celts, Teutons, Gauls, and Anglo-Saxons who conquered earlier European people were descended from the Lost Tribes. It was, even in the late 1600s and early 1700s, a marginalized idea. Richard Brothers was an ex-British Navy officer who embraced the Lost Tribes story and declared himself Prince of the Jews and a direct descendant of the Tribe of David—or to use Brothers' term, House

---

70   The anti-Semitic "blood libel" claims that Jews slaughter Christian children in a ritualistic manner and drink their blood in a ceremony that mocks the Christian sacrament of holy communion. This anti-Jewish propaganda has existed from the earliest days of the printing presses in Europe, to Henry Ford publishing "The Protocols of the Elders of Zion" in his *Dearborn Independent* newspaper in 1927, to modern-day QAnonists claiming "elites" sacrifice children in satanic rituals to harvest the chemical compound product of adrenaline (adrenochrome) found in human blood.

Richard Brothers.

of David. Brothers preached on street corners and was in and out of the workhouse on charges of poverty, and private asylums on charges of insanity. But in 1794 he published the seminal tract that birthed the British-Israelite (Anglo-Israelite) movement. Titled *A REVEALED KNOWLEDGE OF THE PROPHECIES AND TIMES, Book the First, wrote under the direction of the LORD GOD and published by His Sacred Command, it being the first sign of Warning for the benefit of All Nations; Containing with other great and remarkable things not revealed to any other Person on Earth, the Restoration of the Hebrews to Jerusalem by the year of 1798 under their revealed Prince and Prophet*, it fired the imagination of enough Londoners that Brothers grew a substantial following. Readers may notice that Brothers makes an error in his prophetic writing that plagues every failed religious visionary: he commits to a date. When the year 1798 arrives without fanfare or restoration, Brothers' followers fade away and he is taken in by a loyal yet skeptical follower who cared for him until his death thirty years later in 1824.

Anglo-Israelism remained in English consciousness but without any formal organization until the 1870s, when a few advocacy groups are incorporated to coalesce the idea that white, Anglo-Saxon Protestants are members of the House of David, and actively work to infuse the concept into the tenets of the Church of England. It was accepted that the Germanic and Celtic tribes were also of Lost Tribe origin but that the English reigned supreme, as they were descended from the anointed-by-God hereditary kings known as the House of David and members of the Lost Tribe of Ephraim. It is this core idea developed by Anglo-Israelites—that white Englishmen and their descendants are the true inheritors of God's bounty, and have absolute right of dominion over the Earth and its inhabitants—that is the foundational germ of modern American Christian Identity white separatist terrorist groups and emerging Christian Nationalists.

What did it mean to believers, once the awesome glory of truth was revealed to them? For the Anglo-Israelites in England it cemented their belief that they were ordained by God to rule the Earth. In practice, because they formed political groups and not schismatic religious sects, the Anglo-Israelites embraced their "Jew-ish" roots but remained Christians, within the boundaries of accepted organized religions who never considered themselves Jews but the inheritors of God's Promise to the Jewish people.

Leaders of the Anglo-Israelites in England came to the United States to establish chapters of the British-Israel Identity Corporation. Others embarked on archeological expeditions throughout Europe searching for physical evidence of their claims. The Hill of Tara, an important historic ancestral ritual and burial site in Ireland, was nearly destroyed in 1899–1901 by believers searching for the Ark of the Covenant. By the early 1900s, Anglo-Israelites expand the Lost Tribes theory to include a head-spinning interpretation of the Christian Bible that declares themselves to be the true Jews of scripture and actual Jewish people to be the Canaanites, the traditional enemy of the Biblical Jews. The Anglo-Israelites also embraced a virulent form of anti-Semitism—virulent even for the era when casual anti-Semitism was the norm.

As absurd as the Lost Tribes theory may sound to modern readers, it was a popular movement during the tumultuous fin-de-siècle period at the turn of the last century. In a survey for the *Jewish Encyclopedia* published in 1904, it was estimated that two million people in England and the United States were members of an Anglo-Israelite group.

British-Israelism in the United States was more religious than political. The emerging Holiness movement adopted the Lost Tribes theory and took the next logical (for believers) next step. If white people were truly the descendants of the Lost Tribe, then they must follow the Old Testament. Believers saw this as a call to embrace the "old-time religion" and live strictly according to the Book. Many Holiness congregations followed the kashrut food rules detailed in Leviticus. Some also embraced the Edenic Covenant and became ardent vegetarians. Because the Holiness churches in the early 1900s were decentralized with no hierarchical oversight, charismatic ministers with unique interpretations of the Bible and the Lost Tribes narrative held great sway in many churches.

In the United States, Anglo-Israelism splits into multiple distinct tracks. Examples are the previously mentioned and still active white supremacist Christian Identity movement, and the quirkier communal-living groups like the infamous House of David based in Benton Harbor, Michigan. Church of Latter-Day Saints founder Joseph Smith was also a Lost Tribe believer, as is revealed in the Book of Mormon: that Indigenous American tribes are "Lammanites" and descendants of a Lost Tribe. White Mormons claim lineage through the "House of Joseph" or the combined tribes of Manasseh and Ephraim. To be absolutely clear, the American and English groups who embraced Anglo-Israelism did not see themselves as Jews. They considered themselves Christian and they saw themselves as the legitimate inheritors of God's promise as outlined in the Bible.

The House of David might be better known for their barnstorming baseball team that traveled the United States during the 1920s and '30s than their religious commune-*cum*-holiday resort. Yet it was at their resort compound in Benton Harbor that the House of David established itself as the leading Anglo-Israelite group in the United States. The House of David cosmology was shared among the many similar breakaway Protestant groups embracing Lost Tribes, like Alexander J. Christ Dowie's City of Zion. Which goes to say, these groups were fundamentalist Christian with Holiness influences who believed they were God's chosen people, and that the end times were nigh. Benjamin Purnell claimed to be the reincarnated brother of the Messiah which, he explained, meant that the end really was nigh. In practice, the House of David was led by the husband-and-wife pastoral team of Benjamin and Mary Purnell, who devised the brilliant scheme of opening their commune to paid visitors.

House of David members were both vegetarian and kosher, which made their new resort, located about one hundred miles east of Chicago and two hundred miles west of Detroit, an attractive holiday spot for vacationing middle-class Jewish families. The House of David members provided the labor to keep the resort running, including baking, cooking, and

Baker at House of David. Benton Harbor, Michigan, c. 1940. Courtesy of the Israelite House of David.

entertainment. The resort was home to early mechanical rides that would soon become the hallmark of amusement and theme parks. But it was the striking look of House of David members that stands out today. Women dressed in modest clothing and kept their hair covered, similar to the Plain Clothes style of modern Mennonites. However, the men followed an edict from Benjamin Purnell to emulate Samson, the most manly hero of the Old Testament/ Tanakh, and not cut their hair. And Purnell required that all men wear *payot* or sidelocks in reference to a Talmudic prohibition against shaving the sides of one's head.

Part of the entertainment for guests, which later became a revenue source, was the House of David's baseball team. The team was begun in the late 1910s when baseball was rising in popularity. The team played area clubs, then expanded to the traveling circuit to play in other cities. The House of David team was a fan favorite due to their strange look and fast hands. Exhibition baseball could be lucrative for league players, and many barnstorming teams took on professional "ringers" during the off-season. But to play for the House of David, a player had to don a wig and fake beard to fit the look of the rest of the team. Many aspiring young players and a few washed-up older ones put on the wig and beard to play ball. Though, to correct a common misconception, Babe Ruth never played for the House of David.

Black pastors, like their white counterparts, found inspiration in the Lost Tribes theory. But unlike Anglo-Israelites, Black ministers embraced a literal genealogy that placed them firmly within the Jewish Diaspora. The question lingers: is there any discernible truth to the claim that there are descendants of the Lost Tribes alive today? DNA testing in the past decade has thrown much of the Lost Tribe doctrine into disarray. Mestizo converts to Mormonism in Peru, believing themselves to be hereditary descendants of Jacob based on Latter-Day theology, have discovered they have zero Semitic DNA. But other people who have long considered themselves Jews and have religious and food traditions of Judaic origins have confirmed their claim of Lost Tribe status through DNA testing.

Cochin Jews have lived in the Kerala State of India since the time of King Solomon. Are they Jews? 100% yes, as confirmed by their religious traditions and DNA. The Bnei Menashe, a group of tribal villages in northeastern India, have long claimed to be among the Lost Tribes. In 2005, the Chief Rabbi of Jerusalem agreed and proclaimed them true Jews. The Beta Israel (formerly known as Falasha) of Ethiopia claim kinship from the Lost Tribe of Dan. Again, DNA has proven them correct. The Lemba people of South Africa and the Igbo of Nigeria also claim Jewish heritage. Many Igbo describe themselves as descendants of a Lost

Poster announcing International Conference of Knights Templar organizations, 1920.

Tribe. Historians have refuted the claims of the Lemba and Igbo, but both groups have adopted traditionally Jewish food and rituals. Researchers have theories that Jewish traders may have introduced some Jewish food customs hundreds of years ago, but not so far back as to be a Lost Tribe.

In the United States, African claims of Lost Tribe status inspired two distinct religious tracks that posit Black people are either part of the larger Jewish Diaspora, or the true inheritors of God's promise to Moses to deliver his chosen people. A few groups came to embrace Ashkenazi Judaism (with a few twists). Others developed an entirely new cosmology and dogma informed by a diverse range of influences that include the Lost Tribes theories. And still others added Islamic philosophy and rites to the polycultural mix. All the Lost Tribe new religions—Black, white, and integrated—have, because of their shared "Jew-ish" origins, adopted variations of kashrut food laws while also incorporating a wide variety of other health, political, and religious food rules that reflect their specific beliefs.

THE STORY OF BLACK ISRAELITES AND BLACK JEWS WAS ONCE RELEGATED TO footnotes in scholarly histories of religion, but a new generation of Black and Jewish researchers are now taking a closer look at these groups. A robust understanding of the dynamic beliefs and influence of Black Israelites and Black Jews on the modern spiritual life and food traditions is emerging. To better understand the nuances, we again must shift our perspective from a white-centered view of Black life in the United States.

Modern Black religions in the Americas were assembled from regional and culture traditions adopted and adapted throughout the six-hundred-plus years Black people have been here. Yes, some traditions are vestigial practices from a cultural African past, but research has shown that Black American spirituality is truly a bricolage that reflects every aspect of the Black experience. Specifically, the confluence of post-Civil War emancipation, Jim Crow Laws, freemasonry, Lost Tribe theory, African American conjuring, Theosophist New Thought, the Great Migration, and separatist emancipation politics. The Commandment Keepers (Black Jews), Rastafari, Nation of Islam, Moorish Science Temple, the Azusa Street Mission, C.H. Mason's Pentecostalism, Daddy Grace, Father Divine, and Jim Jones—all of whom have had an impact on American life and food—have their beginnings in the work and beliefs of a small group of charismatic Black ministers who saw themselves and not white people as the Lost Tribe.

A common misconception is that Black people in the post-Civil War era primarily lived in the South. This wrongheaded notion was perpetuated by Jim Crow-era films and books that traded in stereotypes and white supremacist narratives. The truth is that Black Americans in 1866 lived in every state and territory. In the larger cities on the Atlantic coast, there was a transnationalism enriched by the two-way flow of people from the Caribbean to New York City, Philadelphia, Washington, D.C., and beyond. At the blossoming of the Harlem Renaissance, census statistics reveal that approximately 20% of the population of Harlem was born on one of the Caribbean islands. In the former slaveholding states of the South, it became apparent to many Black people that Reconstruction reforms were undermined by states enacting oppressive disenfranchisement laws. The same western frontier that called to the Latter-Day Saints and The Brotherhood of New Life called to the hundreds of thousands of Black people searching for a chance to build *their* future.

Kansas and Oklahoma had thriving cities wholly run by Black people. These towns were founded by visionary businessmen and religious leaders. Many were inspired by the message of Booker T. Washington and the Tuskegee mission to build self-sufficiency as the pathway to success for Black America. These pioneers were dubbed "Exodusters," as Black Americans had found analogous comfort in the Old Testament/Tanakh story of Exodus—of God's promise to Moses that if the people of Israel believed in the one true God, he would lead them out of bondage. In the self-sufficient towns of the Midwestern Plains, Black people were free to explore new ways of believing in God while incorporating the food traditions of their ancestors.

The Lost Tribes philosophy dominant in Christianity was not the only influence on the development of Black Israelite, Black Muslim, and Black Jewish sects. During the late 1800s, Masonic brotherhoods were at their height of popularity. A census from 1900 claimed that 20% of all American men—Black and white—were members of a fraternal brotherhood organization. Three-quarters of the "founding fathers" were members of Masonic lodges. Professors, lawyers, and yes, churchmen too were members. It was considered, much as joining the right golf club would be today, that Masonic brotherhood provided entrée and networking with fellow elites. Without giving away the secrets of the brethren, many of the rituals associated with the Masons revolve around the legends of Solomon, the mysteries of the Kabbalah, and recognition of Anglo-Saxon supremacy as *thee* Lost Tribe.

Prince Hall was a Black resident of Boston during the second half of the 1700s. He was a free man, though he may have been enslaved as a child. Hall was an advocate for abolition of slavery and the universal education of Black children. He and a few other prominent Black Bostonians applied for membership to the Grand Lodge of Massachusetts in the early 1770s; they were turned away. Hall believed in the Masonic promise of Liberty, Brotherhood, and Equality, and applied to the Grand Lodge of Ireland, whose members established an outpost in 1775 for British soldiers stationed in Boston. He was admitted but found that the Master limited his and other Black men's access and participation. In frustration, Hall applied to the Grand Lodge of England to start a new Lodge. The Grand Master, the Duke of Cumberland, granted Hall his charter. The African Lodge was invested in 1784 with Hall as the Master.

Hall's African Lodge proved wildly popular among the Black population in Boston, then Philadelphia, and quickly spread across the country and to the Caribbean. The African Lodge adopted the same mysteries and precepts as the European lodges. Though Hall gained the charter from the England Lodge, his group still faced discrimination and was ostracized from joint events and parades in the United States. (Masonic brotherhoods traditionally share an "amity" between different Lodges.) None of the white lodges recognized the African Lodge. The African Lodge formally broke away from the England Lodge in 1827 to become the first independent Masonic organization and became known as Prince Hall Freemasonry, named after its founder.

Hall's Masonic legacy is steeped in his political and social activism. He fought for equality and education, and like other Black leaders of the day, explored the feasibility of a return to an African homeland. Prince Hall Freemasonry lodges became a place for true fraternity between Black men as well as a place to share philosophical and religious ideas, including the prevailing "mystery" of the Lost Tribes. It is difficult to state as fact whether the hundreds of thousands of members truly believed they were descended from a Lost Tribe of Israel, but we do know that the narrative analogy of the story of the Lost Tribes, and Masonry's focus on King Solomon of the Old Testament/Tanakh, passed into Black culture.

In the Black cities of the West, the center of Masonic activity was Guthrie, Oklahoma. The region was also home to the Holiness preachers who traveled from their birthplaces in the South to settle in the frontier west. (Holiness as a definition of religious practice had morphed by the early twentieth century into a shorthand to describe what we would now recognize as Pentecostalism. American organized and unorganized religions were schisming and expanding at an exponential rate.) These ministers adapted the Lost Tribe narrative as gleaned through Masonry and transformed it into a Black history. William Saunders Crowdy of Kansas, and later Oklahoma, spread this message with fervor. Crowdy was not alone. Many white evangelists were sharing the same fundamentalist interpretation of the Bible of who were and who were not God's chosen people. Crowdy's newly formed church, the Church of God in Christ and Saints, was the first to claim that Black people were Israelites and that Jesus and his disciples were Black people. And like the British-Israelites, they differentiated themselves from Jews while incorporating Hebraic holidays, chiefly the embrace of Saturday as the day of the Sabbath, and select kashrut food rules.

The idea of Blacks as the true Israelites spread east to New York City and then throughout the world. The widely-read independent Black newspapers reported on these newer schismatic beliefs, often with disdain from a lofty perspective of the "respectable" religions like the African Methodist Episcopal church, but nevertheless the press exposed people to the ideas. Travel throughout the Black Atlantic region and to Africa spread the Holiness and Black Israelite message at breakneck speed. Crowdy was named Bishop of his church and sent missionaries to South Africa and Nigeria. His message was one of equal rights for Black people insomuch as everyone was equal in the eyes of God, so all people must integrate. The theme of "color-blindness" was one many Black religionists at the turn of the twentieth century returned to again and again. The early Black Holiness movement led by Crowdy, like the Spiritualist Church, and other New Religious Movements prior to Jim Crow Laws, were fully integrated movements that preached and recruited Black and white members. The cultural struggle to fight racism— either by integration or total separation—was a growing theme in American religious life that sees food as signifiers of both freedom and oppression.

Inspired by Crowdy and intrigued by the Holiness movement within Protestant sects, Baptist preacher Charles Harrison Mason visited the infamous Azusa Street Mission, led by William Seymour, in Los Angeles in 1908. Mason stayed with Seymour, taking in his preaching and teaching for six weeks where he came to be "sanctified." (In this context, sanctified means that his soul was cleansed and purified by God.) He began speaking to his parishioners and other clergy about this revelation of God's mysteries—that through baptism in the Holy Ghost, a soul can be saved forever and given divine gifts such as speaking in tongues and divine healing. Mason was one of hundreds of clergy who visited Seymour at Azusa and then began spreading the new Holiness message movement that came to be called Pentecostal. (The name Pentecostal comes from the Biblical story of Christ's apostles visited by the Holy Spirit fifty days after Jesus' death.)

Bishop Mason was more than a zealous convert; he was a gifted organizer. He built on Crowdy's ideas of an interracial church based on love of God and a commitment to disciplined prayer and fasting. Scholars have also documented Mason's connection to traditional "root work" and Black Atlantic spiritual practices that influenced his ideas about worship. As a preacher, he integrated praise-song into his spoken sermons, and is credited with introducing the now common refrain of "Yes, Lord" as a continual prayer during a sermon. Bishop Mason viewed his experience as part of his Baptist identity, yet the Baptist church hierarchy was in opposition to Seymour's vision of sanctification on theological grounds. Mason felt abandoned by his church, but was compelled to share what he believed was God's message. Bishop Mason preached at any church that would welcome him, preaching throughout the Midwest and Appalachia before settling in Memphis, Tennessee, to consecrate the Mother Church of the Church of God in Christ (COGIC). (The name of the church references its connection to Crowdy's church, the Church of God in Christ and Saints, and numerous offshoots adopt a variation of the name.) COGIC grew, and the Pentecostal message spread as Bishop Mason ordained Black and white ministers to preach, hold revivals, and form churches everywhere, giving rise to the very American entity: the storefront church.

Mason's advocacy for fasting as a form of physical prayer differed from many of the other religious leaders of the era and even within the Holiness movement. The Church of God in Christ takes explicit direction from a short passage in the New Testament, Matthew 17:21: "However, this kind does not go out except by prayer and fasting." Bishop Mason taught that fasting magnified prayer and was a vital way to communicate with God. He personally prayer-fasted for days on end when wrestling with difficult issues within the church and for followers. He recommended that followers bedeviled by doubt, temptation, or

Commemorative Founder's Day image of Bishop C.H. Mason, 1953.

fear fast and pray to God for his mercy in the form of an answer to the problem. The modern COGIC church remains actively involved in fasting[71] as a physical component to prayer. Pastors and bishops may call for collective fasting as a method to focus prayer energy to resolve a larger community or societal issue. COGIC recently organized a worldwide prayer-fast to end the coronavirus epidemic, and St. Louis parishes claim success in reducing murder by 30% in 2021 after their forty-day prayer-fast.[72]

The largest denominations in the Black community of the early twentieth century—like African Methodist Episcopal and Baptist—incorporated community feasting that featured what we now call Soul Food. Women were the primary attendees to formal church services, but everyone attended church-sponsored celebrations. Baptisms, Easter, Christmas, and Fellowship gatherings were where home cooks took center stage as they brought dishes made from recipes handed down through generations. From these "proper church" meals and later extended family gatherings, Soul Food emerged as a distinct cuisine. Southern food has become intertwined with what we think of as Soul Food, but that is a credit to the thousands of Black cooks who fed millions.

There is an ongoing debate about what is Soul Food. The term was coined by '60s-era activists like Malcolm X and Amiri Baraka to describe the foods associated with Black people from the Southern states. The origination of these dishes is a complex fusion that mixes traditional West African recipes with Indigenous techniques and ingredients, all prepared within the constraints of the deprivations endured by the enslaved. Plantation owners provided limited

---

71   The Church of God in Christ today defines fasting as a tiered practice and encourages followers to pick the type of fasting that works for them. They are: 1. No food, water only. 2. Water and juice only. 3. One meal a day. 4. The Daniel Fast.
72   They also note that crimes against churches—all churches—was reduced by 92%.

Holy Food

Feast at the Church of Universal Triumph.

access to meat proteins both to keep their costs down and because they believed too much made enslaved workers lazy. Soul Foods were protein-rich bean and pea dishes and nutritionally rich greens. Soul Food— out of necessity—used the rejected and secondary parts of livestock to add flavor and nutrition. What seems decadent today—fried catfish, cheesey noodles, cracklings—were then supplemental to the near-vegetarian diet of enslaved people.

Dr. George Carver (as mentioned earlier) was a proponent of a nutritionally dense vegetarian diet that could be wholly grown by Black people. Yet millions of now-free people with memories of hunger embraced meat eating. The cooking techniques of breading, frying, and fat-laden sauces that added much-needed calories to an enslaved person's diet were now used on all cuts and types of meat proteins. Barbeque cooking techniques, honed by enslaved cooks to make poor cuts of meat palatable, began to use better quality cuts. Black cooks whose repertoire included both French and Black cuisines, and had once been rewarded by plantation owners, now found their skills in demand in fine hotels and even the White House. Freedom meant the freedom to eat whatever the hell one wanted. Pentecostalism embraced the ecstatic extremes of fasting in humbleness to God and feasting to celebrate his glory.

Soul Food spread throughout the United States during the Great Migration to the Northern industrial cities. Soul Food, now separated from its celebratory religious feasting roots, became a regular part of the Black diet. Families would serve these dishes at weekly suppers instead of at occasional events. Soul Food restaurants sprouted up to serve homesick factory workers who came north without their families. The next generation of Pentecostal preachers inspired by Crowdy, C.H. Mason, and William Seymour of the Azusa Street Mission continued in the Black church tradition of Soul Food celebrations to mark holy days and revivals. It was common for missionary revivals, in a nod back to the camp meetings of the early 1800s, to feature elaborate picnics and barbeques to entice attendance. Black and white believers shared prayer and meals together in this color-blind iteration of evangelical Protestantism. This message of unity and equality for everyone spoke to lower- and working-class white Southerners and Westerners as believers of all races joined the Pentecostal churches.

Yet not all converts to Pentecostalism believed in racial equality. A group of three hundred white Pentecostal ministers convened in Little Rock, Arkansas, in 1914 to separate from Bishop

Mason's Church of God in Christ, and formed the Assemblies of God.[73] The split marked the end of the short-lived racial unity that was a hallmark of the Pentecostal movement. Yet the strands of Lost Tribe theories and the food culture that grew around Pentecostal rituals remain in both groups. Modern Assembly of God congregations now de-emphasize their historical connection to the Lost Tribe theory, yet there is a growing movement within white churches to adopt rituals associated with early Anglo-Israelism and Judaism itself, as evidenced by Christian celebrations of Passover. Though the origins of Pentecostalism are rooted in the Black church experience, white churches adopted the practice of shared potluck feasts on holy days and fellowship gatherings featuring *their* version of Soul Food. Although Soul Food represents comfort and home to many, it began to take on political significance for the Black New Religious Movements.

AS MUCH AS BLACK PEOPLE WORKED TO FREE THEMSELVES, WHITE PEOPLE SOUGHT to yoke them. *Plessy vs. Fergusson* was decided in 1896 which allowed states to enact "separate but equal" laws. States and municipalities codified anti-Black statutes nearly overnight. Jamaica-born Harlem resident Marcus Garvey started a Black nationalist group, Universal Negro Improvement Association and African Communities League (UNIA), and a newspaper, *Negro World*. Garvey was a pan-Africanist who advocated for a return to Africa and self-governance for Black people around the globe. He too embraced the Lost Tribe narrative and saw Black people as the children of Solomon, and Ethiopia as Black people's historic homeland. Ethiopia and Eritrea were under Italian colonial rule until the spring of 1896 when the Abyssinian army of over 100,000 men quashed the Italian defenses. The victory of the Ethiopians over a European power in contrast with the dehumanizing verdict in the *Plessy vs. Fergusson* case served as further inspiration for Black Americans to emancipate themselves in all ways.

Barbados-born Harlem resident Arnold Josiah Ford embraced the Black Israelite message differently, as he claimed, unlike Christian ministers, that he and other Black people truly are authentic Jews. He was a friend of Marcus Garvey and worked with him at the UNIA headquarters, teaching music and Black history. Ford was a prodigiously talented man who taught himself multiple languages, including Hebrew. He eventually began, with the limited support of New York City's Ashkenazi Jewish community, a synagogue for Black Jews. Fellow Caribbean native Wentworth Matthew, who differed with Ford on theological and cosmological issues, founded his temple, the Commandment Keepers, in 1919. Rabbi Matthew's Judaism hewed closer to European Orthodox Judaism but retained esoteric influences. The Commandment Keepers followed the most Orthodox interpretation of the kashrut food laws, as they do today. Rabbi Matthews established a shul for children and institute to train Black Rabbis. He sought to be recognized by the New York Jewish community as full members of the tribe, yet formal acceptance never came. The Black Jews of Harlem stood alone as they practiced their faith. To be clear, Ford and Matthew's claim to Jewishness was not through conversion; they believed that Black people—especially those with Caribbean

---

73 The Assemblies of God also schismed a few years later due to an idea called Oneness, which is a rejection of the trinitarian God (God-Jesus Christ-The Holy Ghost) to accept that Jesus Christ is the singular Godhead. Accepting or rejecting the notion of a God in three parts and when exactly a soul is saved fuels many New Religious Movements.

Holy Food

Rabbi Arnold Josiah Ford and Congregation Beth B'nai Abraham, Harlem, 1929. James Van Der Zee.

roots—have a genealogical connection to Judaism through both the Lost Tribes and Sephardic Jews migrating to the Caribbean during the 1600s to 1700s.

During the Spanish Inquisition (1478–1834), when Sephardic Jews were either expelled, forced to convert to Catholicism, or executed, those who were lucky or wealthy enough escaped to Portugal and the Netherlands—the only European countries who would tolerate them. It is how Manasseh ben Israel landed in Amsterdam, but also how thousands of Jews emigrated to the European colonies in the Caribbean. These Jews worked as overseers on large private and government-owned plantations populated with enslaved Africans. There are anecdotal stories of convivial intermarriage, but historians have more solid proof that men begat children by enslaved women. Many of the children of these Caribbean Jews were educated and given religious instruction per the father's wishes, but were not allowed into the small synagogues serving the white population. This same scenario was repeated on American soil by Jewish plantation owners in the South.

Rabbi Matthew claimed his Jewishness via his mother, who he said was descended from a Lost Tribe in Nigeria and from Sephardic Jewish immigrants. But Ford and Matthew's Jewish practice also incorporated Black nationalism, Masonic rituals, and of course the Apostolic-style Holiness Christianity prevalent in Harlem at the time. Another element influenced Ford and Matthew: New Thought and conjuring, which Ford called "cabalistic science." During the early 1900s, books published by the Chicago-based former hypnotist Lauron William de Laurence on New Thought and Theosophical topics found their way to millions of readers. De Laurence's books focused on the New Thought concept of the immanence of God, that God is contained within or manifested in the material world, and that God is within people and all living things and, most importantly, knowable by humans. (In contradiction to mainstream Jewish, Christian, and Islamic religions that teach that God is transcendent and without

The Moorish Jews of Harlem, 1929. James Van Der Zee, Birmingham Museum of Art.

physical constraints, and unknowable to mankind.) De Laurence's books were extraordinarily popular in the Black Atlantic region and their influence found in all the Black Israelite-inspired religions as well as with Santeria and Vodou.[74]

Rabbi Ford left Harlem for Addis Ababa, Ethiopia, in 1930 with a small group of followers. He sought to establish a new colony of Black Jews that would take their rightful place in their ancestral home. While the colony failed to thrive, many other Black leaders would visit Ethiopia under the rule of Emperor Haile Selassie and find inspiration that Black people can and will be freed to manage their own affairs, and their own country. Leonard Howell was a Jamaican who traveled to New York, Europe, and Ethiopia. His 1935 pamphlet on the meaning of Selassie to Black people as a harbinger of freedom, and divine incarnation of a Black savior, is considered the originating document of the Rastafari movement. The Rastafari, in addition to the influences already noted, also incorporated Hindu practices as learned from Indian migrants brought to Jamaica by the occupying English.

Rabbi Josiah Ford failed to keep his Jewish enclave viable and died in Ethiopia in 1935. Rabbi Matthew remained in New York until his death in 1973. During his lifetime, he trained rabbis who then founded new congregations throughout the country. The Commandment Keepers are active today with headquarters in Brooklyn, New York. There are also independent congregations of Black Jews and Black Israelites throughout the United States that espouse

---

74   The Jamaican government finds the De Laurence books so bothersome that they are banned from importation to this day. From the Jamaican government customs website listing banned items: "All publications of de Laurence Scott and Company of Chicago in the United States of America relating to divination, magic, cultism or supernatural arts."

Holy Food

beliefs that fall along a spectrum of Jewish orthodoxy to Black Nationalist Christianity to, at the most extreme, separatist polycultural communes that can be defined as cults. There is a growing interest in the Black American community in these more extreme groups as they actively recruit high-profile members from the world of sports and entertainment.

Sadly, a few modern versions of Black Israelite groups embrace an oppressive version of the Old Testament that sees women as servile to men. News reports in the past decade have highlighted groups and leaders who have crossed criminal boundaries in enacting their new theologies. Former professional football player Muhammed-Kabeer Olanrewaju Gbaja-Biamila (known as KGB by Green Bay Packer fans) has been under legal scrutiny for his attempts to set up a highly securitized Black Israelite Christian commune, and for his threatening behavior toward his ex-wife and former pastor. CarbonNation, a group that began as a hippie-esque nudist group inspired by Rastafari ideas, has evolved to become a small, high-control group led by "Nature Boy" Eligio Bishop. Bishop was recently arrested in Atlanta for raping women followers. Musician Kendrick Lamar has referenced the Israel United in Christ (IUIC) group in lyrics and public statements. The IUIC is a sect that traces its lineage back to Rabbi Matthew Ford's Commandment Keepers. The IUIC has been identified by the Southern Poverty Law Center as a group of concern due to their nationalist and separatist beliefs. Israel United in Christ also advocates for male-led society with women as lesser and subservient to men, much the same as white nationalist fundamentalist Christian groups do. The excesses and potential for psychological and physical harm are always underlying concerns for anyone seeing their loved ones embrace a New Religious Movement.

Black Israelite groups also embrace kashrut food rules, in addition to using access to food as a means of punishment for women and children. These groups—and there are too many to list—value physical fitness and health for religious and political reasons. For men, the emphasis is on physical strength in preparation to defend all attacks against their family or the larger group. For women, the emphasis is on beauty and optimal health to bear children and sexually satisfy her husband. The IUIC counsels members to follow kashrut rules and avoid all processed foods. They believe that processed, nutritionally empty foods filled with salt, fat, and sugar have been introduced to the Black community to undermine their natural strength. The IUIC also believes that sickness is a judgment from God and can be remedied by prayer and a healthy diet. In the case of CarbonNation, they advocated a vegan diet and made numerous YouTube videos about how to prepare their recommended dishes. In our modern era, technology has allowed small groups to spread their message further and faster, and with followers amplifying their influence. Where one hundred years ago Black Israelite groups attracted hundreds of followers, the internet has given these groups the ability to reach millions.

HOUSE OF DAVID

Years active: 1903–1930 (A schism in 1930 led to a small offshoot group that claimed three living members as of 2020.)
Affiliation: British-Israelite
Founders / Leaders: Benjamin and Mary Purnell

ENGLISH WALNUT LOAF
(Vegetarian. Serves 4 to 6.)
Tools: Bread pan, 9x12 baking dish
Oven temperature: 350°F

Ingredients:
2 cups cube-style breadcrumbs
½ cup water
½ cup whole milk
2 cups chopped walnuts
2 eggs, slightly beaten
½ cup minced onion
1 Tablespoon melted shortening
1 teaspoon salt
1 teaspoon ground sage
½ teaspoon ground black pepper

Steps:
1. Preheat oven to 350°F.
2. In a small bowl, add breadcrumbs, milk, and water. Let soak for 30 minutes.
3. In a medium-sized bowl, add the remaining ingredients. Then take the breadcrumbs, pressing out the extra liquid and add to bowl.
3. Mix everything together in bowl and set aside.
4. Grease bread pan with shortening (can substitute vegetable, coconut, or olive oil). Then place mixture into the prepared bread pan.
5. Fill baking pan with 1 inch of water. Carefully place filled bread pan in center of baking pan. Place into oven and bake for 40 minutes.
6. Remove from pan and serve with a tomato or other sauce as desired.

Holy Food

RINKTUM DITTY

(Vegetarian. Serves 4 to 6.)

Tools: Medium frying pan

Ingredients

1 small onion, chopped fine

1 Tablespoon butter

1 15-ounce can stewed tomatoes

1 egg, beaten

8 ounces cheddar cheese, grated

Salt and pepper to taste

Steps:

1. In a medium frying pan add butter and finely chopped onions. Cook at medium heat until onions are tender.
2. Add in can of tomatoes. Season with salt and pepper.
3. Add grated cheddar cheese and stir constantly until cheese is melted.
4. Slowly add the beaten egg to mixture and cook for 1 minute.
5. Remove from heat and serve immediately on buttered toast points.

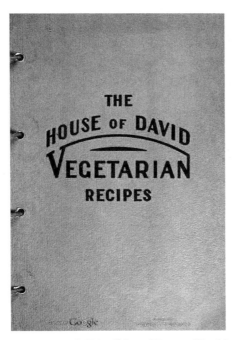

Front cover of 1920 edition of *House of David Vegetarian Recipes*. Author's collection.

EGG CUTLETS

(Vegetarian. Serves 4 to 6.)

Tools: Large saucepan, 9x12 baking pan

Ingredients:

4 Tablespoons shortening

5 Tablespoons flour

1 teaspoon salt

½ teaspoon celery salt

½ teaspoon paprika

1 cup whole milk

1 Tablespoon chopped parsley

3 Tablespoons chopped pimiento

1 Tablespoon minced onion

8 hard-boiled eggs

½ cup flour

1 egg, beaten

½ cup water

2 cups saltine crackers, crushed

Steps:

1. Hard-boil 8 eggs. Set aside to cool.

2. In heavy-bottom saucepan melt shortening. Add in flour, salt, and paprika, then stir until blended.

3. Add in milk and whisk together as sauce cooks to a smooth and thick consistency. Remove from heat.

4. Peel and finely chop hard-boiled eggs. Set aside.

5. Add in the chopped parsley, pimiento, onion, and chopped eggs to saucepan.

6. Line baking pan with parchment paper then pour mixture into pan. (Should be about 1 inch thick.) Chill mixture in the refrigerator until stiff.

7. On a small plate, pour flour. In a small bowl, beat egg with water. And on a larger plate, fill with cracker crumbs. Line up items in the following order: flour, egg and water, cracker crumbs.

8. Using a 2½-inch round cutter, cut circles of the chilled mixture. Dip each disk into the flour, then the egg mixture, and then roll in cracker crumbs. Set each on a plate or cookie sheet to rest for 15 minutes.

9. In a large skillet, fill with 1 inch of shortening or other frying oil. When oil is at 375°F, carefully place 2 or 3 cutlets into the pan and fry until golden brown. (Flip halfway through cooking.) Remove from pan and drain on absorbent paper.

10. Serve as an entrée, alone or with a cheese sauce.

CARBON NATION

Years active: 2016 to present day
Affiliation: Composite
Founder / Leader: Eligio Bishop (a.k.a. Nature Boy)

PIZZA

(Vegan. Makes 1 pizza pie.)
Tools: A small and medium saucepan, large bowl, rolling pin, large baking sheet or pizza stone
Oven temperature: 400°F

Ingredients for pizza crust:

2 cups whole-wheat flour

1 teaspoon baking powder

½ teaspoon baking soda

1 Tablespoon salt

1 Tablespoon apple cider vinegar

1 cup warm water

Optional: 1 Tablespoon onion powder and 1 Tablespoon olive oil

Steps:

1. Preheat oven to 400°F.

2. In a large bowl, add the dry ingredients and whisk together.

3. Make a well in the center of the mixture.

4. In a large measuring cup, mix water, apple cider vinegar, and olive oil (if using). Pour liquid mixture into the flour mixture.

5. Mix together with spatula or wooden spoon until dough takes a ball shape.

6. On a lightly floured flat surface, knead dough ball for a few minutes until dough is no longer sticky. (Add a tablespoon or more of flour if needed.) Set aside and begin other steps.

Ingredients for marinara Sauce:

1 clove garlic, chopped

16 ounces plum tomatoes (can substitute canned plum tomatoes OR fully prepared marinara sauce)

Steps:

1. Peel and mince garlic. (Note: you can peel and mince the garlic for both the marinara and garlic sauce.)

2. In medium-sized saucepan over medium heat, sauté chopped garlic until lightly browned. Add in tomatoes (or premade marinara).

3. Simmer for 10 minutes. Remove from heat, cover with lid, and set aside.

Ingredients for garlic sauce:

4 Tablespoons coconut oil

2 cloves garlic, chopped

1 Tablespoon lemon juice

1 Tablespoon onion powder

1 Tablespoon dried basil

1 teaspoon salt

Steps:

1. In small-sized saucepan over medium heat add coconut oil and garlic. Sauté chopped garlic until lightly browned.

2. Add in salt, onion powder, basil, and lemon juice. Stir together.

3. Remove from heat, cover with lid, and set aside.

Ingredients for toppings:

1 small to medium onion, chopped

1 small to medium bell pepper (any color), chopped

½ pound baby spinach (Note: best if pre-wilted in olive oil over medium heat in a small frying pan.)

1 medium zucchini, washed and chopped

Steps:

1. Wash and chop into bite-sized pieces, onion, pepper, and zucchini. Set aside.

2. Wash and dry spinach. Wilt in small nonstick frying pan over medium heat. Set aside.

Steps for assembling:

1. Roll dough into circular shape between ⅛ to ¼ inch thick. Place dough onto baking sheet or stone.

2. Gently spread garlic sauce over top of dough. Gently spread marinara sauce over the garlic sauce.

3. Carefully and evenly place wilted spinach on top of sauced dough. Spread chopped vegetables evenly atop sauced dough.

4. Place pizza into oven. Bake for 12 to 15 minutes. Remove from oven. Cut and serve.

ISRAEL UNITED IN CHRIST

Years active: 2003 to present day
Affiliation: Black Israelite Christian / Lost Tribes
Founder / Leader: Bishop Nathanyel

BLACK-EYED PEA MEDLEY

(Vegan. Serves 6 to 8.)
Tools: Large skillet or frying pan, jelly roll sheet pan

Ingredients:

2 (15-ounce) cans vegetarian black-eyed peas

1 (16-ounce) bag baby spinach

3 cloves finely minced garlic

1 red bell pepper, diced small

1 red onion, diced small

¼ cup extra virgin oil (used in Tablespoon measurements throughout recipe)

Spices: Cajun blend, garlic, salt & pepper

Steps:

1. Open canned black-eyed peas. Rinse, drain, and set aside.
2. Prepare vegetables. Wash and dry spinach, set aside. Wash, deseed, and dice red pepper, set aside. Peel and dice onion. Peel and mince garlic.
3. In a large skillet over medium heat, add 2 tablespoons of olive oil. When oil is heated, add and sauté onions and peppers until lightly browned but have color and crunch.
4. Add half of the minced garlic to the sautéed vegetables and stir. Cook until the garlic begins to brown.
5. Add in the drained black-eyed peas with another tablespoon of olive oil. Sauté until moisture is reduced.
6. Add spices and another tablespoon of olive oil. Continue to sauté until all moisture is gone. Pour mixture from skillet into sheet pan. Set aside.
7. Without rinsing skillet, add tablespoon of olive oil to pan. Add remaining garlic and stir until lightly browned.
8. Add another tablespoon of olive oil, bring to heat then add rinsed spinach. Stir until spinach is wilted but not browned. Remove from heat.
9. Add black-eyed pea and vegetable mixture back to skillet and warm through. Serve hot.

Note: Reheat in the microwave or flash sauté in a highly heated skillet before serving.

RAW VEGAN CARAMEL DIP

(Vegan. Serves 6 to 8.)

Tools: Food processor or blender, medium-sized bowl

Ingredients:

1 cup of pitted Medjool dates

1 Tablespoon coconut oil (recommended to seek out "butter flavored" coconut oil but recipe will still work without it)

2 Tablespoons of your favorite plant-based milk

1 teaspoon lemon juice

¼ teaspoon pure vanilla extract

Hot water for soaking dates

Steps:

1. In a medium-sized bowl, add the dates. Fully cover dates in hot water and soak for 10 to 30 minutes until plump and soft. (Soaking time depends on dryness of dates.)

2. Once dates are soft, add them to blender. Add in remainder of ingredients.

3. Process or blend until smooth and fully blended. Serve.

Recipe Note: Raw Vegan Caramel Dip can be used a fruit dip or as a frosting for a cake.

Seven

ISLAMIC INFLUENCES

WHILE THE INFLUENCE OF MAINSTREAM ISLAM ISN'T AS PERVASIVE ON NEW Religious Movements in the United States as other Bible-based religions, Islam provided cultural inspiration for the Nation of Islam, the Moorish Science Temple, and their respective offshoots. These modern belief systems were born from the same roiling tumult that birthed so many others, and share similar origin stories. The leaders interacted with each other as they developed their respective dogma and rituals, and many of the Islam-based New Religious Movements were born from internal dogmatic schisms and power struggles. It is common for religions without a hierarchical system to undergo frequent schismatic breaks where new sects emerge. If it hasn't become apparent thus far, every New Religious Movement in the United States has a traceable lineage from leader to acolyte to new leader and so on. Yet in understanding the history of Islamic-influenced religions in America, we see the enormous influence a few people had on millions and how they eat, and why Islam had distinct appeal to Black Americans.

Islam wasn't unknown in colonial-era United States. Thomas Jefferson owned a Quran. In the colonial era, Muslim merchants and traders made their way to America. And researchers note that 10 to 20% of enslaved people brought to the United States were Muslim. On Southern plantations, Islamic worship was forbidden—more so than any other spiritual practice—and enslaved Muslims were forcibly converted to Christianity. While fragments of Islamic worship practices were passed to successive generations, Islam as a religious practice and distinct community faded. There is also evidence of Muslims from the areas under Ottoman Empire control during the mid-1700s making their way to America. The "Turks of South Carolina" are descended from a settler who fought in the Continental Army and was granted land near Ft. Sumter, South Carolina. We do need to make a distinction between immigrants who came to the States with their traditional and widely recognized Sunni and Shi'a versions of Islamic worship, versus the form of Islam created in the States without lifelong immersion in Arab and African Islamic cultural practices.

The second wave of Muslim immigrants who came to the States after the Civil War settled primarily in Chicago and Detroit, where there were readily available jobs in the factories. The Detroit car factories were notorious for their brutal conditions, and took advantage of both immigrant Muslim and Black workers who came north as part of the Great Migration. Chicago, too, had factories that broke men's backs and spirits. The brutal conditions in the factories led many workers to socialism and religious beliefs infused with community-focused direct and Mutual Aid concepts. Many branches and sects of Islamic belief had long encoded a rigorous system of hospitality that included everyone from strangers to family, so the emerging socialist ideas of communal empowerment resonated with disenfranchised people of all races. Mix in a few other ideas, and Islam in America begins a new divergent pathway.

Portrait of Omar ibn Said, born in Senegal in 1770, who held on to Islamic practices while enslaved for decades. Beinecke Rare Book and Manuscript Library, Yale University.

Most Islamic branches follow the dietary laws as laid out in the Quran, with secondary rules and restrictions discussed in the Hadith, the record of what the Prophet Muhammad said, did, and approved or disapproved. These dietary rules are similar to the kashrut rules found in Judaism. Foods are either *halal* (acceptable) or *haram* (forbidden). Pork, horses and donkeys, and the meat of carnivores are haram. Animals must be painlessly slaughtered. Food animals cannot be sick or injured, poisoned, or stunned prior to slaughter. And the animal must be treated with respect while alive and when killed by a practicing Muslim who recites a prayer in the name of Allah. For modern Muslims, halal butchers and supermarkets ensure that all food items conform to Quranic standards. Alcohol and other intoxicants are haram, though there is debate as to what percentage of alcohol qualifies, and there are some sects that allow drinking.

Modern Americans are familiar with the Ramadan fast.[75] During the ninth month of the Islamic calendar, faithful Muslims refrain from eating and drinking from sunup to sundown. They break the nightly fast with a large family meal, often inviting friends and neighbors to share their bounty. During the fasting hours, followers are to reflect on their actions and ask forgiveness for transgressions through thoughtful prayer and Quran readings. Followers are to give up sex and any immoral behaviors during Ramadan and focus on the Islamic practice of restraint. Exercising self-control against desires is considered one of the pillars of Islam, and Ramadan month offers the faithful the opportunity to practice this. People who are old, very young, or ill are excused from Ramadan fasting. In the United States, restaurants that

---

75 The Islamic calendar does not match to the Western Gregorian calendar, which means that Ramadan will occur during a different season of the year. Young non-fundamentalist Muslims have been heard to quietly lament when Ramadan happens during the long daylight hours of summer which results in fourteen- to eighteen-hour fasts!

Holy Food

Ahmadiyya promotional poster, c. 1920s.

serve Muslim communities have begun offering all-you-can-eat *iftar* (fast-breaking) buffets.

In 1920, a *mufti* (scholar and legal expert) missionary from India established the first Ahmadiyya Muslim Community in Chicago, which became the Al-Sadiq Mosque. The Ahmadiyya branch of Islam was founded by a messianic figure who claimed to be the Mahdi, or Messiah, in Punjab in 1889. Akin to the millenarianism in the Christian world, Ahmadiyya believes that the end is coming sooner rather than later. The Ahmadi emphasized missionary outreach, and dispatched representatives to evangelize and educate. The tenets and worship practice are similar to Sunni Islam, but emphasizes a belief in angels as fully formed entities with distinct personalities that act as emissaries to Allah for man, and messengers to mankind from Allah. Ahmadiyya belief liberally embraces other religious figures as prophets, accepts Confucius, Buddha, Zoroaster, and Krishna as valid messengers of God's word, and sees the Hindu Vedas and other religious texts as instructive in learning about God's work. The Ahmadi are considered heretical to Sunni and Shi'a believers. Ahmadiyya beliefs had direct influence on the development of homegrown American Muslim beliefs and practices.

Muslim evangelical missions to the United States accelerated in the early 1900s. Emissaries from all branches of Islam came to spread the message of Muhammad, and stressed that Islam was a religion of peace and equality. Becoming Muslim ensured solidarity with all other followers of Muhammad throughout the world. But in practice, the various sects offered different messages to hearers. Missionaries rarely emigrated to the States but spent an average of two years before returning to their home country. Missionaries focused their work in urban areas that already had a core Muslim population. Detroit, Chicago, and Newark were well-known Muslim enclaves, with immigrants from Syria, Lebanon, North Africa, and Turkiye.

Missionaries showed no preference toward Black and white communities and recruited among both populations, though many of the African and Middle Eastern-born missionaries experienced the racism that American people of color endured, and discovered that Black people found the Islamic message of unity appealing and converted in significant numbers. Conversion to Islam is quite easy—one declares: There is no God but God and Muhammad is his messenger. But to practice the faith can be much more complicated, depending on the sect, and entails rigid prayer schedules, rituals, and behavioral proscriptions. The challenge for Islamic missionaries and followers was understanding which message and what pathway to follow. Sunni evangelists were more rigid in their dogma than the Ahmadi ministers whose syncretic beliefs were easier for American Christians to understand. A letter from a Sunni missionary to his imam complains that a particularly active Tunisian Ahmadi missionary in Newark named Sadiq was causing problems for him. In his telling, Sadiq converted many people to Ahmadiyya Islam which allowed for the new believers to continue many of their beloved and familiar Christian rituals. While there were many first- and second-generation immigrant Muslims in Detroit and Newark who followed Sunni Islam, there were just as many Lebanese and Syrian Christians and Druze[76] who did not. In the face of the energetic Ahmadi missions, many of the other sects ceded their territory and went home.

This evangelical activity coincided with a fascination with "orientalism"—a catch-all phrase used to describe the art, fashion, music, and culture from every corner of the enormous Asian continent. And as mentioned when discussing New Thought and Spiritualism, many people absorbed the notion of esoteric wisdom as coming from the "mysterious East." To paraphrase noted scholar and cultural critic Edward Said's definition of orientalism, it is to view every aspect of the Arab world through the lens of Western imperialism, paternalism, romanticism, and racism. Orientalism as an aesthetic was so culturally dominant in the United States that it inspired a group of Freemasons to adopt "Eastern" symbology and a hazy understanding of Islam to form an offshoot group dedicated to fraternal fun and fundraising, colloquially named Shriners, in the late 1870s.

We associate Shriners today with clowns, Vidalia onions, and large men driving tiny motorcycles in parades. They emphasized brotherhood and fun, and membership is open only to male master Masons. As stated on their website, "Not all Masons are Shriners, but all Shriners are Masons." The group's official name at its founding was The Ancient Arabic Order of the Nobles of the Mystic Shrine (A.A.O.N.M.S). The anagram is a schoolboy joke as it spells out A MASON. The Freemasons used stories of Solomon and adopted a pastiche of Jewish iconography, including naming their headquarters Temples, while the Shriners adopted the popular pan-Arab Orientalism theme for their symbols and décor. Shriners wear a Moroccan-style fez headgear. Their symbol is a scimitar and star, which is from the southwest region of Turkiye. The Sphinx head is taken from the Egyptian landmark. Shriners named their lodges after cities and events important in Islamic history, with the first New York location called the Mecca Shriners #1.

It is relevant to note both the religious and cultural ideas floating in the zeitgeist in the 1910s and '20s. Religious missionaries, fraternal organizations, New Thought, Pentecostalism, anti-Black "rapture" theology, vaudeville and circuses, vegetarianism, spiritualism, Lost Tribe theory, food fads, economic booms and busts, and finally, a growing Black liberation movement. From this heady mix of influences emerges arguably the one person responsible for Black American Islam: Noble Drew Ali. His personal biography is elusive. There are hagiographic origin stories told that burnish his reputation as a holy seeker and keeper of

---

76   Druze is a small offshoot religion from the Ismaili branch of Islam. The beliefs are a syncretic blend of Christian, Muslim, Zoroastrianism, Pythagorism, and Gnosticism. Believers have experienced persecution at the hands of fundamentalist Sunnis but still hold political power in Lebanon and parts of Syria. Druze do not consider themselves Muslim.

Holy Food

Walter Brister (Noble Drew Ali) as a member of the Sotankis Hindoo Fakir troupe. From the "Official Route Book of the Pawnee Bill Wild West Show Presenting a Complete Chronicle of Interesting Events, Happenings, and Valuable Data for the Season of 1900." Courtesy of Illinois State University.

secret knowledge. Other stories, like those told of Paschal Beverly Randolph, tell of worldwide travel and study with gnostic and Sufi masters. What we do know is that the man known as Noble Drew Ali developed an entirely new religious movement that gained international attention and legions of followers in less than a decade.

The Moorish Science Temple history is challenging to verify. Two researchers working separately, historians Patrick Bowman and Jacob Dorman, acknowledge each other's work but diverge as to the born identity of Noble Drew Ali. Bowman's research shows that prior to becoming Ali, he was a factory worker in Newark, New Jersey, by the name of Thomas Drew. (Many other researchers say his name was Timothy Drew, but Bowman and Dorman both agree that it was Thomas.) At various times, Ali was given Cherokee, Egyptian, and Sudanese heritage, but Dorman and Bowman believe that he was born in Virginia to formerly enslaved parents. Dorman diverges from Bowman, with a documentation-filled theory that Ali adopted the name of his much younger half-brother, Thomas Drew, after faking his own death in Chicago in 1913. Both agree about Ali's identity before that: Walter Brister, a renowned child performer in early minstrel shows and later "Hindoo" magician in traveling circus and vaudeville shows.

Ali began his new life as Thomas Drew exploring careers that used his performance skills. He advertised himself as "Dr. Drew" and sometimes "Professor Drew," who could heal people of a variety of ailments. He was arrested twice in New York and in New Jersey for practicing medicine without a license. In the Moorish Science Temple narrative, Ali founded the Canaanite Temple in Newark in 1913 that introduced a new style of Islam to followers, but Bowman's research shows that a different man, Abdul Hamid Suleiman, also known as Prince de Solomon, was the founder, and Thomas Drew was most likely a member of the Temple. Suleiman in 1913 is guessed to be in his fifties during the time of the Canaanite Temple founding, and had previously spent time in New York associated with Marcus Garvey's UNIA group and tangentially connected to Rabbi Arnold Ford's Commandment Keepers. Suleiman was said to be Sudanese by birth and active in the Black Shriner group,

The Ancient Egyptian Arabic Order Nobles Mystic Shrine.[77] It is presumed that Suleiman had a functional knowledge of basic Sunni practices, and introduced both elements of Shriner culture and Ahmadi-style syncretic openness to religious practices at the Canaanite Temple. Suleiman was an active proponent of the idea that Islam was the God-given religion of dark-skinned people. He was an active proselytizer until he was arrested in 1923 for "carnal abuse of a child." Suleiman was convicted and sentenced to eighteen months in prison. Bowman notes and research does uncover a pattern of arrests of Black religious leaders by white authorities on morals charges. That's not to say there isn't a long sordid history of religious leaders of all stripes abusing followers, but we must acknowledge the role weaponized policing has played in suppressing both New Religious Movements and Black civil rights.

Suleiman is the one dietary influence on Noble Drew Ali that emerges in all groups born from the Moorish Science Temple. For all the polyculturism in the Canaanite Temple, they adhered to traditional Sunni food practices that focused on what was *halal* and *haram*. Consumption of pork and alcohol were forbidden.

Names are important signifiers, more so in esoterically informed spiritual practices and in oppressed communities. The appellation "noble" comes from Shriner culture and denotes an acolyte. The word "Canaanite" was a Biblical catch-all phrase meaning foreigner or person outside of the Semitic tribes. The words "bey" and "el" were used by Moorish Science followers to note their belief and rank, and were either added to or took the place of a surname. By the 1920s, there existed, aside from Garvey's group, other Black leaders talking about reclaiming Black identity and reconnecting with an African past—specifically, rejecting names from an enslaved past and adopting names that reflected an empowered future. This idea dovetailed with the Islamic practice of adopting a name from the Prophet Muhammad's lineage upon conversion. Important too was the notion of genealogical identity. Suleiman was not only dark-skinned, but he was also Arab. In the Moorish Science Temple telling, Noble Drew Ali wasn't a dark-skinned man from Virginia, he was a mix of Native American and Arab blood who played the role of an Oriental mystic and magician during his early career. The word "Moor" taps into the Orientalism narrative that intrigued white people, while serving Black people as another way to differentiate themselves from negative stereotypes associated with Blackness. The pervasive racism of white people and their fascination with Orientalism meant that a Black person in America could forge better opportunities for themselves by embracing white expectations of "Hindoo" and Arab people and their culture. When one's identity is marginalized, creating a new one offers different opportunities.

Noble Drew Ali was familiar with Chicago from his time spent performing there in various capacities. He was acquainted with the city's "Black Belt," the highly segregated neighborhoods on the south side of the city that were home to the Black population, when he set up the first iteration of the Moorish Science Temple in 1926. It was housed in the Unity Building, which was owned by the secretive millionaire who ran Chicago's Edison

---

77   Note the slight difference in the name from the white group. Black Shriners, after being banned from joining the white Shriners, started their own group in 1893 adding the word "Egypt" to the name. The AEAONMS won (on appeal) a landmark 1929 lawsuit against the white Shriner group based in Texas that attempted to ban them from using Shriner regalia.

Noble Drew Ali with Chicago Temple congregation, 1928.

power company and elevated trains, Samuel Insull. The building also served as a de facto headquarters for the Black alderman and ward bosses beholden to Insull. Aside from the glorified legend of Al Capone and the Mafia, Chicago during the 1920s maintained a blatantly corrupted government. Each job, from the lowliest street cleaner to department heads, was a reward given to loyalists of Mayor "Big Bill" Thompson. It was he and his cronies who controlled the myriad rackets and kickback networks squabbled over by an ever-changing cadre of men scrambling their way up the system. Chicago was home to numerous esoteric movements, from Mazdaznan to the Bahá'í Temple and the Moody Bible College, as well as the influential publisher of gnostic and New Thought books, the de Laurence Scott Publishing Company. When Noble Drew Ali claimed that the Midwest was "closer to Islam," he understood that the city was tolerant of New Religious Movements. What he may not have understood as well was that tolerance was purchased through the network of ward heelers and vote counters.

The Moorish Science Temple published its sacred text, *Holy Koran of the Moorish Science Temple of America*,[78] that was intended to be a spiritual guide for followers. The book resembles nothing of the Quran and is an assemblage of various New Thought and spiritualist texts. The main sections are taken from the 1908 book by Christian mystic preacher Levi Dowling, *The Aquarian Gospel of Jesus the Christ*, that was purported to be a testament of Christ's "lost years" spent with Indian spiritual teachers, and with heavy borrowing from the Rosicrucian tome *Unto Thee I Grant,* which is a detailed prescription on the correct lifestyle one should follow. Ali dictated the last chapters on his own as he could neither write nor read.

---

78   Also referred to as Circle 7 based on the cover image of the number seven in red or black encircled in blue or red. The colorways varied in subsequent editions.

Members of the Moors, Chicago, Illinois, 1941. Photo by Russell Lee. Courtesy of the Library of Congress.

Moorish Science Temple beliefs were quite conservative and in line with what other Protestant denominations advised. Women were subservient to their husbands. Modesty and chastity were advised for men and women. Alcohol and smoking were forbidden. Ramadan and its fast was anchored to the Western calendar, beginning each year on October 1st and ending on the 31st. Men wore black fezzes and women wore turban-style headwraps. Theologically, Ali emphasized love and equality between all races and, given his bent toward New Thought, believed in the immanence of God in man. He wanted his followers to discover God within themselves through his teaching. The Moorish Science Temple also became an economic engine on the south side of Chicago. Ali set up the Moorish Science Corporation, which manufactured and sold healing oils and herbs. The Temple owned and ran a grocery store that sold the herbs, oils, and teas made by the group, as well as fresh fruit and vegetables and halal meats. The store was opened to provide followers access to approved foods, but many neighborhood residents shopped there as well. The Temple also owned and ran a trucking operation that employed members.

Ali attracted several successful and highly educated Black Chicagoans who rose to leadership roles in the organization. With the assistance of Claude Green-Bey and Aaron Payne-El, the Temple quickly expanded to 35,000 followers in cities throughout the Midwest and East. The Chicago Temple experienced internal struggles between Drew Ali and his lieutenants. Ali proclaimed that Islamic law allowed him to take multiple wives, which he did. His high-ranking followers did not. There were financial irregularities that caused ongoing issues. There was pressure from both mob- and politically connected operators to pay 'tariffs' and kickbacks, which Ali refused to do. It is said that Al Capone preferred using the Moorish Science truckers because they never drank or stole from him.

Holy Food

A key outpost in Detroit became the source of friction when leaders experienced similar Mafia pressures and internal dissent due to questions about money and power. Noble Drew Ali made the mistake of asking his loyal inner circle to take care of the now problematic business manager Claude Green-Bey the Chicago way: by killing him. Ali had been in Detroit on the March 15th day of the murder to deal with James Lomax-Bey, who was supportive of Green-Bey's proposed change in leadership that would oust Drew. The killers made the mistake of not understanding that Green-Bey wasn't just a member of the Moorish Science Temple, Ali was also employed by Samuel Insull to manage the Unity Building and the Black politicians seeking Insull's support. Insull was outraged that Ali's men had killed Green-Bey in *his* building and took retaliatory action.

Police arrested Noble Drew Ali for the murder of Green-Bey and mercilessly beat him. He was never charged, and released. Noble Drew Ali died on July 20th, shortly after his release from jail. The cause of death was noted as tuberculosis, but loyal followers suspected foul play. Whether his death was caused by the police beating or, as some suspected, poisoning, Noble Drew Ali was gone but his religion, Moorish Science, lives on in many forms.

The death of Noble Drew Ali threw the Moorish Science Temple into chaos. There were numerous power struggles for leadership as Ali's lieutenants and the Sheikhs of temples throughout the country claimed to be the new head of the Moorish Science Temple. In the organizational chaos, it was discovered that hundreds of thousands of dollars had disappeared from the Temple coffers. Within a few years the remaining Moorish Science Temple followers accepted Charles Kirkman-Bey as the new Grand Advisor, as chosen by the board of governors. Two Chicago-based members of Prophet Noble Drew Ali's inner circle also laid claim to leadership. Edward Mealy-El claimed that Drew Ali had named him as successor, while John Givens-El declared himself the reincarnation of the Prophet. Both men broke off from the Kirkman-Bey-led incarnation of Moorish Science Temple and started their own rival temples.

During the 1930s all the Moorish Science groups consolidated their following in their respective headquartered cities, with Kirkman-Bey's Chicago Temple having the largest membership. As the Moorish hierarchy fell away, leaders of the fractious sects and local Temples incorporated new ideas and practices. In the years leading to World War II, federal authorities closely monitored all Moor activities, as their claims to an Asiatic identity led to suspicion of seditious activities because they met with Japanese representatives. The Moors were never indicted but consistently harassed by the FBI. At its heart and whether organized or independent, Moorish Science is a conservative and patriarchal belief structure that expects followers to adhere to worship rules and cultural practices. The Moors struggled for relevancy during the 1950s, as the first generation of leaders were not inclined to embrace the growing civil rights movement on the grounds that Moors were not Black, they were Asiatic Africans. Second-generation leaders, often the sons of Moorish Science followers, began to spread a message of separatism. This message of separation led to a variety of Moorish Science followers to embrace a millenarian view that they were awaiting the total Islamization of the African continent to signal a return to God's plan, or conversely, to claim, based on a broad reading of early American documents, that Moors are sovereign citizens and not subject to American laws. Interestingly, the most extreme of white nationalist Christian groups make the same claim of sovereign citizenship. In recent years, the sovereign citizen Moors have caught the attention of media when they are confronted with the force of the United States legal system. Moors have been indicted for numerous bureaucratic violations, from failure to register the birth of children to tax evasion.

John Givens-El's claim as the reincarnation of Prophet Noble Drew Ali caused conflict within all the Moorish sects. He led the Reincarnation Moors through successive leaders while focused on prison outreach recruitment. Givens-El died in 1945, and his successor was a member of Drew Ali's inner circle, Ira Johnson-Bey. Johnson-Bey assumed leadership from prison, where he was incarcerated for the murder of a Chicago police officer during the 1929 armed stand-off between the Moors and police after an attempted kidnapping of Kirkman-Bey. Under Ira Johnson-Bey's leadership the Moors increased outreach and recruitment in prisons, with the message that Moorish Science offered them discipline and a path forward after prison. Johnson-Bey died in 1950 and after a short-lived internecine squabble, his son George Johnson-Bey assumed control of the Reincarnation Moors. Under George Johnson-Bey, the group began to embrace traditional Sunni beliefs and practices that supported and enhanced Moorish Science tenets.

From this early history of the Moorish Science Temple, dozens of groups and independent Moor leaders and thinkers have emerged—each with beliefs honed through interpretation of Noble Drew Ali's *Holy Koran of the Moorish Science Temple of America* and the subsequent embrace of Islamic traditions from Ahmadi and Sunni sects, and, depending on the specific group, black liberation and the Lost Tribes theory. The Moors resist definition as a singular group. Moorish groups highlighted by the media are those with the most outsider and extremist ideas about cosmology, ritual, identity, and politics. Of note are two groups, the Washitaw Nation and Malachi York's Ansarullah group, which morphed into the Yamasee Native American Moors of the Creek Nation, and finally, the United Nuwaubian Nation of Moors. The Washitaw Nation was a small sovereign citizen Moorish group based outside Baton Rouge, Louisiana, and earned revenue by selling 'how to live as a sovereign citizen' pamphlets and diplomas from a fake school, The City University of Los Angeles. Their leader, rare in Moorish groups, was a woman named Empress Verdiacee Tiari Washitaw Turner Goston El-Bey. She died in 2014 and with her demise, the Washitaw Nation was no more.

At the other end of the spectrum is Malachi York's group, known colloquially as the Nuwaubians. He began the group in New York City in the early 1960s and eventually moved to an enclave in Putnam County, Georgia, where his followers erected a fantastical "Moorish" homeland-slash-resort. The move to Georgia in the early '90s was the catalyst for York to embrace different and at times contradictory ideologies. He made claims that Nuwaubians were an Indigenous American people based on ancient Africans intermarrying with Olmec peoples. He adopted the Lost Tribe theory as an origin of the Nuwaubians. He later fashioned the group as devotees of the ancient Egyptian god Kemet. He also became involved in local politics and ran followers for local county offices. (They lost.) As time passed, the Nuwaubian group in its reconstituted forms grew more cult-like, with York making increasingly harmful demands on followers. In 2002, it was revealed that he had a decades-long history of sexually abusing children of Nuwaubian members. He was convicted of child molestation and racketeering and

W.F. Muhammad with Detroit police, November 1932, from the *Detroit Free Press*.

is currently serving a hundred-plus-year term in a federal prison. The Nuwaubian idea of a separate Black nation with God-given rights to the American landmass is not new. The ongoing struggle within American culture is defining who gets to be *American*.

The most significant offshoot of Moorish Science and the legacy of Noble Drew Ali is the most famous. The Nation of Islam was begun in Detroit in 1930 by the enigmatic Wallace D. Fard, to use his most recognized name. Fard was, we can say with caution because researchers are still working to create a definitive biography, either a light-skinned Black man or of Pakistani or Afghan or Syrian heritage. He was a member of the Detroit branch of the Moorish Science Temple, and while working as a door-to-door fabric salesman he took the opportunity to share Noble Drew Ali's message with Black housewives. But after Ali's death and the chaos that marked the power struggle among the Moorish Science leaders, Fard left the Temple. His name was styled differently during these early years; sometimes he used Wallace Farad, Abdul Wali Farrad, Mohammed Ali, but came to be known as Wallace Fard Muhammad.

The Nation of Islam incorporated a diverse range of elements to build its cosmology. Like Moorish Science, it incorporated a new origin story for Black people that placed them in a historically powerful position. Instead of Moors, Fard Muhammad taught that Black people are descended from the tribe of Shabazz, created by Allah as the first Black people blessed with innate inner divinity. The other element of the founding mythos is that white people were created by the evil scientist Yakob who then escaped captivity to cause havoc upon the Earth and oppress Black people. Because these proto-white people were not created by Allah, they are not divine and wholly violent. They overthrew the Tribe of Shabazz and have spent the rest of eternity working to subjugate Black people, the chosen people.

The theology and rituals of the early Nation of Islam were, like Moorish Science, quite conservative. Fard Muhammad called for followers to live a life of discipline and service in the quest to regain their rightful place in the world. The strict dress code of suits and bow ties for men, and ankle-length skirts and dresses with a turban head covering for women, became a distinctive sight on the streets of Detroit. Fard Muhammad also stressed health and prescribed a diet that emphasized a combination of fasting and fresh fish and vegetables. Yet the practice and beliefs were similar enough to Moorish Science that Fard Muhammad's Nation of Islam gained many followers in the wake of the collapse of Moorish Science in Detroit. A former Moorish Science follower, Elijah Poole, who had come north to work in the factories, joined the Nation of Islam and rose to a high rank within a few years. Where Moorish Science followers took on the addition of -El or -Bey to their surname, the Nation of Islam rejected American surnames assigned during enslavement altogether, with followers using "Muhammad," "Shabazz," or in later years, the letter "X."

The great mystery that has never been solved is what happened to Wallace Fard Muhammad? The *Detroit Free Press,* in a blitz of stories during November and December of 1932, tells the story of a "Voodoo Cult" led by Wallace Farad, who claimed to be the King of Islam. Sensationalist quotes about ritual murder and child sacrifices set the city on edge. Black Christian leaders in Detroit promised white city officials to dissuade their members from joining the group. Farad wasn't brought up on criminal charges but was told to leave Detroit for his own safety, as citizens and police were demanding justice, or if left to the loudest of agitators, vigilante retribution. After 1934, W.D. Muhammad, who was already known to have used multiple names, simply disappears from all records. Associates say that he left Detroit to visit followers in Chicago and never returned. Did he change his name and embark on a new life? A few researchers make a case that he was murdered. What we do know is that Elijah Muhammad, formerly Poole, stepped into the role of leader as the Nation of Islam and formalized the theology and practice of the group.

Fard Muhammad's story of man's creation also included references to the Mothership, and that Allah and his prophets may not be of this planet. Elijah Muhammad expands on this. He explains Fard Muhammad's disappearance as a holy event which becomes an important part of the Nation of Islam's cosmology. In the telling, the Mothership, which is of celestial origin, recognizes Fard Muhammad's divinity and transports him to Mecca where he lives on in his divine state. The notion of the Mothership, and other off-planet prophets and scientists, gives more details about Yakub (Jacob in Biblical and Quranic texts), the rogue scientist who created the scourge of planet Earth, white people. Elijah Muhammad embraced a variation of millenarism in his teaching, saying that Allah allowed the white people to rule the planet for 6,000 years, but their timeline was coming to an end and Black people would be restored to their rightful position as rulers of Earth. Most importantly to the culture of the Nation of Islam, this adversarial stand against white people and whiteness is the polar opposite of the Moorish Scientists and Black Pentecostals of the same era who preached a color-blind theology and equality for all. By the 1950s, as the civil rights movement gains support from mainstream black leaders, the separatist Nation of Islam continues to grow and is wary of alliances with the mainly Christian leaders.

While the Nation of Islam followed a nominally Islamic-style halal diet, Elijah Muhammad expanded the Nation's dietary rules and practices, collecting his teaching in the 1967 book *How to Eat to Live.* The slim book provides insights to Elijah Muhammad's thinking about food and how it shapes lives. In the cultural tradition of Black Islam groups, he stresses self-discipline to refrain from not only alcohol, but over-consumption of food itself. The diet is nearly vegetarian, allowing only for small fish, beef, lamb, camel, squab, and chicken only in emergencies, and he exhorts followers to try to embrace vegetarianism. The Nation of Islam diet was considered controversial because it sought to associate traditional Black Southern foods with white oppression, as Elijah Muhammad directed followers to reject any and all foods emblematic of their enslaved ancestors. *How to Eat to Live* reflects politicization of Black foodways that had been growing among civil rights activists. From the Nation of Islam perspective, foods filled with fats, sugars, and salt were a tool to control and subdue Black people, and to keep them unhealthy and unable to fulfill their Allah-given potential.

Specifically, in *How to Eat to Live*, followers are forbidden to eat a long list of items that Elijah Muhammad associated with slavery and poor health. These included: sweet potatoes, sometimes white potatoes (there are contradictions on the prohibition against potatoes), rice, pasta, grits, corn in all forms. Vegetables should be cooked. Collard greens were out, but others allowable. No soybeans or cowpeas. He cautioned against consuming too many nuts as he believed they reduced one's lifespan. He admonished against eating fried foods, margarine, and commercial breads and pastries. He was wary of spices and allowed for the use of sparing amounts of kosher salt. He warned against soda pop and sugared beverages. He taught that navy beans are the ideal food for Black people. He embraced fasting to both cure illness and reconnect with the faith. However, he never claimed divinity, and told followers that he too succumbed to the very human urge to eat "bad" foods.

In *How to Eat to Live*, Elijah Muhammad also goes to great lengths to describe when to eat. His dietary advice aligns with modern views on intermittent fasting. He recommends that adults eat a single nourishing meal per day and only when hungry. Fasting every other day is also recommended. He warns about overeating and how sugar-filled candy and sweets were tainting the blood of Black people. (A prescient observation in light of the looming diabetes epidemic in Black Americans.) Elijah Muhammad rails against the modern (for the late '60s) diet filled with overprocessed foods filled with chemicals. He suggests these foods are marketed to Black people as a form of slow-acting poison with a goal of keeping Black people oppressed by making them obese, sickly, and stupid.

Elijah Muhammad, in the tradition of separatist religious leaders, developed and implemented what was called the Three-Year Economic Plan in 1964. The goal was a resurrection of George Washington Carver's call to self-sufficiency and food sovereignty for Nation members and the larger Black community. The plan required those who had the financial ability to contribute a minimum of a tenth and up to a third of their income to the new Nation of Islam investment fund. With the funds, the Nation purchased commercial real estate to house the new businesses started and staffed by members. Grocery stores, newspapers, restaurants, dry cleaners, barber shops, farms, meat processors, food wholesalers and distributors, bakeries, and more transformed the south side of Chicago and, to a lesser extent, Detroit and New York. At the Nation's financial peak in the early '70s, they took controlling interest in the Guaranty Bank and Trust Company based in Chicago, which resulted in a marked increase in Black homeownership and Black-owned businesses.

To ensure the Nation-operated grocery stores and restaurants had a steady supply of preferred foods, the Nation of Islam purchased farms in Michigan and Georgia where they grew vegetables and commodity crops. These farms attracted members who felt displaced from their agrarian roots, becoming a small part of the larger "back-to-the-land" movement of the early '70s that saw Black and white people seeking to build separatist utopias. The dietary proscriptions (including forbidding bottom-feeding fish like catfish) led to a long-term business partnership with fisheries in Peru. By the mid-'70s, the Nation of Islam was the largest importer and distributor of whitefish, which was considered nutritionally superior to other allowable fish. The Nation also embraced and produced their own brand of sardines. *How to*

Eat to Live never fully advocated for a vegetarian diet but encouraged followers to restrict meat consumption to allowable fishes and sometimes poultry. The Nation nearly achieved George Washington Carver's dream of Black food self-sufficiency.

The Nation of Islam experienced a schismatic and philosophical shift upon Elijah Muhammad's death in 1975. His son, Warith Deen

Nation of Islam brand sardines advertisement, c. 1960s.

Muhammad, began moving away from the founding origin story and cosmology and toward traditional Sunni Islam. He renamed the group he inherited the World Community of Islam in the West, which is still operating in a much smaller capacity than in the peak membership of the Nation of Islam. Deen Muhammad sold off many of the wholly-owned Nation of Islam businesses, including the 4,000-acre Muhammad Farm in Georgia.

Longtime follower and high-ranking member Louis Farrakhan took great exception to Deen Muhammad's changes and reconstituted the Nation of Islam under his leadership. The Farrakhan-led iteration of the Nation of Islam became more politically active and, to much controversy, embraced a more virulent anti-white stance that included anti-Semitic attacks. The modern Nation of Islam remains socially conservative and patriarchal, with very few women attaining leadership positions within the group. Farrakhan also fulminates against homosexuality and bars LGBTQ people from joining. Farrakhan did embrace, like many religious leaders before him, church-supported businesses that serve the needs of followers and their community while creating self-sufficiency and economic opportunities. In 1991, Farrakhan implemented a new Three-Year Economic Plan that mirrored Elijah Muhammad's original vision. A component of Farrakhan's second-generation economic plan, the Nation of Islam continues to encourage members to start businesses as a pathway to financial independence. In 1994, the Nation of Islam purchased about 1,800 acres of the original Muhammad Farms, and continues to raise money and recruit members toward that long-sought dream of a utopia on Earth while paradise awaits.

Though membership in the nineties waned, Farrakhan's public profile was highly visible, culminating with his visionary 1995 Million Man March. The event grew from Farrakhan's idea to successfully bring a million Black men to the Washington, D.C. Mall as a show of unity and strength that captured Black America's imagination. On October 16, 1995, an estimated 837,000[79] Black Americans marched on Washington to affirm their equality and demand their rights. Controversially to many outside Nation of Islam culture, women were not encouraged to attend, as the event was to be a demonstration of the power and humanity of Black men.

---

79   This number is the total estimated by Boston University at the behest of ABC News when National Park officials published that 400,000 people attended. Both organizers and journalists felt this number was a significant undercount. The Boston University crowd study estimate comes with a plus/minus 20% variable. That variable means attendance could have been upwards of 1,001,400 people to a statistical minimum of 666,000 people.

Holy Food

Women and those who could not make the trip to Washington, D.C., were asked to engage in a general strike called the "Day of Absence" in solidarity. Farrakhan, now in his eighties, remains in control of the Nation of Islam, and no lieutenant or next-generation leader has emerged. Yet the Nation has produced a small number of offshoot groups that have taken the roots of Noble Drew Ali, Wallace Fard Muhammad, and Elijah Muhammad's ideas in increasingly extreme directions. As is the pattern in American religious movements, there are a few small schismatic groups that, due to conflicts within leadership and sometimes deviation from the accepted theology, to use Black Muslim terminology, leave the Mothership. Many of the groups in the Moorish Science-Nation of Islam lineage find themselves either embracing traditional forms of Islam or, like the Five Percenters, rejecting the notion of religiosity altogether.

Though often referred to as the Five Percenters, the current name of the organization is The Nation of Gods and Earths. They were founded in Harlem in late 1964 by Clarence 13X, who then assumed the name Allah the Father. There is no clear reason why Allah broke with the Nation of Islam, as numerous versions include everything from excommunication to theological revelation. Prior to beginning the group, Clarence 13X was shot in early 1963 by unknown assailants and experienced a psychological breakdown. He was institutionalized by New York state as a schizophrenic but released a year later with the United States Supreme Court decision that determined mentally ill people, even if they committed a crime, could not be categorically imprisoned without a trial, as Clarence X was.

Regardless of his mental state, Clarence X, now Allah the Father, led the Five Percenters to embrace a decidedly different Black Muslim story. The group rejects the divinity of Wallace Fard Muhammad and is essentially Quranist, also rejecting the Hadith as not coming from the Prophet Muhammad. Five Percenters reject the notion that they are a religion as they teach that God is manifested in each individual. Their teachings—the Supreme Wisdom—are based on early Nation of Islam ideas and share the same origin of man story. Unique to the Five Percenters are the rich and complex numerology and semantical concepts on the esoteric meaning of numbers and words. To that end, importance is given to specific words that communicate spiritual identity to both followers and outsiders. Nation of Gods and Earths members call their teachings "science." The word "supreme" is capitalized and used when talking about concepts related to Five Percenters to their teachings. In use, Supreme Alphabet is the understanding of the hidden meanings in words in accordance with the teachings. For example, the word ISLAM represents I Self Lord And Master and incorporates their core tenet that Allah the godhead resides within Black men. Like many of the American Black Muslim groups, there is a gender division upheld by patriarchal hierarchies, yet women are considered not lesser than, but different from men. The word "wisdom" is often used in lieu of saying "woman," and women followers will incorporate the word into their conversion name.

Five Percenters follow a diet similar to the Nation of Islam. The Nation of Gods and Earths advise against eating any pork products, shrimp, lobster, crab, clams, oysters and other scavengers. Allah the Father was a proponent of fasting, like Elijah Muhammad, and recommended eating a single meal per day at most or, for more devoted followers, eating once every two or three days. New candidates for admittance are encouraged to fast for a few days as part of the induction process. Many Five Percenters are at the forefront of the growing movement among Black Americans adopting a vegetarian and often vegan diet. Awareness of the group's message and dietary culture has been spread through their public proselytizing in New York during the ascendancy of hip-hop.

While not every rapper and DJ who emerged from the Harlem and Brooklyn rap scenes was a Five Percenter, many musicians were aware of the group and their combination of Supreme Alphabet and ciphered language. The message that every Black man was a Godbody, and their advocacy for Black supremacy, resonated with many disaffected teens in the late '70s and '80s. Some joined the Nation of Gods and Earths while others absorbed the teaching and culture without formal membership. Members of the Wu-Tang Clan shared Five Percenter philosophy in their lyrics and publicly talked about the lifestyle but have embraced traditional Sunni Islam in the past decade. Erykah Badu, Talib Kweli, Nas, Big Daddy Kane, all have used Five Percenter Supreme Alphabet ciphers in their lyrics. Badu, Raekwon, RZA, and GZA of the Wu-Tang Clan have followed a vegan diet since the 1990s, influenced by Five Percenter teaching.

Many hip-hop fans and artists are unaware of the connection to the group while adopting the language and lifestyle. This can be seen in fans of the *Supreme* brand of clothing and products as buyers miss the significance of the name, as well as that it was appropriated by a white British/American New York City entrepreneur. The Beastie Boys, an all-white group from middle- to upper-class Jewish homes, liberally sprinkled Five Percenter terms in their songs, most famously using the line "dropping science," which in Nation of Gods and Earths culture means to teach the Supreme Wisdom, and has come to mean "telling the truth" in hip-hop slang.

In the years since Allah the Father's assassination by unknown killers in 1969, new leadership emerged and restarted Five Percenter recruitment that focused on outreach in their Harlem neighborhood to at-risk youth. Though the group was initially labeled by the FBI as a gang, by the late '60s their positive influence on young people was recognized and supported by New York City government officials. The group is often accused of anti-white rhetoric and advocating violence, yet there has been no verified criminal behavior by the Nation of Gods and Earths group. Whether people are formal members or casual followers, Five Percenter terminology and diet have transcended into mainstream hip-hop culture.[80]

Christian dominance in European religious traditions meant that the immigration and colonization of the United States resulted in fewer white converts to any form of Islam, let alone adherence to schismatic sects. The Moorish Science Temple and the Five Percenters did have white members—not many, but they were there. The designated "freedom" to worship enshrined in the First Amendment of the Constitution allowed for Black Americans to see themselves in a new narrative—a story of a Black God creating a paradise for Black people, despoiled by evil as manifested by the white people who oppressed them. The lasting legacy of Black esoteric religions and movements is hope. That a better future is available to Black Americans. And maybe, just maybe, if we free our minds, our stomachs will follow.

---

80 While researching *Holy Food*, I interviewed Black chef-owners of vegan restaurants as to what, if any, religious notions or experiences influenced their choice to serve vegan food. I was surprised to learn from this informal and unscientific polling that half of the restaurants using terms and symbolism from historically Black New Religious Movements were unaware of the history of those words and symbols, or had adopted them for "cool" cultural associations—Rastafari to denote a "chill vibe" and pastiches of Nuwaubian images to convey "Blackness."

MOORISH SCIENCE TEMPLE

The Divine and National Movement of North America, Inc.;
The Moorish American National Republic

Years active: 1928 to current day

Founded in: Chicago, Illinois

Affiliation: Black Islam

Founder: Prophet Noble Drew Ali

Current Leader: National Grand Sheik J. Bratton-Bey

MOOR SALAD

(Vegan. Makes 4 to 6 servings.)

Tools: Stand blender (immersion blender can be used), one medium and one large bowl

Ingredients:

For Salad:

1 pound baby greens (spinach, kale, and a mix of greens can be used)

1 medium salad or Persian cucumber, sliced into bite-size pieces

1 pint strawberries, destemmed, sliced or quartered, if large

1 small apple, sliced into bite-size pieces (Granny Smith, Gala, and other tart varieties work best)

1 bunch scallions

1 medium bell pepper, any color

½ cup sun-dried goji berries (dried mulberries or golden raisins can be used)

1 cup shredded carrot

For Dressing:

1 avocado

2 small seeded oranges (navel, Valencia, or satsumas work best)

2 Tablespoons grapeseed oil

1 Tablespoon liquid amino acids (Bragg or other brands are available at most health and large grocery stores)

1 Tablespoon of your favorite 'garlic and herb' spice blend (most 'garlic and herb' blends contain these ingredients: garlic, paprika, sea salt, onion, parsley, black pepper, basil, oregano, thyme, marjoram)

Steps:

1. Wash and dry greens and place into medium-sized bowl. Then wash, peel, and cut other vegetables and add to bowl. Set aside.

2. Make dressing. If using an immersion blender, use a large bowl; if using a stand blender, then all dressing ingredients can be placed into blend chamber.

3. Peel and cut avocado. Remove seed. Place avocado chunks into blender or bowl.

4. Peel and remove seeds from oranges. Remove as much pith as possible. Break into sections and place into blender or bowl.

5. Add in grapeseed oil, liquid amino acids, and spice blend. Blend until emulsified and thoroughly blended.

To serve: Pour dressing over greens and gently toss together.

Muhammad Farms, owned by the Nation of Islam, Georgia, c. 1970s.

Holy Food

NATION OF ISLAM

Years active: 1930 to current day
Founded in: Detroit, Michigan
Affiliation: Syncretic Islam
Founder: Master Wallace Fard Muhammad
Current Leader: Louis Farrakhan

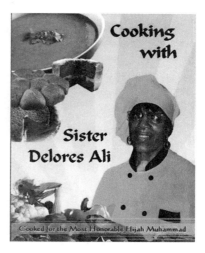

Sister Delores Ali, who worked as cook for Elijah Muhammad from 1960 until his death in 1975 and was then appointed by Louis Farrakhan as the Cooking Instructress for the entire Nation of Islam, wrote *Cooking with Sister Delores Ali* in 2019, and it is filled with Nation of Islam-approved recipes, including the ones below.

Front cover of 2019 edition of *Cooking with Sister Delores Ali*. Author's collection.

The recipes for Bean Pie and Bean Soup are closely identified with the Nation of Islam due to their use in fundraising and recruiting. During the 1970s to early 2000s, entrepreneurial Nation of Islam women set up bakeries specializing in Bean Pies and other approved baked goods. Bean Soup was always served to guests at open meetings.

BEAN PIE

(Vegetarian. Makes 1 pie.)
Tools: 9-inch pie plate, food mill or ricer
Oven temperature: 450°F, then reduced to 350°F

Ingredients:
2½ cups of sugar
2 Tablespoons ground cinnamon
3 cups cooked navy beans, mashed through food strainer (a conical sieve, Foley food mill, or ricer can be used)
½ pound unsalted butter
4 well-beaten eggs
1 teaspoon lemon extract
2 Tablespoons corn starch
1½ cups evaporated milk (one 12-ounce can)

Steps:

1. Preheat oven to 450°F.
2. Rinse beans and soak overnight. Rinse again, then place in medium pot. Fill with water to cover beans approximately by about 3 inches. Cook over medium-high heat for approximately 2–3 hours, until beans are soft.
3. Strain water from beans, then using sieve, ricer, or food mill, mash to pulp then set aside.
3. Prepare pie crust (see recipe below).
4. In medium-sized bowl, cream together the sugar and butter. Add in the cinnamon and corn starch and blend well. Add eggs, one at a time, beating in thoroughly after each addition.
5. Add bean mash and mix until well blended. Then add evaporated milk and extract. Mix thoroughly. Set aside.
6. Pour mixture into unbaked piecrust and place into oven and cook at 450°F for 20 minutes. Then reduce heat to 350°F and continue baking for approximately 45 minutes. Top and crust will be browned. Remove from oven.
7. Let pie cool until set before serving. (Pie will have a browned, crunchy top.)

Flaky Pie Crust

Tools: Pastry cutter

Ingredients:

1 cup flour
4 Tablespoons butter, cold
1 teaspoon sugar
1½ Tablespoons baking powder
1 egg
1½ Tablespoons cold water
Pinch of salt

Steps:

1. In a small bowl, sift flour and whisk in salt, sugar, and baking powder.
2. Cut in butter with a pastry cutter (or fork) until mixture is "mealy."
3. Beat egg in a cup then add to dough. Add in 1 tablespoon of the cold water and mix dough. (Dough will be soft.)
4. On a floured surface, roll dough to fit 9" pie plate. (Make sure there aren't any holes in the dough.) Place in pie plate and press sides and bottom.
5. Place prepared crust in fridge while preparing filling.

Tasters of the Bean Pie were uniformly impressed by how good it is. Testers found that you may have a small amount of filling left over. Two testers experienced a variance in the baking time, while two others did not. (A good reminder to check your oven temperature with a thermometer.) Check your pie at end of the prescribed bake time, knowing that you may need to bake it 10–15 minutes longer. The pie is best served when chilled for at least 8 hours after cooking.

Holy Food

OUR FAMOUS BEAN SOUP

(Vegetarian. Makes 2 quarts.)

Tools: Small stockpot, immersion blender (can use stand blender if needed)

Ingredients:

2 cups navy beans

3 stalks celery

2 Tablespoons butter

½ six ounce can of tomato paste (3 rounded tablespoons)

½ cup onion, chopped (1 medium onion)

1 garlic clove

½ cup carrots, diced

½ cup green pepper, chopped (1 medium green pepper)

1 Tablespoon salt

8 cups water

1 teaspoon paprika (optional)

½ teaspoon black pepper (optional)

Steps:

1. Soak beans overnight in water that covers beans by about 5 inches.
2. Drain and rinse the beans with lukewarm water. Remove any floating outer coverings or other foreign material. Set aside.
3. Chop the carrots, onion, and green pepper.
4. In a small stockpot, place the rinsed beans and chopped vegetables. Add the remaining ingredients to the pot.
5. Cover and cook over medium heat until boiling, then turn heat down to low and simmer for 2 to 3 hours. (Until beans are soft.)
6. Remove from heat. With an immersion blender, blend the contents of the pot together. Adjust seasonings for taste.

A recipe note from Sister Delores Ali's cookbook: "Blended beans are best for consumption. It is easier on the digestive system. However, if you do hard labor, the whole bean is good for consumption."

A few tasters felt that the soup needed more salt. That is your choice, but let's remind ourselves of what Prophet Elijah Muhammad said about sodium "...which may have a bad effect on our brains and human reproductive organs. The scientist that wants to use such poisons on human beings wants to minimize our birth rates or cause the extinction of our people."

NATION OF GODS AND EARTHS
(FIVE PERCENTERS)

Years active: 1964 to current day
Founded in: New York City
Affiliation: Black Islam
Founder: Clarence X, later Allah the Father
Current Leader: NGE follows a localized leadership structure that defers to elders.

SPICED LENTIL TACOS

(Vegetarian. Serves 4 to 6.)
Tools: Large skillet or frying pan

Ingredients:

1 Tablespoon olive oil

1 cup finely chopped onion

1 clove garlic, chopped

½ teaspoon salt

1 cup dried brown lentils, rinsed

1 package (2.25 ounces) taco seasoning

2½ cups vegetable broth

8 taco shells

1¼ cups shredded lettuce

1 cup chopped tomato

½ cup shredded reduced-fat (2%) cheddar cheese

Optional: ½ cup fat-free sour cream

1 chipotle chili in adobo sauce, finely chopped (use half for less heat)

2 teaspoons adobo sauce

Steps:

1. Heat oil in large skillet over medium-high heat.

2. Cook onion, garlic and salt until onion begins to soften, 3 to 4 minutes.

3. Add lentils and taco seasoning. Cook until spices are fragrant and lentils are dry, about 1 minute.

4. Add broth; bring to a boil. Reduce heat, cover and simmer until lentils are tender, 25 to 30 minutes.

5. Uncover lentils and cook until mixture thickens, 6 to 8 minutes. Mash with a rubber spatula.

6. Spoon ¼ cup lentil mixture into each taco shell.

7. Top with favorite taco fixings, lettuce, tomato, and cheese.

8. Optional: Mix sour cream, chili and adobo sauce in a bowl and top lentils with mixture of sour cream, chipotle, and adobo.

Eight
A NEW AGE

THE STRUGGLE TO BUILD A BELIEF SYSTEM AND COMMUNITY THAT SUPPORT ONE'S humanity with dignity is a common thread for numerous American religious movements. Existentialist philosophers argue that man creates his own meaning, while nihilists proclaim that existence has no meaning. Within these modern philosophical ideas is a struggle to impose structure and importance to the work of being human amongst other humans. Religion, of course, has long served as a framework to guide individuals and society. Yet within this struggle, no framework for existence is more fraught with obstacles than wrestling with notions of divinity and humanity. It is the modern American quest for a fully realized physical, emotional, and psychologically stable existence, which in the terminology of psychologists, is when one becomes self-actualized.

German psychologist Kurt Schneider defined self-actualization in 1943 as the goal of every living organism growing into its true self. This notion when applied to an apple tree makes sense: the entire existence of that tree is to produce the fruit that protects and spreads seeds to propagate itself. Applied to humans, the concept becomes complicated. American psychologist Albert Maslow expanded on Schneider's work to include this definition of self-actualization, that it was a particular state when a person recognizes the depth of potential within themselves and can act upon that realization. In Maslow's infamous "hierarchy of needs," he lists self-actualization as the peak of the representative pyramid; that self-actualization—the synthesis of internal ego and external influences—is possible when one's basic and escalating complex needs are met. Only when one is physically and emotionally safe with stable housing and nutrition, within a network of others who recognize and appreciate one's value to the social group, does one have the ability to explore their own potentiality. Sadly, far too many people in the United States were (and still are) unable to experience bodily and psychological autonomy and safety to get to the point of personal discovery, let alone actualization.

Religion can offer a safe harbor, community, and step-by-step manual for becoming self-actualized within that specific belief system. For many New Religious Movements, living to one's potential is the ultimate goal, but the price paid for that journey often comes at an outrageous cost. Rarely do people trade their full autonomy to have their needs met, yet often find themselves in communities that escalate the demands made on the individual that

Illustration of the Women's March on Versailles, on 5 October 1789.

result in an unhealthy and dangerous situation. In this trade-off between basic needs and self-actualization, people create new narratives about their lives, their gods, and themselves to keep them alive.

American knowledge of the French Revolution of 1798 usually begins and ends at "Let them eat cake,"[81] an inaccurately translated phrase misattributed to about-to-be-deposed Queen Marie Antoinette. The phrase is useful shorthand for understanding the chasm between the wealthy and the poor. When the common people are starving, the socially and economically removed ruling class offers sops and untenable ideas. From this perpetual tension of the Haves and Have-nots grew the socio-economic-political philosophy of socialism. An idea that, like "Let them eat cake," is purposefully misunderstood.

Socialism, as it was first phrased in 1832, is a construct conceived as both an idealized society and practical economic and governing system where bounty and deprivation are shared equally by all. It is an idea born of the Industrial Revolution, when people moved away from their agrarian work to cities. The feudal aristocratic system was a form of closed economic system where the lord of a bounded geographic area was responsible for the maintenance and wealth-generating operations of that patch of land. The tenant farmers, herders, and assorted supporting workers relied on the local lord—depending on the era and specific region—to either pay a fair wage or take a fair percentage of the wealth created by their labor. The failure point is, as it always is, personal greed. Without a legal and actual consensus in place, a lord or master is a law unto themselves. Even Fanny Wright's friend, economist Adam Smith, noted that wealth holders will always pursue their own selfish aims and collude with other wealthy

---

81 The phrase is: *Qu'ils mangent de la brioche.* Which is better translated as « They should eat brioche. » Brioche is a fat-enriched soft bread that is more expensive than either white flour batards and rye flour brown breads. The phrase has been attributed to out-of-touch rulers since the seventh century with only a change in the type of food the peasants should eat, and reveals disdain for the common people.

Holy Food

people to ensure their wealth is not distributed to the workers and poor. It was by no means an ideal system, but the socialistic aspects of closed economic systems inspired thinkers to ask: can we create a society that spreads the profit and loss equitably across all strata of a community, and is managed by those whose labor creates the wealth? The changing nature of what work was in the early nineteenth century left millions of people without the guarantee of a (maybe) benevolent lord to (maybe) provide them with a livelihood, and without access to capital and education. Regular Joes were left with very little recourse to change their lot in life.

Socialism can be modeled like Owen, Bellamy, and Fourier's utopianist thinking. Nineteenth- and twentieth-century socialism shared many ideas and tenets with utopianists who embraced proto-socialistic theories as a political ideal. But there was a fundamental difference in the two schools of thought: Utopianists tended toward separatism and building self-contained communes, while socialists were less agrarian-focused and sought to equalize access to wealth and food for all residents of a community. We see this in many modern utopian movements that are socialistic in thinking and separatist in practice. But how did socialism become a popular socio-economic movement in early twentieth-century America?

The post-Civil War era saw the United States in tumult and reckoning with change. During the Reconstruction years, the country sought to rebuild the destroyed cities and economy of the South. Railroads grew apace and the western frontier was no longer Missouri but the California coast. It was the time of the Gold Rush, the railroad and oil boom, and the exponential growth of factories and industrial mechanization, mass deportations and relocations of Native Americans, and the scramble to fully colonize the United States landmass. All this furious economic growth created winners and losers and fabled excesses only matched by the conspicuous consumption of today. In fact, the disparity between the wealthiest and poorest Americans in 1890 is comparable to current (2020) statistics.[82]

What is often forgotten about the waning decades of the 1800s is the economic instability that made the lives of working people so very precarious. The first Great Depression of 1873 (so-called until the much bigger Depression begun in 1929 set a new standard of how bad things could be) was quickly followed by the 1893 Panic. The economic debacle that began in 1873 was caused by several interrelated disasters, real and fiat. The Chicago Fire of October 9, 1871 decimated the city. On the very same day, the Peshtigo Fire in northeastern Wisconsin burned 1.2 million acres and killed approximately 2,000 people. It was widely believed by scientists that both fires were begun by debris from Comet Biela, while the religiously inclined thought it was God's hand signaling the apocalypse or the coming of extraterrestrial beings. There was, as today, a divide between those who embraced eschatological beliefs and those who did not about the meaning and fallout of destructive astronomic events. There also was a railroad investment bubble that unceremoniously burst in 1873 when two large banks failed and triggered a stock sell-off that crashed the entire market. Railroads and the myriad industries that supported them were bankrupted. Railroad workers organized to demand fair treatment and staged work stoppages. Militias, police, and private armies were assembled to protect factories from striking workers.

---

82   In 1890, the richest 9% held 75% of the total wealth in the United States. In 2020 the top 10% held 70% of the total wealth. Also of note is that the total pool of wealth has increased since 1890, making the rich richer.

The Haymarket Riots in Chicago in 1886 were followed by the Bay View Massacre in Milwaukee a few days later as strikers marched for basic rights that many take for granted today: the eight-hour workday and the five-day work week.[83] Workers continued to organize by industry into labor unions, while churches and social organizations incorporated popular socialist ideas into their missions. Though the 1893 panic is considered a separate event by economists, an argument could be made that it was a continuation of the same bad news begun twenty years earlier. The international commodities markets failed in 1890, causing prices for American-grown wheat to bottom out. The silver market crashed and the dollar's value in the world economy was barely hanging on as a viable currency. Unemployment was at a record high of 8.25% in 1878, then leveled off for a few years and spiked again in 1896 at 8.19%. It was a boom-and-bust cycle that could not sustain a national economy. There was, literally, rioting in the streets.

Politically, the country experienced, not to put too fine a point on it, terrible leadership. Numerous scandals during successive presidencies exposed the influence of the wealthy robber barons[84] and deepened the chasm between the working and monied classes about who should be making the laws and policy for the United States. Homegrown socialist theories were integrated with those brought to the States by previous generations of European intellectual émigrés to form a powerful workers' rights movement. There was growing momentum toward electing a populist, reform-minded government that served the needs of the many and not the few.

In the South, white leaders in the former Confederate states worked to undermine the racial equality mandates of Reconstruction and regain control of state legislatures. After the landmark 1896 *Plessy v. Ferguson* ruling by the Supreme Court that deemed segregation by skin color laws legal, laws (Jim Crow laws) were enacted throughout the country to restrict voting, education, and land-owning rights of Black Americans. Blacks also faced a more direct threat of violence in the South than in the North and West. The Northern and Western regions weren't perfect by any stretch of the imagination, but living conditions were considered better than in the South. Black Americans traveled to the industrial cities of the North to find new opportunities in the factories of Detroit, Cleveland, Pittsburgh, Buffalo, Chicago, and Milwaukee. Others traveled west following the pioneer trails to find opportunities in Los Angeles and the San Francisco Bay area. The Great Migration saw an estimated 1.6 million Black people leave the South during the years 1900 to 1940.

It can be difficult to imagine, let alone enumerate, how the composition of the population of the United States changed in the years from 1870 to 1910. Where people chose to live

---

83 At Haymarket, four worker protesters were killed by police in the chaotic aftermath of a bomb exploding during the strike at McCormick Harvesting Machine Company on May 4th. The next day in Bay View (Milwaukee), Governor Rusk ordered the Polish militia to open fire on the 14,000 striking workers marching to the gates of the Illinois Steel Rolling Mill; six workers and one thirteen-year-old boy playing hooky from school to watch the protest were killed.
84 The Robber Barons were the small group of rich and overly influential men who held a disproportionate amount of the total wealth in the United States. Some of the names will be familiar to all readers and others familiar to those in the regions of the country where they held sway. They were: John Jacob Astor, Andrew Carnegie, William A. Clark, Jay Cooke, Charles Crocker, Daniel Drew, James Buchanan Duke, Marshall Field, James Fisk, Henry Morrison Flagler, Henry Clay Frick, John Warne Gates, Jay Gould, E.H. Harriman, William Randolph Hearst, James J. Hill, Charles T. Hinde, Mark Hopkins Jr., Collis Potter Huntington, Andrew Mellon, J. P. Morgan, John C. Osgood, Henry B. Plant, John D. Rockefeller, Henry Huttleston Rogers, A.S.W. Rosenbach, Charles M. Schwab, Joseph Seligman, John D. Spreckels, Leland Stanford, Cornelius Vanderbilt, and Charles Tyson Yerkes.

influenced the food and religious culture of a city or town. In addition to the internal migration of Black people, twelve million people immigrated to the United States from Europe and Asia during those years. Unlike previous waves of immigrants, these newcomers came as refugees fleeing years of brutal wars, economic collapse, and as always, religious persecution. The immigrants followed the same path as Black Americans as they moved west to homestead the newly seized Indigenous lands in the far Western Plains, and to the growing Great Lakes cities to take up jobs in the factories that sprouted up like mushrooms after the rain.

Immigration from Italy and Ireland brought Catholics to the industrial powerhouse cities. Each respective group built a church and parish that reflected the style of worship in their homeland— often within walking distance of each other. Immigrants from Eastern Europe brought Poles and Czechs, adding to the mix of ethnic-specific Christian churches. Eastern Rite Catholics and Orthodox followers came from Serbia and Greece. This wave of European migration also brought, for the first time, Ashkenazi Jews to join the millions of others coming to America.

The Jewish population in 1840 numbered about 15,000 people and were mostly Dutch, English, and Germans with education and a vocation, who filled the ranks of the professional and merchant classes. By 1880, the Jewish population increased to 250,000 (primarily Germans), and then exponentially increased between 1890 and 1914 as two million immigrants escaped the pogroms and religious persecution in the area now known as Poland, Belarus, Ukraine, and Russia.

During this same period, Chaldeans from Syria (both Muslim and Orthodox Catholic), Lebanese, Palestinian, and Bosnian Muslims emigrated to escape the wars and economic depression in the Ottoman Empire. These immigrants found work in the factories of the Midwest, with the largest community of Chaldeans settling in Dearborn and Detroit, Michigan, and the Bosnians settling in Chicago. There were Syrian settlements in Iowa and North Dakota, where communities built mosques and integrated into the fabric of the community. Historians estimate that nearly one million Islamic immigrants came to the United States from the end of the Civil War until 1924, when the Asian Exclusion Act set restrictive quotas on immigrants from "Asian" countries.

America had become a different country in a relatively short amount of time.

WHILE IT'S TRUE THAT THE GREAT AWAKENING INSPIRED A NEW VERSION OF evangelical proselytizing in the Christian faith that resulted in the growth of professed believers—about 34% of the total U.S. population, based on the 1850 Census data— there were many more people unchurched and those who were actively anti-religious. The 1900 Census shows that the percentage of believers in the United States grew to 45% through a combination of conversation and immigration.[85]

The churn of the decades-long financial crisis eroded American's confidence in their government and economy. This was a time before nationwide governmental social programs to directly address issues of poverty and hunger. Social aid programs were religious-sponsored

---

85   The current (2020) statistics show that church attendance is declining with 50% of the population identifying themselves as religious but only 40% actually visiting a house of worship. Even more telling is the increase in population affirmatively identifying as atheist or not caring about religion which is a significant 32% of the population.

(as many are today) and used their assistance as proselytization, recruiting new members among those in need. There were state-funded institutions, like poor farms, that took in the most indigent of people, but those places were built on a punitive model, often mirroring the Puritanical notion one sees in "prosperity gospel" ministries, espousing that wealth is a manifestation of God's blessing and poverty is the direct opposite and, of course, a moral failing. As Gilded Age excesses revealed the vast disparity between rich and poor, progressive reformers looked to the ideas that drove utopian socialism of 1830s

Thomas Nast political cartoon on immigration bans, *Harper's Weekly*, March 25, 1882, p. 192. Courtesy of the Library of Congress. October 1789.

and '40s to envision pragmatic and solutions-focused outreach based on a new, progressive-minded version of Puritanism.[86] The once-held goal of building a separatist, rural ideal was replaced with a determination to build religious-minded communities while alleviating the suffering of workers in the cities.

There was a dark side to this progressive movement toward state-sponsored indigent care. As remembered from the Oneida Community's experiments with stirpiculture, charitable Christian workers embraced eugenics as a scientifically reasoned theory. Not only were poverty and amorality considered a failing of spiritual practice, but that moral bankruptcy was passed along genetically. The theories, and the resulting havoc they caused, are rightly abhorrent today, as they mixed a smattering of proven genetics (like passing along eye color) with the idea that intellectual deficiencies and psychological composition were also bred in the bone. Early eugenicists theorized that interventions were needed to stop defective persons from creating more defective people. This idea led Margaret Sanger to begin Planned Parenthood to control population within impoverished neighborhoods. It also led to Protestant pastors involved in social crusades conducting family "studies" to prove that morality was a tangible trait that could be cultivated and bred into humans. Which conversely meant that amorality was to be excised from society.

In practice, progressive Christian reformers believed that charity for the poor was to be meted out to only those who deserved it—to those who showed their moral goodness as measured by adherence to social norms and the ability to work for wages. It is without surprise that these

---

86   The notion of 'progressive Puritanism' may seem contradictory at its outset, but the abolitionist movement intersected with the feminist movement that found many women embracing a socially conscious outlook within their Congregationalist churches.

Holy Food

reformers found that people of color and non-Christian immigrants were morally lacking and therefore defective. So prevalent was eugenics in mainstream American Protestantism that their activism spurred major sociopolitical changes intended to remove the threat of defective, lesser humans from the population. Lobbying efforts by Christian pastors and other "America Firsters" after World War I ultimately resulted in the 1924 Immigration Act that set quotas for immigrants coming from Southern and Eastern Europe and banned immigrants from Asia altogether. There was also the growth of lunatic asylums and poorhouses. These were, essentially, prisons where people deemed incompetent by the state were housed. Some of the reasons one could be found incompetent: sexual relations outside of marriage, refusal to work, refusal to marry, disobedience to parents (often used against young women), failure to attend religious services, squalid living conditions; the list goes on. Women were forcibly sterilized. In hindsight, it is obvious that moral failings fall disproportionately on the poor and non-conformists. But before the immigration bans and sterilization surgeries, a group of progressive reformers thought that these immigrants and impoverished internal migrants could be taught how to be morally upstanding citizens, breaking the chain of defectiveness. Not all could be saved, but those untouched by moral disease could be lifted from their circumstances.

Jane Addams, educated at the Rockford Women's Seminary, imported the British "settlement house" concept to Chicago and opened Hull House in 1884. Hull House was an organization that worked directly with immigrants and their children to, in Addams' words, "lift them from poverty." Addams not only encouraged the wealthy to donate money but to move into the House and live communally as they donated their time and expertise. It was political stance as much as it was a religious mission, driven by the prevailing capitalist idea of "scientific philanthropy" and moral underpinnings of Congregationalist Protestantism that believed in teaching people skills to earn money instead of giving money directly to them. Addams was able to garner wealthy backers and political allies. Hull House encouraged rich and poor to work together, yet the baked-in notions of class that the United States had claimed to shed still prevailed. Very few of the wealthy benefactors chose to live at Hull House or work directly with people in need. Food and how to eat became a central focus at settlement houses, as alleviating the hunger resulting from poverty was a cornerstone to turning indigents into workers. To her credit, Addams *did* improve the quality of housing, access to food, and working conditions for the poor. The work she did was exported throughout the country by secular and religious alike.

Settlement houses inspired by Hull House sprouted up in cities under a variety of names. Many followed Addams and operated under the sponsorship of a religious organization. Dorothy Day used the Settlement house model for her Catholic Workers' group. Religious groups of all denominations sponsored Settlement Houses that served as community centers in poor and working-class neighborhoods throughout the United States, educating, feeding, and assimilating millions of immigrants and internal migrants. Part of the assimilation process was learning how to eat and cook like "Americans," which meant the cuisine recommended by popular food experts like Fannie Farmer's Boston Cooking School and the many magazine and newspaper "Ladies' Pages" writers. These early food educators and advocates helped shape what immigrants understood as American food—and when viewed through the lens of

Chicago Hull House Dining Hall. Jane Addams, head of table at the far left, 1925. Courtesy of the University of Illinois-Chicago.

religious evangelism, reveals subtle proselytizing. To become American was to adopt the food and traditions of those in power.

Successive waves of immigrants to the industrial cities of the North were welcomed by established members of a religious or ethnic group via settlement-house-style organizations. The model of helping new arrivals proved successful as they taught people the skills and connections needed to survive in the new locale. For Black Americans coming North during the Great Migration, mainstream denominations like the African Methodist Episcopal church offered social outings mixed in with lessons on how to conduct oneself in a city. Many middle-class Blacks believed the Southern migrants were culturally backwards. This power imbalance set up conflict within the Black community about religious and food traditions. While the Great Migration spread Soul Food to the North, the meaning of the cuisine took on a complicated nuance as a marker of identity. In the city, to be considered "country" was to be socially inferior. Foods associated with the South were cast as a vestige of an oppressed past and not a successful future. Because much of Black family life was centered around a faith community, the political positioning of food became an ongoing source of conflict within established churches and New Religious Movements.

ALL POLITICAL AND RELIGIOUS MOVEMENTS FOLLOW NON-LINEAR TIMELINES. IT would be easier for readers (and this author) if all ideas and subsequent events unfolded neatly along a calendar. The simplest summary is that by the second half of the 1800s, due to worldwide cataclysmic economic crashes, multi-country wars, and the advances of technology, millions of people were suffering and angry. People increasingly recognized the unfairness in how laws treated the poor and people of color. They began to see that their

Holy Food

"The New Man on the Job" by John Scott Clubb, 1913. Courtesy of the Library of Congress.

government wasn't acting on their behalf but for the benefit of monied interests, who were also in government. No longer willing to be exploited by unsafe working conditions for twelve hours a day, six days a week, people began organizing and agitating for a fair share of the fruits of their labor.

Mainstream religions established soup kitchens and food pantries to help those in need. Most churches saw their work in helping the poor as a Good Work as detailed in the New Testament. A number of verses speak of doing right by one's neighbor and those worse off, but Ephesians 2:10 (sometimes called Paul's letter to the Ephesians) is often cited as direct instruction, which says: "For we are God's handiwork, created in Christ Jesus to do good works, which God prepared in advance for us to do." Their aid was framed as doing God's work in acts of charity, which was also rooted in class and race, yet for American religions their operating structure changed when charity was married to seemingly innocuous changes in how the United States funds itself. The seismic change so critically important to the story of religion and food in America? The tax code.

Taxation in the United States has always been fraught with dissent. The founding myth of "taxation without representation" was and still is a national battle cry intended to rally voters. But in practice, tax collection during the 1800s was localized and left up to the states and municipalities to decide on both the levy percentages and the allocation of funds. The federal government paid for its responsibilities through a combination of excise taxes (the tax paid by suppliers of designated goods like alcohol, tobacco, and firearms),[87] land sales, and import/export tariffs. When the United States was small, less federal government was required to manage the country, but the expansion of both territory and people at the end of the nineteenth century required a larger government with new fiscal policies.

It had been commonly accepted by legislators and taxpayers that churches provided an overall benefit to the community and culture and had, by tradition, not paid taxes of any kind. This practice was enacted into the tax code reform of 1894. The first nonprofit status laws codified the lasting definition that an organization, be it religious or secular, must be primarily engaged in activities that are to the benefit of their community. In exchange for their "good works," the

---

87 This historical tidbit answers the modern question of why in the world are those three seemingly unrelated things are managed under their own federal department (the Bureau of Alcohol, Tobacco, and Firearms, or ATF). Those three products were the original revenue generators for the United States.

government waives its right to collect taxes. The law was tightened up in 1909 to spell out that any income earned by a charitable group could not benefit an employee or shareholder of said group. (Greedy preachers and shady do-gooders prompted *that* revision to the tax code.)

The national income tax paid by wage-earners was enacted in 1917, and a provision of the law allowed for individuals to donate to a nonprofit organization accredited by the Internal Revenue Service and receive a tax credit. Churches are officially nonprofit entities that can solicit money (and valuables) from people and businesses. They can also "own" businesses. Additionally, if the product or service is deemed part of a church's religious practice or sacramental, that product or service is exempt from *any* government regulation under the 1952 Uniform Commercial Code. Subsequent and ongoing adjustments to the U.S. tax code have allowed for new loopholes and categorizations that allow religious nonprofit groups to build thriving businesses and congregations. With these historical and legal elements in place, the table is now set for the next generation of entrepreneurial New Religious Movements to discover the power of food in both their belief systems and business models.

Socialism and capitalism are set against each other at the start of the twentieth century. A subversive political theory, set in motion by anarchist Peter Kropotkin, began to shape American religious and secular charities. Published in 1902 as *Mutual Aid: A Factor of Evolution,* Kropotkin's ideas indelibly marked twentieth-century new religious and utopian movements. The core philosophy of Mutual Aid upends philanthropy and charity's unbalanced power relationship between donor and recipients. Mutual Aid assumes a shared struggle and equality between all people. It also assumes that the struggle is temporary and can be remedied, and that governmental solutions are oppressive by their very nature. Mutual Aid is communal self-sufficiency. Mutual Aid is the direct opposite of social Darwinism and the individualized competition that determines might is always right. Mutual Aid was in direct conflict with the prevailing mainstream beliefs in eugenics and that poverty was both God's judgment and punishment for amorality. Holding (and withholding) access to money, shelter, and food to a community is a great power indeed. We see this destructive individualism in practice during war when combatants cut off food and water supplies to civilians. We see it in action when legislatures erect bureaucratic hurdles to education, voting, and basic human rights. Mutual Aid is the condition when people—most often people marginalized by outside forces—organize to help themselves. And it is in direct conflict with the hierarchical nature of modern government and mainstream religions.

Mutual Aid was also in conflict with the newly encoded tax laws that rewarded philanthropy and charity. Mutual Aid groups were decentralized and did not reward contributors with laudatory celebrations, tax credits, naming rights. Mutual Aid was the unnamed practice of most small communities in the United States. It was, in our naïve media portrayals of nineteenth-century America, the ideal of small communities of intrepid pioneers helping each other and helping strangers. (Think of 1970s television dramas like *The Waltons* and *Little House on the Prairie,* or western films like *The Magnificent Seven* and even *Blazing Saddles* that depict isolated communities setting aside differences to come together for a common good or to assist a suffering neighbor.) Native American communities have shared resources since long before the Puritans enjoyed their Thanksgiving dinner. Mormon pioneers institutionalized a prototype form of Mutual Aid with the creation of the Relief Society, providing food and care assistance to struggling families.[88] George Washington Carver engaged in a form of Mutual Aid in his work with the Tuskegee Institute Extension Office. We see the twenty-first-century iteration of Mutual Aid in the form of online fundraising platforms that seek money from friends, family, and strangers on the internet when faced with catastrophic medical bills. In the struggle for autonomy and self-sufficiency, Mutual Aid networks were then and remain a lifeline for millions. But during the first decades of the twentieth century, Americans were again tested by politics and circumstance to find new ways to thrive.

There were economic movements that sought to address the lack of social safety nets—especially for the elderly—that developed from the 1890s to 1940s. Simply described, these private retirement plans intended to provide a weekly or monthly guaranteed income to anyone who was a member of the cooperative. But because they were unregulated, these private programs were rife with corruption and fraud. Today, we would call these programs pyramid schemes (or multi-level marketing), where the monetary reward only flows to those who recruit a sufficient number of others to generate enough revenue to warrant a payout. Not every private basic income movement was a scam; notably, those based in Los Angeles in the 1930s at the height of the Great Depression—Ham & Eggs, and Upton Sinclair's EPIC (End Poverty in California)—sought to change laws in California and to create a basic income guarantee to the impoverished and elderly. The private basic income schemes petered out when President Roosevelt instituted the Social Security Administration to address the issues of endemic poverty among the elderly in the United States.

Mutual Aid also took the form of co-operative food buyer's clubs. Buyer's clubs were limited to specific industry, ethnic, religious, or political groups as they sought to collectivize. To become a member, one had to either commit money or labor to the group to access the benefit of shared food commodities. In practice, a co-op would leverage their numbers to buy a large quantity of food from an agricultural partner with member funds, and then use group labor to—depending on the level of organization and number of members—sort and allocate the foodstuffs. During the Great Depression, many of these groups used labor in lieu of money to obtain foods from farmers. A member would be required to donate a specific number of work hours to gain the food benefits. Problems often arose in these groups in calculating labor equivalencies and management hierarchies. If the buyer's club model sounds familiar, the basic principle is the operating template behind cooperative grocery stores that blossomed during the '70s, and Community Supported Agriculture farms (CSAs) during the early 2000s.[89] Even capitalistic businesses like Costco and Sam's Club operate on the idea that buying in bulk quantities reduces costs.

Because these guaranteed basic income and food distribution schemes were membership-only, they were free to accept and deny members according to who fit into their defined affinity

---

88   See page 71 for more about the Relief Society.
89   Modern CSAs often resolve the "labor" issue by creating tiered membership. Most members buy in to the cooperative with cash, and only people who prove agricultural skills (or specific skills needed by the farm such as accounting, food preservation, or machine repair) are offered labor-based membership.

group. Sadly, there is a documented history of groups denying membership to Blacks, Jews, Latinos and, really, anyone who was considered Not Our Kind. This sad truth drove marginalized people further to the margins, where they began to develop their own form of Mutual Aid societies and cooperatives. Religious and ideological groups used the Mutual Aid model to form hybrid versions that supported new ideas about spirituality and how people should eat. And of course, the most extreme of these twentieth-century New Religious groups used the ideal

Self-help cooperative, Burbank, California. Supplies food, vegetables and milk to members, Dorothea Lange, 1936. Courtesy of the Library of Congress.

of "shared burdens, shared rewards" to exploit the faith of seekers and circumvent the law.

California during the first thirty years of the 1900s saw an influx of internal migrants. Wealthier retirees from the Midwest seeking to settle in a more hospitable climate, economic refugees from ecologically decimated southern plains, and Black farmers and agricultural workers from Southern states. By 1930, a third of the population of Los Angeles County originated from the Midwest. The white Midwesterners and Plains dwellers were considered by longtime Angelenos as socially backward, intellectually stupid, and blinkered by fundamentalist religion. The city of Long Beach was derisively called "Iowa by the Sea" as 46% of its residents were born in Iowa. These demographics are important to note because the influx of conservative Midwesterners stood in both contrast and resistance to the easy acceptance of New Thought, Buddhist, and Theosophist groups that had made California, specifically southern California, their home.

The Azusa Street Revival was very concerning to the conservative Methodists, Baptists, and Presbyterians from the Midwest. Mainstream Protestantism had long embraced the "rightness" of separating races, so a mixed-race church, drawing thousands of devotees every day, was entirely problematic for the new Angelenos. The Black preachers who came to see the miracle of Azusa were quickly disillusioned by the reality of California and its legally entrenched racism that saw towns enact laws barring Black homeownership and subjecting Black people to police abuses. What those visiting ministers did take away from visiting Seymour's church was the revelation of Azusa—the gift of fiery speech and a new pathway to redemption. Hundreds of pastors, ministers, and preachers returned to their homes with a new message for the disaffected Americans searching again for something new in the wake of the deprivations under Jim Crow laws. It is again worth noting that Black Americans saw their societal and economic gains during the late nineteenth century eroded by the thousands of Jim Crow laws passed by states and upheld by the landmark 1898 Supreme

Court case *Plessy vs. Ferguson*, giving the United States its cover for racist policies and laws: "separate but equal." (Noted earlier was how *Plessy vs. Ferguson* changed the composition of the integrated Spiritualist churches.) The combined effect of the ruling and the simmering political upheaval as workers demanded rights boiled over into new ideas about what *is* the role of a religion and church to its congregation. When socialism and Mutual Aid concepts were added to the theology of the next generation of new religious thinkers, it created distinct and formidable twentieth-century movements, led by a few unlikely leaders who cherry-picked religious and political ideas, and created lasting impact on American food and religion.

T HE HOLINESS AND PENTECOSTAL MOVEMENTS MOVED IN MULTIPLE DIRECTIONS in the early 1900s. The numerous souls who visited the Azusa Street Mission in Los Angeles and the second generation of ministers who continued to spread the Pentecostal truth saturated the country. Discussions and arguments about practices and scriptural interpretations made the Pentecostal movement split, grow, reform, and divide again, until there were hundreds of denominations identifying themselves as either Holiness or Pentecostal. Of particular interest are two organizations that built their reputations on food. Both Father Divine and Daddy Grace share similar theological influences, and in building their respective new movements influenced each other's restaurant businesses.

Cape Verde-born Marcelino Manuel da Graça grew up on the predominantly Black, Catholic Portuguese colony when the first Protestant missionaries were allowed to preach. Pastors from the Church of the Nazarene, an evangelical Methodist sect, came to the island to spread their version of Holiness and individual salvation. Da Graça emigrated to the United States in 1903 and worked on the railway until he was "born again" in Christ and began his own mission. Da Graça changed his name to an anglicized version: Charles Manuel "Daddy" Grace.

Bishop Grace began the United House of Prayer for All People in West Wareham, Massachusetts, in 1919. The theology was similar to other Pentecostal churches, and Grace never claimed that the House of Prayer was a different church or religion from any other form of Christianity. Daddy Grace did put forward the idea that a church can only be led by one man, and used Biblical history to make that point insomuch as God only chooses one prophet at a time for his people. Like many Holiness preachers of that era, Grace claimed, and witnesses confirmed, that he had healing powers. He claimed that he received an anointing from God as a young man in Cape Verde. Grace was also a savvy businessman who rejected debt financing for church buildings and invested church donations into real estate and revenue-generating projects.

The United House of Prayer for All People grew to multiple locations in the industrial cities east of the Mississippi as Daddy Grace barnstormed throughout the South and Northeast, preaching to (uncommon in the Jim Crow era) mixed Black and white congregations—though by the early 1930s the House of Prayer congregations were predominantly Black. When Daddy Grace visited his New York congregation, he encountered Father Divine's Peace Mission restaurants in Harlem. Soon after, Daddy Grace began a new project that would support his church and his followers: cafeterias.

United House of Prayer for All People restaurants and cafeterias were housed in or adjacent to the church buildings, and employed members as cooks and waitstaff. The cuisine was and still is focused on Southern-style Soul Food. The restaurants are often the top-rated Soul Food dining spots in their respective cities, with long lines waiting for lunchtime meals of fried chicken and fish, greens, macaroni and cheese, and their signature pound cake. The New York City location is located a few blocks from the famous Apollo Theater and became a gathering place for musicians and residents. At their founding in the mid-1930s during the Great Depression,

Bishop Daddy Grace, April 1958 at his residence.

Daddy Grace's United House of Prayer for All People cafeterias didn't charge customers for meals. They began charging a nominal fee at the beginning of World War II, but the need for meals and souls ensured that the House of Prayer Cafeterias and the Peace Mission restaurants engaged in low-level competition when found in the same city. As one church member and cafeteria volunteer told the New York Times in 2003, "The philosophy and doctrine of Daddy Grace was, you can't preach a sermon to a hungry man. Once you feed his stomach, you can speak to his soul." The House of Prayer is active today with restaurants in churches throughout the Southeast and in New York City.

Daddy Grace was, as many businessman-preachers have encountered, accused of taking advantage of his followers and funneling money to himself. He was never formally investigated nor charged with theft. He was accused of deifying himself as a god in 1942 by folklorist Arthur Fauset, himself a mixed-race man active in the Harlem Renaissance.

The conflict between Daddy Grace and Fauset is a good example of the tension between the Holiness-inspired churches and independent preachers, and the mainstream Black church. The tension was exacerbated by the influx of migrants from the South who, by and large, followed newer, charismatic and schismatic Christian religions, and Northerners who made up the congregations of long-established American religions. The Black Church, as the group of traditional Protestant sects is often referred to, was the embodiment of Black success. Followers took pride as they worked to "move up" the unspoken socio-economic class rankings and become the elite of Black America. Within that struggle between new and old religion is reflected the philosophical conflicts between Booker T. Washington, who

Holy Food

advocated for a separatist, self-sufficient vision for Black Americans, and W.E.B. DuBois who championed education and Black excellence as the key to fully integrating society. Fauset, who grew up in the traditional African Methodist Episcopal church in Philadelphia, received his PhD from Penn State and taught high school (after being dissuaded from teaching college because of his race). He was an anthropologist and historian by training and began his life's work of documenting folktales and folklore among the Black Atlantic diaspora.

Fauset interviewed members of the United House of Prayer for All People in the early Forties and noted a phrase commonly used by the parishioners: "Salvation is by Grace only. Grace has given God a vacation, and since He is on vacation, don't worry about Him. If you sin against God, Grace can save you, but if you sin against Grace, God cannot save you." In Fauset's brief study of the group, which was included in his 1944 book *Black Gods of the Metropolis: Negro Religious Cults in the Urban North,* he didn't elaborate nor give context for the quotes and interviews. Later readers and writers incorrectly cited Fauset and took this as reference to Daddy Grace and not "grace" as a tenet of Protestant belief.[90]

It is important to illustrate the constant tension between mainstream and New Religious Movements. It is our human nature to be wary of the unknown or an alternative worldview, especially a view that recasts our understanding of history and challenges our long-held beliefs. The United House of Prayer for All People and Daddy Grace are often lumped into the category of cult, yet the group doesn't exhibit any of the high-control behaviors that define a cult. Sometimes people throw labels at groups and movements that discomfit them. In the case of Daddy Grace, his vision of an open-to-all, integrated version of charismatic Christianity threatened many traditionalists when segregation was the law of the land. Though Daddy Grace indulged in expensive suits, houses, and cars, he also built a church that gave members a pathway to financial independence. It can be argued that Daddy Grace was a proto-prosperity preacher, as he claimed God's blessings would be bestowed on those who both worked hard and kept the faith.

Daddy Grace died in 1960 and was succeeded by Bishop McCollough (after a short internal power struggle). Sweet Daddy McCollough expanded Daddy Grace's mission to the community by building more churches and investing in low-income housing for members. He also established a scholarship fund for church members who wish to attend college that covers their entire tuition. United House of Prayer for All People, as of 2020, was around 40,000 people strong and enjoys outstanding ratings on Yelp.

Father Divine and his Peace Mission were contemporary with the United House of Prayer for All People. Where Daddy Grace brought Soul Food and Pentecostalism to his Washington, D.C.-based movement, Father Divine added New Thought and health food to his Peace Mission, and for a few short years was the toast of Harlem. Father Divine's early attempts at building his Peace Mission followed a path that many inspired pastors follow to this day: plant your church where the message is needed. And more importantly, feed your flock.

Much of what we know about Father Divine comes from historian Jill Watts' 1992 biography, *God, Harlem U.S.A.: The Father Divine Story*. Her research offers a sketch of his background, a story that is familiar as his trajectory of early exposure to charismatic preaching, New

---

90 American history scholar Danielle Sigler untangles the decades-long misinterpretation in her 2009 paper, "Grace has given God a vacation: The history and development of the theology of the United House of Prayer for All People."

Thought writing, and reinvention is shared with other religious leaders of this era. Father Divine was born in a poor suburb of Baltimore with the name George Baker around 1876. As a young man, he struggled to find work as a gardener. He had a curious mind and read deeply the religious thinkers of the day. Charles Fillmore's Spiritualist-inflected New Thought writings on developing new interpretations of the Bible and how the Spirit works were profoundly influential on Baker. Where Crowdy and other Christian ministers embraced a fundamental reading of the Bible and the Spirit Gifts of speaking in tongues and healing, Fillmore explored New Thought philosophies and how they related to

Father Divine at Communion Banquet, c. 1935. Photo by Bettmann, courtesy of Getty Images.

God. Fillmore's Unity Church spread a Spiritualist and New Thought version of Christianity through magazines and newspapers published by the group. For all the slight variations in New Thought and Spiritualist philosophies of the time, it is the New Thought concept of godly immanence—that God is within mankind—that is the schismatic tenet at the core of Father Divine's Peace Mission and many modern American New Religious Movements.

In an echo of the first Great Awakening that saw traveling preacher Charles Finney meet with the first wave of religious thinkers in the early 1800s, the Azusa Street Mission led by William Seymour was a magnet for seekers and a catalyst for many influential religious leaders in the early twentieth century. George Baker traveled west to Los Angeles in 1906 to see for himself what the national media were writing about the Azusa Street Revival. Baker visited the Mission, and though skeptical of Seymour's Pentecostal Holiness movement, he experienced a spiritual energy and renewal while attending services. He was quoted many years later, using a New Thought term, that the experience at Azusa gave him "consciousness of himself as a spiritual being, knowing himself to the Christ of God, he is I AM,[91] and ready to recreate the world." Los Angeles was home to other New Thought groups who maintained libraries that allowed patrons to review materials and attend lectures on elements of New Thought philosophies. Baker also saw the growing socialist movements among organized labor, and he witnessed how Mutual Aid cooperatives could be harnessed to assist people to gain financial prosperity. When he returned

91   His use of the phrase "I AM" reflects the influence of Theosophist beliefs. The I AM Activity Movement was a Theosophist-influenced proto-New Age group founded by Guy Ballard in Chicago in the early 1930s. Though it was only active as the I AM iteration until Ballard's death in 1939, it was very popular. It worked to continue and expand the ideas of Madame Blavatsky and the existence of "Ascended Masters," who were/are a hierarchy of supernatural beings that includes the original Theosophical Masters such as Jesus Christ, El Morya Khan, and Maitreya, plus several dozen more.

Holy Food

to Baltimore later that year, his entire notion of who he was, and the nature of God, had changed. It took several more years of study, preaching, and for a few years, partnership with two other like-minded ministers, before he struck out on his own with a more developed concept of his Peace Mission. But it was Baker who became what Fauset accused Daddy Grace of becoming: a god. Because Baker's interpretation of godly immanence determined that God does not reside in all mankind but only within him. He now was Father Major Jealous Divine.[92]

After spending a few years in Georgia developing his doctrine—and encountering violent pushback, including beatings and jail—Father Divine moved his entire congregation to Brooklyn, New York, in 1914. They lived communally in a small apartment building purchased with the shared funds of members. The group adopted its official name, the International Peace Mission, during this period. Father Divine required followers to commit to a life of abstinence forgoing alcohol, tobacco, "profane language," and sex. Divine married one of his earliest followers, Peninnah, in what was defined as a godly marriage without sex. The group later moved from the Brooklyn apartment building to a mansion in the wealthy Long Island enclave of Sayville in 1919.

During the 1920s, the Peace Mission began to attract as many white followers as it did Black followers. This integrated group, some who lived together in the Sayville house and others who came to weekly meetings, disturbed his wealthy white neighbors. While neighbors complained and launched rumor campaigns, Father Divine was preaching his theological doctrine to all comers. He preached that poverty and racism were manifestations of negative thinking. That a person, through study and devotion to God's word while following the exercises of positive thinking, could change their personal circumstances and bring about world peace. And most controversially in the Black community, Father Divine claimed that races did not truly exist and that he saw no color when he looked into a person's face.[93] He felt that racism existed but that it was a manifestation of the negativity carried by Black people, and they had the responsibility to change minds by becoming successful and freeing themselves from the mind-prison of racial constructs.

It was in Sayville that Father Divine began the tradition of free weekly feasts open to everyone and anyone. Father Divine called these feasts "Holy Communion Banquet Service" and attracted hundreds of people who descended on the residential neighborhood to hear Father Divine and seek his blessing. The dining was always formal, with multiple courses passed at the tables. Peace Mission archivist Dr. Christopher B. Stewart kindly shared details about what was served at a typical Holy Communion Banquet:

"There were salads, cheeses, breads, semi-sweets (like scones), cooked vegetables, meats, pickles, desserts, nuts and ice cream that (I think) were served in that order at every Banquet. In the past, there could be 10 choices or more for each of those categories. The most exhaustive menu in the archive shows over 150 entrées."

---

92   The name "Major Jealous" comes from the Old Testament/Tanakh passage Exodus 34:14 (King James version), "For thou shalt worship no other god: for the LORD, whose name is Jealous, is a jealous God."
93   Father Divine's belief that there is no race among humans was also shared by his contemporary Noble Drew Ali.

The Peace Mission hasn't publicly disclosed historic membership demographics, but based on published newsletters and archival pictures, women outnumbered men by nearly a three-to-one margin. The female-to-male ratio would cause internal issues, as sitting near Father Divine was a high honor and members often engaged in petty antics and small squabbles to gain that coveted position. The Peace Mission

Peace Mission Grocery Store, c. 1935. Photo by Bettmann, courtesy of Getty Images.

newsletters throughout the decades are filled with Father Divine's admonitions against currying favor with him. He scolds followers to focus on their behaviors and not sully the names of others. His sermons presented during the Banquets are a fascinating insight into how challenging managing a large group of followers actually is.

By 1931, the Great Depression had upended the economy of the United States, but Father Divine continued hosting his weekly Holy Communion Banquet Services which became a lifeline for many hungry people. But the neighbors in Sayville had had enough. They demanded that the local police arrest Father Divine on charges that the Peace Mission was a sex cult and that they were loud late into the night.[94] They also claimed that Father Divine was a charlatan bilking followers of money. The money issue is often contentious for communal groups. It was true that Father Divine drove a Cadillac and owned multiple properties funded by contributions. Yet the money was also used by the Peace Mission to expand its collective property holdings in New York and New Jersey in the form of apartment and commercial buildings, called "Heavens," and rented to followers at a substantial discount.

The Peace Mission funds also served as a de facto central bank for members who sought loans or the Mission's investment to start a business. Successful members donated a portion of their earnings and assets to the Mission, and then the Peace Mission underwrote more new businesses begun by followers. Businesses associated with the Peace Mission were allowed to use "Peace" in their name as a signal to all that the businesses were blessed by Father Divine, but if that proprietor should violate church rules or behave unscrupulously, the Peace Mission would rescind its favor and demand that any branding be immediately removed and all loaned and invested funds returned.

---

94 Father Divine was arrested for disturbing the peace in May of 1931. He paid the bail and increased the size of his weekly Holy Communion Banquets for the entire summer before his May 1932 scheduled trial. This antagonized the community and law enforcement who again arrested him and a few hundred followers on November 8, 1931. The ensuing press frenzy only served to increase Father Divine's popularity. The May trial was a circus. The jury found Father Divine guilty but recommended a light sentence. The judge in the case felt otherwise and sentenced Father Divine to one year in jail on June 5, 1931. Father Divine appealed and won and was released on June 25th. The presiding judge, Justice Smith, died on June 9, 1931, of a heart attack. Father Divine is quoted as saying this about Smith's death: "I hated to do it. I did not desire Judge Smith to die. … I did desire that MY spirit would touch his heart and change his mind that he might repent and believe and be saved from the grave."

Though Father Divine was the sole leader of the Peace Mission, there were long-standing members who assisted in the bureaucracy of running the organization. Yet the group did not have a formal hierarchy, or really any organization to vet or manage followers and the businesses created in the Peace Mission's name. If anything, the hotels, restaurants, clothing shops, and other sundry businesses begun by members with assistance from the Peace Mission could be considered informal franchises. Dr. Stewart clarifies:

"Many people have the idea that the Peace Mission was centralized and that FATHER DIVINE micro-managed the Movement. This is far from the truth. Extensions[95] were each and all founded by cooperative members pooling their resources and were expected to operate and maintain themselves completely independently of other Extensions. Most Extensions outside the northeast were never Personally visited by FATHER DIVINE (there were more than 150 internationally at the peak). What food an Extension or one of its Enterprises served was, within reason, entirely up to the Head Waitress or Housekeeper (who is a de facto priestess administering and pacing the Communion Service). An Extension that could not support itself was deemed to necessarily be inharmonious with the Teaching. We believe that FATHER managed the Peace Mission by His Spirit imputed into each sincere Follower, seldom externally and never dictatorially except when some severe repeated transgression demanded the expulsion of an individual. If word reached FATHER that something was not up to standard, He would intervene by letter, and if it persisted, would demand that His Name and the words 'Peace' and 'Thank You, FATHER' be removed from display, and if FATHER were asked by Followers for advice on any particular question, He would provide it."

In line with Father Divine's doctrine that negative thoughts result in bad outcomes, the Peace Mission rejected ideas of charity. Father Divine believed in the redemptive power of work and felt that no person should rely on the state or church, and evangelized that joining the Peace Mission could lift a person from poverty and addiction. And in many individual cases, that was true. The Peace Mission's work grew as they opened restaurants in Harlem and Newark, New Jersey, that served bounteous nutritious meals for ten cents during the height of the Great Depression. These restaurants became both a beloved establishment in the community and an opportunity to demonstrate the power of Father Divine's message of directed Mutual Aid and communal action.

The Peace Mission is sometimes cited as a proto-civil rights group but that isn't quite accurate. The integrated Peace Mission during its heyday of the 1930s avoided taking public stances on politics. Father Divine did meet with Communist Party officials who sought an alliance throughout 1934. He agreed with the Communist Party's views on equality for all and equal legal and voting rights for Black people, but never formally joined, nor did he encourage followers to do so. An event in 1935 changed his mind about the Peace Mission's role in American political discourse regarding race and civil rights.

The Harlem Riot began on March 19th when a Black Puerto Rican teenager was severely beaten by either a white shop owner or the police. The situation escalated as residents

---

95   "Extensions" is the Peace Mission term used for businesses started and managed by members.

demanded justice and the police erected barricades around the neighborhood. All of Harlem was on tense alert. Angry activists set fire to white-owned businesses and buildings. Police violently retaliated. When the melee was over a few days later, 125 people were injured and the neighborhood suffered over one million dollars in property damage.[96] In the aftermath, Father Divine used his position as a Harlem property owner and religious leader to work with politicians and form his Divine Righteous Government Convention to educate and train followers to advocate for issues aligned with his doctrine. The Peace Mission worked to support legislation to dismantle New York Jim Crow laws and end racial segregation, mainly in schools. The Peace Mission assisted in crafting anti-lynching legislation for New York state and gained 250,000 signatures in support of the proposed law. Yet Father Divine was not a member of any political party. In modern political ideology, his stance could be described as libertarian. He believed in American capitalism and that hard work would result in success, but that the opportunities must be equal and accessible to all. He was vehemently opposed to Roosevelt's New Deal, because it supported, in his words, "too many handouts," and believed that creating small businesses and paying fair wages was the pathway for man to make a success of himself. His beliefs align with other New Thought and "positive thinking" teachers of the era, as those leaders shared a relative continuity of ideas that were independently discovered through the hundreds of newspapers, books, and magazines filled with research and revelations.

Father Divine saw himself as a patriotic American, and when in 1939 President Franklin D. Roosevelt set the third Thursday of November as the designated date of the Thanksgiving holiday, Father Divine celebrated with a feast to be remembered.[97] He invited men of Hoboes International, a loose confederation of itinerant workers, to dine with him for the holiday. According to Dr. Stewart, the menu on Thanksgiving Day 1939 included:

"Chicken, duck, turkey with dressing, creamed potatoes, baked macaroni, creamed carrots, greens, pickled beets, other vegetables, many kinds of bread, pumpkin pie, ice cream, and everything that goes to make up a 'real Thanksgiving dinner' including cranberry sauce."

Father Divine's hands-off style of management led to a few lurid incidents that became fodder for the tabloid press. A follower in Colorado declared himself God and kidnapped the seventeen-year-old daughter of a fellow member, and declared the girl the Virgin Mary whom he would impregnate so she could birth the reincarnated Jesus. A few former followers accused Father Divine of sexual coercion. (Father Divine denied this at the time and the Peace Mission states that he lived a wholly celibate life.) There were financial irregularities in the ownership of property and businesses as some were held in Father Divine's name and others by the Peace Mission. As the country's focus turned away from the economic devastation of the Great Depression now remediated by Roosevelt's New Deal policies, and shifted to the coming war, the Peace Mission's form of Mutual Aid wasn't as needed, and membership declined.

---

96   One million dollars in 1935 is the equivalent of $21,335,474.45 in 2022.
97   Until FDR designated the third Thursday of November as the official national Thanksgiving holiday, the annual celebration date was set by individual states.

Holy Food

Father Divine was sixty-six years old in 1942. Mother Peninnah Divine had been ill for several years, much to the embarrassment of Father Divine. The Peace Mission doctrine about health bore the imprint of Father Divine's early reading of Christian Science and equated poor health with negative thinking, poor nutrition, and lack of belief. He purchased a home in Philadelphia and moved there with Mother Divine and only a few followers. Mother Peninnah Divine died in 1943, and Father Divine married a twenty-one-year-old Canadian woman named Edna Ritchings who became the new Mother Divine in 1946. Their marriage signaled a change in the Peace Mission. The weekly Holy Communion Banquet Service downsized but was still open to the public. As economic prosperity grew after World War II, Father Divine's promise for wealth, health, and peace for all seemed to be coming into view.

Archivist Dr. Stewart also shared that Father Divine was interested in and recommended eating natural and unprocessed foods. Father Divine felt that a poor diet added to followers' ill health, and according to Dr. Stewart: "Naturopathic principles were emphasized, particularly avoidance of refined, over-processed foods; there is a recording of FATHER speaking with a Naturopath during the Holy Communion Banquet."

Dr. Stewart also said of the cuisine served at the restaurants, especially beginning in the 1960s: "They emphasize general organic and macrobiotic foods (there was a period, I think centered in the 1980s, when macrobiotic diet was emphasized and encouraged by MOTHER DIVINE, though never very rigidly)." The Peace Mission did not formally nor completely embrace vegetarianism as part of their doctrine, but Mother Divine curtailed the excess at Holy Communion Banquets to serve one course per category of meat, fish, and vegetarian option, along with vegetable side dishes and dessert.

In 1953, a loyal follower gave the Peace Mission the historic Woodmont Estate, located in the bucolic Philadelphia suburbs. The aging Father Divine moved there with Mother Divine and a small coterie of followers who served in administrative and household capacities for the Peace Mission. Father Divine was now viewed by the press as a somewhat comical figure and sometimes as a religious crank, yet he still worked for civil rights in his particular way. He was never accepted by the postwar civil rights movement as he remained steadfast in his claim that he was not Black, and that race truly did not exist. He advocated for reparations to be paid to the descendants of enslaved people, and the elimination of redlining and other discriminatory practices that prevented Black and brown people from purchasing homes wherever they wanted. But his time had passed, and the country had moved on to new leaders seeking new ways of finding divinity. Father Divine died in his sleep of natural causes in 1965.

The Peace Mission Holy Communion Banquets were still held on Sundays for the remaining followers of the Peace Mission and led by Mother Divine, until the COVID pandemic shut the doors of Woodmont to visitors. There remain less than a dozen people, including Mother Divine, residing at Woodmont as of 2022.

The Peace Mission and the United House of Prayer for All People had a lasting ripple impact on American food culture. It demonstrated how food, in the form of free meals and low-cost restaurants, can attract potential believers. The Peace Mission demonstrated the effectiveness of how polycultural hybrids of spirituality, religion and Mutual Aid could unite and inspire believers. The Holy Communion Banquets brought together new listeners and those who may have never otherwise heard Father Divine's message and doctrine. Not every person attending the weekly Banquets became a member of the Peace Mission, but it can be argued that those non-converted attendees did as much to spread Father Divine's message of spiritual immortality through positive thinking and abstinence. The Peace Mission also created an important template for future New Religious Movements: that of the revenue-generating restaurant. In postwar United States, many more groups used the business of food to advance their reach and their wealth.

THERE IS A CODA TO THE STORY OF FATHER DIVINE. IT SHOWS THE INTERCONNECTIVITY between New Religious Movements and their charismatic leaders. And it illustrates the dangerous consequences of a man becoming God.

Like the "begats" in the book of Genesis detailing the genealogy of Adam and his descendants, New Religious Movements are linked by a lineage of spiritual and operational influence. The Pentecostal-inspired and food-centered movements noted here have a terrible culminating endpoint in the Peoples Temple.[98] Americans are familiar enough with the Jonestown, Guyana, tragedy to have it pass into cultural shorthand for the worst outcome for any New Religious Movement. "Drinking the Kool-Aid" is casually used to describe anyone embracing suspect ideas or pledging allegiance to flawed leaders.[99] Glossing over what Jim Jones believed and attempted to build with Peoples Temple diminishes the lives of those who died at Jonestown.

Jim Jones was born into abject poverty in rural east-central Indiana in 1931. His father was a disabled World War I veteran who suffered from the debilitating effects of chemical gas attacks throughout his life. Jones' mother is noted as being indifferent to both husband and son. Jones was often alone as his parents left home to search for food and work. Later, extended family and neighbors would "look after" him. He was remembered by former teachers and neighbors as prodigiously intelligent, socially awkward and without friends, and—because of the Holiness tutoring given along with meals from the local Nazarene pastor and his wife—obsessed with the Bible. His parents were divorced by 1945 and Jones moved with his mother to Richmond, Indiana, where he finished high school and married Marceline, who was to remain by his side until their death. Jones began attending classes at Indiana University before dropping out and moving to Indianapolis. (He completed his degree in secondary education nearly fifteen years later at Butler University's night school in 1961.) Outside of formal schooling, Jones was a student of political science and fascinated by various ideologies from fascism to communism and every iteration in between. He was said to have experienced a racial epiphany during a baseball game when he witnessed a group of whites attack Black fans. By all telling, Jones was eccentric.

Jones, as noted by first-hand accounts from early church members, claimed Native American heritage through his mother. There are unconfirmed accounts that Jones also claimed lineage

98   For anyone interested in learning more about the details of the people who were part of Peoples Temple and their daily lives, please visit the "Alternative Considerations of Jonestown & Peoples Temple" archive held by San Diego State University. The site contains interviews, transcribed audio, and personal remembrances of members and their families. jonestown.sdsu.edu/

99   At the risk of pedantry, the mass poisoning at Jonestown was delivered via Flavor Aid, not Kool-Aid.

Jim Jones standing in a cornfield, c. 1974. Courtesy of The Peoples Temple Collection at San Diego State University Special Collections.

to the Tribe of Ishmael—a now-debunked theory that a mixed-race group of Native, Black, Arab-Islamic, and impoverished whites formed an extensive nomadic tribe with a circular territory that encompassed northern Kentucky and southern Indiana.[100] Jones, as noted by witnesses, was disturbed by the violent racism he encountered in Indianapolis. He was, since his teenage years, a vocal civil rights supporter and activist. As remembered by those who knew him as a young man, Jones was very outside of the mainstream white Protestant culture of Indianapolis of the early 1950s.

In 1951, twenty-year-old Jones began attending meetings of the Communist Party and officially joined the Party. Of all his political readings, Marx's theories about racial equality, the value of labor, and the equanimity of collectivization to bring about true revolutionary change became a central tenet of his belief system. Jones had already felt the pressure from the FBI, who harassed him due to his Communist Party membership and activities associated with the Party, but continued searching for a new way to spread his message of equality. Jones' fascinations with religion, civil rights, and Marxism fueled his decision to become ordained. Jones told a Temple-affiliated interviewer in the early 1970s, "I decided, how can I demonstrate my Marxism? The thought was, infiltrate the church."[101]

Marceline Jones grew up in the Methodist Church and encouraged her husband to join a local congregation and pursue his ordination. The conservative church was misaligned with his values though he was encouraged by the District Superintendent to pursue the ministry, which Jones took as a sign that it was ready for his brand of Christian Socialism. His tenure with Somerset South Side Methodist Church lasted less than two years. He was fired in 1954 as an apprentice pastor for either embezzlement, as the church claimed, or because Jones was working to integrate the congregation, as he claimed. Jones was aware, as were many, of Father Divine and his Peace Mission. The national press tended to focus on the most outré elements of the Peace Mission, but Jones understood Father Divine's underlying Pentecostal style coupled with Mutual Aid ideas that drove Divine's organization. Jones also embraced the early twentieth-century Black liberationist stance that race is an artificial construct and declared that he too was a Black man insomuch that there was no such thing as race.

---

100 Writings from members of the Moorish Science Temple have made the claim that Noble Drew Ali was from the Tribe of Ishmael.
101 Quote is from Transcript Q134 of the "Jonestown Tapes" held and transcribed by the Jonestown Institute at San Diego State University.

During this time, Jones was active in local Pentecostal churches offering his services as a guest preacher. He was associated with the "Latter Rain" movement of evangelicalism and spiritual healing growing out of the Assemblies of God sect that sought to revive Pentecostalism after World War II. (Other preachers associated with the Latter Rain movement were Billy Graham and Oral Roberts.) The Latter Rain movement also embraced a form of Lost Tribes theory, British-Israelism, that elevated white Christians as God's preferred and chosen people. Latter Rain also believed—and this tenet resonated with Jones—in "the Manifested Sons of God," which taught that certain men would

Peoples Temple advertisement, Indianapolis, Indiana, 1955.

be so thoroughly imbued with the spirit of Christ that they themselves would become divine and physically manifest Jesus Christ, becoming Christ himself remade on the Earth to save and heal the world. These "Sons of God" believed the words in Psalms 82:6, "ye are as Gods."[102] Jones broke with Latter Rain leaders as they embraced an increasingly virulent racism leading Jones to denounce the Assemblies of God and strike out on his own.

With these elements firmly in mind, he sought ordination with the Disciples of Christ, a non-denominational Christian group born of the Second Great Awakening in northern Kentucky. Jones claimed in taped interviews that he felt a kinship with Pentecostals as they were considered outsiders by mainstream Protestants, but sought ordination through the Disciples of Christ because they were decentralized with no hierarchical oversight, which allowed him to build the church he envisioned. Jones held his first service in Indianapolis in 1955 with twenty followers as The Healing Way and Wings of Deliverance before changing the name of his church to Peoples Temple.

Jones' work building his church in Indianapolis focused on a tried-and-true method used by Father Divine and so many others: he fed people. The Peoples Temple operated a food pantry and hosted free meals after services. He and his followers focused on service to elderly and infirm Black residents who fell through the cracks of social services and without family support. He openly preached about shared struggle and the power of collectivizing resources. In living his mission, he and wife Marceline adopted non-white children of similar ages to their biological children. Within a few years, Jones had built a robust and integrated church recognized by Indianapolis officials as doing important work. In 1960, Jones was named to the local Human Rights Commission, which further empowered Jones' work toward racial

102 The Assemblies of God are the fastest growing denomination in the world with, as of 2020, over 70 million members. It is estimated by the Pulitzer Center that 35,000 Americans are "born again" every day. Approximately one in ten of what are described as "mega-churches," with congregations over 2,000 people, are affiliated with the Assembly of God.

justice. With his parishioners, he organized "stings" to call out and publicly shame Indianapolis businesses that refused service to Black residents. Peoples Temple became a frequent target of white supremacists, including the very active Indianapolis branch of the KKK. The church was threatened with bombing and frequently defaced with swastikas and hateful graffiti.

Jones received public recognition for his work with Peoples Temple yet was privately fascinated by the Peace Mission. He became convinced that he was the inheritor of Father Divine's Peace Mission. Jones and followers visited Woodmont multiple times throughout 1962 to 1964 but could not convince Father or Mother Divine to appoint him as successor. Jones became increasingly frustrated but also concerned that Indianapolis was not the best place for his next phase of Peoples Temple. Jones was, as were many people in the States during the Cold War era, convinced that nuclear war was not only possible but imminent. He wanted to find a new location that would be least likely to be affected by nuclear fallout and could provide a communal and sustainable living for his followers. After traveling to Cuba and Brazil, he settled on rural Mendocino County (north of San Francisco) in California and proceeded to relocate the congregation.

The move to Mendocino County allowed Peoples Temple to expand their work growing food. They built housing throughout the area and quickly expanded with locations in San Francisco, Oakland, and Los Angeles. Peoples Temple encountered the Black Panthers and Jones took from them actionable ideas about civil rights, revolution, and access to food. Jones continued to provide free meals and operate food pantries as he did in Indianapolis. Yet Jones' son-in-law and high-ranking member Michael Cartmell clarifies, "We publicized that we were feeding everyone who wanted to eat but actually, we were primarily feeding our own members and potential recruits."[103] And as happened in Indiana, Jones was recognized by local government officials and asked to serve on local human rights councils. Peoples Temple's relocation to California also brought about a new focus on communal living. The Temple purchased apartment buildings to house followers, who were then encouraged to give their assets and any earned wages to Peoples Temple on the promise that the Temple would provide for all their material and spiritual needs. For younger, college-age members, Jones encouraged and paid for them to attend college and pursue areas of study that could benefit the Temple. Jones encouraged studying medicine and law. They expanded their revenue streams and social services in a particularly lucrative manner. Jones encouraged Temple members to sign up for any Social Security and welfare benefits that were available. This arrangement allowed for Peoples Temple members to use the government payments to cover the costs of the elder care they were already providing. Jones was building his Marxist utopia.

There are former members of Peoples Temple alive today. Michael Cartmell married Jones' adopted daughter Suzanne and was part of Jones' inner circle: "There is no one Peoples Temple experience." He detailed the many ways Jones used food to exert coercive power over members, potential recruits, and politicians. In hindsight, Cartmell thinks that all decisions made by Jones were based on a power calculation—that Jones would leverage followers to support causes that would make Peoples Temple look good and increase political clout. He

---

103 Michael Cartmell's recollections and quotes taken from an interview conducted by the author in January 2021.

Jonestown pioneers celebrating the banana harvest, c. 1975. Courtesy of The Peoples Temple Collection at San Diego State University Special Collections.

said, "Politicians in the San Francisco area knew we can put five hundred people anywhere we wanted on the West Coast [for a rally or protest]." Cartmell also notes that he was part of the ongoing recruitment strategy. Jones would target small, independent Pentecostal churches and offer to preach for free and bring followers in with food, with the goal of absorbing the membership and whatever assets they have. "Jim was a great PR guy," says Cartmell. Jones chose Cartmell as a trusted ambassador for Peoples Temple to engage what was termed "cake diplomacy." Cartmell explained that Jones would identify a church, political, or civil rights group by reading local newspapers to discover which organizations were recognized for "good works." Cartmell was then sent to that group with a congratulatory note from Jones and a cake. Cartmell recounts how surprisingly effective cake and flattery were for recruiting new members. When asked about "the cakes," Cartmell laughed and said they really weren't anything special or fancy, usually made from Betty Crocker mixes by Temple kitchen volunteers. "Cake diplomacy" only lasted a few years—specifically in the Mendocino County area—where residents quickly became suspicious of the Peoples Temple's intentions. Cartmell, in a rare light-hearted memory, said, "There was a man we asked to paint our school bus in Ukiah, but he was adamant that he was going to get paid and didn't want to join the church and then yelled, 'I don't want a damn cake either!'"

The Peoples Temple kitchens in Indianapolis and later in California were primarily staffed by older Black women who cooked meals based on what was available. Cartmell explained that in the Temple hierarchy, there were a few trusted assistants who oversaw procuring commodities to supplement their agricultural program. The cooks tended to make Southern-style dishes that reflected their—and Jones'—regional traditions. Cartmell remembers that in 1966, Jones gave followers the message that Peoples Temple was now vegetarian. The experiment lasted one year before Jones abandoned it with the message, "[Followers] were not sufficiently evolved to be vegetarian." Cartmell remembers Jones instituting faddish and sometimes quack dietary rules. Jones required that pork liver and onions be served once a week because he had read that there

Holy Food

were, unknown to Cartmell, health benefits. Jones also told followers to drink a glass of water with two tablespoons of vinegar and eat apricot seeds every day for presumed health benefits. Cartmell made clear that the food served to followers in the communes was not the same food eaten by Jones. He ate separately with family and whoever was most favored at the time.

Father Divine died on September 10, 1965. He was eighty-nine years old. Though Jones had success in California, he was still obsessed with the Peace Mission and, in 1971, made a final trip to Woodmont with two busloads of followers to plead his case with Mother Divine to take over the Peace Mission. In Jones' account, she stripped naked and offered herself to him in Father Divine's crypt. In Mother Divine's account, she resoundingly told him "No" while extending him the hospitality that was a hallmark of the Peace Movement. Jones and Peoples Temple members sent letters to Peace Mission members exhorting them to join Jones and his improved version of Father Divine's mission. In 1972, Mother Divine published an official rebuke:

> *"We have entertained Pastor Jones and the Peoples Temple. We were entertaining angels of the 'other fellow!' We no longer extend to them any hospitality whatsoever! Not a one of them is welcome in any Church under the jurisdiction of the Peace Mission Movement, here, or in any other Country! They are not welcome in any of our public hotels; they are not welcome in any of our public dining rooms. They are not welcome!"*[104]

Was this rejection a catalytic moment for Peoples Temple and Jim Jones? Numerous biographies and studies suggest that while Jones embraced socialism and racial equality, he was also a pathological liar. He had a history of verbal abuse. He was sexually promiscuous and was known to drug and rape women. He became increasingly violent and out of control, lashing out at followers and imposing harsh punishments on those who offended or defied his commands. Researchers have not found documented proof that Mother Divine's banishment signaled the next phase of Peoples Temple, but the failure to secure the Peace Mission accelerated Jones' apocalyptic sermons and increased his paranoia that he and his followers were under attack by the KKK, Nazis, and assorted fascists. The theology of the Peoples Temple changed as well, as it became less about Christian Socialism and more about Jones as the redeemer of his people. He no longer baptized new followers in the name of Jesus but in the "holy name of socialism." He began taking cocaine and other stimulants. He formed an armed "security force" of loyal followers and increased the day-to-day rules for followers. Reports began to surface about forced labor, psychological torture, and prolonged denial of food and water experienced by members.

In 1973, Jones again made plans to move followers to a remote location purported to be safe from nuclear fallout: Guyana. It was the same year that Suzanne Jones and Michael Cartmell left the group, as Suzanne disagreed with her father's actions. By 1974, an advance team was 175 miles north of the capital city of Georgetown clearing the land that would become the new utopia of Jonestown. The settlement was envisioned as an entirely self-contained and self-sufficient community, except that neither Jones nor any of his lieutenants had any experience

---

104 'The other fellow' is the Peace Mission term for the devil. This passage taken from Mother Divine's 1972 recorded message from the Peace Mission archives.

with agriculture in the Guyanese jungle. They quickly built small cottages and larger communal buildings and kitchens. Jonestown was barely livable when the first arrivals showed up. Mike Touchette was there.[105]

Touchette's mother Joyce joined Peoples Temple in the early 1960s when it was still in Indianapolis. She was active in the civil rights movement and responded to Jones' message of revolutionary equality. When Peoples Temple relocated to California, she and her children—eleven-year-old Mike and his younger sister—did too. The Touchettes lived at the Ukiah-area commune where his mother worked as a caretaker, a supply clerk, and later in the kitchens. He remembers teenage life in the commune as hard work but not much religious indoctrination or any kind of rituals. "It was more of just a commune. There was no 'you're going to hell,'" he says. Touchette notes that as he grew older, he resented Jones' control over his life choices and how little he saw his mother. Jones, as he did with many young men who defied him, banned Touchette from the communes and Peoples Temple. Mike Touchette's banishment lasted from 1968 to 1972, when he sought out his mother and Jones allowed him to rejoin. And in December of 1974, Jones sent Touchette and a small crew that included his mom, stepfather, and sister to build the new home of Peoples Temple in Guyana.

Mike Touchette says that there was a distinct difference in life at Jonestown in the early days, when it was a small group of fifty people living together and building Jones' utopia, and after March of 1977 when large groups of members and Jones himself arrived. In the spartan early days, Touchette remembers eating simple meals of rice and beans with either chicken or meats provided by local hunters. They subsisted on commodities brought from the States as they did the work to clear lands and establish farms. They soon discovered the soil was poor and not conducive to growing the same crops they did in California. Touchette remembers project leader Archie Ijames telling Jones that Jonestown wasn't ready for more residents, but Jones, after a brutal exposé by Marshall Kilduff and Phil Tracy in the August 1977 issue of New West Magazine[106] about abuses within Peoples Temple, accelerated the plan to move people to Guyana. Touchette remembers, "We were cooking for fifty people one day and then hundreds the next." His mom Joyce become both Head Cook for Jonestown and Jones' personal cook. The foundational crew quickly scrambled to secure World War II-era rations and freeze-dried meals to feed people. Touchette recalls how terrible the hamburger and Salisbury steak were.

New Jonestown residents were shocked to find that there were barely enough supplies to feed them. And most worryingly, as more and more people came to Jonestown, they discovered that there was no way to go back home to California. Jones officially moved Peoples Temple headquarters to Jonestown in spring of 1977 but traveled back and forth to San Francisco to transfer Temple funds to offshore accounts. (The FBI estimated that Jones transferred over ten million dollars of Temple funds during this time.) Touchette remembers how everyone was despondent and how concerned about the health of the elderly and kids they were. He says that Jones ate very differently from the residents. His mother, by Jones' command, cooked only

---

105 Mike Touchette's recollections and quotes taken from interviews done by author in January 2021.
106 Scans of the New West article. Kilduff & Tracy waived copyright and donated contents to the Jonestown archive held by San Diego State University: jonestown.sdsu.edu/wp-content/uploads/2013/10/newWestart.pdf

Holy Food

FBI image of the Experimental and Herbal Kitchen at Jonestown, November 1974. Courtesy of the Jonestown Institute.

his favorite meals. "Nine people [Jones' family and favorites] ate like kings," he said. Touchette says that he was very lucky that his mom was the head cook as she would set aside food for him and his sister, and ill residents, to supplement their daily ration.

Jones faced the issue every apocalyptic preacher has confronted—apocalypse when? Recently transcribed recordings noted Jones had decided in 1975 to bring the apocalypse to his followers. He twisted a Black Panther political concept of "revolutionary suicide" to, essentially, make the case that because the end of their world was imminent, they should kill themselves before their enemies could.[107] It was a grim, nihilistic message. The details are now all too well known: nearly one thousand men, women, and children died drinking cyanide-laced Flavor Aid drink mix on November 18, 1978. Jim Jones shot himself after taking a high dose of phenobarbital.

Michael Cartmell remembers a 1977 phone call to his mother and stepfather pleading with them to leave Jonestown. He realizes now how much Jones took advantage of his mother's loving nature, activism, and loyalty. In recently transcribed FBI files, Cartmell learned that she acted as a spy to monitor other members' activities and helped arrange for sexual liaisons between Jones and women he selected. Mike Touchette was a member of the Jonestown basketball team along with Jones' three sons. The team were in the capital city of Georgetown on the night of November 18th for a game. As officials became aware of the murder of Congressman Leo Ryan by Temple loyalists at the Georgetown airport and later, the massacre at Jonestown, the young men were held under house arrest. It was days

---

107 "Revolutionary suicide" as coined by Huey P. Newton in his book of the same name defined the concept as: "a death brought about by forcibly challenging the system and repressive agencies that can lead a person to commit reactionary suicide."

later that Mike Touchette learned that every member of his family was killed. Touchette shared his memories in a phone conversation and after a long pause said, "I'm making barbeque as we're talking. The way my mom made it. I feel closer to her when I'm cooking." He lives forever with the last picture taken of his mother and sister as was splashed across newspapers throughout the world: still bodies locked in an embrace among the hundreds of corpses of men, women, and children.

The events at Jonestown changed the United States. The casual tolerance for New Religious Movements and communes among mainstream Americans vanished. Anyone exploring a new spirituality was met with concern and often fear. For traditional Protestant denominations, the tragedy of Jonestown was met with a retrenching of conservative values in their churches. Jonestown became an anathema uttered against deviation from accepted dogma. And as time passed, Jonestown stood in to describe every religious-inspired catastrophe and a caution against blindly following charismatic leaders.

FBI photo of Jonestown kitchen, November 1978.

Holy Food

Nine
NATURE BOYS

E ARLY TWENTIETH-CENTURY AMERICANS WERE SICK. A DIET FILLED WITH MEATS AND starches resulted in the middle classes suffering from persistent constipation. Germ theory wasn't yet part of popular consciousness, so very real diseases such as tuberculosis, polio, influenza, smallpox, scarlet fever, measles, and more were blamed on everything but germs: industrialization, lack of fresh air, poverty, immigrants, sexual deviance, drug and alcohol addiction, overcrowded cities, and lack of faith in God.

Vegetarianism and veganism were more common in the 1910s and '20s than modern Americans may think. Scientific recognition of vitamins and nutrients in foodstuffs led to a better understanding of what fuel we need to survive. But as made evident by the still prevalent diet and supplement industry, science still has a long way to go to fully understand the relationship between what we eat and how our bodies are affected. Religious reformers seized on early studies showing the benefits of a plant-based diet. Moralists used the data correlating the Gilded Age penchant for multi-course, meat- and fat-laden meals to diseases like gout and dyspepsia, and called for a war on gluttony. Abstentious lifestyles publicly signaled one's moral and spiritual superiority.

What we know about the things we eat is constantly evolving. What we knew about nutrition science in the early twentieth century was really not much at all. We knew we needed to eat, and that food was fuel, but science was in the early days of figuring out how what we ate transformed into human energy. For all that we do know, there is much we still don't know, and yet we hold on to even the most spurious or outdated facts when they reinforce our beliefs about food choices. Pythagoras hinted at the notion of a molecule containing a life force that was transmuted through consumption. He was correct. Calories, vitamins, nutrients, and all the components that are the building blocks of human growth are contained in our food. And at the dawning of the twentieth century, scientific advances in nutrition instigated an explosion of what were called "food faddists." Scientist Casimir Funk coined the term "vitamine" in 1912, but the evolving progress in understanding the component parts was as Richard Semba's 2012 paper on the history of vitamin research (and really, all science research) describes so well:

> The puzzle of each vitamin was solved through the work and contributions of epidemiologists, physicians, physiologists, and chemists. Rather than a mythical story of crowning scientific breakthroughs, the reality was a slow, stepwise progress that included setbacks, contradictions, refutations, and some chicanery. Research on the vitamins that are related to major deficiency syndromes began when the germ theory of disease was dominant and dogma held that only four nutritional factors were essential: proteins, carbohydrates, fats, and minerals.[108]

Professional home economists and physicians focused on the proteins, carbohydrates, fats, and minerals in calibrating and recommending specific diets that ensured the correct amount of k-calories were consumed. There wasn't much thought about the types of food eaten as long as one hit the caloric requirements. Women's magazines of the day featured regular "expert" columns that guided housewives in how to add calories to their family meals. Vegetables are lower in calories and were thought to have lesser nutritional value unless boosted with heavy cream sauces.

Victorian-era experts told home cooks that eating meats and carbohydrate-heavy foods to fuel labor was the main goal in feeding their families, but by the early 1910s people were now being told that too much meat was bad and led to gout and dyspepsia. The heavy carbohydrate and protein diet was mostly offset by the active manual labor most work entailed in the late nineteenth and early twentieth centuries, yet many Americans suffered from digestive issues and what was euphemistically called "poor hygiene," or to be succinct, constipation. Absent the fiber provided by whole grains and vegetables, Americans were plugged up. A review of newspapers and magazines shows countless advertisements for patent medicine remedies to improve "hygiene." These medicines contained a mix of herbs, alcohol, and a purgative. There is a psychological and physical relief in seeing—I struggle a bit for the appropriate phraseology—tangible evidence that the cause of discomfort has been dislodged.

The state of bowel hygiene and general health intersected with the new field of food science and became of interest to a few New Religious Movements. The fixation on successful elimination as a reflection of bodily health has been traced back to Egyptian medical writings detailing the use of enemas as a curative for sickness. The theory was in line with similar notions of unbalanced "humors," and a buildup of waste needed to be removed. Yet no connection was made between what was eaten and how the body processed food. Enemas used as a medical cure appear in every culture, with variations on when they should be administered. In Hindu and Muslim cultures, the practice was limited as an extreme measure only to be undertaken when other cures have failed. In Saharan and west African cultures, emetics were more popular and often administered to ill children. The Dutch physician De Graaf's 1668 treatise on enemas was a landmark in noting the history and uses of enemas as a cure-all. Notably, De Graaf documents and recommends the "nutritive enema" where a

---

108 Semba, R.D. "The discovery of the vitamins." *International Journal of Vitamin and Nutritional Research*. October 2012.

A physical fitness class at the Battle Creek Sanitarium, c. 1890s. Courtesy of the University of Michigan Bentley Historical Library.

sufferer is rectally administered milk, wine, barley soup, broths, and coffee as a method to deliver nourishment to one unable to eat.

As indelicate as fecal matter may be when also discussing food, the prevalence of enemas, euphemistically called "colonics" by the early 1900s, is another attribute of how religion shapes our approach to food and duty to our body. Bowel health was, until about sixty years ago, a prevailing theme in determining overall health. This fascination when viewed at the intersection of medical and nutrition knowledge during the early 1900s becomes more understandable. In the wide swath of Christian denominations and sects, bodily health and cleanliness were believed to reflect one's moral health. Just as gluttony is reviled as a cardinal vice, so too are the related health issues caused by poor nutrition. Religious-minded health advocates viewed the rapid advances in science as a validation of their beliefs and practices. Dr. Kellogg of the Seventh-Day Adventists was an advocate for colonic irrigation at his SDA-run health spas, where he paired abstinence from meats, heavy dairy, and alcohol with a course of enemas as a cure for every ailment. Colonic therapies appear in health guides produced by members of modern Black Israelite groups, who recommend the use of coffee enemas. Modern non-aligned New Age wellness groups also recommend enema therapy. What was once a cure-all medical practice, relegated to the past by scientific advances, is currently enjoying a resurgence in popularity. In modern New Age circles—where followers are spiritual but not religious—one finds numerous debunked medical and nutrition advice monetized. The new generation of spiritually-minded health faddists still follow the successful recipe concocted over a century ago: a surefire pathway to physical health and spiritual peace for a price.

Alongside the purgative therapies were the newly formed marketing companies and food lobbying groups, who used the new medium of radio and the widening reach of magazines and newspapers to proclaim the health benefits of certain foods. The Citrus Growers Association touted the healing properties of vitamin C-filled oranges and grapefruit. The marketing around bananas was, indeed, bananas, as promoters claimed that the fruit could cure everything from anemia and heart disease to ulcers.[109] Religious sects that professed vegetarianism, especially those coming out of the Adventist movement, saw science as validating their religious teachings and the opportunity to expand their message.

The Seventh-Day Adventists were the founders of the American health sanitarium, where chronically ill people recover from illness via "natural treatments." The most famous director of the Battle Creek, Michigan, location, Dr. John Harvey Kellogg, described the system as "a composite of physiologic methods comprising hydrotherapy (hot and cold baths, douches, and enemas), phototherapy (sunlight), thermotherapy (heating pads), electrotherapy (electric shocks and stimulation), mechanotherapy (chiropractic and massage), dietetics (vegetarian diet), physical culture (exercise), cold-air cure (cold exposure), and health training (sexual continence)." The SDA Sanitarium diet of low-fat and low-protein foods was considered advantageous for healing invalids of all sorts. The SDA opened the second Sanitarium in Glendale, California, in 1902.

The diet and healing program begun by the Adventists in 1866 was replicated in the low-moisture climates of the American Southwest as a cure for tuberculosis. The new sanitoria followed the SDA guidelines of vegetarian meals and vigorous outdoor exercise, and were dubbed the "heroic cure." By 1910, the population of Albuquerque, New Mexico, was 13,000, 3,000 of whom were patients at the eight sanitoria in the city. Each curative residence was operated by a religious group; the Catholic Sisters of Charity erected the first "lunger" residence in 1902 and soon followed the Methodists, Presbyterians, Episcopalians, and more.[110] Arizona, New Mexico, and California had become the locus of the new health movement. The influx of newcomers demographically changed the Southwest. Yet more influential to the story of religious food, these newcomers carved out a new identity for the region. What was once a land inhabited by Native peoples and encroaching ranchers became associated with health and healing, and became a magnet for those seeking respite from every type of ailment, including the increasingly burdensome societal illness of modernity.

The Adventists had already published many cookbooks—primarily written for believers—with detailed instructions on how to create meat-substitute meals. Aside from the widely known Kellogg's cereals created and marketed to everyone, Adventist companies, some owned by believers and others owned directly by the Seventh-Day Adventist Church, developed meat substitutes which were then packaged and sold.[111] The business of creating easy-to-prepare, Adventist-approved food opened a revenue stream far beyond cookbooks.

---

109 My previous book, *American Advertising Cookbooks: How Corporations Taught Us to Love Spam, Bananas, and Jell-O* (Process, 2019), is a deeper exploration of the overall effect colonized food and marketing had on American culture.

110 It is noted in most modern New Mexico state histories that white federal officials encouraged wealthy, white "lungers" to come to Albuquerque for the "cure" to increase the total white population and supplant the Latino and Indigenous residents. Many of the white TB migrants stayed in New Mexico, and because of the "whiteness" of the voting citizens, helped it become a state in 1912.

111 The quest for the perfect meat substitute has been thrust into popular culture as companies, including Adventist-owned Worthington Brands, race to create a product that appeals to carnivores rather than exclusively to vegetarians and vegans. The motivation, besides profit, is the awareness that large-scale animal-meat production is detrimental to the environment.

Other industrialized societies were questioning the negative effects of the so-called modern lifestyle that kept people inside buildings working long hours sustained by poor-quality food. Essentially, the recommendation was: free yourself of sexual and cultural restrictions, eat fresh vegetables, and be one with nature by stripping off your clothes and frolicking out of doors. German doctors and health activists named it *Lebensreform*, or life reform. While there was no singular organizing belief for *Lebensreform,* most devotees believed in some form of "monoism," which is another version of the concept—as put forth by Jains, Pythagoras, Zoroaster, Swedenborg, and . . . you get the idea—that all life contains the same and singular life force or sacred energy. For *Lebensreformers*, living within and in balance to nature as an equal energy was the goal. *Lebensreform* writ large intended to reform laws and society based on science, as it was believed that science revealed the spiritual nature of everything. Writ small, *Lebensreform* was about transforming one's physical, mental, and spiritual self to become tuned in to the energy of the universe. As a movement it grew very popular, albeit decentralized, with localized groups focusing on one or two aspects of the back-to-nature lifestyle. Some advocated for vegetarianism. Others called for a rejection of modern work culture. Yet others embraced nudism as a return to basic and primitive connection with the Earth.

As science progressed throughout the early 1900s, *Lebensreformers* rejected vaccination and Western medicine for holistic medicines that embraced what can be considered quackish theories. Yet many people today, unfamiliar with the origins, embrace homeopathic medicines and plant extractions to cure disease, and *Lebensreformer* Rudolf Steiner's biodynamic agriculture methods. Earlier advocates of various *Lebensreform* ideals came to the United States to share their methods. Naturopath Albert Ehret began advocating for long-term fasting and adopting a mucus-free diet for better health in the 1930s. He published *Mucusless Diet Healing System* in 1924. The thoroughly debunked theory stated that white blood cells were the waste by-product of mucus, and caused illness. Ehret prescribed a combination of fasting and a diet that limited mucus production as ideal for optimum health. The Ehret diet is essentially fruitarian. He had legions of devotees to his diet and fasting programs in the United States.

Lebensreform as cultural movement was apolitical and secular, except when it wasn't. The National Socialists in Germany embraced many of the recommended lifestyle changes including vegetarianism. The children's political indoctrination groups of the *Hitlerjugend* for boys and *Bund Deutscher Madel* for girls, that taught healthy eating and an idealized, physically strong body type and conservative presentation, were a rejection of the urbane cosmopolitanism of Berlin and Vienna. The National Socialists used *Lebensreform* and American-style eugenics with the goal of perfecting German citizenry. German naturopath doctors enjoyed widespread acceptance in developing treatments that addressed the whole person. They used plant-based medicines, hydrotherapy, and diet as a pathway to optimum health. Their followers came to the United States to establish places where people could live to sustain a health-focused lifestyle. German-trained natural medicine doctors like Arnold Erhut came to the States and established practices that touted strict vegetarian diets, chiropractory, biodynamics, therapeutic baths, nudism, and even Ayurvedic concepts.

During the same era of the tubercular migration west and *Lebensreformers* in Germany, was another, smaller group of Germans moving to California: the Nature Boys. These were followers of the *Naturemenschen* movement—a part of the larger *Lebensreform* movement—that prescribed varying degrees of ascetic practices and living as close to nature as possible, and formed clubs and rural retreats where one could embrace a raw food and nudist lifestyle. But then the idyllic vacation ended, and one had to return to everyday life in an office or factory. The dream of many was to live where a person could truly become one with nature and live as a *Naturemensch* all the time. California became an idealized place in the minds of many Germans because of the writing of one man: Karl May.

May was a con man and fabulist who lived by his wits, cycling in and out of jail for decades before settling down to become a novelist in the late 1800s. From about 1875 to 1899, May wrote numerous books about the American West featuring a noble "Indian" named Winnetou. The stories were thrilling and steeped in what we now know as a romanticized version of "cowboys and Indians." Nonetheless, the German reading public[112] loved May's novels and the imagined Western Frontier he brought to life. As a result, the *Naturemenschen* left Germany with the idea of living like and among the "Indians" they idolized.

One of the earliest émigrés was William (Wilhelm) Pester, who came to the States in 1906 and traveled throughout the West until settling near Palm Springs, California, in 1916. He built a hut in the desert and lived off the land. He was called the Hermit of Palm Canyon, yet for a hermit he enjoyed a constant stream of visitors, who bought his carved walking sticks and listened to him lecture on the benefits of a raw food diet. Pester wasn't alone.

In 1881, German-American Theophilus Richter worked in a Chicago factory when he took a natural healing course based on Kellogg's system developed for the SDA, and began his journey to becoming one of the most influential proponents of vegetarianism and raw food. Richter continued his studies to become a certified naturopath doctor in 1900. He traveled throughout the Midwest, giving lectures and seeing patients. He moved with his second wife Vera to Los Angeles in 1918 and set up practice as John T. Richter. Within the year, he and Vera established what is arguably the first raw food restaurant in the United States.

Eutropheon (meaning "good nourishment" in Greek) served breakfast, lunch, and dinner, all featuring raw fruits, vegetables, and nuts. The Eutropheon became a second home to German naturopaths and *Naturemenschen*. The Richters sponsored and hosted lectures by visiting practitioners and saw themselves as evangelists for healthy living. Vera Richter published the very popular cookbook (well, anti-cooking recipe book, to be accurate) *Mrs. Richter's Cook-less Book* in 1925, which featured favorite recipes from the restaurant. Dr. Richter published his book *Nature the Healer* in 1936 to generally positive acclaim. In it, he proclaimed that humans could live to be 140 years old if only they followed a raw diet and abstained from coffee, sugar, salt, meat, dairy, alcohol, and tobacco, in addition to cooked and refrigerated foods. Their books brought more attention to Eutropheon as they connected with other vegetarians from the Buddhist and Yoga communities, as well as Adventist and

---

112   Karl May's popularity cannot be overestimated. His books remain in print with over two billion copies in circulation as of this writing.

Advertisement for Vera Richter's Eutropheon Restaurant, c. 1920s.

other health-focused food faddists and bodybuilders.

The Richters hired young men to work at the restaurant. This crew of next-generation health food enthusiast *Naturemenschen* came to be known as the Nature Boys. Among them was the songwriter and sometime mystic eden ahbez, who sold his tune "Nature Boy" to Nat "King" Cole. And Robert "Gypsy Boots" Bootzin, raised as a Jewish vegetarian, fully embraced the natural lifestyle of living off the land after his older brother's death from tuberculosis. Boots founded one of the first health food grocery stores in the States in 1958; Health Hut was a favorite of Hollywood stars and organic food enthusiasts. Boots was a natural showman and became a Los Angeles celebrity appearing on *The Steve Allen Show* in his manic evangelist style, showing viewers the power of healthy living. Boots was the most famous of the Nature Boys, but Jim Baker was the most notorious.

James Baker was born in Ohio and moved to Los Angeles at the end of World War II as a decorated Marine looking for stunt work. He had met Paul Bragg of Bragg's Cider Vinegar fame as a teenager and embraced the organic, vegetarian, and mucusless diet Bragg advocated. Baker also met Jack LaLanne at the Veterans Hospital where LaLanne worked as a nutritionist when Baker was recovering from a lingering shrapnel wound. He hung out at the Richters' Eutropheon restaurant during its final years, where he connected with the Nature Boys and LaLanne bodybuilders. Baker also attended lectures on esoteric and Theosophist teachings at the Philosophical Research Society, all while doing (maybe) criminal odd jobs and (possibly) robbing banks.

Baker and his then-wife Elaine opened the Aware Inn organic restaurant in 1958 (the same year Boots Bootzin opened Health Hut). Elaine Baker was not immersed in California counterculture. She was more interested in running a business than exploring new ways of being. She divorced Jim Baker in 1963 after tiring of his extramarital affairs cloaked in spiritual discovery. Baker was arrested for manslaughter later in 1963 when he accidentally killed the husband of one of his girlfriends; he served three months in jail after pleading self-defense. Through all this, he kept the Aware Inn profitable and opened a second restaurant. After jail and the divorce, he indulged in a drug-fueled hedonistic binge through the dark side of Hollywood. He sought out Sikh Sant Mat yoga guru Yogi Bhajan[113] in 1969 when he decided to clean up and reclaim a healthy lifestyle.

---

113   More about Yogi Bhajan on page 228.

**Above: Source Family working at the Source Restaurant;
Below: The Source Restaurant, c. 1973. Courtesy of Isis Aquarian Archive.**

It was on a pilgrimage to India in 1971 with fellow 3HO devotees that Baker became disillusioned with Bhajan as a guru. Baker decided to start his own group. His Source Family quickly grew to 150 members by 1972. They ran his Aware Inn—renamed The Source—as a vegetarian restaurant popular with hippies and Hollywood alike. Following the model established by Father Divine and Daddy Grace, The Source restaurant used Family members for labor. The restaurant was frequented by locals interested in healthy cuisine, and because local was Hollywood, enjoyed the patronage of many actors. The Source restaurant became well-known outside of Los Angeles after it was featured in a prominent scene in Woody Allen's film *Annie Hall*. (Allen's character sits uncomfortably and orders "alfalfa sprouts and mashed yeast.") The Source restaurant was sold to new (non-cult) operators in 1974 and remained open for a few more years before permanently closing in 1980.

Holy Food

Aside from his experience in the restaurant industry, Baker gleaned the best practices of Yogi Bhajan, the Nature Boys, and Western esotericism as taught by Manly Hall at the Philosophical Research Center, and created a belief system that was both accessible and enjoyable for members. Baker claimed to have twelve wives in the group and indulged in a young man's fantasy life of having a rock 'n' roll band. As Baker transformed himself into Father Yod (then Ya-Ho-Wah), he combined all the spiritual and dietary influences brought to California throughout the years to its logical endpoint—a syncretic polycultural new religion based on all beliefs but with no specific religious tradition, and which only required that one be young, good-looking and willing to work for free in exchange for cool robes, a mansion in the Hollywood hills, and hanging out with God (Father Yod).

The Source Family, tired of Los Angeles, moved en masse to Hawaii in 1974. It was there that Jim Baker, at age fifty-three and always in good physical shape, on a whim and without any training, attempted hang-gliding. He crashed to the Earth and died of internal hemorrhaging on August 25, 1975. The Source Family has taken its place in the modern psyche as the quintessential American cult.

Yet the California Nature Boys weren't the only people spreading the good news of the Germanic natural health doctrine. Ann Wigmore brought a popular social and lifestyle movement to Boston when she opened her natural healing institute in 1961. She had immigrated from Lithuania as a young woman, married, and raised her family before embarking on her career as a healer and advocate of a vegan, raw food diet.

Ann Wigmore taught her version of *Lebensreform* to Bostonians interested in learning a new way of eating. She also took inspiration from Bible verses in her search for the most beneficial plants. Wigmore is considered one of the first health food advocates to recommend wheatgrass juice as a healing restorative. Her inspiration? The book of Daniel 4:33, which tells the story of King Nebuchadnezzar driven mad and taking to eating grass. *Lebensreformers* were proponents of the idea of "man as animal" and that humans should look to our mammalian cousins for clues to healing. In the case of wheatgrass, Wigmore noted that dogs eat grass to purge themselves when ill. Wigmore also recommended raw food as it contained more solar energy, and that cooking leached the nutritive value out of fruits and vegetables. By the early 1970s, as her institute grew more popular, she incorporated more "alternative" healing practices, including specialized foot baths, astrology, intravenous vitamin protocols, yoga, and spiritual healing. The Institute expanded to Florida, New Mexico, and Puerto Rico under the guidance of disciples in the late 1970s and early '80s.

The Institute attracted a high-profile supporter in the artist Peter Max, who contributed art to their 1979 cookbook *Light Eating for Survival*. The cookbook is interesting in that it features an introduction about following a "yogic diet" by Sri Swami Satchidanandaji Maharaj, who was the leader of LOTUS (Light of the Universal Shrine) whose ashram in Virginia is host to hundreds of visitors and long-term residents. The cookbook also recommends and provides a guide to eating foods that "vibrate" with different organ systems and emotions according to color. The group continued to incorporate different practices and beliefs throughout its many incarnations.

Wigmore's institute was legally a nonprofit church under the name of Rising Sun Christianity. Wigmore herself held dubious credentials of Doctor of Divinity from the College of Divine Metaphysics in Indianapolis. She also claimed doctoral degrees in naturopathy and philosophy. None of this was illegal until she and her disciples began advertising that their regimen could cure cancer, and later AIDS. (Wigmore declared that AIDS was a disease of a malfunctioning digestive system and that cancer toxins could be removed with chlorophyll from wheatgrass.)

The Institute-*cum*-church was cited in the 1980 Pepper Report, published by the United States Congress, as an example of medical quackery that preyed on desperate patients. Soon after, the group changed their name to the Hippocrates Institute and carried on. Wigmore died in 1994 of smoke inhalation caused by a small fire at the Boston location of her Institute. After Wigmore's death, the group split into the Hippocrates Health Institute in West Palm Beach, Florida, which hosts retreats at its luxury campus for intensive "Life Transformation" and weight loss programs. And the Ann Wigmore Natural Health Institute in Guayabo Aguada, Puerto Rico, that offers two-week certifications in becoming a "natural foods practitioner" (which includes learning how to make Rejuvelac). The groups have embraced the wellness trend and have abandoned Wigmore's version of Christian philosophy. Both groups lost their nonprofit status in 2012.

The Source Family acknowledges that many of the recipes served at the Source Family restaurant originated with Ann Wigmore, but there is another spiritually inspired cuisine that gained popularity in Boston and spread to California, and served as inspiration for the Source Family and other natural food restaurants: the macrobiotic diet. The diet is pescatarian (with many wholly vegan dishes) and has waxed and waned in popularity since its inception in the early 1930s, and enjoys periodic bursts of resurgence when celebrities mention following the restrictive and complex dietary plan. (Gwyneth Paltrow claims to follow a macrobiotic diet. So does Sting, who has written a macrobiotic cookbook.) Macrobiotics was begun by a sickly young man in Japan who desperately sought to cure himself from the ravages of tuberculosis. George Ohsawa was only a teenager when his mother and siblings died of tuberculosis; this traumatic event fueled his will to live. He felt that Western-style medicine and diet was the cause of their illness and his own. He sought out tutelage in *Shokuyō*, a method of natural healing and food-based medicine developed by Imperial Army doctor Sagen Ishizuka. Ishizuka was trained in Western medicine, but by his retirement in 1894 he was convinced that health came from within and could only be obtained through proper diet.

Shokuyō and Chinese medicine were banned in Japan in the early 1900s, but Ohsawa found a mentor and learned enough to control his tuberculosis. He soon left for Europe where he embarked on a writing career and refined his ideas about health and food. He noted that the seven markers of health were a lack of fatigue, having a good appetite, enjoying good sleep, having a good memory, having good humor, precise thought and action, and gratitude. He wrote in French and Japanese about his theories of balancing yin and yang energies for health. In the late 1920s he returned to Japan to begin an institute to teach his philosophy and methods. Ohsawa blended the food-as-medicine theories of his mentor Ishizuka with the teachings of Austrian naturopath physician (and Illuminati member) Christoph Hufeland, who titled his 1796

Aveline Kushi. Date and photographer unknown.

manifesto on health *Makrobiotik oder Die Kunst*. Ohsawa took the name "macrobiotics" for his syncretic blend of *Lebensreform, Shokuyō,* and Zen Buddhist-influenced cuisine.

Ohsawa felt that following his practice would lead practitioners to better physical, mental, and spiritual health, but that if enough people followed, they could positively affect the health of the world. Ohsawa lived in Japan during World War II and was disturbed by the violence of war and the world-ending possibilities of nuclear arms. He refined an ancient Japanese diagnostic technique used to assess fatigue, *sanpaku,* to diagnose the emptiness or weariness of world leaders, going as far as to predict their deaths. Some hailed him as a visionary. After World War II, Ohsawa traveled regularly to France where he met with European and American acolytes. In the United States, William Dufty, who credited his good health to a macrobiotic diet of brown rice, was given the mission to translate and publish Ohsawa's writings in English. This was achieved in 1965 by fellow macrobiotic adherent and Trotskyite publisher Felix Morrow, and the book *You Are All Sanpaku Now* introduced macrobiotic diet and philosophy to American readers.

But it was the married Japanese-American couple of Michio and Aveline Kushi who brought the macrobiotic diet to the United States in 1951. Aveline was a member of Ohsawa's group in Japan and came to the States to study at the University of Illinois and Columbia University where she met fellow Ohsawa follower, Michio. They married and moved to Boston in the early 1960s where Aveline opened the first health food store, Erewhon, in the city. Aveline taught classes in macrobiotic cooking at the store. She wrote and published cookbooks and became the most visible ambassador of Zen cookery, as it was called in the press after the name of Ohsawa's cookbook. Michio ran the business and expanded the Erewhon concept to Los Angeles. The Boston store eventually closed and the Kushis sold the business while continuing to espouse the philosophy of peace and health through macrobiotic cooking. If the name of the Kushis' store sounds familiar, it's because the Erewhon store in Los Angeles has become a fashionable center of celebrity sightings and favored social media influencer photo location.

ANN WIGMORE/ RISING SUN CHRISTIANITY

Years active: mid-1960s to present day
Affiliation: *Lebensreform* / Christianity
Founder / Leader: Ann Wigmore

REJUVELAC

(Vegan, raw, and slightly fermented. Makes 16 ounces.)

Notes from *Light Eating for Survival*: "Rejuvelac is a delicious enzyme-packed drink made from soaked grains. It contains vitamins B complex, K, E, lactic acid, and water-soluble minerals. It aids in digestion and acts as protection against harmful bacteria in the intestinal tract. Spring or distilled water is best to use for soaking. It allows the Rejuvelac to stay active up to two months if the seeds are of good quality. All soaking water from seeds (not beans) and dried fruit is good to drink."

Ingredients:

1 cup of grain (wheat is preferred but can also use rye, millet, oat, brown rice, barley, or buckwheat)

2 cups of pure, distilled water

Steps:

1. Find a warm place to ferment. The best temperature is between 60–80°F.
2. Always rinse your seeds first and use the best-quality organically grown seeds.
3. Use 1 cup of grain to 2 cups of water.
4. Soak seeds for 24 hours covered.
5. Drain and refrigerate soaked water (Rejuvelac) for drinking and for use in any food preparation that calls for water.
6. Add the same amount of water as before and repeat the process.

Note: If your Rejuvelac has an offensive odor or bad taste, pour off the water and start again. If it reoccurs, compost the seeds and start new ones. Good Rejuvelac has a pleasant odor and tastes somewhat lemonish and sour.

If this recipe seems slightly terrifying yet oddly familiar, then you're seeing that "Rejuvelac" is a variation of kvass. Kvass is a lightly fermented grain drink popular in Eastern Europe. In the Slavic variations, kvass adds a touch of sugar to boost the fermenting yeasts. Acceptable

Holy Food

sweeteners range from cane sugar to fruit or vegetable, or in very old recipes, kvass is made by putting stale rye bread in water and letting it ferment. Try it the Wigmore way, then try adding a few pieces of dried fruit.

Rejuvelac is, at its core, a lacto-fermented grain juice. There are some that claim it is unsafe to drink, but experienced fermenters will feel comfortable making this. Rejuvelac has enjoyed a resurgence in the recent decade as more people experiment with fermentation, and vegan cheese makers have found that Rejuvelac works very well as a substitute for rennet, an animal product used to make cheese.

DAYAS ASHRAM FRUIT SOUP

(Vegan and raw. Makes 4 servings.)
Tools: Blender

A recipe note from the *Light Eating for Survival* cookbook: "These are complete meals and eaten alone. Do not mix fruits and vegetables if possible."

Ingredients:
2 cups chopped apples
2 cups sliced bananas
1 cup reconstituted raisins (soaked in purified water to plump up, about 1 hour)
½ cup ground sesame seeds
½ cup ground sunflower seeds
1 Tablespoon lemon juice
1 cup apple juice
Dash of ground nutmeg and cinnamon
Steps:
1. Wash and peel fruit. Chop as needed.
2. Place all ingredients in blender. Blend until smooth.
3. Serve chilled in soup bowl.

PEA CROQUETTES

(Vegan and raw. Makes approximately 12 croquettes.)
Tools: Food mill or food processor

Ingredients:
2 cups fresh peas
½ cup diced celery
½ cup grated carrots

½ cup finely chopped buckwheat greens (can substitute with other hearty sprouted greens)

½ cup sunflower cheese (can substitute with your preferred brand of vegan "cream cheese")

1 teaspoon paprika for garnish

Steps:

1. Wash all vegetables. Shell peas if needed. Dice and grate carrots and put into medium-sized bowl.
2. Using a food mill or food processor, grind peas, celery, and carrots together. Put mixture back into bowl.
3. Add the chopped greens and "cheese" to mixture.
4. Take approximately 1 heaping tablespoon of the mixture and roll into a ball. Place on serving dish. Sprinkle with paprika.

Front cover of 1978 edition of *Light Eating for Survival*. Art by Peter Max. Author's collection.

OHSAWA (MACROBIOTICS)

Years active: 1931 to present day
Founded in: Paris, brought to Boston in 1949
Affiliation: Zen Buddhist/*Lebensreform*
Founder: George Ohsawa
Leaders: Michio and Aveline Kushi in the United States

SHRIMP VEGETABLE PIE

(Pescatarian. Vegan if you omit the shrimp. Makes 1 pie.)
Tools: 9-inch pie plate, rolling pin, medium sauté pan
Oven temperature: 450°F

Pie Dough Ingredients:

1 cup whole-wheat flour

3 teaspoons vegetable oil

½ teaspoon salt

1 Tablespoon cold water

Steps:

1. Mix dry ingredients in a medium-sized bowl.

2. Add oil and blend well.

3. Add the water and form dough ball.

4. On a lightly floured surface, roll dough out to ¼- to ½-inch thickness. Place on pie plate and place in refrigerator until needed.

Filling Ingredients:

1 onion (sliced on the diagonal into small pieces)

1 small carrot (cut in half lengthwise and then sliced)

3 green cabbage leaves (cut into half-inch squares)

½ turnip (cut in half then sliced thinly)

2" Japanese (daikon) radish (cut in half, sliced thinly)

2 teaspoons vegetable oil

12 small shrimp (optional)

1 cup water

½ teaspoon salt

Steps:

1. Preheat oven to 450°F.

2. Sauté prepared vegetables in oil until lightly browned.

3. Add water and fish to sauté pan and bring to boil. Simmer until tender. Add salt.

4. Set aside and make béchamel sauce.

Béchamel sauce Ingredients:

1 cup whole-wheat flour

½ cup vegetable oil

3 cups vegetable stock or water

Salt (1 to 2 teaspoons)

Steps:

1. Heat oil slightly. Add the flour gently and toast, stirring constantly. Toast until brown but not burned, about 15–20 minutes. It will have a nut-like fragrance.

2. Add stock or water and boil for 20 minutes, stirring occasionally. Salt to taste.

3. Reduce heat to simmer until ready to use.

Assemble the pie:

1. Remove prepared crust from refrigerator.

2. Place vegetables and shrimp in crust and pour the béchamel sauce to cover the ingredients.

3. Place in oven and bake for approximately 20 minutes, until crust is browned. May take 5 to 10 minutes longer, depending on oven.

4. Remove from oven and serve.

Tasting Notes: Testers tried both the shrimp and a vegetable-only version and recommend using vegetable stock in the béchamel. Unlike familiar "pot pies," the crust does not harden. Tasters felt the flavor was unexpected and interesting.

CHOU FARCI

(Vegetarian. Makes 4 servings.)

Tools: Heavy, enameled cast-iron casserole dish

Oven temperature: 375°F

Ingredients:

8 green cabbage leaves carefully pulled from the head, so they stay whole

2 eggs

1 cup buckwheat groats

2 cups water

½ teaspoon salt

2 Tablespoons vegetable oil

Steps:

1. Preheat oven to 375°F.

2. In a medium-sized bowl, mix buckwheat with water and salt. Set aside.

3. In a smaller bowl, add and beat the eggs.

4. In a heavy iron casserole dish, add the vegetable oil and spread until pot is completely coated. Lay a leaf of cabbage on the bottom, pour a layer of buckwheat mixture over this, and then a layer of egg and top it off with another cabbage leaf. Alternate in this manner making sure to have a cabbage leaf on top when finished.

5. Cover and bake in a moderate oven for 1½ hours.

6. Remove from the pan by inverting over a platter. Cut at the table while still hot. Or you can serve directly out of the casserole. Serve with tamari soy sauce.

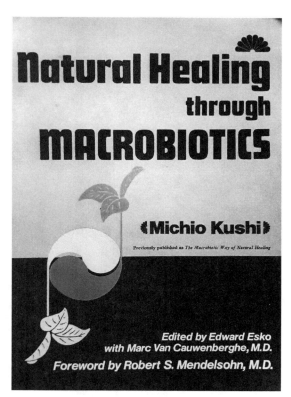

Front cover of 1978 edition of *Natural Healing Through Macrobiotics*. Author's collection.

PAUL BRAGG'S HEALTH CENTER OF LOS ANGELES

Years active: 1921
Affiliation: *Lebensreform*
Founder: Paul Bragg

CORN AND TOMATO CASSEROLE

From Paul Bragg's *Cure Yourself* (1929)

(Vegetarian. Serves 6.)

Tools: Casserole dish

Oven temperature: 350°F

Ingredients:

2 cups corn (frozen or canned; if fresh, cook corn prior to using)

2 cups tomatoes, chopped (fresh or canned)

1 cup whole-wheat breadcrumbs

2 Tablespoons butter

Steps:

1. Preheat oven to 350°F.

2. Pour corn into casserole dish. Add tomatoes on top of corn.

3. Cover with breadcrumbs. Cut butter into small pieces and place on breadcrumbs.

4. Put into oven and cook for 20 to 30 minutes.

5. Remove from oven and serve.

THE SOURCE FAMILY

Years active: 1971 to 1975

Affiliation: Yoga/Sikhism/New Age

Founder / Leader: Father Yod (Jim Baker, Ya-Ho-Wa)

According to Source Family archivist and one of Father Yod's wives, Isis Aquarian, "Foods were 'consciously prepared for the highest vibration,' and served by hip young women and men with long hair who radiated health and serenity. Jim [Baker] transformed the fireplace in the dining room into a waterfall, and he would light candles over it. The melted wax made colorful, psychedelic designs on the mantle. The Moody Blues, Jethro Tull, or Zen meditation music played in the background."

MUSHROOM BARLEY SOUP

(Vegetarian. Makes 12 servings.)

Tools: Sauté pan, stockpot

Ingredients:

2 cups barley

1 onion, diced

½ cup celery, diced

2 pounds sliced fresh mushrooms

1 Tablespoon butter

2 Tablespoons olive oil

3 cloves crushed garlic

½ cup sour cream

Salt and pepper to taste

12 cups of water (3 quarts)

Page from Source Family Restaurant menu. Courtesy of Isis Aquarian Archive.

Steps:

1. Clean and prepare onion, celery, and mushrooms. Crush garlic.
2. Add olive oil to sauté pan and warm over medium heat. Lightly sauté celery, onion, and mushrooms.
3. Add butter and garlic and continue to sauté.
4. Place stockpot over medium heat. Add sautéed items, barley, and water. Cook until barley is soft (approximately 1 hour).
5. Remove from heat. Add sour cream and gently stir until thoroughly blended.
6. Serve.

SOURCE FAMILY VINAIGRETTE DRESSING & AWARE INN SALAD

(Vegan. Makes 4 servings.)
Tools: Large and small bowls

Vinaigrette Ingredients:

¼ cup + 2 Tablespoons extra virgin olive oil

2 Tablespoons water

½ teaspoon dry mustard powder

1 teaspoon prepared Dijon-style mustard

3 Tablespoons fresh lemon juice

¾ teaspoon lemon-pepper seasoning*

1 Tablespoon white wine vinegar

⅛ teaspoon garlic powder

⅛ teaspoon onion powder

¼ teaspoon dried Italian herbs

¼ teaspoon salt

¼ teaspoon ground black pepper

*Penzey's Spices brand of Lemon Pepper blend is recommended.

Steps:

1. In a small bowl, add all ingredients EXCEPT olive oil.

2. Whisk together until blended.

3. Add the olive oil. Slowly whisk until oil emulsifies. Set aside and prepare salad.

Salad Ingredients:

1 head romaine lettuce (outer leaves removed), torn into bite-size pieces

1 cup finely grated carrots

1 cup finely grated beets

1 medium-sized cucumber, thinly sliced

2 ribs celery, finely chopped

1 cup finely shredded red cabbage

2 plum tomatoes, cut into quarters

1 ounce alfalfa sprouts

¼ cup raw sunflower seeds

¼ cup raw pine nuts

1 avocado, peeled and pitted, thinly sliced (sprinkle with lemon juice to prevent browning)

Assembling Salad:

1. In a large bowl, layer ingredients in the order they are listed, starting with the romaine lettuce.

2. Drizzle dressing over salad until gone.

Ten

HINDU... BUT MAKE IT AMERICAN

THE RICH COMPLEXITY OF HINDUISM CAN BE CHALLENGING TO UNDERSTAND IF one grew up in the United States isolated from believers. The American pop culture presentation of Hinduism (until very recently) relied on casual racism and terrible accents to convey exoticism. Again, only in the past few decades has American culture begun to shift its focus from a pastiche version of spiritual beliefs originating in Asia to something else. This fundamental lack of understanding of the religious philosophies from the Indian subcontinent set into motion successive waves of self-styled gurus who, like ravenous magpies, took elements of sacred teachings and secret revelations to build something new. Something American.

The word "guru" has slipped into American English to mean leader. Usually without any religious context. A popular exercise trainer is now a fitness guru. A modern-day cryptocurrency billionaire has become a financial guru. The word has passed into common usage and as with all things common, the meaning is lost in translation. In the Hindu and a few Buddhist traditions, the Sanskrit word *guru* is used as an honorific, a title given to a spiritual teacher recognized for the quality of their lessons and saintliness. It literally means "dispeller of darkness." A guru is a light-bringer.

To understand how millennia-old spiritual philosophy traditions morphed into hundreds of New Religious Movements, communes, ashrams and, yes, cults with numerous food prohibitions and rules, we take a closer look at how Hinduism and Sikhism came to America. Hinduism, like all religious beliefs, isn't monolithic. There are regional practices, sects, and of lesser importance on the Indian subcontinent but of significant influence in the United States, *Sant Mat* gurus. The Beatles may have introduced millions of Westerners to their first guru when their 1968 visit to Maharishi Mahesh Yogi generated global news reports, but *Sant Mat*—"teachings of the saints"—began in thirteenth-century India and came to the United States long before the Beatles did.

The Sant Mat movement elevated religious teachers revered for their devotion to a specific god or a specific spiritual practice—like meditation and yoga, or to qualities ennobled by a god. Sants lectured followers in their shared common language and not the religious language reserved for priests which most common people didn't understand. (The Sants were a few hundred years ahead of Luther in advocating for holy texts in local languages.) Though most Sants and sects share a common spiritual touchstone based on the Bhagavad Gita, there is a vast chasm between the individual personalities and teachings of the Sants. Regardless of their specific teachings, Sants were schismatic to traditional, caste-driven Hinduism because they rejected priest-led religious rituals and promoted the idea of a personal relationship with God(s).

A guru can be described as a profoundly wise and gifted teacher, but a guru is much more than our American notion of a teacher. A guru is someone who not only teaches but exemplifies the spiritual nature of the holy concepts

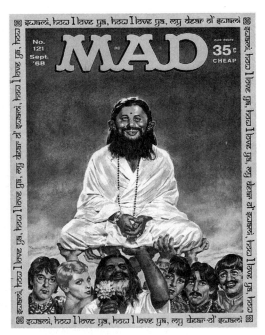

September 1968 cover of *Mad* Magazine featuring the Beatles and Maharishi. Courtesy of MadMagazine.com.

taught. The spiritual ideas and practices espoused by a guru and passed along to students follow in a tradition that is nearly nine hundred years old. A popular Sant Mat guru will establish an ashram, a school, or a communal living environment to reach as many students as possible. Genealogies documenting the lineage of a guru, identifying the teacher with whom he studied, and with whom that guru studied, and so on is a vital element in establishing the credibility of a guru. This lineage becomes a reliable catalog of influences and an imprimatur of approval that whatever the guru says and does is aligned with the philosophies and personal character of those who taught him and the teachings of that tradition.

The guru concept is also found in Jainism and Sikhism.[114] Jainism is an ancient religion practiced in India before the Aryan invasion and the development of Hinduism, and may be linked to earlier, indigenous belief systems. There is no deity in Jainism. For ordinary people, the practice focuses on living the four tenets of belief: nonviolence, well-roundedness, non-attachment to the world, and abstinence from pleasure. Jains also have the option to join a monastery and follow an ascetic life as a monk. Jains are always vegetarian as they view killing animals for food as an egregious violation of their code of nonviolence. *Ahimsa*, the word embodying sacred nonviolence, appears in many of the Jain, Hindu, and Hindu-inspired religious movements. Jains also abstain from eating root vegetables as consuming such items would kill the plant, a much greater violation of *ahimsa* than picking a fruit or seed pod.

Sikhism grew out of Sant Mat tradition to become an entirely new religion. Sikhs revere Guru Nanak (1469–1539) as the revealer of a transcendent God without form or gender. In Sikhism,

114 Gurus are also loosely associated with some Buddhist sects, especially within Vajrayana (tantric) Buddhism.

Mandeep Ahuja (left) and Jasbir Dulai (center) make roti for the *langar* at the Oak Creek, Wisconsin, temple. The Sikh Temple was the target of a racist attack by a neo-Nazi in August of 2012 that killed seven and wounded four people. Photo by Gary Porter for the *Milwaukee Journal*.

followers strive to balance spiritual development with a lived moral good in their daily life. Most of the world's Sikh population lives in the Punjab region of Northern India, with thriving communities in Great Britain, Canada, and the United States. In contrast to Jains and many Hindus, Sikhs eat meat. Though meat cannot be served in the Gurdwara (temple), religious leaders leave it up to individuals to make a personal choice. "Fools wrangle over flesh" is how a Sikh guru in the early 1900s put it. Sikhs are forbidden from eating meat that has been ritually killed, i.e., avoiding Muslim halal and Jewish kosher meats. There are just as many Sikh vegetarians as there are Sikh carnivores. The issue of carnivore vs. vegetarian informed by holy tradition is unresolved. The Sikhs believe in communal dinners to share their bounty and good will. It is considered a blessing to offer food to strangers and people in need. In the United States, Gurdwaras serve *langer*, a free vegetarian meal, to all who wish to eat on Sunday afternoons.[115]

The Indian subcontinent had suffered with small European trading outposts run by the British, Portuguese, and Dutch since the early 1500s. But in 1757 the British East India Trading Company, de facto, occupied the entire region. The Company turned its governing charter over to the British government in 1858, but religious practices and food influenced by the colonizers and traders remained. To this day, there are Zoroastrian enclaves in Goa and a robust and fully integrated Jewish-Indian population founded by shipwrecked merchants in Maharashtra and Konkan. And the third largest religion in India is Christianity.

115 On Sunday, August 5, 2012, a white supremacist opened fire on the Oak Creek, Wisconsin, Gurdwara as they opened the doors to visitors for *langer*. The murderer assumed the Sikh temple was a mosque. Seven people were killed. The Oak Creek Sikh community, after a period of mourning and increased security, still offers *langer* on Sunday afternoons.

Christianity had been brought to the Indian subcontinent in the earliest days; legend has it that St. Thomas preached in Kerala in 50 CE. But it was the hundred-plus years of British occupation of India during the nineteeth century that brought Anglican-style Protestantism to people, often by force. Christian converts were given preferential treatment and jobs. Young Indian men from the middle and upper classes were educated in schools sponsored and run by the English. Students were mandated to learn the English language and the Christian Bible. Thus, the Indian religious leaders and monks who became the first gurus to visit America were well versed in Christian parables and the tenets of Church of England Protestantism.

But we must talk about yoga before we get to our American gurus. Yoga is one of the six schools of Hindu religious philosophy and began around 1000 BCE, but it is the practice that has made the most inroads into American culture. Yoga emphasizes a physical relationship between the body and spirit. Yoga then developed different aspects that emphasize a particular teaching or philosophical study. The styles include *karma* yoga—the yoga of action; *bhakti* yoga—the yoga of devotion; *jnana* yoga—the yoga of knowledge; and *ashtanga* yoga—the teaching of all paths. *Hatha* and *kundalini* yoga are considered "modern." Hatha was first noted in the eleventh century, and kundalini was developed in the ninth century and focused on the "feminine energy" and was later adopted into *Hatha* yoga practices. Neither hatha nor kundalini yoga are considered part of the spiritual-based philosophies, though the postures have been widely adopted by other spiritually-minded yoga gurus and practitioners—especially in the United States, where the hatha yoga *asanas* (postures) are what most Americans associate with yoga.

Yet the mainstream American view of the Indian gurus during the early 1900s was one of skepticism. Aside from genuine seekers and members of the avant-garde, main-street Christian U.S.A. held fast to the belief that their way of life was under siege by agents of the devil. There had, of course, been earlier, white American-born teachers who, absent of guru lineage, taught yoga poses devoid of the spiritual practice. One of the most notorious was Pierre Bernard ("The Great Oom" or "Oom the Omnipotent"), who traveled the country during the 1890s as part showman, part Pied Piper, combining hatha yoga with carny-geekdom as he would entrance himself and pierce his cheeks with long needles. Bernard was also interested in hypnotism and sex. He settled in Nyack, New York, where he marketed yoga as a metaphysical practice that would improve one's sex life. Bernard is the man who forever linked tantric yoga with sex in American minds. He was later accused of using his power to corrupt young women who claimed to be unable to stop his yogic-hypnotic seduction. In many ways, Bernard created the template used by "yoga gurus" to attract and exploit followers.

It is from the Sant Mat tradition of lineages and schools that Hindu guru Yogendra brought modern, asana-based yoga to the United States in 1919. His school, The Yoga Institute in Harriman, New York, began teaching American enthusiasts asanas that were praised by the German-influenced back-to-nature and physical health fans. Yogendra met with German-American naturopath doctor and fasting advocate Benedict Lust and Adventist doctor and food pioneer W.H. Kellogg. Both doctors found Yogendra's hatha yoga accessible because it was decoupled from the rigorous monastic asceticism associated with yoga in Hindu culture. Two other influential Indian gurus who were catalysts for changing American food

Paramahansa Yogananda purchased the Mount Washington Hotel in 1925 for his new center. Courtesy of the Self-Realization Fellowship.

and health culture were the Ayurvedic doctor and scholar Krishnamacharya and the teacher Paramahansa Yogananda.

Yogananda was the first Indian-born guru to fully immigrate to the United States in 1920. He founded the Self-Realization Fellowship in Los Angeles to bring *Kriya* yoga spiritual practice to Americans as a balance to Western materialism. In the Kriya tradition, a combination of meditation and poses allows practitioners to energize their blood and transmute their cells into pure energy. The advanced student, it is thought, can heal diseases, materialize and dematerialize their body at will, and at the highest level, join their energy with God. The Kriya lineage of gurus is unique in that from their founding in 1861 by Babaji,[116] they inclusively adopted the prophets and messiahs of other religions as divine beings equally holy and viable as the Hindu pantheon. This integrated approach allowed many Americans to accept and embrace the yoga practice as another way to pray without abandoning or contradicting their familiar belief systems. While yogic practices were, and still are, denounced in fundamentalist religions in the United States, Indian gurus like Yogananda saw no conflict with Christians, Jews, or Muslims studying yoga.

No one was surprised that Norman Paulsen had an interest in spiritual matters. His father, Charles Paulsen, a respected lawyer and judge in Lompoc, California, was one of eleven white ordained ministers in Shin Buddhist temples during the late 1930s. His son Norman was familiar with the Shin Buddhism of his father but felt the call to seek further. He left the family home at age eighteen in 1947 to pursue his spiritual quest when he became acquainted with the writing of Yogananda. Norman Paulsen moved to Los Angeles and became one of Yogananda's devoted students.

He spent four years at the Los Angeles monastery then left in 1951, motivated by a vision that there were more answers to be revealed by the universe. He worked as a bricklayer, and a telephone lineman while experiencing visions and at least one accidental drug overdose. But he had his epiphany while thirty feet above ground working on a telephone pole in Santa Barbara,

116 Many twentieth-century gurus claim lineage through Babaji.

California. As he lost a step and was about to fall, he thought of wanting to say farewell to his father before his imminent death. But then he realized that he could communicate with his father through the spirit and thusly convey his love and respect and remain alive. Paulsen fell thirty feet and did not die.

Paulsen had been teaching meditation to interested people, but with the settlement payment from his fall from the telephone

The Sunburst Family Bakery stand, c. 1983. Courtesy of the Sunburst Family.

pole he was able to purchase his first mountain compound near Santa Barbara. Paulsen expanded on the Kriya philosophies to include pastiches of indigenous Hopi beliefs and an increasingly phantasmagorical UFO narrative. In 1971 Paulsen filed for nonprofit status as a church and built his new self-sustainable religious community and businesses. Sunburst Farms provided organic produce to the Lompoc area community through their health food stores. They expanded their offerings to include a bakery and then a restaurant. They formed satellite communes in Nevada and Arizona. Paulsen and the Sunburst Community seem to defy the odds and be a healthy and financially successful organization. In 1982 the façade slips: Paulsen is said to have spent $60,000 to $200,000 worth of farm profits on illegal drugs in a few years. A large weapons cache is found on the property. Those who left the group tell tales of Paulsen claiming to be Jesus of Nazareth.

Members began to question Paulsen's wife Patty about the disparity between his profligate spending and their unpaid twelve-hour workdays. Followers decamped over the next few years leaving Sunburst in a reduced state. Gone were the multiple farms, restaurants, and grocery stores. The community was able to sustain itself in a smaller incarnation and slowly retreated from public activities until the last grocery store in Solvang, California, closed. Norman Paulsen's death in 2008 brought new changes as Patty Paulsen took on the role of spiritual and operational leader of Sunburst. Today, the group has approximately forty residents living on the Lompoc property. They have transformed the original commune into a yogic retreat, spiritual healing and meditation center while continuing to expand their organic farming operations.

K RISHNAMACHARYA NEVER SET FOOT IN THE UNITED STATES, BUT HIS STUDENTS who later became gurus, and *their* students who proclaimed themselves gurus, created the robust network of Sant Mat in America. This lineage is important to trace. From Krishnamacharya comes his student B.K.S. Iyengar, who went further than Yogendra and completely separated the physical practice of the yoga postures from his guru lineage of Visistadvaita Hinduism and developed an entirely secular yoga practice. (In contrast to Yogananda, who took the asanas out of the monastery and invited all the gods.) Another Krishnamacharya student, Indra Devi (born Eugenie Peterson, a Russian-Swedish aristocrat), began teaching yoga at her Los Angeles studio in 1948. Devi met natural health advocate and apple cider vinegar mogul Paul Bragg—who came to Los Angeles in 1921 as part of the *Lebensreform* movement—and became a vocal proponent for eating organic foods. Devi had spent time at the Theosophist compound in Chennai, India, when Annie Besant and Charles Leadbeater were extolling Krishnamurti[117] as the Maitreya, and was familiar with many of the New Thought ideas that were coalescing to become described as New Age.

Los Angeles had long been the home of newer religious movements. Manly Palmer Hall headed up the Philosophical Research Center, documenting and disseminating research on esoterica from Western and Eastern traditions. Buddhist missionaries set up temples to serve Japanese immigrants and their families while also welcoming curious non-Japanese learners. But it wasn't just Eastern religions that captured the imagination of Californians. Southern California was awash in preachers, gurus, masters, and teachers keen on sharing their revelations about, well, everything.

When seventy-year-old A.C. Bhaktivedanta Swami Prabhupada arrived in New York City in 1965 from his Kolkata monastery, he embraced a different pathway to teaching. Instead of ecumenical outreach or courting wealthy seekers Los Angeles-style, he went to the places where the hippies hung out. Prabhupada brought a message that he called Krishna Consciousness that was the animating force of a five-hundred-year-old Hindu sect, Vaishnava. In the Vaishnava tradition, followers direct their worship to Krishna (avatar of Vishnu) as he (for them) represents the Supreme God. Prabhupada also taught *bhakti* philosophy, which is an all-encompassing concept of worship that had seven elements: 1. Listening to stories about Krishna and his companions. 2. Praising, in the form of group singing. 3. Fixing all thoughts on Vishnu. 4. Rendering service to others. 5. Servitude. 6. Friendship to all others. 7. Surrender of the self. Specific to Vaishnava and Krishna Consciousness is the practice of *kirtan* as a form of praise, which is the repetitive chanting of prayers and holy words called mantras.

Prabhupada formed the International Society for Krishna Consciousness (ISKCON) in 1966, not long after renting a run-down storefront on 2nd Avenue in the crime-ridden Bowery neighborhood. Allen Ginsberg, who had been exploring Eastern religions, heard about the geriatric Indian holy man and sought him out. Ginsberg and Prabhupada led a *kirtan* of the *Krsna* mantra in Tompkins Square Park, drawing a large crowd . . . and the *New York Times*. Newspaper coverage generated more interest in Prabhupada from young hippies and intellectual academics experimenting with new ways of being human. During the early years, both *sannyasins* (student monks) and critics referred to the group as the Hare Krishnas.[118] Prabhupada set up communal living spaces with kitchens in San Francisco, New York, and throughout the States. According to the tenets, cooking and feeding people helped fulfill the *bhakti* of serving others and offering friendship. For ISKCON believers, no job was too menial for anyone to perform regardless of their rank or level of spiritual attainment.

---

117 Jiddu Krishnamurti was a philosopher, speaker, and writer. In his early life, he was groomed to be the new Maitreya, but later rejected this mantle and withdrew from the Theosophy organization behind it. His interests included psychological revolution, the nature of mind, meditation, inquiry, human relationships, and bringing about radical change in society. He stressed the need for a revolution in the psyche of every human being and emphasized that such revolution cannot be brought about by any external entity, be it religious, political, or social.

118 The Hare Krishna name came from the mantra chanted by followers: *Hare Kṛṣṇa Hare Kṛṣṇa/Kṛṣṇa Kṛṣṇa Hare Hare/ Hare Rāma Hare Rāma/Rāma Rāma Hare Hare.*

Prabhupada shares a meal prepared in accordance with the rules of Hare Krishna prasadam. Photographer Roger Siegel (Guru Das), 1968

ISKCON followers are vegetarian. They believe in the concept of *ahimsa* (nonviolence) common to Hindu, Sikh, Jainist, and Buddhist traditions. They also embrace *prasadam,* which is the practice of offering all food to Krishna before eating. Yet, the concept is more profound than an obligatory ritual; it transforms and sanctifies the food. Foods are prepared in silence, and the cooks focus their energy and intention on Krishna as they work. The cooks should hold in their hearts and minds a devout intention to make the food worthy of Krishna. The food is then served to Krishna, who accepts the offering and bestows his blessing upon the food, allowing everyone else to eat. Food is a gift from Krishna.

Food is central to Hare Krishna life. Prabhupada built into the structure of ISKCON a charitable arm that distributes food to people after natural and man-made disasters. Krishnas provided food in Chechnya during the 1990s war and in New Orleans after Hurricane Katrina, to cite a few examples. He also instructed temples and ashrams to open restaurants that served ISKCON favorite dishes. The group published cookbooks highlighting recipes served at Govinda's Restaurant locations worldwide that included shortened lessons on *prasadam* and written teachings from Prabhupada. (True *prasadam* meals never include onions and garlic as they are considered offensive to Krishna because of their Ayurvedic values of causing sexual excitation and slowing the mind.) To this day, ISKCON is affiliated with most restaurants named Govinda's throughout the States, and OmNom in London. ISKCON also encouraged devotees to open their own restaurants inspired by Prabhupada and following *prasadam* practices. Kitchen of Krishna was a vegetarian restaurant in Charlottesville, Virginia, run by devotees who lived in a rural commune and spawned their own cult-like following due to their 1975 cookbook *Vegetarian Gothic* written by the restaurant's cook, Mo Willett. Even today, two trendy New York City restaurants are run by Krishna chefs, Doughnut Plant and Divya's Kitchen.

The first ISKCON ashram was established in New Vrindaban, West Virginia, in 1968. More ashrams, both urban and rural, soon followed. At the group's peak, the group claimed to have over a million members, most living in India. But something about the Hare Krishnas fired the American imagination. Yes, the Krishnas became a conspicuous presence in public spaces with their orange draped robes and dhoti, cheerfully offering anyone who crossed their path a copy of the Bhagavad Gita and an invitation to a meal. But in the late 1970s, especially after the events in Jonestown, antagonism toward the Krishnas reached a fever pitch. There were news stories that ISKCON was a cult luring young and susceptible teenagers away from their families. A landmark lawsuit was filed against ISKCON in 1976 by a family who accused the group of brainwashing their daughter. ISKCON won the suit, which established that the group was a legitimate religion entitled to all the protections afforded under the First Amendment.

After Prabhupada died in 1977, ISKCON experienced decades of internal conflicts and scandals. A swami at the West Virginia ashram was removed and later stood trial for fraud and racketeering. ISKCON faced claims of rampant child abuse at their schools in India and the United States in the early nineties. Today, devotees attend temples near their homes and live and work like most other Americans. Gone are the striking orange robes. Today, the American ISKCON temples are filled with worshippers with a cultural connection to India, and rarely does one find a young, white, middle-class teenager chanting on a street corner.

A lesser-known contemporary of Prabhupada was Amrit Desai, who came to Philadelphia in 1960 as an art student and taught yoga on the side. His inspiration was his teacher, Kripalvanda, who developed a form of kinder, gentler hatha-kundalini hybrid yoga that Desai named Kripalu after his teacher. Desai developed a following and purchased small compounds in Pennsylvania and Massachusetts to house his ashram. Desai lived in the United States, but frequently traveled to India to continue the work of his now-global group, Kripalu Yoga Fellowship. At its zenith in the early '80s, the group had 350 residents living at its main retreat center, a former Jesuit monastery in Stockbridge, Massachusetts.

The food served to retreat and seminar attendees reflects the early days when the community followed Hindu food rules and reflected Desai's personal tastes. The group published *Kripalu Kitchen: A Natural Foods Cookbook and Nutritional Guide* in 1980. The book is filled with mostly vegan recipes favored for their cleansing and nutritive qualities. The recipes also reflect Ayurvedic medical philosophies that prescribe and prohibit types of foods based on a person's Ayurvedic profile. These profiles are based on the energy pattern or *dosha*, of which there are three. *Pitta, Vata*, and *Kapha* are the three doshas and each person has all three, but one is more naturally dominant.[119] Ayurvedic eating recommends foods that complement and balance the three energies, resulting in a physically healthier and spiritually stronger person. *The Kripalu Cookbook* has been revised and updated throughout the years with the most current edition published in 2019.

---

119 How to discover your *dosha* type? A simple primer: People with a dominant *vata* dosha are considered creative, active, and bright; they walk, talk, and think fast, but get tired easily. *Vatas* are usually thin with a light frame and suffer from gastro-intestinal problems like constipation and bloating. *Pittas* are intelligent but can be short-tempered. They usually have a medium build and have a healthy appetite, a strong metabolism, and good digestion. *Kaphas* are known for strength, stamina, and sharp intelligence. They are also usually very sweet and grounded. *Kaphas* are often larger-framed and muscular, and they have a slow metabolism.

While the beliefs espoused by Desai are traditionally Hindu and The Fellowship was incorporated as a religious organization in the United States, the group had a relatively small reach. In 1994 it was fully revealed that Desai had numerous sexual relationships with women living at the Center throughout the decades. He was summarily fired. In 1999, the American Yoga Fellowship changed its nonprofit status from religious organization to a secular nonprofit. The Kripalu Center today hosts over 25,000 visitors per year who come to experience yoga, post-trauma therapy, weight loss, meditation, and other wellness retreats. The new Kripalu Center—absent of its guru—has standardized its yoga practice and offers teacher training and licensure for a nominal fee. The Center employs over six hundred community members, and reported revenue in 2019 of $42,476,051.00.

ANT MAT GURUS IN THE UNITED STATES CAME FROM A VARIETY OF INDIAN RELIGIOUS philosophies. Bhagwan Rajneesh was not born a god. Nor was he Rajneesh. Chandra Mohan Jain was born into a large Jainist family in 1931. He was raised by his maternal grandparents, who doted upon him and, many biographers note, gave him free rein. He was intelligent and a prodigious debater. He bucked against all authority, rejected traditional Jainism, advocated for pure capitalism, and rejected sexual norms. He was interested in esoteric practices and explored yoga, breathing meditations, fasting, and hypnosis. He claimed to have attained enlightenment at the age of twenty-one while sitting under a tree.[120] He was precocious.

He began teaching philosophy at Jabalpur University in 1958. He was a popular lecturer who contravened popular beliefs, calling Gandhi a "worshipper of poverty," and called for the liberalization of laws surrounding sex and, indeed, for a loosening of repressive sexual mores in general. By 1962 he was traveling India, giving lectures, and leading meditation retreats. He resigned from teaching in 1966 to lecture full-time. He railed against conservative orthodoxies in Hinduism and Jainism. At a large gathering of religious leaders in 1969, he scandalized the assembled holy men by declaring, "Any religion which considers life meaningless and full of misery and teaches the hatred of life, is not a true religion. Religion is an art that shows how to enjoy life."

In 1970 Rajneesh accepted his first disciples, whom he called *neo-sannyasins*. He instructed followers in his new method of Dynamic Meditation that incorporated accelerated breathing rhythms joined with ecstatic dance. True to his 1970 denouncement, his new pathway was joyful. The group moved to Pune in western India, near Mumbai, to build their ashram and retreat center. At the Pune ashram, Rajneesh began welcoming more Western visitors and seekers. He also incorporated "Encounter" groups in the style of the Esalen Center as part of the Human Potential Movement.[121] During these years, Rajneeshies would act out aggressive scenes and sexually violent role-play that were supposed to help followers evolve. Instead, it

---

120 The Buddha also claimed to have attained enlightenment while sitting under a tree. If one is generous, then much can be said about the power of meditation among trees. If one is not as generous, then Rajneesh most likely cribbed his enlightenment story from the Buddha. Remember too that Joseph Smith incorporated elements of his spiritual mentor Finney's spiritual awakening in a wooded glade as part of his own story.

121 Esalen was founded in 1962 by two Stanford psychologists wanting to incorporate counterculture thinking into traditional psychological therapies. Esalen became the center of practices and beliefs that make up the New Age movement, from Eastern religions/philosophy, to alternative medicine and mind-body interventions, to Gestalt Practice. Esalen has faced controversies for using experimental techniques on the fragile psyches of paying attendees.

Bhagwan Rajneesh a.k.a. Osho, c. early 1980s. Unknown photographer.

resulted in rape and broken bones. In addition, there was open drug usage and drug smuggling; Rajneesh himself was not involved and claimed to be unaware.

He sent high-ranking *neo-sannyasins* around the world to establish outposts in American and European cities. Given Rajneesh's embrace of capitalism, the group also started restaurants, all named Zorba the Buddha—named for Rajneesh's claim to be a Buddha reincarnated and for his love of the movie *Zorba the Greek*, which he said embodied the joy one should feel in the face of all challenges. In later years, he used the name Zorba the Buddha.[122] The Zorba restaurants were vegetarian and offered dishes that reflected their geographic location, and traditional Indian dishes. The Rajneesh group published a cookbook in 1984 featuring favorite recipes from their global restaurants.

Rajneesh's move to the United States was precipitated by threats of crackdowns by the Indian government. A decade of free(ish) love, violent personal growth sessions, and drug smuggling, combined with Rajneesh's outspoken criticism of the Gandhi family and Indian-style socialism, had pushed the ruling politicians to the breaking point. Rajneesh left the Pune ashram in 1981. The American ashram, initially called "Rancho Rajneesh," was a 64,000-acre

---

122 Osho, *From Death to Deathlessness*, *Talk #3*: "My discos, my restaurants are called 'Zorba the Buddha.' First I am a Zorba, and then I am a Buddha. And remember, if I have to choose between the two, I will choose Zorba, not Buddha because the Zorba can always become the Buddha, but the Buddha becomes confined to his own holiness, he cannot go to the disco and become the Zorba. And to me, freedom is the highest value; there is nothing greater, more precious, than freedom."

tract of land purchased by a devotee in rural Jefferson County, Oregon, and donated to the Rajneesh nonprofit foundation. *Neo-sannyasins* spent the first months of 1981 building a town before welcoming the Bhagwan in August of the year. Much has been written about the battles between the Rajneeshies and the local population. For most outsiders, having 2,000 members of a religious commune decked out in orange robes paying adoration to a guru waving at them while riding in the back of one of his ninety-three Rolls-Royces was beyond their comprehension. After years of escalating strife, the federal government arrested Rajneesh on visa violations. A plea agreement barred Rajneesh from entering the States unless he had written permission of the Attorney General, but he did not serve any prison time.

Orient Occident Associates and "New Consciousness" presents

Yogi Bhajan, Master of Kundalini Yoga

Saturday, July 19th
3 to 6 p.m.
Ellison Hall
Room 1910
"Yoga -
A New Way of LIfe"

Yogi Bhajan comes from Vishwayatan Ashran in New Delhi.

"Breath is the tender charge of the divine through which God- realization can be achieved, through which the voltage of a person can be increased to make him bright and high."
Yogi Bhajan

Poster advertising yoga classes taught by Yogi Bhajan, Los Angeles, c. 1969.

Rajneesh moved back to the Pune ashram. There he denounced the United States and declared that many of the people close to him were seeking to destroy him, as evidenced by the failures in Oregon. He changed his name to Osho, declared himself free of all religion, and focused his final years on studying and teaching Zen philosophy and meditation. His highest-ranking assistant, Ma Sheela, was arrested for arranging the mass salmonella poisoning via restaurant salad bars in The Dalles, Oregon, in 1984. Rajneesh died on January 19, 1990, at age fifty-eight. There are a handful of Zorba the Buddha restaurants still in operation in India and Nepal.

Arguably the wealthiest American Sant Mat guru, Yogi Bhajan was born Harbhajan Singh Khalsa in Pakistan's Punjab region to a wealthy family. His father was Sikh, and his mother was Hindu. He was raised as a Sikh but attended Catholic schools. When the Partition of 1948 happened, his family fled south to New Delhi. He continued his formal education and took a job with the Indian tax and customs office. However, he was interested in spiritual matters and used his work-related travel to visit Sikh ashrams. He continued his yogic studies until he left his job and emigrated to Toronto to teach his version of Kundalini yoga. He developed a loyal following and in 1969 moved to Los Angeles, where the hippie movement and openness to spiritual teachers was well known. It was the beginning of the 3HO—Happy, Healthy, Holy Organization.

The Southern California free-thinkers and yoginis embraced the guru who told them to keep their hair and beards long. Yogi Bhajan, like Rajneesh, borrowed from a variety of Indian philosophies and incorporated New Age thought into his teachings, mixing Western astrology into the Sikh tradition, and proclaimed that founding guru and Sant, Guru Nanak, was the perfect guide for the Age of Aquarius.

Bhajan was an impressive speaker and earned acclaim in 1970 at the "Holy Man Jam" with fellow gurus and commune leaders, including The Farm's Stephen Gaskin. Weeks later, Bhajan led prayers for 200,000 attendees at an outdoor concert in Atlanta. As a former government worker, he understood the power of establishing relationships with politicians. He never hesitated to let elected officials know his stance on issues, insinuating that *his* position would be the position of his thousands of followers. Bhajan also embraced the interfaith movement in the United States, met with clerical leaders from different religions, and spoke at the United Nations.

Bhajan personified American religion-based entrepreneurial capitalism. The 3HO Foundation was (and still is) incorporated as a nonprofit entity. There are other groups related to and under the 3HO umbrella that are incorporated as churches. In the eyes of the American revenue collectors, a church does not have to report its income, spending, or holdings, while a nonprofit organization does. Bhajan and his family used—just as many religious organizations and churches do—the American corporate structure and complex tax codes to grow a vast network of companies, holding companies, and decentralized churches to build and retain wealth.

Bhajan began with yoga. According to an early follower, Bhajan's 1969 yoga classes were filled to capacity, but Bhajan wanted faithful adherents, not casual faddists.[123] He wanted to, in his words, separate the "yogis from the bogis." To achieve this, he mandated a three-day fast that required new students to eat three cloves of garlic three times a day while only drinking water. If you completed the garlic fast, you were allowed to take the yoga classes.[124] Bhajan began offering communal meals at his yoga studio. His teaching spread throughout the West via emissary teachers dispatched to large cities in the United States and Europe.

Sikhism is neutral on meat-eating, but Bhajan was a vegetarian and recommended his followers eschew meat as well. Contrary to the Hare Krishnas, Bhajan also embraced onions and garlic as cleansing foods for the digestive system. It is noted by early followers that Bhajan loved cooking and often would create meals from his imagination using whatever ingredients on hand. The first Golden Temple restaurants opened in Europe in 1972, then expanded to the United States with locations in Arizona, Virginia, and Los Angeles. A few years later in 1978, 3HO published their first cookbook, *The Golden Temple Cookbook*. In the introduction attributed to Bhajan, he says:

> *"The vegetarian diet alkalizes the blood, regulates circulation and preserves the elasticity of the arteries, besides making us less susceptible to diseases of the skin and joints and to congestion of the internal organs."*

(Nearly fifty years of science has proven Bhajan correct about the benefits of a vegetarian diet.)

---

123 Though there are no records of exactly who attended Bhajan's early Los Angeles yoga classes, it is known and confirmed by personal memoirs that members of the Hog Farm Commune and influential comedy collective The Committee attended classes. (The more notable members of The Committee include Rob Reiner, Howard Hesseman, David Ogden Stiers, and Peter Bonerz. The Committee also provided many of the actors in the Tom Laughlin counterculture hit movie *Billy Jack* in 1971.)

124 Groups that are considered cult-like often have high-control environments and purity tests to weed out casual interest and potential resistants.

Many groups would have been satisfied running a lucrative restaurant chain and publishing a successful cookbook, but Bhajan had bigger, American, dreams. He wanted an empire.[125] He started the Golden Temple Natural Foods Company, which operated health food stores and distributed health food products to other stores. He launched companies that manufactured 3HO-approved foods, including Sunshine Oils, Peace Cereal, Golden Temple Granola, Kettle Chips, Yogic Herbs, Nanak's Cookies, and their most famous product, Yogi Tea.[126]

3HO leadership and Bhajan were accused of exploiting followers by demanding what amounted to unpaid labor. Bhajan also required followers to sign over their assets to 3HO. The group had moved its headquarters to its New Mexico ashram in the early 1970s. He also began survivalist training with followers giving lectures on the coming apocalypse and yoga postures to heal from radiation poisoning. Yet his excesses remained hidden from the public as Bhajan continued his political activism and donated to Democratic and Republican candidates alike, but became close to then-Governor Bill Richardson. Critics accused Bhajan of using his political alliances to protect him from the worst financial and sexual abuse allegations. Like so many religious leaders in American history, Bhajan exploited the trust of his followers and sexually assaulted women and girls. The most egregious abuse occurred during his trademarked Kundalini brand of yoga teacher training. An independent investigation in 2020 concluded that the witness testimony and pattern of behavior were consistent with abuse. Women are still coming forward with stories of abuse at the hands of Bhajan.

Bhajan and his family set up trusts and other financial instruments to protect the sprawling business empire. Yet because the main oversight group, Sikh Dharma, is registered as a religious entity, the leadership council of 3HO was able to retain control of all the religious and business entities after Bhajan's death in 2004, effectively removing Bhajan's wife Inderjit Kaur Puri and their children from any future business dealings. In 2010, the board of directors sold Hearthside Food Solutions (maker of Peace and private-label cereals) for $71,000,000. Conflicts escalated between the board members and Bhajan's family about control and ownership of the companies. All came to a dénouement when Puri filed a lawsuit in Oregon (corporate home to Sikh Dharma and many of the related entities) accusing the Board of Directors of malfeasance. The case was dismissed in 2018, and Puri continues to appeal the decision. A review of 990 tax forms filed in the past five years shows a diversified and complicated web of churches, nonprofit groups, real estate trusts, and companies—some of the nonprofits fund related church activities, and vice versa. Yogi Tea is still owned by 3HO.

As a final comment on the 3HO organization, many Americans view Sikhism solely through the lens of 3HO and Bhajan's teachings. He met popes and presidents and fashioned himself the authority on Sikhism in the United States. But traditional Sikh organizations and leaders

---

125 My research on 3HO, Bhajan, and their companies does not find any documented references or knowledge of Seventh-Day Adventist-owned companies, but the SDA would have been a logical model for 3HO to follow.

126 3HO also started a private security company named Akal born from Bhajan's need for bodyguards. This business grew to be the largest provider of private security for United States federal courthouses. They also have worked with the federal Immigration and Customs Enforcement to provide security at immigrant detention centers. When Akal began it was wholly staffed by 3HO members. After September 11, 2001, the company expanded and opened employment to people outside the group. Akal Security had 15,000 employees when it closed in February of 2021. This closure is thought to be part of the general restructuring of the larger Siri Singh Sahib Corporation, the holding company for the non-church companies owned by 3HO.

Holy Food

dismissed Bhajan's beliefs and the 3HO as heretical. Which version of Sikhism will prevail in the United States? Unknown. Through his teaching, yoga training schools, and food businesses, Bhajan attracted two generations of white Americans to grow out their hair and become initiated as Khalsa—members of the greater Sikh community. Yet as the traditional Sikh community grows in the United States and Americans learn more about their beliefs, Bhajan's version of Sikhism is fading. The 3HO group is still wealthy, and the next few years will show if they can shed the cult accusations and, as Bhajan said, "Love the teachings, not the teacher."

The arrest and deportation of Bhagwan Rajneesh in November of 1985 signaled the end of American cultural tolerance for large-scale religious communes. Years of reported excess coupled with increasingly hysterical pop culture movies, television, and books about the dangers of cults had done its work. Yet, the long-lasting impact gurus had on American culture cannot be overstated. Yoga is everywhere. And Indian-inspired and influenced cuisine continues to become more American with each passing year.

SUNBURST FARMS AND SANCTUARY

(formerly known as Solar Logos, and then Brotherhood of the Sun)
Years active: 1969 to present day
Affiliation: Syncretic Protestant, Buddhist, mysticism, Kriya yoga, and Hopi
Founder: Norman Paulsen
Leader: Patty Paulsen

LENTIL LOAF

(Vegetarian. Makes 2 loaves.)
Tools: Stockpot, large frying pan, 2 bread loaf pans
Oven temperature: 375°F

Ingredients:
2 cups lentils
2 Tablespoons vegetable oil
2 small onions, chopped
4 cloves garlic, minced
6 celery ribs, chopped
1 cup breadcrumbs
⅔ cup rolled oats
1 cup chopped walnuts
1 cup chopped almonds
6 eggs, beaten
2 teaspoons sea salt
1 Tablespoon dried basil
2 teaspoons dried thyme
8 cups of water (for cooking lentils)

Steps:
1. Preheat oven to 375°F.
2. In a stockpot, fill halfway with water. Add in lentils and cook over medium-high heat until boiling then cover tightly and reduce heat and simmer until lentils are tender, approximately 15 to 20 minutes. Drain any remaining liquid and set lentils aside.
3. While lentils are cooking, clean and prepare onions, garlic, celery, and nuts. Set aside.
4. In a large frying pan, add oil and warm under medium-high heat. Add onions, garlic, and celery and sauté until tender.

5. Add cooked lentils, salt, basil, and thyme to frying pan and continue to simmer for 5 minutes then remove from heat.
6. In a large bowl, add in breadcrumbs, oats, nuts, and eggs. Add in cooled lentil mixture and mix well.
7. Lightly grease 2 loaf pans. Divide lentil mixture equally between loaf pans, gently patting mixture in.
8. Place in oven and bake for 60 to 75 minutes.
9. Serve plain or with a tomato sauce or gravy.

Variations recommended by the Sunburst Farms:
    Add 1 cup chopped tomatoes and 1½ cups cheese.
    Add 2 cups chopped, hard-boiled eggs.

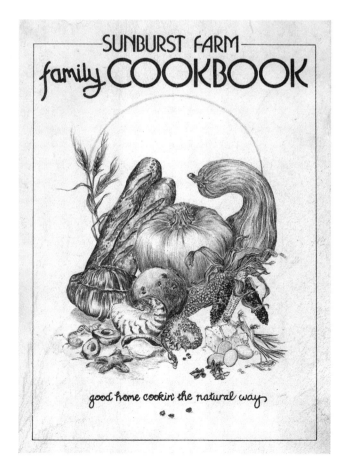

Front cover of 1978 edition of *Sunburst Farm Family Cookbook*. Author's collection.

BLUEBERRY RICOTTA REFRIGERATOR PIE

(Vegetarian. Makes one 9-inch pie.)

Tools: Pie plate, food processor

Ingredients for crust:

½ cup raw or roasted walnuts

½ cup raw or roasted almonds (not smoked or flavored!)

¼ cup almond butter

¼ cup honey

1 teaspoon cinnamon

½ teaspoon sea salt

Steps:

1. Grind nuts using hand grinder or food processor until coarse to fine texture. (You can purchase pre-ground nut meats, but freshly ground is better.)
2. In medium-sized bowl, add ground nuts and remaining ingredients and mix.
3. When thoroughly mixed, press into pie plate. Place plate in freezer until chilled, about 30 minutes. Make filling while plate is chilling.

Ingredients for filling:

1½ cups ricotta cheese

½ cup maple syrup

1½ cups fresh blueberries

½ teaspoon sea salt

Steps:

1. Rinse blueberries in cool water; remove any remaining stems.
2. Hand mash with a fork or back of spoon ¾ cup of the blueberries in a medium-sized bowl, then mix in remaining berries.
3. Add in maple syrup and salt and mix until berries are completely covered.
4. Add in ricotta cheese and fold mixture together.
5. Pour into prepared crust, then refrigerate for 3 hours before serving. For an extra flourish, add dollops of freshly whipped cream and decorative blueberries.

Testers and tasters loved this pie. Testers declared they were going to use the nut-based crust for other refrigerator-style pies. Further experiments led to suggested variations. Try substituting the blueberries for fresh cherries or peaches. You can also change up the nut combinations; pecans and almonds worked well, as did a combination of pecans and walnuts with tahini substituting for the almond butter. Cashew butter worked well too but can be a touch expensive.

APPLE-CORN COOKIES

(Gluten-free. Makes approximately 2 dozen cookies.)

Tools: Jelly roll pan, parchment paper

Oven temperature: 350°F

Ingredients for cookie:

¾ cup honey

¾ cup butter

2 eggs, beaten

1¾ cups fine ground cornmeal

1¾ cups soy flour (can substitute a gluten-free baking flour mix, example: Bob's Red Mill)

¼ teaspoon sea salt

1½ teaspoons baking powder

Ingredients for filling:

½ cup apple sauce (unsweetened)

¼ teaspoon ground cinnamon

¼ teaspoon lemon juice

2 teaspoons honey

Steps:

1. Preheat oven to 350°F.
2. In a medium-sized bowl, cream together honey and butter. (You can use a stand mixer or hand-held mixer.)
3. Add in beaten eggs and mix.
4. Add the cornmeal, flour, salt, and baking powder and mix together. Set aside.
5. In a small bowl, add all the filling ingredients and mix until blended.
6. Line jelly roll pans with parchment paper. Place tablespoon-sized scoops of dough onto pan in 3 rows of 3 for a total of 9 cookies per pan. (The batter spreads as they cook.)
7. With the back of a spoon, gently press a well indentation into the middle of the dough ball.
8. Fill each cookie with ½ to 1 teaspoon of applesauce filling.
9. Place in oven and bake for 10 minutes. Cool before eating.

Tasters loved this gluten-free cookie. Test bakers preferred batches using a pre-made gluten-free baking mix with Bob's Red Mill cited the best overall.

HARE KRISHNA (ISKCON)

(International Society of Krishna Consciousness)
Years active: 1965 to present day
Affiliation: Hindu
Founder / Leader: Prabhupada

It is said that Krishna is a hungry little boy. In speaking with a former high-level member of the group, he said that Prabhupada himself taught that eating food is one of the sources of human joy. And while monastic ISKCON members eschew sexual pleasures and worldly material goods, they do enjoy eating. "Peter" has a theory: because so much is forbidden in the ISKCON monasteries, food is the only pleasure allowed to members. ISKCON cuisine tends toward the sweet. Peter also thinks that the additional sugar in many dishes is due to the fact that it is the only stimulant allowed. Which would also account for the large array of dessert recipes included in the ISKCON cookbooks of the past fifty years.

COCONUT BURFI

(Vegetarian. Makes 1 pan.)
Tools: Stockpot, jelly roll pan, parchment paper

Burfi is a popular dessert served at ISKCON restaurants and temples. There are endless variations and additions that make it a delicious treat. This recipe is taken from the ISKCON *Higher Taste* cookbook and makes no claims as an authentic recipe but *is* the version made by the Krishnas.

Ingredients:
1 cup ground fresh coconut (can substitute a combination of frozen pureed coconut and bagged shredded coconut)
1½ cups sugar
6 cups whole milk
½ teaspoon ground nutmeg
¼ teaspoon ground cardamom

Steps:
1. If using fresh coconut, grind with food grinder. (If using substitute, use 4 ounces of frozen puree and one 16-ounce bag of shredded coconut that has been pulverized with a food processor.)
2. Put the coconut and sugar in the stockpot and cook over high heat for 10 minutes, while constantly stirring.

3. Add the milk and continue cooking over high heat for 30 to 45 minutes, until mixture has thickened.
4. Add in spices and keep stirring. Remove from heat when mixture doesn't release liquid when moved.
5. On a parchment-lined jelly roll pan, either scoop and roll into balls or pour into pan. Allow to cool. If poured, cut into squares or diamonds when cooled.

A note from our recipe tester: You must be fearless when making this recipe; keep the heat high and keep stirring. The mixture burns easily, and ideal burfi is snow-white as its name implies.

KOFTA
(Vegetarian. Makes 6 servings.)
Tools: Stockpot, blender or food processor, large frying pan

Note: It is recommended to make the sauce first and while it's simmering, make and fry the kofta. ISKCON restaurants will serve kofta in various ways. Some serve it as it appears here (the fried balls with sauce); others add lemon rice.

Ingredients for sauce:
10 to 12 plum tomatoes, chopped (about 4 cups when cleaned and prepped)
½ teaspoon whole cumin seed
½ teaspoon crushed chilis
½ teaspoon whole coriander seed
¼ teaspoon asafetida
¼ teaspoon ground ginger
1 teaspoon salt
2 bay leaves
½ teaspoon oregano
2 Tablespoons ghee

Steps to make sauce:
1. In a small stockpot—without oil—add cumin seeds and chilis. Stir until both are browned. Add asafetida and ginger and continue to heat while stirring for 5 minutes.
2. Add 1 cup of the chopped tomatoes and simmer over low heat for 10 minutes.
3. Using a blender or food processor, puree remaining tomatoes and add to stockpot.
4. Add bay leaves and oregano. Continue to simmer over low heat for 30 to 60 minutes. Remove from heat when fully cooked to taste.

Ingredients for kofta balls:
2 medium heads cauliflower, grated
2 potatoes, peeled and grated (about 2 cups when cleaned and prepped)
1½ teaspoons turmeric

1½ teaspoons salt

½ to ¾ cup chickpea flour

pinch asafetida

ghee for deep frying

Steps for kofta balls:

1. Clean and prepare cauliflower, potatoes, and tomatoes. Set aside.

2. In a large bowl, grate the cauliflower and potato. Squeeze excess liquid out of mixture with hands or strain through cheesecloth. Return mixture to bowl.

3. Add turmeric, salt, asafetida to mixture. Add in ½ cup of chickpea flour. Mix until dough holds shape. If dough is too wet, add remaining ¼ cup of chickpea flour and mix again.

4. With hands, take approximately 2 tablespoons of dough and shape into 1-inch balls. Set aside until dough is gone.

5. In a large frying pan, add approximately ½ cup ghee for frying. Over medium-high heat, warm ghee until hot for frying.

6. Carefully place kofta balls into hot oil. Use fork to gently turn balls to ensure they cook evenly. When golden brown, remove from pan and place on plate covered with paper towels to absorb excess ghee. Finish frying all the kofta balls and set aside.

To serve: Pour ½ cup of tomato sauce into a shallow bowl then add 3 to 5 kofta balls.

Prabhupada, 1968. Photo courtesy of Roger Siegel (Guru Das).

Close-up of Hare Krishna shared meal, 1968. Photo courtesy of Roger Siegel (Guru Das).

Holy Food

VEGETARIAN GOTHIC/ KRISHNA'S KITCHEN

Years active: Mid-1970s
Affiliation: ISKCON/ Independent Commune
Head Cook: Mo Willett

ACORN SQUASH-POTATO SOUP

(Vegetarian. Makes approximately 2 quarts.)

Tools: Stockpot, medium frying pan, immersion blender (or standard blender)

Ingredients:

6 cups acorn squash, peeled and cubed (Can substitute butternut squash. Can also use leftover baked squash; if using leftover baked squash then omit cooking squash again and add to cooked potatoes at blending stage.)

5 white potatoes or 3 white potatoes and 2 sweet potatoes

1 cup onion, diced

2 cups instant milk powder

1½ teaspoons sea salt

¼ teaspoon black pepper

3 Tablespoons tamari

⅓ cup butter

1 quart water

Steps:

1. Peel and cut the squash and potatoes into large pieces. Place into stockpot and cover with water. Cook until soft over medium-high heat.

2. Remove from heat. Add the milk powder then blend with immersion blender. (If using standard blender, puree in batches.)

3. Dice the onion and sauté with butter in frying pan over medium-high heat. When onions are golden brown, add to stockpot.

4. Add remaining ingredients to the pot. Cover and simmer over low heat for 40 minutes.

5. Remove from heat and serve.

Front cover of 1975 edition of *Vegetarian Gothic* Cookbook. Author's collection.

CAULIFLOWER WITH CHEESE AND NUTS

(Vegetarian. Makes 6 to 8 servings.)

Tools: Medium saucepan with steamer insert, casserole baking dish

Oven temperature: 350°F

Ingredients:

1 head cauliflower, chopped into bite-size pieces

1 cup milk

1 medium onion, diced

1 cup chopped cashews

1½ cups grated mozzarella cheese

1 teaspoon sea salt

½ teaspoon garlic, minced

⅓ cup softened butter

Steps:

1. Preheat oven to 350°F.

2. Clean and prepare cauliflower, onion, and cashews. Set aside.

3. Fill saucepan with 1 inch of water and place steamer insert. Add the chopped cauliflower into the steamer and bring to boil over medium-high heat. Steam for 5 to 6 minutes until tender but not mushy.

4. In a large bowl, add the steamed cauliflower, diced onions, milk, cashews, sea salt, garlic, and butter. Add 1 cup of cheese. Mix until ingredients are equally blended.

5. Pour mixture into casserole baking dish and sprinkle with remaining ½ cup of cheese.

6. Place in oven and bake for approximately 25 minutes until cheese is melted and golden.

7. Remove from oven and serve.

EGGPLANT-MUSHROOM CASSEROLE

(Vegetarian. Makes 6 to 8 servings.)

Tools: 9x13 casserole baking dish

Oven temperature: 350°F

Ingredients:

2 medium eggplants, sliced into thin strips

1 large onion, chopped

¾ pound fresh mushrooms, sliced thin

2 cups tomato paste

4 cups grated mozzarella cheese

¾ cup sesame seeds

Vegetable or sunflower oil for greasing baking dish

Holy Food

Steps:

1. Preheat oven to 350°F.
2. Clean and prepare onion, eggplant, and mushrooms. Set aside.
3. Lightly coat baking dish with oil. Layer the eggplant, mushrooms, onion, and 3 cups of the cheese in the baking dish.
4. Cover layered dish with tomato paste.
5. Sprinkle remaining cup of cheese on top. Sprinkle the sesame seeds on top.
6. Place into oven and bake for approximately 60 minutes or until eggplant is tender and cheese is melted and golden.
7. Remove from oven and serve.

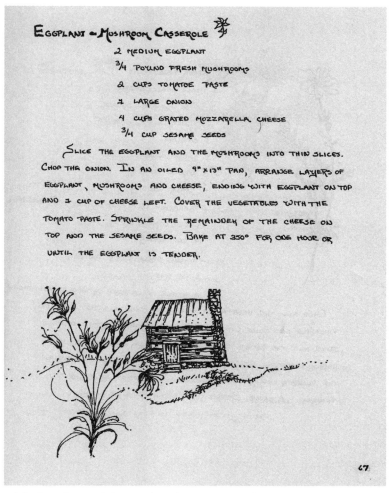

Original recipe and illustration from 1974 edition of _Vegetarian Gothic_. Author's collection.

RAJNEESH MOVEMENT/OSHO

Years active: 1974 to present day (though the group changed focus
   to a spiritual retreat center after Osho's death in 1990)
Affiliation: Syncretic Sikh, Buddhist, and New Age
Founder / Leader: Bhagwan Rajneesh

CORN DELICACY

(Vegetarian. Makes 4 to 6 servings.)
Tools: Large frying pan or small wok

Ingredients:

4 Tablespoons butter

2 medium onions, finely chopped

2–3 Tablespoons ginger, peeled and grated

2 green chilis, finely chopped

1 cup cashews

1½ teaspoons salt, or to taste

1 teaspoon paprika

3 cups corn (can be fresh, frozen, or canned)

2 teaspoons garam masala

2 teaspoons lemon juice

½ bunch (approximately ⅓ cup) coriander leaves (removed from stalk, washed, and finely chopped)

1 lemon, halved and sliced

1 tomato, sliced

Steps:

1. Clean and prepare onions, ginger, chilis, and coriander leaves. Set aside.

2. In frying pan, add butter and warm over medium heat.

3. Add onions and ginger and fry until soft and fragrant.

4. Add chili peppers and cashews and cook for 5 minutes.

5. Add salt, paprika, and corn. Continue to simmer for 5 to 10 minutes until fully tender.
   Remove from heat.

6. Add garam masala, lemon juice, and coriander leaves. Mix together.

7. Garnish each serving with lemon and tomato slices.

Holy Food

PIEROGI

(Vegetarian. Makes 4 to 6 servings.)

Tools: Frying pan, jelly roll pan, parchment paper, stand mixer (optional)

Ingredients:

Dough:

¾ cup butter, room temperature

¾ cup cream cheese, room temperature

2 Tablespoons heavy cream, room temperature

2 small eggs, room temperature

1¾ cups flour

¾ teaspoon salt

Filling:

10 ounces fresh mushrooms

½ cup onion, finely diced

1 teaspoon dill weed

2 Tablespoons butter

1½ slices black bread, dried or stale (can substitute whole wheat or rye bread)

¼ cup sour cream

¼ cup cream cheese

½ teaspoon caraway seeds

2 hard-boiled eggs

1 cup mushroom, onion, or vegetable stock

For egg wash:

1 egg

2 Tablespoons water

Steps for dough:

1. Make sure that all ingredients are room temperature. In a medium-sized bowl (or stand mixer with paddle attachment) mix butter and cream cheese.

2. Add the heavy cream and eggs, then mix until thoroughly blended.

3. If using stand mixer, change to dough hook attachment. Add flour and mix until dough forms ball. (You may need to add an extra tablespoon or two of flour.)

4. Wrap dough ball in plastic wrap and place into refrigerator to chill.

Steps for filling:

1. Peel and finely dice onions. In a medium-sized frying pan over high heat, place butter, dill, and onions and sauté until onions soften.

2. Finely dice mushrooms and add to onions. Cook for additional 5 minutes. Set aside.

3. In a small bowl, pour stock and place dried bread. Set aside.

4. Hard-boil eggs for 10 minutes. When done, peel, place in medium-sized bowl, and mash with fork.

5. Remove bread from stock. Tear soaked bread pieces and add to mashed egg. Then add sour cream, cream cheese, salt, pepper, and caraway seeds. Then add cooked onion and mushroom mixture. Mix together, then set aside to cool.

Steps to assemble and bake:

1. Prepare a well-floured bread board (or cutting board). Place dough on board and roll out until approximately ¼" thickness. (Turn dough over, adding more flour as needed to prevent sticking.)
2. With a pastry cutter or knife, cut 3" squares from dough.
3. In a small cup, crack 1 egg and mix with 2 tablespoons of water. Brush edges of dough squares with mixture.
4. Place 1 tablespoon of filling in the center of the square. Fold each corner to the center and gently press together to seal. Carefully press the edges together to seal.
5. Place each pierogi on jelly roll pan spaced 1 inch between. Brush tops with egg wash. Place into oven and bake until golden brown. (Approximately 15 minutes.)

Serve as a side dish or main dish. Can be topped with browned butter or sour cream.

Front cover of 1984 edition of *Zorba the Buddha* Cookbook. Author's collection.

Holy Food

PARATHAS

(Vegetarian. Makes 12 parathas.)

Tools: Rolling pin, large, heavy-bottom skillet (a cast iron frying pan or skillet works well)

A tasting note from the 1979 cookbook *Zorba the Buddha* introducing parathas to primarily white, American cooks: "Parathas are an Indian delicacy. They are stuffed flat breads, spicy and filling."

Ingredients:

Dough:

2 cups whole-wheat flour or chappatti [*sic*] flour
   (chapati flour is finely milled whole-wheat flour)

½ teaspoon salt

3 Tablespoons vegetable oil

½ cup water (more if needed)

Filling:

2 cups cauliflower, finely chopped

2-inch piece ginger, peeled and finely chopped

1 chili, finely chopped

salt to taste

½ cup coriander leaves, finely chopped

Cooking:

¼ cup ghee or clarified butter, melted (for cooking)

Steps for dough:

1. In a large bowl, mix flour, salt, oil, and water together with hands until the mixture binds together.

2. Knead in bowl until dough has a soft and smooth appearance. Set aside.

Steps for filling:

1. Clean and prepare cauliflower, ginger, chili pepper, and coriander leaves and add to a large bowl. Add salt.

2. Mix together then set aside.

Steps for assembling and making:

1. Prepare a counter or bread board and lightly sprinkle with flour.

2. Separate the dough into 10 to 12 smaller balls of dough.

3. One at a time, flatten a dough ball with your palm, then place on prepared surface. Roll dough out to 6-inch circle.

4. Place approximately 2 to 3 tablespoons of filling in center of dough circle. Bring edges to the center so filling is covered, then pinch together.

5. Sprinkle surface with flour, then carefully roll out filled dough ball into 6-inch circle. Repeat until all dough balls are filled and rolled.

6. In a large, heavy-bottom skillet, heat pan over medium-high burner. Place 2 paratha and grill in the dry pan, turning it over until it begins to brown. Brush both sides with ghee or butter and continue grilling until paratha is golden brown and crispy. Repeat until all are cooked.

*Tester's note: You can cook two at a time if your pan is large enough. Also, wipe pan clean of butter and any crumbs with a paper towel between parathas.

POTATO MASALA
(Vegetarian. Makes 10 to 12 servings.)
Tools: Large and small frying pan, medium stockpot

Ingredients:
14 cups white potatoes, peeled and cut into ½" cubes
½ cup + 2 Tablespoons vegetable oil
2 ounces onions, sliced into half moons
5 Tablespoons fresh ginger, grated
¾ teaspoon turmeric
1 teaspoon paprika
1 teaspoon cumin seeds
1 teaspoon mustard seeds
½ teaspoon crushed red chili
1 teaspoon green chili, chopped
salt to taste
2 teaspoons garam masala (your favorite blend, homemade or commercial will work fine)
6 ounces roasted cashews, chopped
5 Tablespoons fresh lemon juice

Steps:
1. Boil potatoes until tender but not soft. Drain, cover, and set aside.
2. In a large frying pan, heat ½ cup of oil over medium-high burner. Add ginger and cook for 2 minutes, then add onions. Cook onions until golden brown. Add turmeric and paprika and cook for another 2 minutes, then remove from heat, cover, and set aside.
3. In a small sauté pan, heat 2 tablespoons of oil over medium-high heat, then add cumin seeds. When browned, add mustard seeds, then immediately remove from heat. Add toasted seeds to onion mixture.
4. Place the frying pan containing the onion mix over a medium-high burner. Heat through, then add the cooked potatoes, salt, and crushed chilies. Mix well. Then add garam masala and lemon juice. Mix well and continue to cook for approximately 5 minutes until heated throughout.
5. Remove from burner. Top with chopped cashews.
Serve as side dish or as a main course.

Testers suggested toasting the spices in the same frying pan when cooking the onions to save time and create less mess.

3HO

Years active: 1969 to present day
Affiliation: Syncretic Sikh, yoga, and Western Astrology
Founder / Leader: Harbhajan Singh Khalsa. Also known as Yogi Bhajan and Sri Singh Sahib

YOGI TEA

(Vegetarian. Makes 4 cups.)

Before Yogi Tea became commercially available at your local health food store and co-op, it was served at restaurants run by acolytes of Yogi Bhajan. The "tea" is a variation on a traditional northern Indian chai and became the bedrock recipe of Yogi Bhajan's billion-dollar food company, Yogi Tea. The commercial blend claims to be Ayurvedic but does not contain milk, which, according to the 3HO *Golden Temple Cookbook,* means it is NOT proper Yogi Tea.

Here's what 3HO cooks say about Yogi Tea:
"The greatest of all hot beverages! This is Yogi Bhajan's original recipe. This beverage is intended to be taken for more than its good taste. It is a great pick-me-up, a substitute for coffee and a blood purifier.

Yogi Tea made without milk is not Yogi Tea. The milk eases the assimilation and prevents irritation to the colon. Herb tea may not be substituted for the black tea; it does not produce the same effect. Many people now add a few slices of ginger root and boil it along with the spices for added zest.

Make at least four cups at one time. The measurements can vary according to your taste but be sure not to put in too many cloves or cinnamon."

Ingredients:
40 ounces water (1 quart plus a cup)
8 whole cloves (see them dance!)
8 whole green cardamom pods, cracked
12 whole black peppercorns
1 stick cinnamon (about 3 to 4 inches long)
1 teaspoon black tea (preferably jasmine)
2 cups milk (you can substitute a non-dairy milk if desired)
6 slices fresh ginger root (optional)

Steps:

1. Bring the water to a boil and add the cloves, cardamom, peppercorns, and cinnamon. Cover, and continue boiling for 10 to 15 minutes, then add the black tea.
2. Let mixture sit for a minute or two, then add the milk and return to a boil. Be careful that it does not boil over. When it reaches a boil, remove immediately from the heat.
3. Strain and serve with honey to taste.

You can increase the total amount made without proportionally increasing the spices.

MINT FRAPPÉ

(Vegan. Makes 1 serving.)
Tools: Blender

Ingredients:

½ cup very strong cold mint tea

1 teaspoon honey

4 ice cubes, crushed

Steps:

1. Blend ingredients together until frothy. Serve immediately.

MUSHROOM STROGANOFF

(Vegetarian. Serves 10 to 12.)
Tools: Large sauté pan

Ingredients:

1 cup chopped yellow onions

½ cup ghee (can substitute butter)

4 to 5 cloves of garlic, minced

4 cups sliced fresh mushrooms

1 Tablespoon dried basil

1 teaspoon dried rosemary

⅓ cup tamari

½ Tablespoon dill seed

½ Tablespoon pepper (cayenne)

10 to 12 black olives

½ cup chopped parsley

½ cup roasted cashews

1 cup milk

3 cups sour cream (reduce as desired, 1 cup for a less dairy-heavy final dish)

Cooked rice or noodles, and toasted bread

Holy Food

Steps:

1. Sauté onions in ghee until clear and cook slowly with garlic. When half-done, add 4 cups sliced mushrooms.
2. Season with basil, rosemary, tamari sauce, dill seed and pepper.
3. Add the black olives, chopped parsley, and cashews. Cook 3 minutes.
4. Then add 1 cup milk and 3 cups sour cream. Heat just hot enough to serve.
5. Serve on rice or noodles, with toast.

Recipe testers noted that the amount of dairy in this dish might overwhelm modern eaters. Feel free to reduce the amount of sour cream to 1 cup.

THE GOLDEN TEMPLE SANDWICH

(Vegetarian. Makes 2 sandwiches.)

Ingredients:

Whole grain bread slices

Guacamole Spread* (see recipe below)

Mushrooms, sliced

Alfalfa sprouts

Tomato slices

Monterey Jack or cheddar cheese slices

Steps:

1. Spread a slice of bread with Guacamole Spread.
2. Add sliced mushrooms, alfalfa sprouts, tomato slices, top with jack or cheddar cheese.
3. Place open-face under broiler until cheese melts.

Guacamole spread ingredients:

1 cup mashed avocados

2 Tablespoons cloves garlic, minced

2 Tablespoons lemon juice

1 Tablespoon vegetable broth powder (optional)

Dash of kelp powder (optional)

4 scallions, finely chopped

¼ teaspoon salt

Steps:

1. Mix all ingredients and refrigerate until time for use. Makes 1⅓ cups.

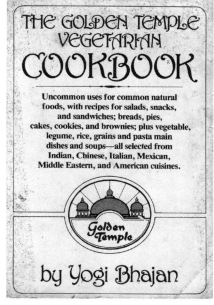

Front cover of 1978 edition of *Golden Temple Cookbook*. Author's collection.

KRIPALU

Years active: 1972 to present day
Affiliation: Kripalu Yoga/Hindu; then secular "wellness"
Founder / Leader: Amrit Desai

SOYBURGERS

(Vegetarian. Makes 12 burger patties.)

Tools: Large bowl for soaking beans, large bowl for mixing, oven and jelly roll pan for baking or large frying pan

Oven temperature (if baking): 350°F

Ingredients:

2 cups dry soybeans
½ cup diced celery
½ cup diced green peppers
½ cup diced carrots
¼ cup chopped parsley
¼ cup peanut butter
1 cup toasted wheat germ
1 Tablespoon tamari
½ Tablespoon sage
¼ teaspoon ground kelp
1 teaspoon cumin
½ Tablespoon salt
¾ teaspoon chili powder
⅛ teaspoon cayenne
½ teaspoon thyme
¾ teaspoon celery seed
Whole-wheat flour for coating patties

Steps:

1. Soak soybeans overnight in large bowl.
2. In a large stockpot, transfer beans and liquid and cook over medium heat until soft. (Approximately 6 hours.)
3. While soybeans are cooking, finely dice celery, green peppers, and carrots. Chop parsley finely. Set aside.
4. When beans are fully cooked, drain liquid and return to cooking pot.
5. Mash the beans until smooth.
6. Add peanut butter, wheat germ, and tamari, and mix while continuing to mash beans.

7. Add the diced vegetables and chopped parsley and mix in. (The Kripalu suggest using clean hands to mix at this point.)
8. Add spices and continue to mix thoroughly until all ingredients are equally blended.
9. Using clean hands, take ⅓ to ½ cup of the mixture and form a patty. Repeat.
10. To cook, dip patties in flour and either bake in oven for 30 minutes OR pan-fry using a tablespoon of vegetable or sunflower oil.

Dress with tomato, lettuce, and condiments on whole-wheat bread, buns, or pita bread.

SECLUSION SPECIAL

(Vegan. Serves 8 to 10.)
Tools: Large saucepan or small stockpot

Notes from the *Kripalu Kitchen* cookbook:
"In 1974, our spiritual teacher, Yogi Amrit Desai, spent an intensive period of seclusion in a small meditation home. During that time, his wife, whom residents affectionately call Mataji, prepared his daily meal and carried it up the hills to his retreat house in the woods. One of her special creations at that time was this light, high-protein dish. Retreat residents became enamored of this dish and dubbed it 'Seclusion Special,' in honor of Yogi Desai's special retreat. You need not enter seclusion to enjoy its flavorful goodness and nutritional benefits!"

Ingredients:
½ Tablespoon oil
¼ teaspoon mustard seeds
½ teaspoon turmeric
1 cup brown rice (dry)
1 cup mung beans (dry)
5½ cups water
1½ teaspoons cumin
1 teaspoon curry powder
¼ teaspoon pepper
¼ teaspoon ginger powder
1 teaspoon salt
½ cup finely chopped cabbage
¼ cup chopped green pepper
½ cup finely shredded carrots
¼ cup raw peanuts (optional)
Ingredients for marinade:
½ cup light vegetable oil
⅓ cup lemon juice
½ Tablespoon salt
½ Tablespoon tamari

1 Tablespoon honey

1 teaspoon basil

¼ teaspoon dried oregano

Steps:

1. In a saucepan heat the oil then add the mustard seeds. When the seeds begin to pop, add turmeric, and stir the mixture.

2. Fold in the rice and beans, coating them with the oil-spice mixture. Add water and the remainder of spices, mixing them thoroughly and letting them simmer until the grains and beans are well cooked (approximately 40 minutes).

3. Wash and prepare the cabbage, peppers, and carrots while the mixture is cooking.

4. When the beans and rice are finished cooking (they should be soft but not mushy) add in the cabbage, peppers and carrots with the cooked rice and beans. Place lid on pan or pot and set aside.

5. Prepare the marinade then pour it over the grain-bean-veggie mixture, blending it in thoroughly.

"This is a hearty dish which can go either hot or cold, depending on your preferences and the time of year."

Recipe testers noted that the marinade may overwhelm the dish. It's recommended to add half of the amount and adjust to your personal preference. Other tasters felt the dish was a bit bland; feel free to increase the spices if you agree. One tester noted that this dish would be a nice addition to a mezze platter or picnic potluck.

BULGUR-SESAME PORRIDGE

(Vegetarian. Makes 3 cups.)

Tools: Large sauté pan with lid

Ingredients:

1 Tablespoon vegetable, sunflower, or canola oil

1 cup bulgur wheat

¼ cup sesame seeds

¼ cup wheat germ

¼ cup unsweetened shredded coconut

¼ teaspoon salt

2–3 Tablespoons honey

3 cups water

Steps:

1. Heat cooking oil in sauté pan over low-medium burner until warmed.

2. Add bulgur wheat, sesame seeds, wheat germ, coconut, salt, and honey and sauté until lightly browned.

3. Add water. Reduce heat to low simmer and place lid on pan. Steam for approximately 25 minutes.
4. Remove from heat and serve.

Note from the *Kripalu Kitchen* cookbook:
"This has a pleasant, sweet, and nutty flavor—helps you off to an energetic day."

THREE BEAN SALAD

(Vegetarian. Makes 6 cups.)

Tools: Large bowl for soaking beans, large stockpot

Ingredients:

For salad:

1 cup chickpeas (dry)

1¾ cups green beans (2-inch pieces)

1 cup kidney beans (dry)

½ cup chopped celery

Marinade:

½ cup oil

1½ cups vinegar

1½ teaspoons honey

¼ teaspoon black pepper

1 teaspoon oregano

½ teaspoon basil

½ teaspoon salt

¼ teaspoon marjoram

⅛ teaspoon dill

pinch cayenne

2 Tablespoons tamari

¼ cup water

Steps:

1. Soak the dry beans overnight in a large bowl filled with water.
2. In a large stockpot, add the soaked beans and cook over medium heat until soft (approximately 4 hours).
3. When beans are cooking, make the marinade by mixing spices, oil, vinegar, tamari, honey, and water in a shaker bottle. Set aside.
4. When beans are fully cooked, drain and rinse. Pour beans into large bowl.
5. Pour the marinade over the beans and mix thoroughly.
6. Cover and place in refrigerator for 24 hours so flavors fully develop and penetrate beans.
7. Serve as a side dish or light lunch on a hot day.

Eleven

MEDITATION MASTERS

BUDDHISM IS HISTORICALLY CONNECTED TO INDIAN RELIGIOUS PHILOSOPHIES. However, Buddhism as a practice spread beyond the subcontinent throughout the sixth century and developed regional variations based on interpretations of Buddha's documented teachings. Chinese- and later Japanese-influenced Buddhism followed immigrants to California, Oregon, and Washington state. Shin and Zen Buddhism gained few white followers until after World War II, when the nascent counterculture began exploring different spiritual pathways. Although generations of Japanese and Chinese Americans were initially wary of these newcomers, eventually the temples opened their doors to committed students.

A prevailing concern of hierarchical religions is the lack of control over the message the further away from "home" the messenger is. Without the reaffirming rituals of a homogeneous community, the more likely a ritual becomes divorced from its meaning. All religions have experienced schismatic dicing by charismatic interpreters of holy books and the erasure of cultural influence on that belief system. The issue of appropriation is just as consequential to religious traditions as it is to food traditions. The question is always: Is the American version of a [insert food item or spiritual practice of your choice] authentic? The answer always is, and with a nod to Buddha, it depends.[127]

Siddhartha Gautama worked out the Four Noble Truths: existence is suffering (*dukkha*); suffering has a cause, namely craving and attachment (*trishna*); there is a cessation of suffering, which is *nirvana*. He then developed the Eightfold Path to guide others in reaching *nirvana*, which would reduce the amount of suffering in the world. The earliest Buddhists lived in communal monasteries and followed Gautama's exact prescriptions to the letter. The Buddha himself was elliptical when it came to specifics regarding deities. He generally dismissed divine beings as being caught in an endless cycle of karmic rebalancing. As Buddhism spread and grew, veneration for Gautama as Buddha and other elevated *dhamma*[128] teachers began to look like deity worship, which led to the development of the varied sects of Buddhist thought. All

---

127 "What is good, what is bad? What is right, what wrong? What ought I to do or not to do? What, when I have done it, will be for a long time for my sorrow . . . or my happiness?" *Lakkhana-sutta* (D.iii.157)
128 *Dhamma* are all the teachings of Buddhism. *Dharma* are the teachings of Gautama (Buddha).

the sects honor the Four Noble Truths, the Eightfold Path, and observe the five moral precepts that compose Buddhist spirituality for general practitioners. They are usually expressed as prohibitions against 1. Killing 2. Stealing 3. Unchaste behaviors 4. Lying 5. Ingesting intoxicants. Broadly interpreted, Buddhists are vegetarians who don't drink or take drugs.

An essential item in the Eightfold Path is meditation. But to still one's mind from causing and revisiting suffering remains a challenge for people today as much as it did during the Buddha's existence. Buddhists have developed many different tools to successfully meditate and further the meditation to achieve transcendence from the material world. The first wave of

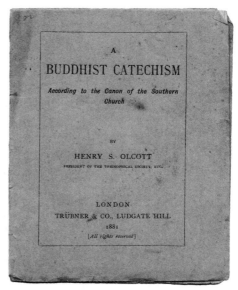

Front cover of *A Buddhist Catechism* by Henry Olcott, 1881. Courtesy of Amherst College.

white American Buddhists (1930s to 1950s) adopted the prohibitions and requirements with few qualms as they embarked on the journey to enlightenment. Later seekers—and teachers—presented challenges to both the doctrines and practices of Buddhism. West Coast Buddhism was influenced by Shin and Zen teachers who closely followed doctrine as laid out by the respective sects' spiritual home in Japan, while two styles of Buddhism flourished on the East Coast thanks to two very different monk-teachers. Theravada Buddhism is considered by scholars to be the most conservative branch in both doctrinal matters and practice. It began in Sri Lanka and then spread throughout Southeast Asia to become the dominant sect in Thailand, Burma (Myanmar), Laos, and Cambodia. Theravada Buddhist monks were closely intertwined with the government of those countries until Western powers began colonizing. Just as colonizing forces did on the Indian subcontinent, schools were forced to teach Christian doctrine. The monks relied on their monastic tradition to keep Buddhism thriving.

Henry Olcott was an American who is considered the first white Buddhist convert. He was, with Madame Blavatsky, one of the founders of Theosophy. He moved with Blavatsky in 1878 to Chennai, India, to open the new headquarters of the Theosophist Society. He also wanted access to libraries and temples to continue his learning by translating religious documents from Hindu, Zoroastrian, and Buddhist groups. After a long correspondence with monastic leader Sri Piyaratana Tissa Mahanayake Thero in Sri Lanka, Olcott secured an invitation to visit a monastery. His long fascination with Buddhism was made more profound by the experience, and he converted. He worked with Thero to open Buddhist schools in Sri Lanka. He and Thero are often credited with reviving Buddhism in Sri Lanka and birthing the Modern Buddhist movement. Olcott translated complex Buddhist doctrine into a format easily understood by Westerners, the catechism. He created the Buddhist Catechism in 1881, which replicated a

Christian-style catechism but was filled with Buddhist philosophy and *koans*. Olcott's stated goal was to ensure that the Buddhist concepts were understood yet remained untainted by Western thought. Regardless of his intentions, the Buddhist Catechism as published reflected Olcott's American Protestantism and Theosophist studies. Here's an excerpt from his Buddhist Catechism:

> **Q:** *What is Karma?*
> **A:** *A causation operating on the moral, as well as physical and other planes. Buddhists say there is no miracle in human affairs: what a man sows that he must still reap.*
> **Q:** *Why does ignorance cause suffering?*
> **A:** *Because it makes us prize what is not worth prizing, grieve for that we should not grieve for, consider real what is not real but only illusory, and pass our lives in the pursuit of worthless objects, neglecting what is in reality most valuable.*
> **Q:** *And what is that which is most valuable?*
> **A:** *To know the whole secret of man's existence and destiny, so that we may estimate at no more than their actual value and this life and its relations; so that we may live in a way to insure the greatest happiness and the least suffering for our fellow-men and ourselves.*

On the origin story of the Buddha:

> *"The astrologers had foretold at his birth that he would one day resign his kingdom and become a Buddha. The King, his father, not wishing to lose his son, had carefully prevented his seeing any sights that might suggest to him human misery and death. No one was allowed even to speak of such things to the Prince. He was almost like a prisoner in his lovely palaces and flower gardens. They were surrounded with high walls; and inside everything was made as beautiful as possible, so that he might not want to go and see the sorrow and distress that are in the world.*
> **Q:** *Was he so kind-hearted that his father feared he might really want to sacrifice himself for the world's sake?*
> **A:** *Yes; he seems to have felt for all beings so strong a pity and love as that."*

A cursory reading of these excerpts shows how the story of the Buddha and *dhamma* was presented to align with the Christian stories about the life of Jesus Christ. In addition, Olcott funded the Theravada Buddhist delegation to the Chicago World Parliament of Religions in 1893,[129] which exposed more Americans to Buddhist thought. Even with his faulty presentation of Buddhist philosophy, Olcott was recognized by the Sri Lankan Buddhists as a revered figure and advocate for Theravada. He remained president of the Theosophical Society in Mumbai as a practicing Buddhist and vegetarian until he died in 1907.

Due to Olcott's writing and advocacy, white Americans' understanding of Buddhism at the turn of the twentieth century was considered by Asian scholars as "Modern Buddhism" or,

---

129 This convocation of religious leaders in Chicago in 1893 also brought D.T. Suzuki and his version of Zen Buddhism from Kyoto, Japan, as well as other religious thinkers representing numerous religions and sects.

Holy Food

sometimes derisively, "Protestant Buddhism." Buddhism, by its very nature, isn't a proselytizing religion. Monks and teachers from Sri Lanka and Thailand would occasionally visit the United States but as emissaries of their country and monasteries, not as recruiters. It wasn't until the 1960s, when Americans sought out new ways to expand consciousness, that Theravada concepts took hold in the cultural zeitgeist.

Another figure looms over modern American Buddhism—Chögyam Trungpa. Trungpa was a larger-than-life teacher whose inconsistencies as much as his wisdom influenced what Buddhism was to be in the United States. He was a hereditary monk born into the Tibetan theocratic tradition. There are four linked schools of Tibetan Buddhism. Important to Trungpa was his study of the Vajrayana tradition, considered the oldest in Buddhism and the source of tantric or mystical studies. He also was affiliated with the *ri-mé* movement, a nonsectarian group that sought to bring all the teachings and practices of the four schools together into a unified Tibetan Buddhism. In his autobiography, he tells of being given the mandate to bring "dharma to the West" by his mentor upon taking his monastic vows. Trungpa left Tibet in 1959 to escape the persecution of Tibetan monks by the occupying Chinese army when he was twenty years old. He came to the Tibetan community in exile in Dharmsala, India, where he founded a school for boys. He left India for Great Britain in 1963 to continue his English and comparative religious studies.

Trungpa's years in England and Scotland are critical to the development of a new, and wholly American, school of Buddhism. He was teaching meditation techniques at Buddhist centers in London and Edinburgh but wanted to reach more people. He studied and began talking about an advanced tantric concept of creating or discovering wisdom from "poison." The earliest of the Vajrayana *mahasiddhas* who roamed Northern India during the first millennium CE were seeking a mystical wisdom and magical powers. The *mahasiddhas* harnessed the power of opposites and created rituals that violated long-standing Buddhist taboos. Tantric feasts were held on holy ground and featured dancing, drinking alcohol, eating meat, and having sex. It was believed that a disciplined student of tantra could transform the energy of these transgressive acts into magic, but more importantly, into spiritual liberation.

Trungpa's time in the United Kingdom changed him and his approach to teaching. He realized that the monastic dress and ascetic lifestyle of a Tibetan monk were off-putting to Westerners. He abandoned his monastic vows and embraced Western culture. He was regularly drinking alcohol—so much that he caused a car accident that left him temporarily paralyzed in 1967. He was sexually involved with favored students. Trungpa moved to the United States in 1970. He traveled the country teaching what he called Vajradhatu Seminaries, which were three-month-long intensive studies of Vipassana meditation and tantric techniques. (Before Trungpa's arrival in the States, these techniques were only taught in monasteries to students with decades of experience.) Trungpa inspired both devotion and criticism. He demanded loyalty and threatened students who abandoned him with severe psychological torment. In the tradition of Tibetan Vajrayana, Trungpa demanded students vow secrecy in all that they observed and learned. The Vajradhatu sessions also taught those who wanted to teach meditation to others.

In 1974, Trungpa and his followers founded the Naropa Institute in Boulder, Colorado. Allen

Rinpoche Chögyam Trungpa in undated photo, c. early 1980s, by Bob Morehouse.

Ginsberg was a friend and student who helped Trungpa establish The Jack Kerouac School of Disembodied Poets at Naropa.[130] (Along with Diane diPrima and Anne Waldman.) By 1976, with over one hundred meditation centers throughout the world and Naropa thriving, Trungpa developed what came to be called Shambhala Buddhism.[131] His Shambhala vision was to develop a training system of meditation without any religious connotations, that was accessible to everyone regardless of their individual background. It was an American Buddhism divorced from the rigid Vajrayana rituals.

Shambhala meditation also introduced the now-common concept of "mindfulness" as a practice. It was the work at Naropa to develop psychological sciences and arts alongside Buddhism to teach students a fully integrated curriculum. Shambhala Buddhism was the realization of *ri mé* in bringing together the various schools of Buddhist thought to a unified and simplified practice for everyone. Trungpa also forged a relationship with Roshi Suzuki, founder of the San Francisco Zen Center and Tassajara Zen Mountain Center, who was the main proponent of Japanese Soto Zen Buddhism in California. Both leaders visited the other's center to work with students. The two men are considered the pillars of American Buddhism. They also personify the different attitudes toward food among Buddhist sects and traditions. Vegetarianism became the dividing philosophy between what was growing into the American Buddhist tradition that embraced mindfulness and vegetarianism, and the tantric and Zen practices that valued discipline while allowing meat consumption as an individual choice.

Trungpa, though regarded as guru by many, was all too human. He died in 1987 at age forty-eight after two years of declining health due to diabetes, alcoholism, and lingering effects from

---

130 Ginsberg had a wide-ranging interest in "Eastern philosophy" and befriended many of the 1960s–'70s-era guru-teachers.
131 Shambhala is a word of Tibetan origination describing a mythical and mystical kingdom. In other words, Shambhala is a utopia.

Holy Food

in 1979 to start a restaurant owned and run by the Zen Center. The restaurant earned published the *Tassajara Bread Book* in 1971 and *Tassajara Cooking* in 1973. Brown left the monastery of breadmaking and explored the possibilities incorporating Zen philosophy into cooking. He asked the cooks to teach him how to make bread, which they did. He took the basic knowledge Suzuki at Tassajara and became fascinated with his memory of an aunt's homemade bread. He the high-quality food served to guests and monks alike. Edward Espe Brown was studying with of intensive study but not necessarily to join the monastery. Those visitors spread the word about Tassajara retreat. Tassajara opened its doors each summer to seekers who wanted a short course book was a best-seller and brought more people to both the San Francisco Center and the lectures were edited and compiled as a book, *Zen Mind, Beginner Mind*, published in 1970. The

With the help of three early followers, Marian Derby, Trudy Dixon, and Richard Baker, Suzuki's was open to American students and those who wanted to become monks. type) monastery in the United States, in 1967. Like his contemporary, Trungpa, Suzuki's center land in the rural Carmel Valley and built the Tassajara Zen Center, the first Buddhist (of any community. With the success of the San Francisco Center, Suzuki and his followers obtained States was home to so many curious and seeking minds that he decided to stay and build a new included it in their works, exposing Buddhism to a wider audience. Suzuki felt that the United of Buddhist teachers and thinkers, but it was the Beat writers who embraced Buddhism and at the exact right time. Americans on the East and West Coasts were familiar with a variety but gives a basic idea of the practice. Suzuki's arrival in San Francisco in 1959 to teach was and chanting. Soto Zen also incorporates a monastic practice. This is an oversimplification practice incorporates silent meditation called *Shikantaza*, and *koan*, or revered words, study too that the leader will make changes to benefit the group and ensure its longevity. Soto Zen style of succession to ensure that the practice remain as unchanged as possible, knowing in China in the early 700s and came to Japan in the 1200s. Soto Zen carefully follows a lineage follows in the tradition of Soto Zen, the largest of the three sects of Zen Buddhism. Soto began The San Francisco Zen Center was established in 1962 by Roshi Suzuki and his followers. It American Buddhism into a distinct subset of Zen, Thai, Chinese, and Tibetan schools of Buddhism. and retreat centers, while writing their own interpretations of various teachers, transformed positions within various organizations, but having Americans in charge of the monastic orders cultural connections to Asia long before the 1970s-era American practitioners attained leadership 1975 with Sharon Salzberg and Joseph Goldstein. Buddhism had already begun to lose the of Buddhism prior to coming to Naropa, went on to start the Insight Meditation Society in the idea of Shambhala Buddhism. Jack Kornfield, who studied Thai and Burmese schools

The first cohort of Trungpa and Naropa students became teachers and writers who expanded heed his teaching.

of his shortcomings, telling students, just as Osho/Bhagwan did, not to mimic his lifestyle but follower of tantric practices, he often ate meat. He was sometimes a bully. Yet he was aware amounts of alcohol and, according to former students, also used cocaine and Seconal. As a mind-altering substances were not in accordance with Buddhism, yet he drank prodigious the 1967 car accident. Trungpa remains an influential and controversial teacher. He taught that

Undated group picture of San Francisco Zen Center students.

rave reviews and remains in business to this day serving inspired vegetarian cuisine, with most of its produce sourced from the Zen Center's Green Gulch Farm and monastery. Fellow Buddhist monk Deborah Madison, who managed the Green Gulch Farm, took over restaurant operations at Greens after Brown's departure. Tassajara and its farm-to-table approach to cooking were instrumental in creating what became California Cuisine. Brown has since retired from monastic life and teaches meditation and cooking for small groups in his home.

Another Suzuki Americanized traditional Japanese-style Zen into an entirely new practice. D.T. Suzuki came to the United States in 1897 to participate in the World Parliament of Religions. Suzuki wrote and taught the Zen he learned—The Kyoto School—to seekers throughout the country. His books, *Essays in Zen* (1927) and *An Introduction to Zen Buddhism* (1934, with a foreword by Carl Jung), stressed that the practice of Zen was difficult. It required willpower. It demanded strict discipline. Suzuki's Zen Buddhism taught that individuals who practiced sacrifices to eliminate ego became spiritually strong. His thinking was influenced by Japanese nationalism, as the country was at war with Russia and engaged in colonizing battles in China and on the Korean peninsula. His idealized warrior was a Zen master who was skilled in all forms of combat.

Suzuki was well aware of the physicality of Indian-style Buddhism. He rejected it with unveiled contempt. "...in Zen there are fortunately none of those marvelously incomprehensible words, as in Indian cults. Neither does Zen play about with complicated Hatha-yoga techniques, which delude the physiologically thinking European[132] with the false hope that the spirit can be obtained by sitting and breathing. On the contrary, Zen demands intelligence and will-power, as do all great things which desire to become real."[133] Suzuki advocated for physical strength and wrote admiringly about *Bushido*, the ethical code followed by Samurai.

As influential as D.T. Suzuki is to Zen Buddhism in the United States, his way was often criticized as not being a true or accurate reflection of Buddhist concepts. He noted in his

132 Suzuki referred to all non-Asian white people as "Europeans" in his writings.
133 Passage from *An Introduction to Buddhism* by D.T. Suzuki (1934).

Holy Food

academic translations of early Buddhist histories and commentaries that additions were made, and just like the Bible, cannot be considered the actual words of the Buddha. His reasoning led him to remain neutral on the question of vegetarianism, as the founding generations of monks *did* eat meat, being that they were required to consume only what was given as alms. As Buddhism spread in the United States, more practitioners adopted vegetarianism because it was a constant reminder to refrain from killing living creatures. Many modern Zen teachers leave the decision to eat meat up to the individual, likening the purchase of meat to scavenging, which was always considered acceptable, insomuch that if the animal has already been slaughtered then the greater offense is to those whose hospitality is rejected, and to the animal itself who sacrificed its life to provide sustenance. Suzuki himself only noted that food was to be eaten only as needed and without "imagination," which is interpreted as focusing solely on the act of nourishment and not letting the mind idly wander. In this, Suzuki is aligned with modernist Buddhist thought as exemplified by Thich Nhat Hanh in his book *Mindful Eating*. In it, readers and eaters will recognize the gentle admonishments to eat slowly and mindfully, the notion evolving from the strict discipline of Suzuki to the very American sentiment of focusing on the self. Yet for many who grew up with convenience foods and eating in the communal lunchroom of schools under a watchful teacher pressed for time, settling one's mind to consider the feelings of hunger and satiation is revelatory.

Critics characterized Suzuki's teachings as less Buddhist and more akin to Western and Theosophist philosophies packaged in "Eastern" dressings. Even Buddhist traditionalists in Japan were quite clear that Suzuki's Zen was a layperson's Buddhism devoid of the spiritual components. Suzuki's American-born wife, Beatrice Lane, was active in Theosophist and Bahá'í[134] groups and is said to have brought these ideas to her husband. For Suzuki, Buddhism was not static but constantly evolving in reaction to "the irritant" that is the world. A modern world required a modern Buddhism.

D.T. Suzuki's version of Zen Buddhism was a vigorous, masculine practice which taught that great spiritual rewards came from intensive individual commitment to its pursuit. There were similarities to self-actualization philosophies and the I AM Activity Movement. Suzuki's tenure at Columbia University put him in direct contact with John Cage, Allen Ginsberg, and Jack Kerouac, all of whom embraced Suzuki's philosophies. Kerouac, through his popular writing, brought a pastiche of Suzuki's Zen to millions of young male readers who saw themselves as dharma bums—setting the wheel of doctrine in motion for the convergence of all the new religions, self-styled gurus, and hapless seekers in the growing counterculture movement.

134 The Bahá'í Faith is a relatively new religion teaching the essential worth of all religions and the unity of all people. Established by Bahá'u'lláh in the nineteenth century, it initially developed in Iran and parts of the Middle East, where it has faced ongoing persecution since its inception.

According to the Bahá'í teachings, religion is revealed in an orderly and progressive way by a single God through manifestations of God, who are the founders of major world religions throughout history; Buddha, Jesus, and Muhammad are noted as the most recent of these before the Báb and Bahá'u'lláh. Furthermore, the Bahá'í Faith stresses the unity of all people, explicitly rejecting racism and nationalism. At the heart of Bahá'í teachings is the goal of a unified world order that ensures the prosperity of all nations, races, creeds, and classes.

Specific food-related beliefs and practices: Adult Bahá'ís should observe a nineteen-day fast each year during daylight hours in March, with specific exemptions. Drinking or selling alcohol is forbidden.

The last of the influential teachers on American Buddhism is the recently deceased Vietnamese monk Thich Nhat Hanh (1926–2022). He was accepted at age twelve as a monk in Saigon in the Mahayana and Theravada tradition. He became an outspoken peace advocate during the French occupation and communist counter-insurgency during the late 1950s, and remained actively against war throughout the escalation of violence in Vietnam. He was exiled a few times prior to being permanently banned from the country in 1966. His work was based on his concept of "engaged Buddhism," the idea that both monastic and lay practitioners must share their work with everyone to further the principles of peace that are foundational to Theravada Buddhism. (Suzuki's version of Zen had more militaristic trappings.) Like D.T. Suzuki a decade earlier, Thich taught Buddhist philosophy at Columbia University. His activism led to friendships with other American religious leaders, and he spent time with Catholic monk Thomas Merton and Baptist leader Martin Luther King, Jr.

His groundbreaking 1975 book *The Miracle of Mindfulness* laid the foundation for his future work in bringing the Buddhist concept of mindfulness in every thought and action to wider audiences. As Thich became more famous he established Plum Village, a monastery in southwestern France that became the headquarters for his growing mindfulness movement. He believed in ecumenical harmony, and worked with religious leaders throughout the world to bring peace and dignity to everyone. He was not outwardly political, yet the philosophy of engaged Buddhism required one to speak and act in the face of injustice. To that end Thich organized for refugee rights and against human trafficking. Through his writing he spread his message that mindfulness is the key to personal and societal harmony. The concept is described by his foundation: "Mindfulness is the energy of being aware and awake to the present moment." The result for Americans is the distillation of Thich's spiritually complex teachings into bite-sized nuggets that are divorced from their larger context.

Thich's foundation published a small book of his thoughts about food and eating in 2004 as *How to Eat*. In 2010, he worked with fellow monk-leaders at Plum Village and Harvard nutritionist Lilian Cheung to publish *Savor: Mindful Eating, Mindful Life*, which gave scientific basis for his vegan diet and mindful system. When asked why he recommended a vegan diet for his followers he said, "By eating meat we share the responsibility of climate change, the destruction of our forests, and the poisoning of our air and water." Most interestingly, Thich's interpretation of Buddha's prohibition against killing had expanded to include not only specific animals but to the planet itself.

Mindful eating continues to be a popular conceptual practice for many people—those many include non-Buddhists. The Slow-Food Movement, which began in Italy in 1989 as a protest against fast food and to retain artisanal food practices, has found alignment with the mindful eating concepts. Psychologists encourage mindful eating as one of many tools used to manage eating disorders. Mindful eating is also touted by social media influencers as a holistic way to lose weight. And in the American tradition, there are a growing number of self-styled coaches and gurus who will teach you mindful eating practices for a price. Still, research shows that mindful eating, absent the rigor of daily Buddhist practice, has benefits for those who try it. As Americans struggle with supermarkets and restaurants filled with overprocessed, nutritionally

Ching Hai and her Loving Hut vegan restaurant chain.

bereft foods, slowing down to think about, savor, and give thanks for what we eat is never a bad idea.

Lest one think the age of master-teachers has passed, a woman living in Taiwan is making spiritual and culinary inroads into the United States. Quan Yin Method is not an American-born group, yet merits mention because, like the Unification Church (Moonies), they are working to attract Americans. As a religious practice, Quan Yin Method is rooted in Buddhism yet has all the polycultural elements that define it as a wholly New Religious Movement. The group has few formal worship locations, and relies on the internet and its satellite broadcast channel to livestream meditation events throughout the world, and is often referred to as a cybersect.

Quan Yin Method was founded in Taiwan by a wealthy Vietnamese-Chinese woman, Trinh Dang Hue. Hue was born in 1950 and as a member of the upper classes was raised as a Roman Catholic—common among the Vietnamese elite due to the country's centuries-long occupation by the French. She traveled the world extensively and was living in Europe at the escalation of the Vietnamese-American war. She married a German national in 1969, but they soon divorced when she embarked on her spiritual journey that took her to Buddhist monasteries in Europe, and finally to India where she studied with multiple teachers. Hue was following a traditional Buddhist pathway to becoming a monk, studying with Taiwan-based monk Jing-Xing, but during the mid-1980s, Hue felt stifled by the sexism within the Buddhist monastery tradition and began to reject all asceticism.

The Quan Yin Method was formally introduced in 1988 when Hue changed her name to Ching Hai and began teaching. The Quan Yin Method (loosely translated from Mandarin as "observation of the inner vibration") owes more to the Sant Mat tradition of Sikh gurus. While not prominent in the histories written by the group, outside researchers have noted that Ching Hai spent several years as an acolyte of the controversial Indian guru Thakar Singh. His teaching also focused on meditation as a tool for connecting to the spiritual world and bringing peace. Singh traveled through Europe but never to the United States, yet he succumbed to the same lures of power and was accused of sexually abusing followers.

The Quan Yin Method as developed by Ching Hai is truly a new movement that decouples teaching and meditation from the guru-teacher lineage so important to traditional Buddhism and Sikhism. Ching Hai calls herself and her group humanitarian and not religious. Most interestingly, and why the group is included here, the group uses the proven recruitment-

cum-revenue model of operating restaurants staffed by unpaid members. A review of their American tax filings show that they do indeed spend the majority of their funds on verifiable charitable works around the world—all funded by the group's Loving Hut Vegan Restaurants, as well as Ching Hai's other businesses selling authorized clothing and jewelry. Only the future can know if the Quan Yin Method will outlast its charismatic leader, but the food is quite good.

HENRY OLCOTT'S WORK IN BRINGING THERAVADA BUDDHISM TO AMERICANS fueled a phenomenon that has only been recognized by scholars and researchers in the past two decades: the rise of the JewBu. A few days after the seventeen-day-long 1893 Chicago World Parliament of Religions ended, Theravada monk Anagarika Dharmapala gave a lecture at the Chicago Theosophist Society. Attending the lecture (and the Parliament) was Jewish business owner Charles Strauss. He lived in New York and was a widower with four young children, and by all tellings was searching for meaning in his grief. After Dharmapala's lecture, Strauss asked to be converted. Dharmapala performed the initiation ritual of *Pancil* as Strauss accepted the Five Precepts of Morality and took vows to abstain from harming living beings, stealing, sexual improprieties, lying, and intoxication.[135] Strauss became the first converted Buddhist living in the United States.

Modern scholars have explored exactly what about Judaism and Buddhism allows for an easy spiritual coexistence. JewBus identify as both Jewish and Buddhist, honoring traditions and rituals from both practices. Many of the monks and leaders in American Buddhism identify as having a Jewish cultural and religious upbringing. Religious scholars note that Judaism and Buddhism have many shared values. Buddhist Karma is akin to *middah k'neged middah* (measure for measure), meaning that negative actions are repaid with negative consequences. Both believe that the suffering of innocents is a test of faith. Modern and Hasidic Judaism believes in a form of soul reincarnation that aligns with Buddhist thoughts on a soul's journey. And Judaic scholars from the outset have accepted and incorporated teachings and wisdom from other religious traditions that do not conflict with the Tanakh— though there are scholarly disputes as to whether a person worships or reveres the Buddha, as there are clear prohibitions against worshipping "graven idols." But the argument against Jews also being Buddhist is made by the most conservative of Judaic sects, as most American JewBus are born and raised in the liberal Reformed Judaism tradition. Yet before Jews found Buddhism, they became American.

Abraham Lincoln House in Milwaukee was founded by a group of wealthy German Jewish women in 1896 to serve the influx of Eastern European Jewish immigrants, and became famous through the publication of a cookbook. The Abraham Lincoln House focused on teaching émigré women how to "keep house" in the States—a far different endeavor in an industrial American city than in the rural villages most had called home. Lizzie Black Kandor led cooking classes for women to teach them how to cook traditional dishes using modern

---

135 *Pancil*, in Theravada Buddhism, is a simple ritual where the convertee asks a monk to give him the Five Precepts. In a ritualized speech, the monk asks the convertee to accept the Precepts and then repeat what they are after the monk declares what they are. This can be done in any language, though many use the Pali language of Sri Lanka, the spiritual home of the Theravada tradition.

Holy Food

ABRAHAM LINCOLN HOUSE

(a.k.a. Jewish Settlement House)

Years active: 1900 to present day (as the Jewish Community Center)

Affiliation: Jewish

Founders: The trustees of B'ne Jeshurun temple, Temple Emanu-El Ladies Society, and the Sisterhood of Personal Service

MUSHKAZUNGE

(Vegetarian. Serves 8.)

Tools: 9x13 jelly roll or baking pan, parchment paper

Oven temperature: 350°F

Ingredients:

7 egg whites

1 cup plus 2 Tablespoons sugar

½ teaspoon cinnamon

rind of ½ lemon, finely grated

½ pound roasted almonds, grated

Steps:

1. Preheat oven to 350°F.

2. In a large bowl, beat whites until stiff enough to hold a soft peak.

3. Add sugar in 4 phases, beating mixture after each addition.

4. Add cinnamon and lemon rind and mix together.

5. Fold in grated almonds.

6. Line baking pan with parchment paper. Spread mixture evenly into pan. Bake for 20 minutes.

7. Remove from oven. Slice into rectangular pieces for serving.

TASSAJARA

(Formal name is The San Francisco Zen Center Tassajara Retreat)
Years active: 1962 to present day
Affiliation: Soto Zen Buddhism
Founder: Roshi Shunryu Suzuki

TAHINI SHORTBREAD

(Vegetarian. Makes 1 pan.)
Tools: 8x8 pan, parchment paper
Oven temperature: 325°F

The Tassajara bakers offer a few suggestions when making these cookies. "Cashew butter or peanut butter could also be used in place of the tahini. And a somewhat drier shortbread can be made without the butter. Much less flour (¾ to 1 cup less) will be needed." Note that making the version that omits butter would make this recipe vegan-friendly.

Ingredients:
¼ cup sugar
¼ cup butter
1 cup tahini
½ teaspoon salt
2 cups flour (add additional ½ cup if dough is too moist)
Optional: 1 Tablespoon minced lemon rind

Steps:
1. Preheat oven to 325°F.
2. In a large bowl, cream the butter with the tahini. (This can be done with a mixer or by hand.)
3. Add the sugar, salt, and then flour. Stir until the mixture is firm, working with the hands at the end.
4. Press the mixture into square pan lined with parchment paper, about a quarter- to a half-inch thick. (It's all right if it doesn't come all the way to the edges.)
5. With a sharp paring knife, mark into pieces and cut about halfway through the dough. (An almond or walnut can be pressed on top of each piece.)
6. Place into oven and bake at 325°F for about 45 minutes, or until the center is firm when gently pressed. Don't overbake or wait for it to brown—the shortbread would be overly hard, dry, and crumbly.

Some tasters reported a slight bitterness. If this is a concern for you, add the optional tablespoon of minced lemon rind. It will add a touch of brightness.

Holy Food

NUT-BUTTERED BEANS

(Vegetarian. Serves 4 to 6.)
Tools: Small stockpot, casserole baking dish
Oven temperature: 350°F

Note from the Tassajara cooks: "This dish can be spiced up with the addition of chili powder, cumin, coriander, garlic, lemon, cardamom. Take your pick, but easy does it."

Ingredients:

1 cup dried cannellini (white kidney) beans (updated from the original soybeans, which can be used if desired)
4 cups water
½ cup sugar-free peanut butter (can substitute with cashew or almond butter)
1 Tablespoon kosher salt (or soy sauce)

Steps:

1. Soak beans, fully submerged in water, overnight in a large bowl.
2. Next day, preheat oven to 350°F.
3. Drain beans. Put them in a small stockpot. Add the water and cook over medium heat for 60 to 90 minutes. (Check beans at 60 minutes, they should be tender but not soft.)
4. Drain beans, reserving the cooking liquid.
5. Pour beans into casserole dish.
6. In a small bowl, add the peanut butter and 2 tablespoons of the reserved cooking liquid. Stir together until smooth. Add a few more tablespoons of the liquid if needed. Pour over beans and mix.
7. Place lid on casserole dish and bake for 20 minutes.

Serve as a side dish or entrée.

If you started with a cup of dry beans, use about half a cup of peanut butter. Add a couple of tablespoons of the cooking liquid a little at a time, mixing well so that the peanut butter becomes a smooth sauce. Again, this dish can be left to simmer or bake. Even better with sesame butter or tahini and more exotic with cashew, almond or walnut butter.

TANGERINE CABBAGE WITH ONION FRENCH DRESSING

(Vegan. Serves 4.)

Tools: Large and small bowl

Ingredients for salad:

1 small green cabbage

1 small red cabbage

2 tangerines (can substitute canned mandarin oranges)

Ingredients for dressing:

1 cup olive oil

½ cup rice wine vinegar (or red wine vinegar)

¼ cup minced onion

1 Tablespoon dry mustard powder

2 Tablespoons fresh (or powdered) garlic

1 teaspoon salt

1 teaspoon black pepper

1 teaspoon sugar

Steps:

1. Wash, then shred both red and green cabbage and place into large bowl.

2. Peel and section tangerines and add to bowl.

3. In a small bowl, make the dressing by mixing all ingredients together. Stir vigorously. Taste. Adjust spices, salt, and sugar until it pleases you.

4. Add dressing to cabbage and tangerine and toss together.

5. Serve.

The Tassajara cooks give wise instruction on achieving the best-tasting dressing: "If it lacks body add salt. If it lacks bite add mustard. If it lacks flavor add garlic." And: "It's not right if I can taste or feel any one particular ingredient."

QUAN YIN METHOD

Years active: 1988 to present day
Affiliation: Syncretic Buddhism
Founder / Leader: Suma or Supreme Master Ching Hai

SINGAPORE CURRY RICE NOODLES

(Vegan. Makes 2 servings.)
Tools: Large, deep-dish frying pan or small wok

Ingredients:

6 ounces rice noodles

1 8-ounce block firm tofu, sliced to ¼-inch thickness

½ cup thinly sliced white onion

1 cup shredded carrots

¾ cup bean sprouts (about a handful)

2 green onions (only use the green leaves), cut into ¼-inch pieces

2 teaspoons salt (or to taste)

1½ teaspoons natural MSG

1 Tablespoon + 1 teaspoon sugar

1 Tablespoon + 1 teaspoon curry powder

1 Tablespoon of vegetable or sesame oil

Steps:

1. In a medium saucepan, boil water over high heat. Add rice noodles and cook for 3 minutes until soft. Remove from heat, rinse, and set aside.

2. Clean and prepare onions and carrots. Set aside.

2. In a frying pan, add 1 tablespoon of oil and warm over medium-high heat. Add tofu slices and fry until golden brown on both sides. Remove tofu slices from pan and set aside.

3. In same frying pan, add another tablespoon of oil and warm over medium-high heat. Add onion slices until fragrant and soft.

4. Add fried tofu, carrots, bean sprouts, and green onions, reserving approximately 1 tablespoon of green onion pieces for final garnish. Stir constantly until all are lightly seared and fragrant.

5. Add cooked rice noodles and turn off heat.

6. Add in salt, MSG, sugar, and curry powder. Mix well.

7. Turn burner back on to medium-high and while stirring, cook
   until noodles are "dry." (Approximately 3 minutes.)
8. Remove from heat and serve with sprinkle of green onion pieces.

A tasting note: I was able to sample this dish as made by the Ching Hai group-owned Loving Hut restaurant chain in San Bernardino, California. Arriving as they opened at 11 a.m., there was already a line of diners waiting to place orders. I sampled a few dishes—all vegan and reflective interpretations of Southeast Asian dishes—and everything was very good. I also noted that the restaurant was staffed by Quan Yin Method followers, but the diners were there specifically for the food.

Front cover and interior from 2021 edition of *Love Is The Only Solution*. Author's collection.

Holy Food

Twelve

TURN ON, TUNE IN, DROP OUT

THERE HAS ALWAYS BEEN A COUNTERCULTURE IN THE UNITED STATES. (Puritans and utopian communards are both examples of counterculture practices.) The country is too geographically spread out, too populous, and too diverse to have a singular mainstream culture. As Americans, our notions about spirituality and religion beliefs are too varied to unite under a simplistic ideology, regardless of the machinations of small groups striving to impose their specific beliefs onto everyone. It is both a strength and weakness of the American experiment.

Academic researchers in the early 1970s theorized that previous American spiritual revivals came about as a societal reaction to cultural change and economic stressors. The Finney-ites of the late 1770s were born of the disconnect between elite aristocrats tied to the hierarchical English caste structure and the hardscrabble farmers seeking autonomy from inherited class systems. The Second Great Awakening was fueled by the changes to the agrarian way of life upended by the Industrial Revolution. And the twentieth-century "New Age" was born out of the conflict between a system of capitalism that valued productivity and return on investments over human experience. Post-World War II generations struggled to find intrinsic meaning to their existence and personal connection with humans. Religious congregations became a cure for the loneliness that was fast becoming the hallmark of modern life, and a new mission of activism to change American culture. Yet there were, as always, conflicts between *whose* vision of America will prevail.

A key commonality among American religious and spiritual revivals was easy access to the message and messenger. It's a point touched on earlier: the desire to find a pathway to spiritual communion without the need for a priestly intermediary. For mainstream religions, direct experience of God requires hard work. Fasting, long hours of prayerful meditation, deprivations, and even bodily endurance feats facilitate mystical experiences. And aside from choosing the ascetic life of a monk, workaday laborers existing in the modern American system did not have access to the tools that brought about a personal relationship with God. Regardless of the religion, 1950s-era thinking was: spend your time with the congregation following your pastor/

rabbi/imam/priest's interpretation of the Book, and his (or the denomination's) rules and God will accept you. Your community will accept you. During the post-World War II low tide of radical activism in the United States, the relatively easy access and participation in spiritual life was enough to maintain a cultural status quo. Yet not everyone was satisfied with their role in the American story nor with their personal experience of spirituality.

Front cover of 1967 edition of *Start Your Own Religion*. Author's collection.

The American mythos is built on a conceptual notion of "frontiers," of seeking and the discovery of the "new." Puritans and pietists came from Europe to escape the dominant culture at home. Americans went west in the mid-1800s to build new communities based on their beliefs about God. Yet by the end of World War II, the American landmass was entirely settled. There were no material frontiers to be crossed and conquered. The last frontier was spiritual. To find a new way to be human in the industrial, capitalist, and increasingly hostile United States, one had to turn inward to discover a place in the world in relation to the spiritual cosmos.

IT WAS DURING THE 1960S THAT A NEW STYLE OF GROUPS AND MARGINALIZED thinkers using nonviolent protest claimed center stage. Through marches, boycotts, demonstrations, and educational campaigns, motivated activists shifted American culture and politics. Ideas of racial and gender equality moved from being viewed as leftist extremism to accepted planks in the Democratic Party. Yet there was always tension from conservative reactionaries who sought to maintain the status quo that hoarded economic and political power for white Christian men. The war in Vietnam became a catalyst and wedge that further divided the nation. The question becomes: when did everything change? When did the vibe shift? As with so much of American history, rather than a singular event, there was a convergence of events that spurred the next decade of new religious and communal movements.

Statistically, the young men who served in Vietnam—whether voluntary or drafted—were predominantly from poor and working-class backgrounds. It was the first war fought with a fully racially integrated military. It was the first war fought after the passage of the 1964 Civil Rights Act. And for many young soldiers, serving with men from racially diverse (including Hispanic and Native American) backgrounds was their first experience living in close quarters with someone outside of their own ethnic group, religious beliefs, and geographic area. Terry

Wilds, a Black war correspondent who wrote *Bloods: An Oral History of the Vietnam War by Black Veterans,* said in 1984, "I'm convinced part of Martin Luther King's dream came true in Vietnam. In his famous 1963 speech at the Lincoln Memorial, he said he had a dream that one day the sons of former slaves and sons of slave owners would sit at the same table. That dream came true in only one place, the front lines of Vietnam." The young men who came home after their combat service came home to a country dismissive of their sacrifice and experience. These were veterans who endured psychological and emotional traumas that would take decades to be recognized by society. They were men who, once marginalized by their race and socio-economic backgrounds, became further marginalized by their service to their country.

Those who were not drafted to go to Vietnam were (on average) young men with wealth and privilege. They were the sons of families who could send them to college and attain deferment until the war was over.[141] They were the sons whose families had connections with the local draft board to ensure they would never be called up. They were the sons who could afford doctors who wrote ridiculous medical diagnoses to exempt them from service. They were the fortunate sons. The obvious class divide between who served and who did not exacerbated veterans' disaffection for a political system that rewarded wealth and power with more power and wealth. Far too many returning soldiers came home to seek an existence that would allow them to remain outside the constant noise of political and cultural battles.

Historians also point to the assassination of Dr. Martin Luther King Jr. in April of 1968 as the event that signaled the death of the '60s. In the weeks following King's assassination, riots and demonstrations erupted as the nation raged. King's murder took on symbolic importance as the end of the era of peaceful protest—of respectfully asking the powers that be to essentially give everyone equal rights and be the best version of the American promise, and not serve the craven desires of a small cadre of politicians and businessmen. Then came the assassination of Robert F. Kennedy a few months later, on June 6, 1968. Kennedy was the most likely presidential candidate to carry forward progressive ideals. His murder left the Democratic Party and activists stunned. Though the Democratic Party was mostly aligned with the values and aims of young activists, not every candidate was. Just like today, the two-party system means that each party has members with a wide range of ideologies. The final event that catalyzed the start of drop-out culture was the Democratic National Convention riots in Chicago in August of 1968. Activists wanted the U.S. out of the Vietnam war. The Democratic Party leadership battled among members whether exiting Vietnam would or would not be included as a "plank of the platform." Activists converged on Chicago in a show of will and determination to make de-escalation part of the Presidential campaign. Most know that the events devolved into police attacks on demonstrators and the Democratic party moved to nominate then-Vice President Hubert Humphrey on a platform of watered-down de-escalation. Republican Richard Nixon won the 1968 election and increased military draft quotas, sending even more young men to war.

---

141 Famous Vietnam-era deferrees include: Joe Biden, George W. Bush, Dick Cheney, Bill Clinton, Mitt Romney, and Donald Trump. None of these American politicians evaded the draft on political or antiwar grounds; instead, they used their relative wealth and access to avoid service to country in service to themselves.

For enthusiastic and hopeful activists, it was a bitter loss. And for many it was a betrayal of promises made—the promise of America and what it can be when its citizens work to make it better for their neighbors and future generations. Why bother? Time to get out.

T HE WORD *ENTHEOGEN* WAS COINED IN THE LATE '70S TO DESCRIBE A PLANT-DERIVED substance "which causes God to be within an individual." Used primarily by ethnobotanists and academics, the word better designates the class of plants that cause psychedelic or hallucinogenic experiences. The study and use of entheogenic plants have passed from universities and pharma labs into popular culture, as evidenced by National Football League superstar Aaron Rodgers openly discussing his use of *ayahuasca* for personal insights and growth. Once again, there is tension between provable facts and pure faith as we seek God.

The entheogenists view the psychoactive compounds as part of God's gift to man, a tool to commune with the deity. But many Christian traditionalists dismiss any drug-induced revelation as escapist rot and the work of the devil. But as noted earlier, many religious traditions incorporated a plant concoction that *did* cause altered brain states. Taking note of the Zoroastrians and others, the focus now shifts to the early seekers who sought God through plant-based and synthetic compounds who influence the next wave of New Religious Movements and their food. The connection is quite clear when we think of plants as food to be consumed, but if the plants we consume contain the essence of god(s) we are closer than ever before to understanding why we sacralize food. Yet before we discover tasty personal saviors through plants, science is still working to understand how these plants affect the brain.

Modern brain research has benefited from technological advances, like fMRI (functional Magnetic Resonance Imaging) tools that allow scientists to "see" what the brain is doing during activities and under the influence of drugs. One fascinating new insight into brain function is the recent discovery that a specific region of the brain influences our predilection to have religious and spiritual beliefs. These are areas within the brain called the Default Mode Network (DMN) which works akin to a computer operating system constantly running in the background of our daily lives as it thinks and daydreams. It is believed that the DMN system is home to our notions of ego and selfhood as it processes experiences and information in the ongoing construction of the self. Two areas within the DMN influence our sense of personhood: the prefrontal cortex in the front of the brain is responsible for reasoning, problem solving, comprehension, impulse control, creativity, and perseverance; and the cingulate cortex in the middle of the brain is responsible for memory formation, emotional responses, and pain responses. All sections of the DMN are awash in serotonin receptors. The functional opposite of the DMN is the CEN—the Central Executive Network. The CEN brain sections are responsible for task-focused work and analytical processes. The CEN has fewer serotonin receptors and less neural connection to the DMN sections of the brain. A simple reductive way to think about the DMN and CEN sections of the brain is that the DMN controls how we feel and the CEN controls how we think.

Experiments in the past two decades have revealed much about how our brains make us uniquely human. We know that our brains are hummingly active when our physical bodies are at rest. We know that damage to a single area of our brain affects very specific aspects of our personality. We also know that we can adjust and manipulate how our brains process information with the introduction of any number of chemical agonists and physical activities to tweak how our DMN reacts to our environment. Harvard researcher Michael Ferguson of Harvard Divinity School conducted fMRI studies in 2018 on people who were known to have a lesion—damage to the brain—to see what those damaged sections looked like. But first, he administered a questionnaire to assess their level of spiritual belief prior to the lesion and if those beliefs changed after discovery of the brain damage. Working on the scientifically informed hypothesis that religious and spiritual beliefs "live" in the DMN section of the brain, he found that people with DMN lesions had less belief in God, while those with damage to the analytic CEN regions had increased belief in spiritual possibilities. And those with severe CEN damage experienced a hyper-religiosity verging on mania. Later studies also found that these shifts of perspective happened in people who also had small or undiagnosed brain lesions, such as those caused by concussions, chronic inflammatory diseases, and unnoticed strokes and seizures. These studies begin to reveal that spiritual matters have an organic human component.

There are other conditions and substances that can change the brain and how the brain communicates with itself. The ascetic practices in monastic religious communities use the body to change the brain. Studies have shown that physical discipline practices like yoga, deep breathing, and meditation all tweak the brain structure into increasing neural flow between sections which, of course, allows for the DMN sections to make deeper connections to CEN. It is the notion of immanence—that God is within us—that a high-functioning and productive DMN can give us. Aside from the SSRI family of pharmaceuticals intended to adjust the flow of serotonin throughout brain sections, modern brain research is now reaching back into our collective history to study the effect of hallucinogenic (potentially entheogenic) plants, and their later chemical-derived counterparts, on the human brain. Research so far shows and confirms the same outcome every time: there are both plant and synthetic chemical substances that can increase neural connections between the DMN and CEN. Consuming these substances can decouple the established construction of the individual self and create a deeply felt relationship to the expansive idea of God and spirituality. This research is why scientists termed this class of plant-derived chemicals *entheogens* as a better descriptor than hallucinogens or psychedelics. The findings, while groundbreaking, are still inconclusive in determining whether god-like entities exist in our universe or are a creation of the brain. Or if God is in our food.

Zoroastrians drank the sacred *haoma* derived from the ephedra plant and psychoactive mushrooms. Indigenous people in North and South America use a variety of plants—marijuana, peyote, ayahuasca, to name a few—to seek communion with other planes of existence; Northern European people consumed amanita mushrooms with hallucinogenic properties. People living in central Africa-based cultures used the bark of the iboga[142] tree in rituals and healing. Indo-Aryans in central Asia and northern India drank soma, a fermented concoction

---

142 The bark from the iboga tree after preparation is called ibogaine in the West. The French colonial powers brought it back to Europe as a stimulant in the late 1800s. American researchers have touted its power to "cure" addiction since the early 1960s. It is a Schedule I drug in the United States whose use is prohibited by harsh legal penalties. The past decade has seen new research into therapeutic uses for ibogaine, including addiction treatment, post-traumatic stress disorder, and traumatic brain injuries.

that researchers believe contained psilocybin or another mushroom-derived compound. Alcohol, too, can affect brain function by reducing CEN operations regulating impulse control and logical reasoning. Christianity symbolically uses wine to represent the blood of Christ ritually consumed by followers. Humans have sacralized eating since our remembered history, and for as long as humans have believed that God has told us what to eat, we eat to find God. But in the mid-twentieth century, entheogens, long restricted in use and cloaked in ritual, were about to go worldwide and give New Age spiritual thought the last element it needed to move from isolated practices to a burning Revival based on the idea that God could be revealed by consuming specific plants and their synthetic cousins.

RICHARD ALPERT WAS BORN TO AN UPPER-MIDDLE-CLASS JEWISH FAMILY AND attended prestigious schools attaining his doctorate in psychology. He has said that he had a happy childhood with loving and supportive parents. He also said in interviews and writings that while he felt culturally Jewish, he never felt any connection to G-d or any sense of spirituality. Alpert followed a straightforward path through prestigious schools earning respect for his research into personality development. His mentor had taken a position at Harvard and encouraged Alpert to join him there as a lab assistant and adjunct professor. At the same Harvard Center for Research in Personality was another lecturer, Dr. Timothy Leary.

Timothy Leary was raised in a traditional Irish-Catholic home in Springfield, Massachusetts. He attended Holy Cross College and then the United States Military Academy. His time at West Point gives insights into his later beliefs and stances. He was loath to follow the rules in the discipline-focused setting. He began drinking and was court-martialed for his refusal to confess to drunkenness and other rule violations. He was vindicated at the trial which found him not guilty, but he remained ostracized until a family friend—a sitting U.S. Senator—intervened. Leary was eventually given an honorable discharge and left to study psychology at the University of Alabama. At the outbreak of World War II, he was drafted into the medical corps and served as a psychiatric assistant. He eventually attained his degree via correspondence school and then pursued terminal degrees at the University of Washington and later University of California - Berkeley. His academic work focused on interpersonal tools to diagnose and assess personality disorders. By 1955, Leary was married with two kids and a clinical job working with patients. He and his wife had become dedicated alcoholics trapped in the quiet desperation of idealized middle-class America. Sadly, his wife Marianne killed herself in October of 1955. Leary took his children to Europe, where he struggled to write and teach until he was given a job at the Harvard labs by a former mentor.

Alpert visited Berkeley in 1961, where he first encountered psychedelic drugs. He was intrigued by the therapeutic potential and upon returning to Harvard, he and Leary began the Harvard Psilocybin Project. Recruiting among students and friends, they administered various doses of LSD, psilocybin, and other psychedelics, and made extensive observational notes about what people experienced. Alpert was fascinated that many users reported spiritual and profound religious visions while using the drugs. Alpert advised in the infamous "The Good Friday Experiment," a double-blind study with Harvard Divinity School students in 1962 that

HUMAN BE - IN
A GATHERING OF THE TRIBES

Timothy Leary
Richard Albert
Dick Gregory
Allen Ginsberg
Jerry Rubin
MANY OTHERS

SATURDAY
JAN. 14th
—1967—
FREE

ALL OF SAN FRANCISCO'S ROCK BANDS

* INCLUDING *
SANTANA
AND
THE STEVE
MILLER
BAND

GOLDEN GATE PARK
SAN FRANCISCO

—BRING—
FLOWERS
INCENSE
FEATHERS
CANDLES
BANNERS
FLAGS

—BRING—
FAMILIES
ANIMALS
CYMBALS
DRUMS
CHIMES
FLUTES (358)

Poster announcing the 1967 Human Be-In.

resulted in more reports of mystical religious experiences. The Good Friday Experiment was the first to use scientific methodology to connect spiritual experiences with entheogenic substances and set humankind on a new course of religious discovery—experiments that would continue to this day, and as mentioned earlier were recreated in 2018 at the Divinity School with the addition of fMRI technology.

Leary and Alpert founded the nonprofit International Federation of Internal Freedom (IFIF) to engage in private fundraising to expand their lab's research, but Harvard was not aboard the magic bus. Alpert and Leary were dismissed by Harvard in 1963 after a series of critical and poorly sourced articles in the *Harvard Crimson* newspaper by their undergraduate assistant, the now-celebrity integrative health expert and supplement salesman Dr. Andrew Weil. Out of academia and inspired by Aldous Huxley's psychedelic-informed books *Doors of Perception* and the lesser-known utopian novel *The Island*, the men worked with IFIF board member Peggy Hitchcock—an heiress to the Mellon fortune—to lease a family property to Leary and Alpert for an experimental communal living psychedelic research lab. They moved to the Millbrook Estate in the Hudson River Valley north of New York City and invited friends, fellow researchers, and others interested in psychedelics to move to the decaying mansion to live together and take all the drugs. Which they did. The Millbrook community hosted visitors from all over the world, and the place developed a reputation as a required stop on the journey to selfhood. They later disbanded the IFIF and rebranded as the Castalia Foundation which offered LSD-assisted psychotherapy in addition to yoga, meditation, and other mind-body spiritual exercises. Leary and Alpert continued writing and lecturing together and independently building interest and access to psychedelic drugs, which were still legal in the United States.

Leary and Alpert were among a small group of psychologists and psychotherapists, along with the CIA, who were experimenting with the naturally occurring and synthetic entheogenic compounds. In hindsight, many of the experiments were dangerously haphazard. While there were therapeutic outcomes, there were also mishaps due to lack of oversight and overdosing that resulted in psychotic breaks and even suicide among users. Sandoz Pharmaceutical stopped LSD production in 1965. The American Psychiatric Association issued strong directives to stop any treatment or research using LSD. Individual states began declaring it illegal, and in 1968 LSD was classified as a Schedule I drug by the United States which made possession, transportation, and selling it subject to federal prosecution.

Timothy Leary felt that psilocybin and LSD held great promise for human evolution. He believed it was a tool that could repair psychological damage in individuals and expand an individual's human potential. His friend Allen Ginsberg joined him at Millbrook for extended stays and encouraged Leary to recruit artists to take a trip. Many did. Jack Kerouac, Charles Mingus, and poet Charles Olson all traveled to Millbrook to try psychedelics. Where Leary advocated for a personal and societal healing, making a transhumanist argument for LSD, Alpert saw the spiritual possibilities, that these chemical compounds could allow someone to see god(s). Leary left Millbrook in 1967 and continued his psychedelic evangelism with his newly founded organization-*cum*-spiritual group the League for Spiritual Discovery and traveled throughout the States delivering lectures and doses. Leary was invited to speak at the 1967 Human Be-In at San Francisco's Golden Gate Park. In front of 30,000 people, he uttered the phrase that became the siren call to the hippie generation: Turn On, Tune In, Drop Out. The event became known as the start of the Summer of Love that saw thousands of young people leave their homes to discover themselves while discovering America. Leary elaborated on his ideas for a new way to exist in his 1967 pamphlet *Start Your Own Religion*. In it, Leary states that all religion is created and that human beings are innately divine and it's one's mission to access the god within. Psychedelic drugs help you find your inner divinity. And if we're all God, then we need to start our own religion to sacralize our individual divine practices. Leary elaborated his Buddhist-influenced intention in 1970: "*Drop Out* – detach yourself from the external social drama which is as dehydrated and ersatz as TV. *Turn On* – find a sacrament which returns you to the temple of God, your own body. Go out of your mind. Get high. *Tune In* – be reborn. Drop back in to express it. Start a new sequence of behavior that reflects your vision."

Many were inspired by Leary's work and the convergence of drugs, counterculture tolerance, Buddhism, Hinduism, and radical politics in late-'60s-era San Francisco spreading throughout California and the country. John Griggs was a working-class Anaheim city park attendant who loved car clubs, motorcycles, and smoking weed. He and his buddies were dealing in marijuana and by 1965 had a good racket. They heard about LSD and learned of a Beverly Hills movie producer with a large stash in his refrigerator. Griggs and his gang robbed the man of 1,000 tabs of LSD and retreated to the Hollywood Hills to try out the new drug. They tripped hard. Griggs had an epiphany. He saw the love within all mankind. And he saw how LSD could bring people together in love. Griggs began giving away LSD and moved to the remote Modjeska Canyon with his family and gang of friends. They rented houses and worked to purchase a large tract of land. It was an attempt to create Huxley's imagined utopia, but after a fire burned their main church building and living quarters, the group moved to the then-remote community of Laguna Beach. There they opened a church/head/surf shop and continued to sell marijuana and give away LSD.

Griggs met Timothy Leary during one of Leary's lecture tours. (Griggs was, by 1966, well-known in psychedelic circles.) Griggs and Leary "clicked" and talked about the immanence revealed by LSD, both describing the experience as sacramental. The state of California was moving to declare LSD illegal and, inspired by Leary, Griggs started a religion. Officially incorporated as the Brotherhood of Eternal Love, their declared mission was "to bring to the world a greater awareness of God through the teachings of Jesus Christ, Rama-Krishnam Babaju [*sic*], Paramahansa Yogananda, Mahatma Gandhi, and all true prophets and apostles of God." The requirements for joining the Brotherhood of Eternal Love were an open mind and the ability to take a lot of drugs.

Make no mistake—The Brotherhood's main operation was importing and distributing large amounts of marijuana and LSD. They made so much money that they ceremonially burned thousands of dollars in an impromptu sacrifice. The money allowed them to engage in their one true mission: putting LSD into as many mouths as they could. In 1967, they expanded their communal property holdings and purchased a three-hundred-acre ranch outside of Palm Springs with cash. Idyllwild Ranch became the new home of the Brotherhood of Eternal Love that welcomed all seekers, while the Laguna Beach properties housed longtime members active in the operational aspects of a global importation business. Throughout 1968, the Brotherhood increased their importation operations but as Sandoz Pharmaceutical stopped making LSD they turned to homegrown chemists. They worked with an underground network of chemists that created the iconic American LSD variant, Orange Sunshine. The Brotherhood held the largest distributorship of Orange Sunshine while still extolling their beliefs that the drug was a pathway to godly revelation. Griggs insisted that the group not engage in violence even when threatened or robbed, which occasionally happened.

Timothy Leary considered the Brotherhood's Idyllwild Ranch a second home, as did many transient teenagers and other young people on the hippie trail heeding the siren call of the Summer of Love. Peace and love took a dark turn when Richard Nixon was inaugurated as president in January of 1969. He declared Timothy Leary public enemy Number One and promised worried parents that he would put a stop to the criminals feeding drugs to their kids.[143] Griggs is remembered as telling fellow members of the Brotherhood that in hindsight, maybe hosting a high-profile wanted criminal like Timothy Leary at the ranch where they stored millions of tabs of LSD wasn't such a good idea. A teenage girl died of an overdose while at the ranch. The police raided when the Brotherhood expanded their marijuana sales to include imported Afghan hashish. Yet, they continued their mission, unaware that the times were quickly turning dark. LSD was now widely available and taken without the "holy" constraints by teenagers, biker gangs, and thrill-seekers. Press ran sensational stories of horrific deaths, psychotic breaks, and permanent brain damage due to misadventure caused by psychedelic drugs. It was during this mainstream backlash against mind-altering drugs that John Griggs received a gift from Switzerland on August 3, 1969—a vial of pure psilocybin crystals liberated from the vaults of the Sandoz labs. As was his way to commune with the creator, he ate a hero's dose and retreated to his private teepee. Reports say that he emerged from the teepee a few hours later to warn the others not to take any of the Sandoz psilocybin as it was too strong. His loyal wife wanted to take him to the hospital,

---

143 A theme throughout *Holy Food* is the interconnectivity of people whose ideas and theories spread throughout the country. Conversely, it is also small groups of interconnected people who opposed these ideas and worked to thwart them in many ways. Specific to this era is G. Gordon Liddy. He was a former FBI agent who became the District Attorney for Dutchess County, New York, from 1966 to 1970. As the Dutchess County D.A., he led raids against Timothy Leary and Millbrook that created the ongoing pressure that ended the Commune in 1967. Liddy also led raids against nearby Bard College resulting in the arrests of many students on marijuana charges, including musicians Walter Becker and Donald Fagen, better known under their band name, Steely Dan. Liddy is immortalized in their song "My Old School." Liddy was recruited by the Nixon administration in 1970 as a special agent for drug and gun prosecutions, where he specifically targeted his old nemesis, Timothy Leary.

but he refused, telling her, "It's just between me and God, and that's the way it's going to be." By the next morning he was near death and was taken to the hospital, where he died on arrival.

The Brotherhood continued living communally and dealing marijuana and other drugs until a final police raid in 1972 broke the group. After John Griggs' death, the Brotherhood lost its naïveté about LSD and understood the realities of distributing illegal drugs. What seemed like a new way of being human devolved into constant police actions and fending off armed biker gangs who wanted to control the illicit drug markets.

WHILE LEARY WAS PUBLIC ENEMY NUMBER ONE, RICHARD ALPERT WENT TO INDIA to pursue the spiritual connection to psychedelics. There he met guru Neem Karoli Baba, a Bhakti yoga practitioner devoted to the Hindu deity Hanuman. In Baba, Alpert found the guidance he sought to understand the spirituality he felt while using psychedelics. He changed his name to Ram Dass and wrote the groundbreaking meditative book, *Be Here Now* in 1971. Ram Dass became one of the most high-profile converts to what was growing into an American-style syncretic Hindu-Buddhism. His philosophy mirrored the reductive nature that many "holy men" of the era espoused: kindness to oneself and others, a commitment to live in the Now, and vegetarianism. At the height of his fame during the '70s and '80s, he was criticized by Jewish religious leaders as the chief instigator of leading young Jews away from their cultural traditions and into Buddhism and Hinduism. But in 1991, during his sixtieth year of life on Earth, he decided to explore Judaism. He told the Religious News Service in 1992, "My belief is that I wasn't born into Judaism by accident, and so I needed to find ways to honor that. From a Hindu perspective, you are born as what you need to deal with, and if you just try and push it away, whatever it is, it's got you." In the New Age, the lines between religion of origin and family were quickly erased by spiritual philosophers and gurus who, like religionists of the prior century, mixed ideas from *every* religion to form an entirely new construct.

Ram Dass still believed that psychedelics could be used to further one's spiritual journey, but he parted ways with Leary's carnival barker style and increasing megalomania. It must also be noted that after Leary's arrest and escape from jail, which was funded by the Brotherhood of Eternal Love and managed by the Weather Underground, he effectively removed psychedelic usage from serious scientific research and discourse. Leary was again arrested in Switzerland in 1974 where he made the decision to work with the FBI as an informant to avoid prison. Based on information acquired through Freedom of Information requests after Leary's death in 1996, it is apparent that he consistently gave the FBI information about radical political groups and other psychonauts. Publicly, Ram Dass would lightly criticize Leary that his methods of indiscriminate LSD distribution absent of a healing or spiritual framework could cause great harm to people, yet they reunited in 1983 and remained friends until their respective deaths.

The difference between Leary and Ram Dass' psychedelic paths neatly encapsulates the divergence in American thinking about New Age spirituality. Leary's ideas that hallucinogenic substances revealed a synthesized notion of a practical and spiritual existence of God and that human beings were individual manifestations of God. Leary had a gift for coining memorable phrases and often said, "You are a God, act like one!" More prosaically, he says in *Your Brain*

Ram Dass with Neem Karoli in India, c. 1968. Photo by Rameshwar Das, courtesy of the Ram Dass Foundation.

on God (2001), "God is defined in terms of the technologies involved in creating a universe and engineering the obvious stages of evolution." It is clear that Leary's version of human evolution includes a belief that psychedelic experiences open the brain's pathway to see humans as linked to other living things.

While Ram Dass had similar revelations about the nature of spirituality within the existence of humans, he sought out older traditions rooted in physical manipulation of the body—disciplined meditation and yoga. Dass returned from his pilgrimage to India at Baba's ashram in 1971. He went to the recently established polyspiritual commune, the Lama Foundation[144] in Taos, New Mexico, where he shared his manuscript for becoming spiritually enlightened, *Be Here Now*. The book contained drawings, koans, poems, observations, and exercises to help American seekers become "yogis." *Be Here Now* has sold over two million copies as of this writing and is often called the "Hippie Bible." Leary and Ram Dass set the course for the 1970s spiritual movements—that then became food movements. Their intersecting journey determined the two distinct pathways: one that furthered a syncretic Hindu-Buddhism and another that focused on carving out a separate existence away from society to become a god.

---

144 The Lama Foundation, begun by then-married couple Steve and Barbara Durkee in 1967, was intended to be an ecumenical spiritual center where one could explore a variety of spiritual practices. Steve Durkee converted to Shadhiliya Order Islam (a Sufi subsect of Sunni Islam) and changed his name to Nooruddeen Durkee. He was respected as a scholar and translator. Barbara Durkee followed Sufi and other New Age practices as she moved with her children to an intentional community in Virginia. The Lama Foundation was one of the first of many communes, ashrams, and spiritual centers that called New Mexico home. Their website gives a clear definition of their beliefs and practices:

"Lama's spiritual practices vary at any given time depending on what people bring or what form grace assumes. Certain core practices are constantly re-discovered and renewed. New practices emerge, diverse and multi-faceted, yet seeking the holy, seeking unity and common ground.

Everyone is invited to taste, savor, embrace the feast:

Morning sitting meditation for the entire community. Friday night Jewish Shabbat service. Sufi dhikr. Periods of community silence. Native American prayers at the tipi circle. Grace sung before meals. Dances of Universal Peace in the Dome. Silent vipassana intensives. Hindu kirtan and all-night Akhanda Nama. Christian centering prayer. Ramadan month of Islamic fasting and prayer. Women's lodge. Zen tea ceremony."

T HERE WERE OTHER GROUPS WHO FORMED AROUND THE NEW AGE HIPPIE IDEALS but weren't outwardly religious in nature. These were groups who were informed by the polycultural religious stew that was California during the sixties, but embraced secular communal practices informed by entheogenic plants. The Diggers Commune was a politically active anarchist group who took their name from an English mid-1600s socialist group of the same name. The English Diggers advocated for access to common lands to be used for farming and access to food as a basic human right in opposition to the feudal system of the time. The San Francisco Diggers saw the influx of teenage runaways and other seekers flooding the Haight and sought to address their basic needs. First came the soup kitchens and free food pantries that fed thousands of people each day. The Diggers were highly organized and very effective. They were instrumental in setting up what later became the San Francisco Free Clinic to address basic and emergency health care. (Clinic records show a high number of sexually transmitted diseases, limb injuries, and oddly enough, foot wounds caused by walking around the city barefoot.) As the Diggers had roots in the agitprop theater, they produced ideological performances that highlighted their anarchist views about private property and consumerism. Digger Billy Murcott was interviewed by the local San Francisco news on December 2, 1966, where he neatly describes who eats at the daily free meal site: "I understand there'll be a few politicians, a few intellectuals, a few hippies, a few acid heads, a few speed heads, a few straight people, a few middle-class people, a few teachers, a few merchants, a few gods, a few devils, a few demons, anything you want."

Hollywood was the birthplace of one of the longest-lived apolitical, non-religious communes, The Hog Farm. Its leaders, peace activists Hugh Romney and his wife Jahanara, informally founded the group as a peace-loving, drug-taking, politically-minded performance collective. They took their name after taking up residence at a former hog farm and later collectively purchased land outside of Llano, New Mexico, to set up a self-sufficient living space. The Hog Farm became known for their peaceful interventions at large events that defused potential bad-vibe situations. In 1969, Hugh Romney was asked by the organizers of the Woodstock Festival to bring Hog Farm members to the festival as a "security" force. The problems of Woodstock are well known. Lack of sanitation. Not enough shelter. And nowhere near enough food and water for the estimated half-million people occupying Max Yasgur's fields.

Romney and the Hog Farm leapt into action, scouring nearby towns for food donations. Residents of Sullivan County heard of the food shortages and quickly set up volunteer brigades to make sandwiches for attendees. Romney set up a field kitchen where the Hog Farm made continual vats of brown rice and vegetables that fed tens of thousands. And they made what became the infamous Hog Farm granola[145] that kept the crowds from starving. Romney announced Saturday morning breakfast to Woodstock with his trademark humor, "What we have in mind is breakfast in bed for four hundred thousand! Now it's gonna be good food and we're going to get it to you. We're all feedin' each other."

Romney, as head of security, took to the stage throughout the festival to give updates and provide reassurance to attendees. The Hog Farm also set up emergency field hospitals to provide

---

145 See page 324 for recipe.

Hog Farm Free Kitchen at Woodstock, August 1969. By Lisa Law.

care to what was essentially a large city sprung up overnight in a rural community. The Hog Farm was so successful in providing peaceful security and food in difficult circumstances that they were asked to do it again a few weeks later at the Texas International Pop Festival. It was at the International Pop Festival that Romney was given his new name by musician B.B. King: Wavy Gravy.

The Hog Farm exists today in multiple locations. Their headquarters is in Berkeley and their main commune is the 600-acre Black Oak Ranch outside of Laytonville, California. Wavy Gravy uses the Ranch as the homebase for his children's theater camps and hosts charity music festivals. Yet for all the work the Hog Farm has done to feed people, build peace, and teach children, Wavy Gravy is best known as an ice cream flavor produced by former communards and hippie food entrepreneurs, Ben (Cohen) & Jerry (Greenfield).

Back in the Haight-Ashbury, the Bethlehem of psychedelic seeking, is Stephen Gaskin, lesser known by name but far more influential to American food as founder of The Farm. Stephen, who used the single-name moniker during his stint as a "holy man," sought to do what Griggs and Leary failed to: build a spiritual framework around psychedelic drug use, and what Wavy Gravy and the Diggers attempted to do: feed people.

Gaskin was born in Denver to Southwestern-born parents of Methodist stock in 1935. The family was not religious and traveled throughout the area as his father Enzell searched for work. Stephen joined the Marines after graduating high school and saw combat as a rifleman in the Korean War. After discharge from the military, he went to San Francisco to attend San Francisco State College (now University) to study literature. He chose San Francisco because of its affiliation with Beat writers Ferlinghetti, Kerouac, and poet Gary Snyder. He earned bachelor's and master's degrees in English with a focus on semantics, and stayed on to teach literature classes.

Gaskin stated in numerous interviews before his death in 2014 that he was never part of the Boomer generation but saw in his young Boomer students a distinct cultural shift. He learned about everything from the Beatles to drugs during the early part of the '60s until he embraced the new ideas about society and culture happenings at San Francisco State and Berkeley. Like many counterculturists in San Francisco in 1965, he took LSD after hearing about its mind-expanding capabilities. Gaskin claimed to have had a spiritual awakening on his twenty-sixth

Stephen Gaskin speaks to followers in San Francisco, c. 1970. Courtesy of the *New York Times*.

LSD trip. Gaskin the literature professor had casually transformed into Gaskin the spiritual leader. He said in a 1970 *CBS News* interview, "I realized all that stuff in the Bible was the truth and the Sermon on the Mount was not just goody-goody Boy Scout instructions but a technical manual about how to survive at a certain level."

Gaskin never purposefully set out to be a guru, yet because of his experience teaching young adults and his participation in the counterculture, he felt he could help young people navigate the new ideas swirling around them. His first Monday night class was held in a community space on the San Francisco State campus in 1967. Gaskin describes the early "classes" this way: "We discussed love, sex, dope, God, gods, war, peace, enlightenment, free will, and what-have-you, all in a stoned, truthful, hippie atmosphere. We studied religions, fairy tales, legends, children's stories, the I Ching, Zen koans—and tripping." That first class of twelve attendees quickly grew to hundreds. They moved to increasingly larger spaces but each class followed the same structure: Gaskin sitting cross-legged on an elevated dais, sometimes silent, always chanting "om," and lecturing about spiritual insights and humanity's role in the universe. Each class ended with a question-and-answer period that would swing wildly depending on who was asking. Some attendees challenged Gaskin's assertions and positions while others would seek out his approval. Not every attendee was impressed. Critics noted that young people, often under the influence of drugs, began to view Gaskin as their spiritual guide.

Gaskin's actual beliefs evolved over time. He referenced Acts 2:44, 45,[146] as many religious communes do, that true disciples should live together in intentional communities. He also spoke simplistically about Buddhist and Hindu notions of karma, and as influenced by his early years in the Southwest, Diné concepts of responsibility to the Earth and all life on it. He believed that entheogenic plants taken with intention to shed the ego and the past will result in a significant mystical experience, one that joins the tripper to the holy and infinite universe.

146 And all the believers were together and had all things in common; and sold their possessions and goods, and parted them to all as every man had need.

Gaskin during this period defended his drug use in multiple "Holy Man Jams" organized in San Francisco and Denver that brought together leaders of New Religious Movements to young seekers. Yogi Bhajan, Alan Watts, and Swami Satchinanda participated and recognized Gaskin's sincere belief that psychedelics were a spiritual tool. Gaskin, who had a knack for aphorisms, said, "Acid is transubstantiation." He equated LSD with Martin Luther as equals in their work in bringing access to God to the people. He taught that Christ "manifested" what he wanted and that his followers should focus their positive energy on building collective agreements to manifest what *they* wanted.

Gaskin's actual cosmology was a polycultural blend of Gnostic New Thought, Christianity, Hindu, and Zen Buddhist concepts wrapped in a semantics-derived "total agreement" collectivized energy. The theology can be summed up as positive moral determinism. Early members of Gaskin's Family saw the ritual of taking LSD as a necessary step in their spiritual growth. Gaskin and the Family also used prodigious amounts of peyote tea and cannabis, with Gaskin saying that "high" was a human's preferred state of being and that the drugs were the tool to remove ego.

By early 1970, his weekly lectures drew 1,500 attendees and gained the notice of the American Academy of Religion, a nonprofit group of religious scholars, who sponsored Gaskin on a barnstorming tour across the States. The goal was to better inform 'middle America' about the hippie movement and its new spiritual ideas. The trip was part evangelical and part educational. Gaskin saw he could share his message with more young people and reassure their parents that all hippies weren't Charles Manson. Yet key to Gaskin's belief system was the idea that psychoactive drugs were a legitimate and effective pathway to spiritual advancement. Many of Gaskin's loyal devotees joined him on the tour. It became known as the Caravan. Men, women, and children convoyed throughout the country in converted school buses to share their experiences. The trip proved to be a crucible for the followers and Gaskin.

The young people who joined in the Caravan were from both a different generation and class than Gaskin. They were in their late teens to early twenties. Most came from wealthy families and had attained college degrees or quality high school education. They were primarily urbanites with little skill or experience with manual labor or understanding of what was needed to build a self-sufficient, albeit transient, collective. Yet they managed to stay on the road for about six months as each day brought new challenges and new rules from Stephen intended to maintain group cohesion and safety among the two hundred travelers. When they returned to San Francisco, Gaskin and the core group decided to take the next step—a step many spiritual and ideological-minded groups were taking—to drop out.

The back-to-the-land movement born of the disillusionment and failure to effectively change American political systems became a national phenomenon. Where the Great Depression-era generation left agrarian life for the promise of factory work in the cities, the wealthier, younger hippie generation reversed the urban migration. The commune-builders and back-to-the-landers sought to carve out a society separate from the mainstream—much like early Pietists. Gaskin and others heard the same evangelical call to utopia and sought to create a new ideal. In early 1971, a group of approximately 250 of Gaskin's followers climbed back aboard their buses and traveled eastward because Gaskin had heard that land was available for around $70 an acre in Appalachia and the South. They explored Kentucky and Arkansas before settling in poor, rural Lewis County in central Tennessee. Lewis County was known for poor quality soil and robust moonshine production, and was not prepared for a hippie invasion. They found an abandoned farm and purchased it from a sympathetic and "with it" family member who helped facilitate Gaskin's introduction to his new neighbors. What Lewis County residents discovered was that this band of hippies was much more conservative in their values than the media portrayed them.

Gaskin's rules for being part of the community had evolved and grown during their caravan trips across the country. He forbade that the group be called a commune, as he felt that it would upset their neighbors who would equate commune with communist. Members of the collective took a vow of poverty and were required to turn over all assets to a central "bank." Members must follow a vegan diet in accordance with Gaskin's views on animal rights and God's directives in various holy books. Again, Gaskin had the right quote for the time: "I've been to animal killings and rice boilings, the vibes are better at the rice boilings." Alcohol and tobacco were forbidden. Refined sugar was considered evil. As vegans, they did not use honey but sorghum for sweetening. Marijuana was considered a sacred plant and ceremonially smoked. Though he had his spiritual awakening during an LSD trip (and took hundreds of LSD trips during the 1960s), his views shifted as more people had access to LSD and psychoactive drugs. He told his Family to stop taking LSD and only use organic, plant-based drugs. While the media often portrayed communes as sexual anarchy, Gaskin had a rule that stated, "If you're balling, you're engaged, and if you're pregnant, you're married."

After the first year that saw the group deal with a hepatitis outbreak, poor nutrition, lack of food, and bitter cold as they lived in army surplus tents, they began to learn how to build their utopia. Gaskin's vision was for an entirely self-sufficient spiritual community where he would continue to teach his evolving philosophy. And in the American entrepreneurial tradition, Gaskin encouraged members to develop skills and start businesses. The businesses were usually outgrowths of activities begun to support the entire collective. For example, The Farm (as it was now called) planted, harvested, and processed the first sorghum crop in Tennessee since the late 1800s. Sorghum syrup was used by The Farm as a food sweetener and the excess sold to Lewis County residents under the brand "Old Beatnik Pure Lewis County Sorghum."

Of the 250 founding members, only four had any kind of agricultural experience. The demographic breakdown in 1974 revealed that there were 750 full-time members, of which 251 were children under sixteen years old. Of the other five hundred residents, half were under twenty-seven years old. Two hundred and seventeen had attained a college degree, including a few with masters and doctorates, while all but twenty-three members completed at least two years of college. Those degrees were overwhelmingly in humanities fields and none in engineering or agriculture. As mentioned earlier, The Farmies came from the cities, with only sixty members coming from rural small towns. As to religious makeup, most identified as non-religious but spiritual. Of those who responded to travel writer Peter Jenkins' questions during his 1974 research visit for his book *A Walk Across America* (1979), 138 members grew up in a Protestant denomination, one hundred in a Catholic home, and forty-six in the Jewish faith.

Holy Food

Members of The Farm harvesting sorghum in Summertown, c. December 1971. Courtesy of the Associated Press.

These statistics reflect the average composition of both New Religious Movement and secular communes throughout the United States during this time. They were unified by their shared work, mission, and belief in Gaskin's vision.

The Farm excelled at monetizing every aspect of their collective operations. They began a printing and publishing arm that published a newspaper and books written by Gaskin, his partner Ina May who was becoming a world-recognized expert on midwifery and maternal care, and by other Farmies who developed specialized knowledge about farming and, to our purposes, cooking.

The first Farm cookbook was published in 1975 and was edited by Louise Hagler. It contains recipes to ensure that Farmies ate enough calories while getting full nutrition—protein was always a concern—and adhering to a vegan diet. *The Farm Vegetarian Cookbook* solicited recipes from the Farm cooks who were known to make dishes that people enjoyed and fulfilled the dietary requirements. The recipes rely on soy-based protein and contain a significant percentage of traditional "Jewish" foods remade as vegan. Soy knishes, vegan blintzes, and sauerkraut soup all make an appearance. One unlikely member helped give Farm cuisine its Jewish flavor; his name was Uncle Bill.

Uncle Bill was born in Poland in 1893 and came to Brooklyn as a child in the early 1900s. He worked at a traditional Jewish delicatessen and caterer until his retirement to a Florida nursing home where he was miserable. His great-niece was a member of The Farm collective and staged a rescue operation to liberate Uncle Bill from his hated nursing home and brought him to live at The Farm. It's noted in various Farm histories and in *The Farm Vegetarian Cookbook* that Uncle Bill was initially unsure about veganism, but once he understood the philosophy, he began adapting his old delicatessen recipes. His recipe for Pickled Herring was adapted to use eggplant. He reworked his recipes for onion rolls, bagels, and remade deli-style potato chips with turnips to the delight and satisfaction of Farm members. Uncle Bill also assigned himself the role of "kitchen supervisor" and taught members how to cook.

From *The Farm Vegetarian Cookbook*, Uncle Bill with Farm community members, c. 1974.

The Farm Vegetarian Cookbook was a best-seller and provided many with detailed instructions on how to create vegan cheese from nutritional yeast, and is the first cookbook in the United States to introduce tempeh to eaters. Louise Hagler added new recipes in an expanded version published in 1988 and continued to write cookbooks published by The Farm's publishing operation, The Book Company, that expanded the depth and breadth of vegan cuisine. Hagler also is a trained midwife and has focused her recent work on vegan cooking for pregnant people and children.

The Farm reached its peak population in 1980 with 1,500 residents living collectively on a few properties surrounding Summertown, Tennessee. Yet for all the business successes, the poor soils of Lewis County could not support large-scale commercial crops and effectively ate the profits created by the other businesses. Members of the collective were no longer impressionable teenagers and college idealists. Gaskin's philosophy and revelations that once seemed profound and spiritual now were accepted as the Farm way. While some members still revered and worshiped Stephen as a divinely inspired sage, many more who had taught themselves the skills to work the land and create a thriving economy from whole cloth realized that Gaskin was essentially a kindly English teacher with a vision and a Holy Man trip, but not necessarily the financial acumen to singularly manage the collective. Disgruntled members left. When they left, it was with only their meager household belongings and clothing, because they had signed away their assets and any income generated by their labor. The Farm also experienced a common problem faced by every commune: freeloaders. The Farm had no requirements about who could join, aside from following Stephen's prohibitions, which led to more loafers than workers. The open-door policy led to overcrowding and hangers-on who were there for the vibe and not the values. The imbalance became untenable.

By 1983, The Farm was in a precarious financial position and disintegrating. Gaskin was the sole leader and decision-maker. In the hippie ethos, the group didn't formalize any governing structure or financial equity systems. People fearing a total collapse of the commune left until there were only approximately 250 people remaining. As the situation grew increasingly worse, longtime financially contributing members asked Gaskin to step down as leader. And in a rare case of a leader acquiescing without struggle, he did. The Farm, much like the Amana Colony nearly a hundred years earlier, decollectivized. The Farm reorganized its land holdings and business operations to function under a nonprofit status while members now became financially

Holy Food

independent and responsible for maintaining their own properties. The remaining members under the new arrangement paid off the nearly half-million-dollar debt within a few years.

The Farm's legacy is that Middle Tennessee is now home to a bustling hive of socially aware entrepreneurism developing high-tech tools like sensitive radiation measurement devices and eco-villages. The Farm's missionary arm, Plenty International, provides food and nutrition services and education throughout the world. And Ina May Gaskin's work in midwifery has trained thousands of women throughout the world on how to birth babies safely without Western medical systems. Stephen Gaskin remained living at his home in Summertown not as a deposed leader but as a lifelong seeker determined to see his experiment through until the end. He died at his home of natural causes in 2014. Ina May continues her work teaching midwifery.

The Farm collective transformed Lewis County and the surrounding region from a poor and declining area into a thriving community. The businesses they founded employ non-Farm community members. The school they began is now accredited by the state and accepts all area residents. Even as The Farm was experiencing internal dissent and financial problems in the early '80s, the image projected to the outside world was one of collective success that attracted other visionary leaders to start communes in the area. One element that made The Farm successful is that Gaskin, while flirting with notions of his personal infallibility, never demanded followers sever relationships with their family of origin or the community at large. He felt that showing others how they could happily reject the material plane of existence for a spiritual one was an attractant. He encouraged followers to invite their parents to visit The Farm and establish healthy relationships based on where they were now and shed past "hang-ups." For this reason alone, The Farm does not fit into the categorization of a cult. The Farm was and remains very American insomuch that a singular leader, inspired by a spiritual vision, recruited followers and removed themselves from mainstream society, and then used the American ideals of capitalism to remake a small corner of the country into their cultural ideal.

THE FARM COMMUNITY ATTRACTED OTHER PEOPLE SEEKING TO CARVE A SEPARATIST lifestyle. Of note is the unnamed collective of radical leftists who moved to Short Mountain, Tennessee, in the late '70s. (Short Mountain is one hundred miles east of The Farm "capital" of Summertown.) The original group members drifted away after a few years and the deed holders sought out new residents. At the same time, gay rights leader and neo-pagan Harry Hay called for a new way for gay men to reengage with their primal self. He and co-founder Don Kilhefner conceived of a group that would support their vision for a magical, new age, pagan, safe retreat and living space for gay men throughout the United States. They called their group Radical Faeries. The Faeries maintain a dozen communal living spaces in rural areas where men can live or visit in absolute freedom and safety. The Faeries shared their vision with the landowners living at Short Mountain, and the space became a Radical Faerie commune known as the Short Mountain Sanctuary. Throughout the '80s and '90s, more small collectives and individuals seeking community and safety moved to the region. There are, as of this writing, approximately a dozen LGBTQIA communes in the area between Short Mountain and Summertown, including IDA (Idyllic Dandy Arts), a commune of queer vegetarians.

Other groups are best described as "family communes" comprised of small collectives of like-minded blood and chosen families who work together sharing labor and its bounty. The Farm and the Short Mountain communities have fundamentally changed the population demographics and culture of rural Middle Tennessee. Lewis County, once dry, voted to repeal its liquor prohibition to support the opening of a Faerie-owned distillery that employs local residents. Queer property owners who came to live gently on the land advocated for environmental protections to stop clear-cut logging operations. Residents use permaculture and organic farming methods. And it was at Short Mountain Sanctuary where Sandor Katz began his fermentation experiments and wrote his seminal book *Wild Fermentation: The Flavor, Nutrition, and Craft of Live-Culture Foods* (2003). Like many who lived at the Faerie Sanctuary at Short Mountain, Katz remains in the area as a homeowner, writing and teaching about food fermentation practices. He is considered by many a catalyst in the resurgent interest in making fermented foods.

Short Mountain and the Radical Faeries were not outliers in the growing gay and lesbian rights movements. Women joined empowerment groups like National Organization of Women but also embraced homegrown consciousness-raising meetings, hosted by an activist and held at a woman's home or in a "safe" space. Women came to discover feminism through many different pathways, but it was clear that the legal, financial, and social subjugation of women must end.

Women who came of age during the hippie era of the late '60s and early '70s soon discovered that while men could easily free themselves from social contracts and expectations, women could not without dire consequences. Mothers who rejected mainstream family structures were legally stripped of child custody. Women who entered the male-dominated workforce could expect sexual harassment and lower pay. The criticism leveled at women ranged from the moronic to the asinine. Yet escaping mainstream society did not give women the equality they sought. One of the chief complaints in communes of the time was the sexist and gendered roles women were expected to fill. A man could find himself, but a woman still had to wash the dishes. Also laid bare were the consequences of "free love." Communal living experiments from the previous century experienced nearly the same thing—free love meant a man could have as much sex as he wanted with any woman he wanted, while women were subject to sexual coercion, assault, rape, and unplanned pregnancies. Nor did women have the social approval to engage in the same style of freewheeling sexual behavior; a man with many partners was to be admired while a woman was a slut. The notion of "safe spaces" and "women-only" spaces was critical to developing political ideologies and personal identities.

In 1977, in a residential neighborhood of Bridgeport, Connecticut, founders Selma Miriam, Samn Stockwell, Betsey Beavan, Noel Furie, and Pat Shea opened a restaurant that served high-quality vegetarian food. With that first service, the Bloodroot Collective was born. The women hosted issue-awareness sessions, book readings, art shows, and performances while serving food that earned rave reviews. They held select days of the week as "women only" nights for lesbians. Bloodroot was one of a growing number of feminist separatist places that sought to empower women. Groups of womyn (often spelled with a "y" to sever the linguistic connection to men) formed music festivals, campgrounds, bookstores, and communes.

The Womyn's Land movement took as inspiration the Women's Commonwealth (1875–1983) of Belton, Texas. It was founded by Martha McWhirter, who separated from her husband when she discovered he sexually harassed a teenage maid in their home. McWhirter was a vision-having Methodist who said that God told her to build a safe place for women to study the Bible. So she did. The home and enclave she built gave safe harbor to women escaping abuse, and to impoverished widows. McWhirter called her

Founders of the Bloodroot Collective Restaurant, Bridgeport, CT, c. 1972. Courtesy of Bloodroot Restaurant.

group Sanctificationists and held the credo that no woman should be compelled to live with brutal, alcoholic, and abusive husbands. They supported themselves with barter, and later developed a women-based economy producing baked goods and handmade goods sold to regional retailers. McWhirter and the Sanctificationists are considered the mothers of the women's shelter system and separatist communities.

The 1970s iteration of Womyn's Land took many shapes. Some spaces were communal living agriculture-based enterprises, others were urban collectives, and still others were enclaves that sprouted near Summertown, Tennessee. Other separatist spaces were temporary autonomous zones where women gathered, free of men. The Michigan Womyn's Music Festival (1976–2015) was a yearly event that attracted thousands of women over the course of the weeklong festival.

Many of the women-only spaces have encountered controversy in the past decade as the second- and third-wave feminists who rely on a gyno-specific definition of woman have excluded transwomen from these spaces and events. So too the lesbian-separatist communes have folded as the original occupants age and younger women are less interested in separatist ideologies.

The Bloodroot Collective and Bloodroot Restaurant have weathered these political machinations as remaining founders and owners Miriam and Furie have straddled each wave of feminist activism with thoughtful open-mindedness. Bloodroot has published four cookbooks, including the first, *The Political Palate: A Feminist Vegetarian Cookbook* (1980), which included recipes from the restaurant, and art, poetry, and feminist theory from the leading women thinkers of the day. Two follow-up cookbooks expanded the recipe offerings and feminist ideology. Miriam and Furie continue to live their ideals and bring refugee women into the Collective to cook and share their different styles of cooking. The food served reflects their Atlantic Coast location and their commitment to locally raised produce. Though Bloodroot closed during the COVID pandemic, the restaurant reopened in 2022 and continues to earn high praise from critics and diners alike.

CALIFORNIA AND NEW MEXICO WERE AND REMAIN HOME TO NUMEROUS SPIRITUAL communes, now 'retreat' or 'wellness' centers. The communards of Middle Tennessee have morphed into active and activist citizens that are, after fifty years, respected elders and leaders in their community. Lesser known are the smaller, family communes of New England. Not every communal living situation was officially documented, but it is estimated by researchers that there were 2,000 to 3,000 communes in the United States in the early '70s. Seventy-five were in Vermont, mainly in the southeastern corner of the state. And like what happened in rural Middle Tennessee, the influx of back-to-the-landers and communes changed the demographics of the state. The population in 1964 was 399,000, the same as in 1864. The population in 1980 grew to 511,546, an increase of 112,546 people, attributed to "hippies" moving to Vermont.

These communal experiments were usually short-lived and followed a boom-bust cycle. Activists and students who came of age during the civil rights and antiwar actions of the '60s were, by the early '70s, weary of the grind of city life and sought rural areas to live and raise children in nature. Many of these reverse migrators had work they could continue to do from their new location, or sought to be self-sufficient and live off the land. Most had college degrees and access to wealth through their families. Peter Simon (scion of the Simon & Schuster publishing family) purchased land and created Tree Frog Farm, a clothing-optional commune frequented by other nepotism kids of the era. Simon lasted two years on his commune before selling the Farm to journalist Andrew Kopkind, who lived and worked there. The Red Clover Collective in Putney (once home to John Humphrey Noyes' Putney Commune, and later an outpost of the Oneida Community) was a political collective comprised of former SDS (Students for a Democratic Society) members who now advocated for a violent takeover of the federal government. Another commune with twenty-five core members was Earth People's Park, set on six hundred acres abutting the Canadian border. Like many communes of the era, the population swelled during the summer months when students hitch-hiked across the country visiting communes to hang out. Earth People's Park developed a reputation of pure anarchy with no rules and all the drugs. It also became a transit point for men going to Canada to escape the Vietnam-era military draft. None of these errant communes lasted for very long. They encountered the problem that has dogged communes and utopias from their very conception: the imbalance between those who labor and those who do not.

The most successful communes were the ones that employed strict rules for admittance and contribution. Total Loss Farm (also called Packers Corners) was founded by the journalists who began the Liberation News Service—an AP for alternative weekly and college newspapers—and moved their families from New York City and Washington, D.C., to a farm outside of Guilford, Vermont, to live and farm collectively while maintaining the News Service. Total Loss residents invited friends to stay for periods of time and would sometimes take in a traveler who could provide a needed skill and get along with others. Total Loss Farm, like other communes throughout the country, provided safe harbor for people wanted by the government for subversive political activity. Total Loss provided a home for Patricia Swinton (a.k.a. Shoshona, Suzanne Davis) of the Weather Underground, who was on the FBI's Most Wanted list for her participation in the 1969 bombings of the Whitehall Street military induction center and the Manhattan Criminal Courts Building in New York City. Swinton was arrested in 1975 at her job at a health food store in Brattleboro, Vermont.

The Total Loss group also included artist and poet Verandah Porche and writer Ray Mungo, who helped document their experiences in the 1973 book *Home Comfort: Stories and Scenes from Life on Total Loss Farm*. The stories detail their successes and failures as they attempt to carve out a different kind of life. The book includes recipes of classic Americana foods adapted to reflect "healthy" ingredients. The banana bread replaces sugar with honey and adds wheat germ to the flours. A carrot bread recipe includes variations for making it gluten-free but also includes full-fat buttermilk.

Tangential to the growth of communes were the communally-run restaurants that began in the 1970s. Like Bloodroot, the Moosewood Restaurant was founded in 1973 as a worker-owned collective. Each member shared labor without hierarchical management. The Collective allowed new worker-members to purchase ownership as the restaurant grew and older members left. Unlike the religion-based restaurants that deem members' labor to be religious work, Moosewood purposefully declared itself "free from dogma." Workers all earned the same wage and "tips" were shared equally among all staff. The focus was wholly on serving food made from locally grown ingredients. In the first year of business Moosewood served meat-based dishes but soon became vegetarian-focused, with an occasional fish entrée offered.

Moosewood would have remained one of the many unknown hippie restaurants that proliferated in college towns like its home in Ithaca, New York, but members saw the value in having an alternative cookbook and created their own. *The Moosewood Cookbook* was written and illustrated by Mollie Katzen using recipes sourced from the Collective that were served at the restaurant. The Collective published it on their own in 1974, and word of the cookbook and the restaurant spread. The recipes reflected the cultural traditions of individual members as well as versions of favorite global dishes. Ten-Speed Press published a revised edition in 1977 that went on to become one of the best-selling cookbooks of all time. *The Moosewood Cookbook* is credited with popularizing vegetarian cooking in the United States.

A group of early Moosewood Collective members also founded the nearby Lavender Hill commune, which was one of the few gay and lesbian communal living groups in the country. The intersectional inclusiveness was and remains a hallmark of the Moosewood Restaurant. The restaurant is now owned by a three-person collective that includes Danica Wilcox, whose mother Kip was one of the founders of the Moosewood Collective. The dishes served at Moosewood have evolved over the years and reflect culinary trends, including the growing mainstream acceptance of veganism. Wilcox plans to commemorate the fiftieth anniversary of Moosewood Restaurant by publishing a revised edition of the *Cookbook* that includes old favorites and new.

Back-to-the-land and "drop-out" experiments in living and eating were not isolated blips on the American landscape. During the 1970s, many small rural communities saw a new type of owner—sometimes with a traditional family structure but often a small group—who came to experiment with new ways of growing food. Organic farms. Cruelty-free farms. Bio-dynamic agriculture. Symbiotic plantings. How could young urbanites disconnected from agriculture learn how to become successful farmers? Feeding a commune or family group has been the singular challenge faced by every communal living experiment since forever, but best evidenced by the failures of Bronson Alcott's Fruitlands where little fruit grew and none of the men wanted to engage in physical labor. Information about best practices was the key to success.

Stewart Brand's *Whole Earth Catalog*, a magazine-*cum*-catalog, featured mail-order products useful to back-to-the-landers, articles on various topics of interest, diagrams and instructions for DIY projects, agriculture research and best practices, and recipes. Brand

Lucy Horton, author of *Country Commune Cooking* at Frog Run Farm, c. 1973.

started the *Whole Earth Catalog* in 1969 with yearly, sometimes quarterly, editions published as Brand determined the information should be updated. His idea was born of a cross-country trip visiting communes, bringing along tools and a reference library in his truck. He wanted to learn more about communal living but also wanted to be useful to any commune they visited. Richard Fairfield started a journal devoted to communal life in throughout the world. Titled *Modern Utopian*, Fairfield traveled and corresponded with communards to get status reports about the health of communal living experiments from 1966 to 1970. Fairfield published a compendium of his reports in the 1970 book *Communes, USA*. If not clear by now, hippies and communes were now an accepted fact of American culture.

Lucy Horton was also aware of the flow of recipes among communes. She spent 1970 on the Vermont commune Frog Run, headed by Robert Houriet and his then-wife Mary Mathias. Houriet had traveled to visit various communes throughout the country to write his book *Getting Back Together* (1971), documenting communes, their leaders, and philosophies, and Horton, a Bryn Mawr graduate, typed his manuscript. In discussions with Houriet, she asked him what was—if there was—a common topic or concern among all the communes he visited, and Houriet replied without hesitation: FOOD. Scarcity. Access. Preparation. Every notion of spiritual journey or shared trip took a backseat when residents were hungry. Finding and developing nutritious meals for a large group is always a challenge, and more so when many groups were impoverished by choice or by circumstance.

Horton decided that she would travel to as many communes as she could and collect favorite recipes. She made no distinction between religious and secular groups. As a communard herself, she was an insider, documenting her culture. *Country Commune Cooking* (1972)[147] is filled with recipes for dishes served and eaten at communes. Horton notes in her introduction that there is consistency in the recipes; many use similar ingredients and techniques. Woks for quick-cooking vegetables. Tamari instead of commercially prepared and preserved soy sauce. Plant-derived oils instead of animal fats. Cider vinegar and lemon juice for acidification. Honey instead of refined sugar. Whole-wheat flours replace bleached white flour. Communes often maintained a "kitchen garden" to supply fresh produce and incorporated it as it came into season. Horton notes that while there were a few communes that ate meat, most adhered to a vegetarian diet loosely informed by Buddhist-Hindu ideas and a reaction to overprocessed and corporatized food. Horton notes that many communes had favorite "ethnic" recipes adapted from the cultural backgrounds of members and the geographic location of the commune. Agriculture-based communes hewed to the traditional farm style of eating and provided one main meal a day. Depending on the size of the group, other meals were made by individual members, or a simple "bread and spread" combination that could be prepared in advance.

In the wake of the success of *Country Commune Cooking*, some of the better-organized communes assembled and published their own cookbooks. Like the Rosicrucians and Seventh-Day Adventists of previous generations, these cookbooks provided income and a cheery version of life on the commune. The True Light Beavers of Woodstock, New York, published *Feast: A Tribal Cookbook* with mainstream publisher Doubleday in 1972. Robert Crumb's then-wife, Dana Morgan Crumb, wrote (with R. Crumb illustrating) *Eat It!*, documenting the recipes cooked at their family's short-lived communal home in San Francisco and Potter Valley, also in 1972. (Dana divorced Crumb in 1978 and went on to become the preeminent caterer of modern, healthy Jewish cuisine in the Mendocino County region.) The Sunburst Family Farm published their *Sunburst Family Farm Cookbook* in 1976. The New Age/UFO group One Family published *Cosmic Cookery* based on recipes served at their commune and restaurant in 1974. *Vegetarian Gothic*, containing recipes from the Hare Krishna-influenced unnamed group who ran Krishna's Kitchen restaurant in Charlottesville, Virginia, was published in 1975. These are but a few of the more infamous "cult cookbooks" that came to readers during the 1970s. The trend picked up on a growing acceptance of "health food" in mainstream American society.[148]

The Farm, Short Mountain Sanctuary, and the numerous Vermont experiments are examples of the changeable nature of spiritual movements and communes. Not every group has a positive impact on their geographic area, nor do they all have a specific food culture. But in areas that saw an influx of counterculture activists, the hippie invasion had lasting impact on the food systems. Ben & Jerry's Ice Cream was founded by two former communards. Socialist Senator Bernie Sanders came to Vermont in late 1968 as an antidote to the violent repercussions to antiwar

---

147 A single recipe from Horton's *Country Commune Cooking* is included here, the recipe she collected from New York City art-activist-anarchist group Up Against the Wall, Motherfuckers, or more commonly known as the Motherfuckers. The group was small, radical, and short-lived, but their take on the cheap, communal staple—the pot of beans—is classic and delicious.

148 See the recipe section for dishes from Sunburst Farms, True Light Beavers, One Family, and Krishna's Kitchen.

and civil rights demonstrations in Chicago. Vermont and Tennessee both have robust organic farming and cooperative food manufacturing and distribution systems because of the food activism of hippie-era communes and back-to-the-landers.

While vegetarianism in the United States has historic ties to Seventh-Day Adventism, Mazdaznanism, and some Christian and Theosophist religions due to scriptural interpretation, by the '70s and '80s vegetarianism had become a political and health statement. Environmental activists at the time looked at the growth of industrial meat farming reliant on chemicals as poisoning the Earth and people, as well as being cruel to animals. There was also growing awareness of worldwide food inequity

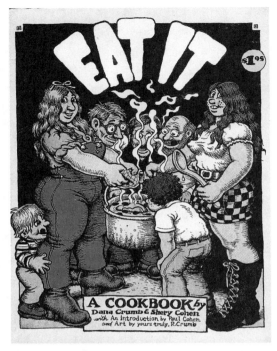

Front cover of 1972 edition of *Eat It: A Cookbook*. Author's collection.

as catastrophic famines decimated populations in Biafra, Sub-Saharan Africa, Bangladesh, Cambodia, and Ethiopia during the '70s and '80s. Meat production to this day is resource-intensive, and in the view of many vegetarians, one of the causes of global warming and food instability. Plant-based "meat" has moved from the primitive kitchens of the commune to corporate-owned factories. Successful restaurants offer vegetarian entrées as part of their standard offerings. Even fast-food restaurants have begun to offer vegetarian versions of their popular menu items. And while there has been some cultural pushback from extremists associating plant-based meats containing soy as part of an evil plan to "feminize" men, only time will tell if the societal embrace of vegetarianism and veganism improves American health and environment or if it is another fad dietary trend.

Thirteen

IS JESUS ALRIGHT WITH YOU?

A N ENTIRELY LOGICAL QUESTION TO ASK, TWO DECADES INTO THE TWENTY-FIRST century, is whether religious ideologies still have influence on American cuisine. The answer, of course, is yes. The framework—First Amendment and tax laws—that successfully allowed for groups to open restaurants and food pantries and to start food businesses throughout the history of the United States still works today. If anything, New Religious Movements are more financially savvy than ever before.

Groups once thought of as beyond the fringe are now accepted as part of mainstream American religious culture. The once-integrated Pentecostal movement of Charles Mason has continued to split along racial lines. The Hot Springs Conference of 1914 that created the all-white Council of Assemblies of God is now the fastest-growing denomination in the United States with 55 million members as of 2020, while Mason's original Church of God in Christ has nearly 9 million majority Black members. In contrast, the traditional Evangelical Lutheran Church of America has 3.1 million members. The United States continues to reckon with what it means to be open to all religious beliefs when the dominant groups that have benefited from those freedoms wish to strip those freedoms for everyone else. This cognitive disconnect between building a religion in total freedom to then imposing those beliefs onto non-believers has been with us from the earliest days of the Puritan colonies. This tension can be described for believers as a hedonic treadmill. Believers are continually validated by their spiritual community that their faith has ensured good things for all and protected them from the bad things encroaching. Members seek to maintain a cultural stasis based on their worldview and fight like demons to return to that perceived stability. Any change to their accepted norms is perceived as a threat. Sexuality, gender, racism continue to be reactive issues for people in more fundamentalist belief systems. Yet beyond the societal issues, the hedonic treadmill works on a personal level to exert a not-so-hidden pressure to conform to the rules and standards of a group. It's why anything from beauty standards to food choices becomes mired in escalating religious-political cant.

Many non-denominational Pentecostal Protestant congregations host diet and wellness programs that recast popular fad diets into a theologically acceptable package. The danger

Nation of Islam stevedores unloading fish, c. 1984. Photo by Nafessa Muhammad.

in this—as with all religiously informed diets—is that while nominally about health and diet, they use food to reinforce destructive ideas about women's bodies and autonomy. The most notorious religious-based diet program was started by Gwen Shamblin, who was a member of the conservative and fundamentalist Church of Christ. Shamblin had both bachelor's and master's degrees from the University of Tennessee in nutrition and dietetics, yet eschewed traditional recommendations of exercise and balanced food choices in favor of extreme calorie restriction and prayer. Her "Weigh Down Workshop" program was adopted by over 10,000 evangelical Protestant churches by the year 2000 when they stopped tracking that statistic. Shamblin wrote books, expanded her programs, and became exceedingly wealthy, which, in fundamentalist churches who have adopted prosperity gospel thinking, means God approved of her work. Her death in a small plane crash in 2018 unraveled the complicated finances of her complex church-business structure, raising new questions about the validity of any religious organization earning and holding large tranches of wealth. While Bing Crosby as the idealized Catholic priest Father O'Malley said in *The Bells of St. Mary's* that the mark of a Catholic parish was its mortgage, today the conspicuous wealth of traditional and upstart religions is suspect in the face of claims of bankruptcy and poverty when ordered to pay for damages inflicted on believers.

It's not just the Assemblies of God that have moved into the mainstream. Other groups that were once categorized as either New Religious Movements or cults are, after a few generations, accepted in the larger ecumenical community. The successful groups are the ones that learned the lessons of the Seventh-Day Adventists and Father Divine and built thriving businesses within and supported by their religious beliefs. A model example is the Unification Church, often derisively called "Moonies."

Reverend Sun Myung Moon was born in Korea where he converted to Presbyterianism after World War II. A few years later he founded the Unification Church based on his interpretation of

Holy Food

the Bible and the personal revelations from God he believed he received. The church subscribes to a conservative and fundamentalist view of scripture with the Moons serving as authoritative parental figures. Moon immigrated to the United States in 1971 where he expanded his evangelical outreach. The Unification Church became identified as a cult during the post-Jonestown backlash against New Religious Movements, but Moon was a savvy marketer who courted politicians for influence and protection. The Unification Church earned money to support its growth through their diverse corporate holdings that include food businesses. To this day, the Unification Church owns International Seafood, based in Alaska and one of the largest cod, crab, and prepared fish processors in the U.S. The Church also owns True World Foods which is the largest provider of raw fish products for sushi in the United States. Again, mentioned earlier, but it bears repeating that the Unification Church also has a long collaborative partnership with the Nation of Islam in political efforts to ensure their mutual freedom to operate as nonprofit entities. That relationship has resulted in further cooperation in the Unification Church's True World Foods business that hires many of its workers from Nation of Islam membership, who are trusted—because of the rigid moral code of the Nation of Islam—not to engage in theft or fraud against the Church-owned business. There also remain small family groups that one only hears of when something terrible occurs. Recently the NXIVM group made news with their single male leader who used sex and restrictive eating to control women in a combination self-actualization meets multi-level marketing cult. The group had all the prurient elements that capture the American imagination. The leader is now serving jail time while former members recover and give interviews to successive documentary filmmakers. More common is a group like Adidam.

Adidam can hardly be called a religion as much as it is the veneration of one man, Adi Da. His beliefs and the followers he inspired to join him could be described as shared madness. Adi Da, to use his final name, is an illustrative example of the phenomenon of the homegrown guru who picked up a little something from each successive religious and food fad he encountered. Born Franklin Jones in 1939 in Queens, New York, to solidly middle-class Lutheran parents, Jones initially went to college intending to become a minister. His time at Columbia University exposed him to many of the newer ideas about religion and spirituality as revealed by hallucinogenic drugs. He changed his major to philosophy and upon graduating went to Stanford in California in pursuit of an advanced degree.

After finishing his master's program in English in 1963, Jones volunteered for an Army study of LSD through the Veterans Administration administered at Stanford. He spent the next year reading esoterica and taking more drugs. He then left California for Greenwich Village and became acquainted with Albert Rudolph, a follower of Muktananda and Gurdjieff, who was also a self-taught yoga teacher. Jones continued to dabble in Eastern religious philosophies until his father convinced Yogi Rudolph to encourage Jones to go back to divinity school. Which he did in 1966. He dropped out in 1968 and made a pilgrimage to India to visit the ashram of Muktananda. The guru told him to study yoga directly from him, which he did until returning to New York, where he discovered and embraced Scientology for a year. After he broke with the Hubbard crowd, he went back to the ashram with Muktananda but became disillusioned by the influx of American seekers. He then had a vision of the Virgin Mary and decided to leave India, and spent most of 1970 visiting European holy sites.

In the fall of 1970 Jones returns to Los Angeles and opens a bookstore. He continues his personal explorations and publishes an autobiography in 1972 detailing his spiritual growth. He is a popular speaker and teacher and accrues followers. As his followers increase, he reveals more insights until he declares that he is "the divine lord in human form." By 1974 he moved to a rural enclave in northern central California near the Mendocino State Forest. At their church property, Jones dictated all behavior. His stated goals were to break down conventional morality, and practice what he called "crazy wisdom." This involved drug-fueled orgies and psycho-sexual theatricals that he filmed. He embraced polyamory but only he could choose who could sexually partner with another member. He often made this determination by demanding the woman give him sex first. By this time, dissatisfied ex-members alerted the press, and from 1985 and for the next few years, Jones and his church were the subject of exposé television programs and newspaper articles. Former members sued for everything from fraud to sexual battery.

Front cover of 1974 edition of *Garbage and the Goddess*. Author's collection.

In 1986, Jones stated that he experienced a physical and spiritual crisis that allowed him to evolve into his next form, that of divinely resurrected being. He took on the name "Adi Da" in 1994 as he quietly wrote books and made art surrounded and supported by a loyal but reduced number of followers. As Jones continued to absorb practices and beliefs, he adopted an increasingly restrictive diet. In the early days, he exhorted his followers to adhere to a vegetarian diet. Later, it became a vegan diet. And after 1994, he touted a raw fruit and vegetable diet. Toward the end of his life, he claimed that practitioners of his method of meditation and yoga would only need one Green Drink per day to thrive. He himself survived on less than that. He died in 2008 at his private island retreat in Fiji.

The post-Jonestown crackdown on "cults" meant that many New Religious Movements went underground; enough time has passed to see these groups embrace their history and become more public. New groups also rise up to meet and reflect current trends. The Yellow Deli is a small chain of cafés scattered throughout the United States, recognized as successful restaurants while their religious beliefs are less known. Visiting a Yellow Deli café or shop one must search for the connection to their owner, the Twelve Tribes Community, a fundamentalist Christian group that traces its lineage back to the Lost Tribes theories and Anglo-Israelite groups of the late 1800s.

The Twelve Tribes group was founded by the husband-and-wife pastors Gene and Marsha Spriggs in Chattanooga, Tennessee, in 1975. Prior to establishing the group, the Spriggs were youth pastors affiliated with the Presbyterian Church in Chattanooga and started a coffee house in the basement of First Presbyterian in 1972. As the Spriggs' theology evolved, they broke with the Presbyterians and embraced the emerging back-to-the-land, organic food, and communal movements. The first Yellow Deli was founded in Chattanooga, inspired by a Biblical verse in Galatians.[149] As the Twelve Tribes group grew, they were accused by concerned citizens of being a cult, and welcomed an invitation to preach from a Vermont church located in Island Pond. The group left Chattanooga for Island Pond, Vermont, where the residents were more tolerant but still suspicious of the group. Over the years the group eroded any goodwill as they faced child abuse charges and more cult accusations. Yet Twelve Tribes has settled into the community and expanded their Yellow Deli business with locations in the Hudson Valley of New York, two in Southern California, and the original location in Chattanooga. Other locations have sprung up and then closed in other cities in the U.S. and Europe.

Core to the Twelve Tribes beliefs and business model is following "Mosaic Law" that includes Leviticus-style dietary rules. The cafés serve no pork or crustaceans, and tend to serve sandwiches Americans recognize as "Jewish deli-style" like corned beef reubens and National Hebrew brand hot dogs. Twelve Tribes also owns the Common Ground Coffee Roasters chain, with most locations in Massachusetts. Key to Yellow Deli's success is that the restaurants are staffed by group members. Their labor is considered part of their service to the group, which has caused Yellow Deli to run afoul of state and federal labor laws on wage minimums and Social Security taxes. Member-workers live communally in homes purchased by the group, where they engage in Bible study and homeschooling. The communal homes ban television and secular entertainment. All Yellow Delis close from late September to mid-October to collectively recognize and privately celebrate holidays associated with the Jewish calendar. They, like many of the Anglo-Israelites, participate in both Christian holidays like Easter and Jewish observances of Yom Kippur and Rosh Hashanah.

If the Twelve Tribes tenets of belief sound like those of nineteenth-century Anglo-Israelite groups, you're not imagining the connection. Twelve Tribes is part of the burgeoning Messianic Judaism movement, which is the latest iteration of the Lost Tribes theory that Christians are the true Chosen People as foretold in the Tanakh/Old Testament. The new version of Anglo-Israelism is entirely Christian-focused with breakaway fundamentalist leaders embracing the old ideas, unlike the well-known Jews for Jesus groups of the 1970s and '80s that recruited among young Jews. Social media has helped raise awareness of the new-style messianic groups though videos showing Christian pastors blowing a shofar (the traditional ram's horn blown during Jewish services to mark ritual elements) to both good and ill outcomes. More Christians are seeking out these conservative congregations, while Jewish communities are offended

149 Galatians 5:22 (NIV) But the fruit of the Spirit is love, joy, peace, patience, kindness, goodness, faithfulness, gentleness, self-control; against such things there is no law.

at the appropriation of their religious practices. There is also concern that the new breed of Messianic fundamentalists is fueling the growing Christian Nationalist/Fascist movements throughout the United States, as the core message has the same racist origins as the Anglo-Israelism that caused the Pentecostals to separate along racial lines.

More challenging to predict is which, if any, religious or spiritual belief morphs into a destructive force. Psychologist and former "Moonie" Steven Hassan developed an assessment tool to help determine if a group—religious or secular—is a cult. The BITE model uses a series of questions to assess the level of control a group (or its leaders) has over individual members. **B** stands for Behavior, which assesses if there are rules in place to dictate or ban individual choices about clothing, sexual activity, family and social relationships, decision-making, and bodily autonomy. The **I** stands for Information, which assesses if individuals are given 100% true facts about their living situation and the world around them, and allows members to have unfettered access to any and all sources of information. **T** stands for Thought and assesses if members can have a private interior life and opinions. **E** is for Emotional and assesses if a member is fully allowed to express their feelings without fear, guilt, or punishment. Thinking about various elements of the BITE model reveals that many religions, families, and social clubs enact one or two of these controls amongst members, but a religion (or bowling league) moves into cultic terrain when nearly all the control elements are used. Because each group is unique, deciding which group is and is not a cult is challenging and often open to interpretation.

Using the BITE model as an assessment tool, there is a clear delineation between harmless and dangerous groups that hold non-mainstream beliefs. UFO-based spirituality has lineage to many of the American New Religious Movements discussed, especially those that connect God(s) to not an ethereal plane of existence but to actual places in galaxies far, far away. The mid-1950s was the golden age of UFOs and aliens in popular culture. Linked to nuclear-age Cold War politics, the promise and peril of new technology was imagined as both hero and villain. The mainstream view was that new technologies would save humanity from unknown invaders, but others saw the so-called invaders as the saviors. A clear line can be seen from Emanuel Swedenborg to Madame Blavatsky to the Urantia Book to the One World Family, who put forward the idea that beings from other planets exist to help humans. A few of these groups came to believe that humans are descended from or were planted by highly intelligent and evolved beings. The Nation of Islam has incorporated the notion of aliens as progenitors after Louis Farrakhan publicly spoke in 1985 about his alien abduction experience. For the Nation of Islam, a cosmology that recasts the horrors of slavery and the Black American experience as part of their hero's journey in overcoming the devil's (i.e., white men) oppression of Black people is an affirming tale versus the banal evil of racism.

On the harmless side of the BITE spectrum is the Unarius Academy of Science, founded in 1954 in Los Angeles by the husband-and-wife duo of Ernest and Ruth Gordon. Both were interested in Spiritualism and met at a conference. Ernest was a channeler who, in the post-World War II UFO craze, wrote about the messages he received from various beings and ascended masters on Mars, Venus, and other places. Ernest died in 1971, and Ruth took the helm of the group and it became a higher-profile organization. Ruth was referred to as Uriel and acted as a benevolent—though

Front cover of 1986 edition of *Transfiguration Diet*. Author's collection.

sometimes critical—parental figure to Unarians. She advocated that human beings had unlimited creative potential that must be nurtured to reveal mankind's spiritual power. She also made a series of predictions that "our Space Brothers" would physically appear on Earth and it was the Unarians' role to welcome them. Her kindly nature and colorful attire made her a popular figure on Johnny Carson's *Tonight Show* and other media outlets who presented character portraits of outré personalities.

As seen throughout *Holy Food*, group leaders often imposed personal tastes onto members. For Unarians, this took the form of cake. Ruth (Uriel) had a sweet tooth. Unarius celebrations focused on artistic creation by members. Dance, painting, costuming, and cake making and decorating. A memorable celebration a few years prior to Ruth's death in 1993 saw members bake and assemble an intricate multi-layered and -level structure that still amazes. While Ruth is still revered by current members, they also made note that she could be critical of individual members' weight, and advised that when the Space Brothers came to Earth, everyone had to be in good physical health. Yet, overall, the Unarians are looked at with gentle humor and tolerated as eccentrics.

In contrast, the Heaven's Gate group ticks nearly every box on the BITE inventory as a dangerous high-control group. Their beliefs are like those of the Unarius group, which are also similar to the Aetherius Society and Raelians: that extraterrestrial beings are fundamentally entwined with humans. A key difference is whether a group embraces a millenarism or end-times tenet in their cosmology. Heaven's Gate did. The leaders, Marshall Applewhite and his partner Bonnie Nettles, had followed a common pathway through New Age beliefs before adopting the idea that human bodies were merely containers to be reunited with the cosmos. Bonnie died of cancer in 1985, which sparked the shift from the group as publicly engaging to one that became monastic and secretive. Marshall, as the group's sole leader, instituted rigid behavioral controls. The core group lived communally, wore the same outfits, and as is common with high-control groups, experimented with regimented cuisines.

There remain few living members of Heaven's Gate, who act as archivists and historians. They are anonymous but will sometimes answer questions submitted via their website or by email.

A 2015 *Vice* article written by Andrew Paul asked them what they ate. "We tried every diet out there to see its effect on the body . . . From fruitarian, to wheatgrass, to low cooked grains to juice-only consumption." As Heaven's Gate beliefs progressed, they believed themselves to be scientists involved in a grand experiment on Earth, albeit one where they are trapped in human bodies. They made the decision to shed their humanness, which involved embracing asceticism in every form, including denial of all pleasure.

They embraced a simplistic diet that served to provide nutrition, and was explained by the anonymous Heaven's Gate member this way:

> "You would have a grain cereal in the morning, followed by a low-fat sandwich for lunch (no fried foods such as French fries). Dinner would consist of a carefully prepared protein with vegetables. But in the end, moderation in small amounts of meat, chicken and lots of vegetables and grains was the key. It provided a balance that could supply us with the energy to work at our regular jobs while [supplying] the mental alertness to keep our focus and direction."

Yet, a sample menu reflects meals that could be served in an average American home:

> MONDAY: Breakfast: Hot cereal w/raisins, Bread
> Mid-Day: Salad, Swedish Meatballs, Mashed Potatoes, Corn, Rolls, Iced Tea
> Evening: Meat Sandwich—Pickle, Chips, Drink

Heaven's Gate did advocate occasional "juice cleanses" intended to focus the mind on pure satiation and break emotions surrounding food.

Like the Unarians, Marshall Applewhite (Do) made unfulfilled predictions about when the alien intelligence would arrive on Earth. Over time, his message changed to a rapture-like narrative where the alien beings would come to take them to their new home away from Earth. In 1997, the reappearance of the Hale-Bopp comet led believers in various UFO cosmologies to declare that Hale-Bopp was a message, while others like Heaven's Gate believed the comet cloaked the long-predicted escape vehicle coming to take them away. Going back to the Heaven's Gate belief that their human bodies were mere containers for their energy, Applewhite declared they must drop their bodies to board the coming spacecraft. Between March 22 and March 26, 1997, the thirty-nine members of Heaven's Gate who collectively resided in a rented mansion in San Diego took their own lives via an overdose of phenobarbital dissolved in applesauce.

In examining the Unarians and Heaven's Gate, we see how seemingly fantastical beliefs can hijack a person's sense of discernment, of self. If one subscribes to one scientifically unproven belief, then it opens a pathway for the brain to accept more. Our innate mythmaking and storytelling brains continually ask, "and then what?" And when that construct is applied to new ideas about spirituality and food, the practices lead to unlikely yet logical outcomes. Like William Miller who popularized and predicted the theologically rogue idea of a physical rapture, when those predictions fail a new story must be told. The Unarians internalized their beliefs to continually strive to be more creative and do their utmost to finally get it right enough that the Space Brothers come. For Heaven's Gate, their chain of logic determined that it was their physical bodies preventing them from merging with the cosmos. Every religious belief is based on faith—faith in something that cannot be scientifically proven to exist. Most religious writing and preaching is about giving evidence of God's realness, of his presence among mankind. Believers of non-mainstream religious ideas also follow an internal logic that determines what happens next. As we've seen, if the outcome is benign and no one is truly harmed, then American society accepts it. Yet if the internal logic begins to dictate adverse outcomes for both believers and, more importantly, those who do not believe, then society may have moral compunction to act in the better interest of all.

These are the difficult moral conundrums faced by Americans. Many cities and counties still have "Sunday laws" that prevent the sale of alcohol on Sundays. The United States also has "dry" counties, where alcohol can never be sold. Both types of laws were written and passed by fundamentalist Christians who at the time of their making held legislative power. In recent years, politicians have used fearmongering tactics to scare fundamentalist Christians into believing that Islamic rules (known as Sha'ria laws) would be implemented in the States, yet these are rules followed by believers and only made legal in theocratic nations. We are in a state of perpetual cognitive dissonance, as we want freedom for ourselves yet are wary of what that First Amendment freedom means for others. Current battles over bodily autonomy could easily be followed by decrees regarding what foods can or cannot be eaten. The step-by-step logic that escalates acceptance of increasingly restrictive rules against, well, anything, is the dark underside of American religions.

The lighter side of American spirituality also brings us back to the First Amendment. While there is rigorous vetting of secular groups who seek nonprofit status with the Internal Revenue Service, the only standard the IRS requires to bestow nonprofit status to a church or religion is that they 1. periodically publish a "newspaper" primarily about issues pertaining to the group and its beliefs, and 2. hold religious meetings, retreats, and/or assemblies. In our modern age, both online publications (like a website) and virtual meetings meet the IRS standard for the 501c3 religious exemption to the United States tax code. Because the First Amendment guarantees the government cannot legally impinge on religious beliefs and the Internal Revenue Service is a government office, then as long as the publication and meeting criteria are met, any group can apply for nonprofit status. The few criteria have allowed for many groups to seek a religious exemption when they are actually irreligious. A 1980 lawsuit by the Peyote Way Church of God argued that the Schedule I enforcement exception given to the Native American Peyote Church should be extended to the Peyote Way group too. The courts ruled that the Peyote Way Church was more political than spiritual in nature and would not be allowed to use peyote in their services. The ruling was a rare hardline stance taken against a legally recognized church. In their wake, other groups—under religious guises—have gained nonprofit status for comedic and often political effect. The Pastafarians were loosely formed by a group of pranksters taking inspiration from writer Robert Anton Wilson's *Illuminatus! Trilogy* where the Flying Spaghetti Monster plays the role of Godhead. The group enjoys casual pranks and is best known for pushing the First Amendment's free exercise clause to ridiculous degrees by wearing pasta strainers on their heads in government-issued documents.

The Satanic Temple—not to be confused with the Church of Satan—is also a legally recognized religious organization. The group uses its legal status and contrarian nature to bring Christian theocratic excesses to public attention and often to legal challenge. The Temple hosts a weekly *Satanic Chef* cooking show via their website that also serves as the virtual meeting place for members and fulfills the IRS requirement. The Satanic Temple has formed after-school Satanist groups in answer to Christian groups who hold religious meetings on school grounds. They have erected statues of Baphomet in and on government-owned properties that display Christian iconography. Most recently, the Satanic Temple has filed lawsuits in states that have banned abortion, claiming that abortion is one of the sacraments of the Temple. And in banning abortion, a governmental body is impinging on the First Amendment protection to practice their religion. The argument, while logically sound, has yet to be fully tested in the courts.

American religions are also inextricably entwined with American business. Corporations have mission statements and organize themselves in hierarchies based on culture, adherence, and success. Some businesses have merged the organizational and control structures found in cults to further their ends. While not outwardly spiritual, modern multi-level marketing companies like Amway and LuLaRoe as well as non-secular self-improvement leaders like Tony Robbins are accused of cult-like operations. The BITE model gives a framework for assessment here as well. Often, the final determining factors are the power dynamics and free will. Is the group or person using a position of power and authority over a person to gain money, sex, and/or more power? Does the person in thrall to the group or leader have free will to make a choice without coercion? Human beings have made poor choices throughout history, yet how do we deal with those who wish to make decisions for us? Adding a religious component only complicates matters. Rules about what and when and why we eat are a checkbox on the BITE assessment, and would move any spiritually-minded group closer into cult territory but would not be the sole determining factor. Each generation of Americans must decide what is widely culturally acceptable and mainstream as well as what is marginally acceptable to remain on the fringes. Mainstream religious culture—for good or ill—has acted as a bulwark against the most outré of fringe beliefs.

It is easy to think that our particular time of existence occurs during the most and worst of political and cultural upheaval. Yet, the United States, as shown throughout *Holy Food*, is and has always been an ideal marred by the limitations of execution. Within that vast space of our utopian vision for what the country should be are the practical problems of how to create and support the actual lives of millions of individuals, each with their own ideas of perfection. Religious historians and philosophers have identified several catalytic elements that seem to drive schismatic and new spirituality. Mainstream American society enjoys a tenuous shared values system that allows for liberal interpretation. We've come to identify with political catchphrases that sum up those values—"a chicken in every pot" (Herbert Hoover, 1928)[150] was

---

150 Variations of this phrase and sentiment have been used by politicians dating back to sixteenth-century France.

understood that all Americans should have the economic prosperity to feed their families. Yet when our understanding of our shared values is threatened by a change in purpose, or in the societal rules, or in our ability to reach those goals, or, more critically, a change in our personal sense of place within our society, many individuals look for new structure and meaning. We may choose to change our personal behaviors to effect change, like many who have embraced plant-based lifestyles to reduce the negative effects of industrial meat production on the environment. Or we may seek out voices, leaders, that reassure us with messages that any change is bad and we must defend the current state of culture, or, conversely, follow leaders who advocate for a rejection of the shared identity and carve out a new way forward that only includes those who share a specific vision. These premises of human behavior and motivation never change, only the circumstances and interpretation.

The other catalyst for societal shifts is access. The availability of cheap paper and printing allowed William Miller to spread his apocalyptic end times message to millions of people in the 1840s. The ubiquity of television showed the horrors of Jonestown and David Koresh's Waco compound to millions of viewers. Today, the internet has facilitated unfettered broadcast of ideas both mundane and dangerous to millions. We are in the midst of another Great Awakening. And like the religious movements throughout our American history, food is a tool to attract followers as well as signal membership to others. For every YouTube channel featuring a neo-pagan all-carnivore diet aimed toward young men seeking to reaffirm their masculinity and bolster their belief that they are supplanted from their societal place at the top of the cultural food chain, there is a Black-Israelite live-streamer showing how a 100% vegan diet cleanses the mind and body from the toxic processed foods of the white oppressors.

My intention when I began *Holy Food* was to show how food and religion are intertwined into American history and our everyday lives. I wanted to show how unlikely characters and ideas about belief and eating contributed to how we define ourselves as American. What I learned is that a few people had enormous influence on both religion and food in the United States— and, most surprisingly, how interconnected these people were. What I also learned is that Americans love food. Not just eating food (though we do love eating), we are curious eaters who want to make everything American. We create a simulacrum of authenticity rooted in our own immigrant and colonist history. New Religious Movements, cults, and communes were part of the structure that introduced sacralized food to believers until capitalism desacralized it and served it up for everyone.

If we're lucky, we meet people from different religious, cultural, and geographic backgrounds and we eat their food. We go to their churches / temples / mosques during festivals and open houses to enjoy the delight of experiencing the unfamiliar. We relish introducing friends to a delicious food discovery, and in doing so support a new business or recent immigrant arrival. We become Americans through our stomachs but sometimes God tells us what to eat.

 # ADIDAM

Years active: 1974 to present day (A small and active following remains after Adi Da's death.)
Affiliation: Syncretic Kashmir Shaivite and Advaita Vedanta blend of Hindu, Scientology
Founder: Adi Da (Franklin Albert Jones, died 2008) a.k.a. Adi Da Samraj a.k.a. Bubba Free
John, Da Free John, Da Love-Ananda, Da Kalki, Da Avadhoota and Da Avabhasa. From 1991 until
his death, he was known as Adi Da Love-Ananda Samraj.

Followers of Adidam adhere to a rigid and restrictive diet, including flirtations with
"breatharianism." Here are their detailed notes on how to make the Green Drink (which, in
their view, is the *only* food one should consume).

"When you begin making blended green drinks, experiment with the amount of fruit. The
general recommendation is to use less fruits than greens, but you may want to use somewhat
more fruit than greens at first, and then over time use less so that you develop a 'greener'
drink. It is also possible to make blended green drinks using greens with non-sweet fruit
vegetables (such as tomatoes, cucumber, zucchini and other squashes, bell peppers, etc.),
or other vegetables, sprouts, etc., rather than with sweet fruits—and, for some, this may be
necessary because of their bodily reaction to sweet fruits.

Further healthful additions to the basic green drink recipe are also possible, such as a spoonful
of ground flaxseed, some chlorella, spirulina, or blue-green algae, or wheatgrass juice, a bit of
lemon juice or lime juice, etc.

It is important to rotate the greens regularly, to avoid micro-accumulation of alkaloids
contained in a single variety of greens, which may over time create toxicity in the body.
Use as wide a variety of greens as possible."

GREEN DRINK

(Vegan. Makes 1 quart.)
Tools: Blender

Ingredients:

2 cups (16 ounces) of any of the following green leafy vegetables: kale, chard, collards, spinach, romaine lettuce, bok choy, and arugula (The greens can also be mixed.)

1 cup of one or a blend of the following fruits: apple, pineapple, papaya, mango, pear, lemon, and berries

2 cups (16 ounces) of purified water

1 Tablespoon of any of the following: ground flaxseed, chlorella, spirulina, blue-green algae, wheatgrass, or lemon or lime juice

Optional ingredients: sprouts (alfalfa, clover, buckwheat, sunflower), herbs (dill, basil, cilantro, mint, parsley), edible weeds (dandelion, lambsquarters, plantain), and aloe vera

Optional additions: "non-sweet fruit vegetables": tomato, cucumber, zucchini, and bell peppers

Steps:

1. Rinse the ingredients before placing them in the blender.
2. Start with 16 ounces of one or more varieties of green leafy vegetable.
3. Add small amounts of one or more fruits (to taste) to make the blended greens more palatable—such as apple, pineapple, banana, papaya, mango, pear, lemon, berries, and so on, but no more than 8 ounces.
4. Add pure water.
5. Blend well. It takes generally about 30 seconds for a high-powered blender. With a lower-powered blender, you may have to blend longer—but do not blend for so long that you heat the drink (or overheat the blender).

Drink as much as you want/need immediately. Any extra can be stored in the refrigerator for 8 hours easily, and even up to 72 hours.

 **THE FARM**

Years active: 1971 to present day
Affiliation: Entheogenic/Polycultural
Founders: Stephen and Ina May Gaskin

SOY "YOGURT" DANISH PASTRY

(Vegan. Makes 3 full-sized Danish.)
Tools: Baking sheet, parchment paper, rolling pin, large and small bowls, cotton kitchen towel
Oven temperature: 375°F

Ingredients:

½ cup soy milk, scalded

1 cup margarine

1 cup unflavored or vanilla soy yogurt

1 teaspoon vanilla extract (reduce to ½ teaspoon if using vanilla soy yogurt)

1 Tablespoon grated lemon peel

1 Tablespoon yeast

½ cup water (room temperature to lukewarm)

2 Tablespoons + ½ cup sugar (separated)

1½ teaspoons salt

5–6 cups flour

Filling:

1 to 2 cups jam, or cooked fresh fruit, or dried fruit and/or nuts

Steps:

1. Preheat oven to 375°F.

2. Scald (using stovetop or microwave) ½ cup of soy milk.

3. Place 1 cup of margarine in large bowl. Pour scalded soy milk over margarine and stir to dissolve. Allow to cool to lukewarm.

4. Beat in 1 cup of soy yogurt, vanilla, and grated lemon peel. Set aside.

5. In small bowl, dissolve yeast in ½ cup of lukewarm water.

6. Add 2 tablespoons of sugar to yeast mixture. Gently stir and let rise in warmth for 10 minutes.

7. Add proofed yeast to soy yogurt mixture in first bowl.

8. Add ½ cup sugar, salt, and 5 cups of flour. Mix until dough comes together and can be worked with hands without sticking to sides of bowl. If dough is wet, add more flour a ½ cup at a time. Mix until kneadable.

Holy Food

9. Knead dough in bowl then cover with cotton cloth and let rise until volume of dough is doubled.

10. When risen, punch down dough. Turn out onto floured surface for robust kneading. Knead until dough is firm yet pliable.

11. Separate dough into 3 sections. By section, roll into rectangle shape approximately 9x12 inches in size and ½ inch thick.

12. Place rolled dough onto parchment-paper-lined baking sheet.

13. Add filling of your choice in a strip down the center third of the dough. Filling suggestions: homemade jam, freshly cooked fruit (cooked to reduce moisture), dried fruit or dried fruit and nut mixture. Can choose instead to sprinkle dough with cinnamon and sugar blend and omit fruit filling.

14. Using sharp paring knife, cut slits in dough approximately 1 inch apart, from the filling out to the edges of the dough.

15. "Braid" the strips of dough by folding each section over the filled middle, alternating sides as you move from top to bottom.

16. Cover with light cotton kitchen towel and let rise until doubled in size.

17. Place into oven and bake 20 to 30 minutes until lightly browned on top.

18. Remove from oven and brush with margarine. (This step can be omitted.)

19. Serve alone or topped with vegan ice cream.

GLUTEN ROAST

Add to 2 cups raw gluten:

½ cup oil
¼ cup soy sauce
1 tsp. salt
½ tsp. garlic powder
1 tsp. onion powder
1/8 tsp. black pepper
½ cup walnuts, peanuts, or almonds, etc.

Grind nuts, and if necessary to mix all the ingredients, grind the gluten in a food grinder. Blend all the ingredients and put in an oiled loaf pan. Cover with equal proportions of oil, soy sauce and water. Bake at 350° for 1 - 1½ hours.

Louise bags a five-pound gluten

GLUTEN BURRITOS

Fry left over roasted gluten in a pan with chopped onions, chopped tomatoes, and a little chili. Fold into large flour tortillas (see page 11).

- 55 -

Louise Hagler, author of *The Farm Cookbook* and gluten model. From *The Farm Cookbook*.

KNISHES

(Vegan. Makes 6 to 8 knishes.)

Tools: Baking sheet, parchment paper, rolling pin, large and small bowls, cotton kitchen towel

Oven temperature: 350°F

Note: This recipe begins with mashed potatoes (no peels). You can peel, boil, and mash a few potatoes for the required one cup or use leftover potatoes, or prepare powdered or flacked "instant" mashed potatoes.

Ingredients for dough:

1 cup mashed potatoes

1 Tablespoon vegetable oil

1 teaspoon salt

3 cups flour

1 Tablespoon baking powder

½ cup cold water

Steps for dough:

1. In a large bowl, combine mashed potatoes, oil, and salt.

2. In a separate bowl, sift flour and baking powder together until thoroughly blended.

3. Add flour mix to potato mixture and mix well.

4. Make a well in the dough mixture and ½ cup of very cold water.

5. Knead dough in bowl until smooth and slightly shiny. Cover bowl with cotton kitchen towel or cloth and rest dough for 30 minutes. (Dough will rise but may not double in size.)

6. While dough is resting, preheat oven to 350°F and prepare filling. See below for 2 filling options.

7. Separate dough into 4 sections.

8. Place 1 sectioned dough piece onto lightly floured rolling surface. Roll dough as thin as possible (¼ inch is ideal).

9. Cut rolled dough into 2x3" rectangles.

10. Place approximately 3–4 tablespoons of filling in center of rectangle.

11. Fold the shorter ends of the filled rectangle toward the center. Then fold the longer ends over each other to totally encase filling.

12. Place onto parchment-lined baking sheet, folded side down.

13. Repeat steps 8 through 12 until all dough is used.

14. Place baking sheets into oven and bake for approximately 30 minutes until golden.

KNISH FILLINGS:

Buckwheat Filling

Ingredients:

3 cups buckwheat groats

4 teaspoons salt

1 teaspoon black pepper

9 cups boiling water

2–3 cups chopped onion

2 cups vegetable oil

Steps:

1. In oven, place groats on parchment-lined baking sheet and roast until browned, approximately 20 to 30 minutes.

2. Remove groats from oven and transfer to large stockpot.

3. Add 9 cups of boiling water, salt, and pepper.

4. Over low-medium heat, cook for approximately 20 minutes until groats are soft. Drain any excess liquid.

5. In a sauté pan, add the oil and warm over medium heat.

6. Add the chopped onions and cook until onions are lightly golden brown in color.

7. Add the sautéed onions and remaining oil to the groat mixture and mix well with large fork.

8. Cool and use for prepared knish dough.

Potato Filling

Ingredients:

1½ cups mashed potatoes

½ cup onions, chopped, sautéed in

¼ cup margarine

½ teaspoon salt

¼ teaspoon pepper

Steps:

1. Add margarine to small frying pan. Warm over medium heat.

2. When margarine is melted, add chopped onions. Sauté until onions are golden.

3. In a large bowl, add mashed potatoes, salt, pepper, and sautéed onions. Mix well.

4. Use as knish filling.

"JANE'S GRINGO POZOLE"

(Vegan. Makes approximately 6 quarts of soup.)

Tools: 2 stockpots, food-grade lime (calcium hydroxide)

Note: This recipe begins with the process of nixtamalization, which requires the use of food-grade lime (calcium hydroxide).

Ingredients and steps for preparing corn:

3 cups dried corn

9 cups water

1 Tablespoon food-grade lime (calcium hydroxide)

Steps to prepare dried corn:

1. Place all ingredients in a large stockpot.

2. Bring to boil. Lightly cover pot and reduce to low boil for 3 hours. Occasionally stir to prevent burning and sticking.

3. Remove from heat and repeatedly rinse until water runs clear. Fully drain and return to cleaned stockpot.

While corn is nixtamalizing, prepare other ingredients.

Ingredients for rest of soup:

3 cups tomato sauce

2 cups water

1 teaspoon dried cumin

½ teaspoon dried oregano

1 teaspoon dried sweet basil

1 teaspoon dried coriander

¼ teaspoon dried thyme

1 Tablespoon sugar

⅛ to ¼ teaspoon dried cayenne pepper (add less to more for level of "heat")

2 jalapeño peppers, diced

1–2 carrots, diced

1–2 stalks celery, diced

1 teaspoon salt

1 clove garlic, minced fine

2 medium onions, sliced and chopped into 1-inch pieces

1 cup chopped greens (collards or cabbage)

2 Tablespoons margarine or vegetable or sunflower oil

Optional: More onions, cut into slices for garnish. Chopped raw
   radish and/or lettuce for additional topping.

Steps:

1. While corn is cooking, in another stockpot, add tomato sauce, water, sugar, and spices.

2. Place lid on stockpot and simmer over low-medium to medium heat for approximately 2 hours.

3. While both pots are simmering, prepare other ingredients. Clean and cut jalapeño peppers, carrots, celery, onions, and greens.

4. In large frying pan, add margarine or oil. Warm oil over medium heat.

5. Add the cut vegetables and salt and garlic to the frying pan. Sauté until vegetables soften.

6. Remove from heat and set aside.

7. When corn is cooked and rinsed, add to stockpot and simmer for 1 hour.

8. Add sautéed vegetables to soup mixture and simmer for final 45 minutes.

BLOODROOT COLLECTIVE

Years active: 1977 to present day
Affiliation: Secular, Radical Lesbian Feminist
Founders: Selma Miriam, Samn Stockwell, Betsey Beavan, Noel Furie, and Pat Shea
Current owners: Selma Miriam and Noel Furie

CHOUCROUTE GARNIE

(Vegan. Makes 6 servings.)
Tools: 2 frying pans

Note from the Bloodroot Kitchen: "Traditional Alsatian sauerkraut is garnished with smoked pork or bacon, sometimes with preserved goose. We have chosen other garnishing and expect you will find sauerkraut cooked in wine and served with potatoes as satisfying a cold-weather meal as we do."

Ingredients:

8 ounces tofu

8 ounces tempeh

½ cup white wine

4 Tablespoons shoyu

32 ounces (2 pounds) fresh sauerkraut

1 cup chopped onions

1 clove garlic, diced (approximately 1 teaspoon)

4 Tablespoons olive or vegetable oil

½ teaspoon crushed juniper berries

½ cup grated white potato

1 cup stale champagne (can substitute white wine)

¾ cup water

1 bay leaf

1 Tablespoon *Kirschwasser* (or any cherry liqueur; can substitute cherry juice)

Steps:

1. The night before, squeeze excess liquid from tofu, wrap in foil and place into freezer. Remove when ready to use and defrost again squeezing out any more excess liquid. Dice and place into a medium-sized bowl. Dice tempeh and add to bowl.

2. Combine ⅓ cup of the white wine and 2 tablespoons of shoyu then pour over tempeh-tofu mix. Mix thoroughly then cover with plastic wrap or pot lid as it marinates.

3. Drain sauerkraut in a large colander in sink. Rinse and drain while squeezing out liquid so kraut is as dry as possible. Set aside to continue draining.

4. Chop onions. Peel and dice garlic. Peel potato.

5. In a large frying pan, add 2 tablespoons of oil and the chopped onions. Over medium-high heat, cook until onions are translucent. Add garlic. Crush juniper berries and add to frying pan.

6. When onions have browned, add in drained sauerkraut, and continue cooking for approximately 3 minutes. While cooking, grate potato into mixture. Turn heat to low.

7. Add 1 cup of champagne (or white wine), water, 2 tablespoons of shoyu, and a bay leaf. Cover and simmer for 1 hour.

8. In another frying pan, heat 2 tablespoons of oil over high heat. Add in the marinated tofu and tempeh. Fry while stirring constantly until browned and crispy. Add to the simmering choucroute. (Include any remaining marinade.)

9. Approximately 5 minutes before choucroute is done simmering, add 1 tablespoon of *Kirschwasser*. Continue cooking for another 5 minutes, then turn off heat.

Serve with boiled parsley potatoes or glazed carrots.

GINGERED PEAR ROLL

(Vegetarian. Makes 1 cake.)
Tools: Jelly roll pan, parchment paper, cotton kitchen towel, stand or hand mixer
Oven temperature: 325°F

Ingredients:
For Filling:
3½ pounds firm Bosc pears
1½ cups unsweetened apple juice
1 teaspoon dried powdered ginger
¼ teaspoon powdered cloves
¼ teaspoon powdered cinnamon
2 Tablespoons lemon juice
1 Tablespoon lemon zest
3 Tablespoons agar agar flakes (can substitute with arrowroot powder or corn starch)
2 Tablespoons maple syrup for sweetening (optional, not needed if pears are very ripe)
For Cake:
6 eggs, room temperature
½ cup pure, unsweetened orange juice
1⅓ cups unbleached all-purpose flour
¼ teaspoon salt
½ cup + 2 Tablespoons honey
1 Tablespoon cream of tartar
carob powder (can be substituted with all-purpose flour)

Steps:

1. Start filling. Peel, core, and dice pears. Put in a pot with apple juice, ginger, cloves, cinnamon, and lemon juice and zest. Cover and simmer ½ hour or until pears are tender.

2. Preheat oven to 325°F.

3. Make cake: Butter jelly roll pan then line with parchment paper. Set aside.

4. Separate eggs and place whites into a medium-sized bowl and yolks into a small bowl.

5. Into another medium bowl, sift flour and salt. Set aside.

6. Using stand or hand mixer, beat egg yolks until thickened and light in color. Add ½ cup honey and the orange juice. Mix well. Set aside.

7. If using a stand mixer, transfer thickened yolk mixture to another bowl. Clean mixer bowl and attachment, then add the egg whites to bowl. (If using hand mixer, wash beaters before using on egg whites.)

8. Add cream of tartar to egg whites and mix until soft peaks form. Add 2 tablespoons of honey, then continue to beat until stiff peaks are formed. Set aside.

9. Fold yolk mixture into flour and gently mix. Fold in stiffened egg white mixture and gently mix until all ingredients are blended.

10. Pour cake batter into prepared jelly roll pan. Bake until cake is light brown in color and springs back when you touch it in the middle, approximately 25 to 35 minutes. (Check it at 20 minutes.) Remove from oven.

11. Lay cotton dish towel on flat counter surface. Sift carob powder lightly onto towel, covering the entire surface. Run a knife blade around the edge of the cake in the pan, then carefully turn cake onto carob-covered towel. Remove the parchment paper. Gently roll cake up into towel. Move to cooling rack.

12. By this time, your pears should be done cooking. Remove from heat and set aside.

13. In a small cup, put 2 tablespoons of apple juice then sprinkle the agar agar flakes over the juice. Set aside.

14. Leaving the pears in the cooking pot, gently mash with a potato masher. Add the agar agar mixture to the pears and simmer again for 5 minutes. Mixture should thicken. If not, repeat the agar agar and apple juice combination. (Can also thicken with either arrowroot or corn starch dissolved in cold apple juice.)

15. When thickened, taste. If too tart, add maple syrup. If too sweet, add 1 tablespoon of lemon juice.

16. On flat counter, carefully unroll cake. Spread the pear mixture evenly over entire cake. Reroll cake. Place in refrigerator to chill for at least 1 hour. Serve with whipped cream or vanilla ice cream.

BEER SOUP WITH SPAETZLE

(Vegetarian. Makes 8 servings.)

Tools: 2 stockpots, stand mixer, baking dish, spaetzle cutter OR colander

Oven temperature: 350°F

Ingredients:

4 large Spanish onions, a total of 3 cups of sliced onion (Spanish onions are a low-moisture, sweeter onion. You can substitute a Vidalia or regular yellow onion.)

6 Tablespoons butter + 3 Tablespoons butter

1 Tablespoon + 1 teaspoon caraway seeds

1 cup chopped celery (including leaves)

¼ cup flour

24 ounces lager-style beer

7 cups water + ¼ cup of water

2 teaspoons crushed garlic

1¼ teaspoons dried thyme

1½ Tablespoons kosher salt

2½ Tablespoons shoyu

2 bay leaves

2½ Tablespoons vinegar

1 Tablespoon miso (optional)

⅛ teaspoon nutmeg

⅛ teaspoon black pepper

1 bunch chopped parsley

8 ounces shredded cheddar cheese

Steps for making soup:

1. Thinly slice onions and set aside.
2. In a large stockpot, add butter and caraway seeds. Over medium-high heat, melt butter then add the onions. Cover and stew for 10 minutes. Stir occasionally.
3. Chop celery and add to stockpot. Continue to cook (with the cover off) for 30 minutes. Add flour and stir thoroughly into mixture.
4. Add beer and water to stockpot then bring to boil. Add garlic, thyme, salt, shoyu, vinegar, and bay leaves. (And miso if desired.) Cover, reduce heat to low medium and simmer for 20 minutes.
5. Make the spaetzle while soup is simmering.

Steps for making spaetzle:

1. Preheat oven to 350°F.
2. Using a stand mixer with paddle attachment, add to bowl flour, eggs, salt, nutmeg, black pepper, and a ¼ cup of water. Beat dough for approximately 10 minutes. (You should hear it "slapping" on side of bowl.

3. In another stockpot, fill with water and bring to boil. Reduce heat to simmer.

4. Using a spaetzle maker or larger-holed colander, position over the simmering water pot. Force the dough through the holes by pressing and moving back and forth. When the pot is filled and the spaetzle cooked in approximately five minutes, use the colander to drain the pot of spaetzle and rinse in cold water.

5. Using a medium frying pan, add 3 tablespoons of butter and under high heat brown the drained spaetzle. When browned, place into baking dish and place in oven to bake for 10 minutes.

6. To serve, place warmed spaetzle in bowls and ladle soup over. Garnish with chopped parsley and grated cheddar cheese.

Front cover of 1984 edition of *The Second Seasonal Political Palate: A Feminist Vegetarian Cookbook.* **Author's collection.**

HOG FARM

Years active: Late 1960s to present day (note that founder Romney considers the Hog Farm as an evolving collective without a specific beginning date)
Affiliation: Secular "hippie" commune
Founder / Leader: Wavy Gravy (Hugh Romney)

HOG FARM GRANOLA BREAKFAST (ROAD HOG CRISPIES)

Tools: Double boiler, small saucepan, large bowl, baking sheet
(Vegetarian. Can be made vegan if honey is substituted with maple or sorghum syrup. Makes 10 to 20 servings, depending on serving size.)
Oven temperature: 250°F

Recipe note: Hog Farm Granola was famously served at Woodstock in August 1969 to the nearly half-million hungry attendees. The recipe can be scaled up to serve a larger-than-expected crowd.

Ingredients:

½ cup millet
½ cup cracked wheat
½ cup buckwheat groats
½ cup wheat germ
½ cup sunflower seeds (without shell)
¼ cup sesame seeds
2 Tablespoons cornmeal
2 cups raw (or rolled) oats
1 cup rye flakes
1 cup dried fruits and/or nuts (Use your favorites or whatever you have on hand. This recipe is very forgiving. You can add either ½ cup each of dried fruit and nuts OR 1 cup of each.)
3 Tablespoons soybean oil (can substitute canola or vegetable oil)
1 cup honey

Steps:

1. Preheat oven to 250°F.
2. Over medium heat, boil the millet in a double boiler for 30 minutes. Stir occasionally to prevent sticking.
3. In a large bowl, mix all the dry ingredients. Add in the cooked millet and mix thoroughly.

4. Over low heat, cook while mixing the soybean oil and honey together until small bubbles appear. Remove from heat and set aside.
5. Spread the cereal in a parchment-lined baking pan. Pour the honey-soybean oil syrup over the grain mix. Toast in oven until lightly browned, approximately 30 minutes. Stir once or twice to ensure even browning. Remove from oven and cool.

To serve: Pour into bowl and eat plain or with milk.

Store leftovers in refrigerator in a covered container.

A note from the Hog Farm cooks: If made in quantity, this fantastically healthy breakfast food will be cheaper than the brand-name cellophane that passes for cereal.

Wavy Gravy (Hugh Romney) with Pigasus, Prime Minister of the Hog Farm Commune and 1968 candidate for President of the United States representing the Yippie Party. Photo by Julian Wasser for *Avant Garde* Magazine, 1968.

THE MOTHERFUCKERS

(The Family/Up Against the Wall Motherfuckers, UAW/MF, Black Mask)

Years active: 1966–1969

Affiliation: Secular/Political/Situationist/Anarchist

Founders / Leaders: Ben Morea & Dan Georgakis

RON'S MOTHERFUCKER BEANS

(Makes 8 servings.)

Tools: Medium stockpot, covered baking dish or Dutch oven

Oven temperature: 325°F

Ingredients:

2 cups dry beans (navy, soldier, pinto, etc.)

8 cups onions, chopped

½ pound piece of salt pork or bacon

¼ cup cider vinegar

12 ounces canned tomato paste

1 cup molasses (blackstrap molasses is sweeter, if using omit honey)

2 Tablespoons kosher salt

2 Tablespoons honey

1 teaspoon Worcestershire sauce

1 teaspoon dry mustard

½ teaspoon cumin

2 teaspoons garlic, mashed

Steps:

1. In a large bowl, cover beans with water and soak overnight. (Do not discard the soaking water.)

2. Place soaked beans in a heavy pot with 2 cups of the onions and the salt pork or bacon and cover with the soaking water.

3. Bring to a boil over medium heat, reduce heat, cover, and simmer until tender. (Add more water if the beans become too dry.) While simmering, preheat oven to 325°F.

4. Place cooked bean mix into a baking dish and add the remaining ingredients.

Cover and bake 2 hours.

5. Uncover and bake another half-hour. Serve as main or side dish.

A tasting note from the Motherfuckers: "Good reheated." All our testers and tasters loved Motherfucker Beans. If you're not a fan of a sweeter-style baked beans, cut the molasses by half and omit the honey.

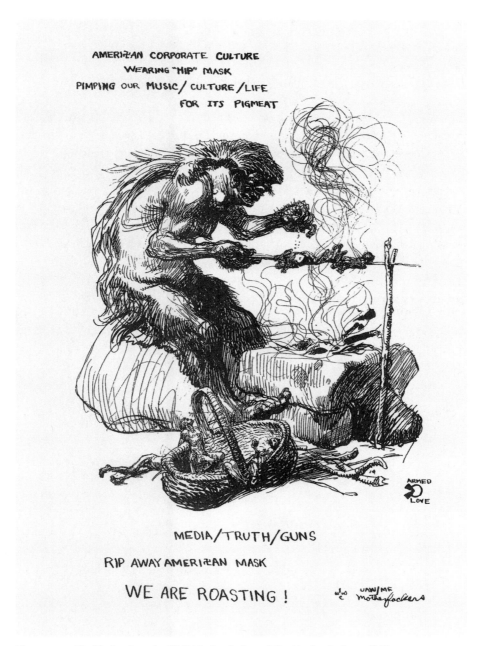

Flyer created by Up Against the Wall Motherfuckers / The Motherfuckers, 1968.

GENTLE WORLD

Years active: 1979 to present day
Affiliation: Animal activism
Founders / Leaders: Light and Sun (Burton Waldbaum and Merle Dunetz)

Gentle World founders met while living with the Children of God group headed by Dave Berg. The Children of God were a high-control, apocalyptic evangelical Christian group that mixed hippie aesthetics with end times prophecy, that abused children. Berg's group went through many iterations but was thrust into the spotlight in the nineties when actor River Phoenix revealed his parents had been members of the group, and he and his siblings spent many years as missionaries in Venezuela. Phoenix's maternal aunt is Merle Dunetz, "Sun," who also left the group and went on to form Gentle World, which is a combination animal rescue and vegan advocacy organization. Phoenix, a committed vegan, often hired his aunt and her group to cater events and parties as a way to spread the message of veganism.

STRING BEAN CHEESE BAKE

(Vegan. Makes 6 servings.)
Tools: Blender, large frying pan, casserole baking dish
Oven temperature: 350°F

Ingredients:
1 pound string beans, cut into bite-sized pieces
2 Tablespoons coconut or vegetable oil
1 cup diced onions
1 cup diced carrots
½ cup diced celery stalk
2 teaspoons + 1 teaspoon diced garlic
2 Tablespoons + 2 Tablespoons tamari
½ teaspoon + ½ teaspoon sea salt
¼ teaspoon + ¼ teaspoon garlic powder
2 to 3 cups vegetable stock or water
⅔ cup nutritional yeast
2 Tablespoons nut butter
¼ cup flour
½ teaspoon paprika
(Can add ½ cup of green peas if desired.)

Holy Food

Steps:

1. Clean and prepare green beans, carrots, onions, garlic, and celery. Set aside.

2. In a medium-sized saucepan, add 2 cups of water. Add the green beans and cook over medium heat for 15 minutes. Remove from heat.

3. Drain green beans, saving the cooking liquid. Set the green beans and pot liquor aside, separately.

4. In a large frying pan, add the oil and warm over medium heat. Add the carrots, celery. 3/4 cup of the onions, and 2 teaspoons of diced garlic, then sauté for approximately 7 minutes.

5. Add 2 tablespoons of tamari, ½ teaspoon of sea salt, and ¼ teaspoon of garlic powder and continue cooking over medium-low heat. Preheat oven to 350°F.

6. While vegetable mixture is cooking, pour reserved green bean cooking liquid, nutritional yeast, ¼ cup of onions, nutritional yeast, nut butter, flour, and the remaining tamari, salt, paprika, and garlic powder into a blender. Blend at high speed until creamy.

7. Remove sautéed mixture from heat and pour into a large bowl. Add the cooked green beans and blended dressing, and mix together.

8. Transfer entire mixture to casserole dish. Sprinkle top with nutritional yeast. Bake for 15 minutes. Serve hot.

CARAWAY PUFFINS

(Vegan. Makes 1 dozen.)

Tools: Blender (regular or immersion), muffin tin

Oven temperature: 400°F

Ingredients:

2⅓ cups whole-wheat flour

2 Tablespoons dry active yeast

2 teaspoons caraway seeds

1 cup soy milk

¼ cup water

2 Tablespoons sorghum syrup (can substitute agave syrup)

1 Tablespoon vegetable oil

1 teaspoon sea salt

1 Tablespoon chopped onion

Steps:

1. Preheat oven to 400°F.

2. In a large bowl, combine the flour, and caraway seeds. Set aside.

3. In a blender, combine the soy milk, sorghum syrup, vegetable oil, salt, and onion. Blend at medium speed for 1 minute until smooth. (If using immersion blender, place the ingredients in a tall blending cup.)

4. Warm water to 115°F in glass or plastic measuring cup. Add yeast and dissolve.

5. Add the blended wet ingredients to the dry ingredients. Add the dissolved yeast. Mix with electric mixer for 3 minutes at high speed or by hand with a large fork.

6. Place dough in an oiled bowl, cover with a light cotton dish towel and allow to rise for 1½ hours.

7. Oil a muffin tin. Divide the dough into 12 equal parts. Fill each muffin cup with batter. Cover and allow to rise for 30 to 45 minutes until doubled in bulk.

8. Bake the muffins for 12 to 15 minutes. Serve hot.

NUT MILK

(Vegan. Makes 1 to 1½ cups.)
Tools: Blender

Ingredients:

¼ cup nut butter

1 cup water

Steps:

1. Put ingredients in blender. Blend at high speed for 30 seconds. (Decrease water to ¾ cup for a thicker nut milk.)

Variations: Use a variety of nut and seed butters for different flavors, like peanut butter, cashew butter, almond butter, sesame tahini butter, sunflower seed butter. You can also add 1 teaspoon of vanilla to mixture while blending for additional flavor.

CAROB BROWNIES

(Vegan. Makes 1 dozen.)
Tools: 8x8 baking pan, parchment paper
Oven temperature: 375°F

Ingredients:

½ cup oil

⅓ cup sorghum syrup (can substitute with agave syrup)

⅓ cup date sugar (can substitute with coconut sugar)

2 Tablespoons soy powder and 4 Tablespoons water, mixed

1 teaspoon vanilla

½ teaspoon sea salt

½ cup carob powder

⅔ cup whole-wheat pastry flour

1 teaspoon baking soda

½ cup mixed nuts

3 Tablespoons soy milk

½ cup raisins, chopped (optional)

Steps:

1. Preheat oven to 375°F.

2. Line baking pan with parchment paper.

3. In a large bowl, add the oil, sweeteners, soy powder mixture, and vanilla. Mix thoroughly.

4. In a separate bowl, combine sea salt, carob powder, flour, baking soda and whisk together. Add nuts and raisins, if desired.

5. Add soy milk and mix well.

6. Pour batter to baking pan and place into oven. Bake for 30 minutes. (Careful not to overbake.) Cut into squares while still warm.

Front cover of 1989 edition of *The Cookbook for People Who Love Animals.* **Author's collection.**

ONE WORLD FAMILY

Years active: 1967 to present day
Affiliation: UFO/New Age
Founder: Allan Michael

HOT CAROB DRINK

(Vegetarian. Makes 4 cups.)
Tools: Large, heavy-bottom saucepan

Ingredients:

4 cups milk (can substitute non-dairy milk)

3 Tablespoons carob powder

4 teaspoons honey

1 teaspoon molasses

Steps:

1. In a heavy-bottom saucepan, add milk, carob powder, honey, and molasses.

2. Over medium-low heat, whisk all ingredients together until fully blended.

3. Adjust heat level if needed to warm mixture until hot, but not boiling. Stir frequently.

4. Serve hot or cold.

MACRO BURGER MIX

(Vegan. Makes 48 small patties.)
Tools: Stockpot, food processor or food mill, jelly roll pan, parchment paper
Oven temperature: 250°F

Ingredients:

5 cups cooked, well-seasoned and drained soybeans (can substitute canned soybeans OR canned black beans)

½ cup soy sauce

4 ounces vegetable or coconut oil

2 Tablespoons cloves garlic, chopped

1 teaspoon chili powder

1 teaspoon cumin

1½ teaspoons dill weed

1 teaspoon dry mustard

¼ teaspoon cayenne

1½ cups toasted rolled oats (toast in oven)

3 cups cooked millet (1 cup dried millet cooked in 2 cups of water)

⅓ cup green bell pepper, chopped fine

½ cup onions, minced

½ cup carrot, grated

1 stalk celery, minced fine

Steps:

1. If using dried beans, soak overnight in a bowl of water. Drain, then cook beans in a stockpot with water to cover and 1 tablespoon of sea salt.

2. Preheat oven to 250°F. Line jelly roll pan with parchment paper and spread oats evenly in pan. Place in oven to bake for approximately 10 minutes, until oats are lightly browned. Remove from oven and set aside.

3. In a large stockpot, cook millet (1 cup of dried millet cooked in 2 cups of water). Bring to boil, then reduce heat to low to simmer approximately 10 minutes. Remove from heat and set aside.

4. If using canned beans, open and drain beans and pour into large bowl. Add the soy sauce, oil, garlic, and spices and mix together.

5. Using a food processor or food mill, puree bean mixture together until mixture is fully blended. Transfer mixture back to large bowl and set aside.

4. Clean vegetables and prepare as noted. Add to bean mixture.

5. Add toasted oats and cooked millet to bean and vegetable mixture and mix until all the ingredients are equally distributed.

6. Shape into patties.

Patties can be sautéed in a frying pan, cooking each side approximately 6 minutes. Can be served on a bun or alone with side dishes.

Patties can be formed and kept refrigerated for up to 4 days. They can also be layered between waxed paper, then put into a freezer bag and kept frozen for up to 3 months.

MOCK TUNA FISH SESAME SPREAD

(Vegan. Makes 2½ cups.)

Tools: Large bowl, food processor or blender

Ingredients:

2 cups sesame meal

3 Tablespoons vegetable oil

1½ Tablespoons garlic, minced fine

2 sprigs parsley, minced

⅛ cup minced carrots

⅛ cup minced bell pepper

⅛ cup minced scallions

⅛ cup minced celery

1½ teaspoons nutritional yeast

1 teaspoon sea salt

4 Tablespoons lemon juice

¼ cup soy sauce

⅛ cup water

¼ cup unflavored yogurt (can substitute an unflavored non-dairy yogurt)

Steps:

1. Clean and prepare garlic, parsley, carrots, bell pepper, scallions, and celery. Place all minced ingredients into a large bowl.

2. Add sesame meal, vegetable oil, nutritional yeast, sea salt, lemon juice, soy sauce, water, and yogurt. Mix all ingredients together in a bowl.

3. In small batches, blend using food processor or standing blender. Return mixture to bowl.

4. Serve as sandwich filling or stuffing for tomatoes.

Notes from *Cosmic Cookery:* Add diced tomatoes and/or soy mayonnaise. Also try adding equal parts of soy mayonnaise and yogurt to moisten.

Front cover of 1974 edition of *One World Family: Cosmic Cookery*. Author's collection.

Holy Food

TRUE LIGHT BEAVERS

Years active: 1969–?

Affiliation: Secular

The True Light Beavers are an example of a secular family commune. They wrote their own biography in their 1972 cookbook, *Feast, A Tribal Cookbook*. This excerpt is pure '70s and gives more insights to the group than any scholarly ethnography.

From Zen basketball team to mountaintop tribe—this is the True Light Beaver Story.

Back in the Summer of '66, when family still meant nuclear, and our heads were into dope, and reclaiming the city streets with flowers, love, and costumes, the True Light Beavers were born, delivered on a back shelf of Moe's Discount Mart. Susan Beaver used to shop at Moe's for old football jerseys, basketball shirts, and the like, finding the beautiful colors and nice slogans ("Courtesy Taxi") just right for decorating body and soul. Her real find was a batch of nine basketball jerseys, white and shiny green, with the words True Light Beavers emblazoned on the front. (The True Light Beavers, we discovered years later, were a defunct Zen Buddhist Basketball team from Chinatown.) We found the name fitting and symbolic of just about everything. Instantly, the shirts were passed out among friends, and True Light Beavers started showing up at sweep-ins, ESSO meetings, psychedelic showcases, be-ins, and finally, at the raising of the Pentagon. When the Pentagon was raised, so were many consciousnesses, and flowers and costumes started being replaced by flags and overalls. A big exodus started taking place: some flower kids took off for Chicago (Yippie!), others for the woods; some dropping out, some digging in.

The True Light Beavers dug in! From a nuclear family of four in New York and three in Boston, the True Light Beavers became seven in the woods of New Hampshire. Brothers and sisters moving together, we became a clan of ignorant Indians, learning, that first year, how much we didn't know. Life-art is where we're at, and that year in New Hampshire meant a lot of life-art dealing with heating a house, making a garden, stringing beads, doing some movies, and a lot of drawing. We grew close in New Hampshire, brothers rediscovering each other, sisters working it out, all of us, with the kids, making it work. We learned a little bit to read the seasons and interpret the messages, we learned a bit that to make the revolutionary alternative first meant getting ourselves together . . . New Hampshire got the clan together, a new order came into being, and we flashed that we were at the beginning of the biggest trip we've ever taken.

CHICKEN MOLE

(Gluten-free. Makes enough sauce for 1 chicken.)

Tools: Stand or immersion blender, medium covered casserole dish

Oven temperature: 350°F

Notes: Modern cooks would be fair to criticize this mole recipe as appropriated and not traditional. Like the pozole recipe used at The Farm (when they maintained a New Mexico commune), communards often adopted and adapted local cuisines to suit their dietary needs. It was also common for people to visit different communes while hitch-hiking throughout the country. There were unwritten rules of hospitality at each commune but knowing how to cook and sharing a good recipe would stand you in good stead with communards. The early-'70s commune dwellers were introduced to food experiences beyond their homogeneous, primarily middle-class, white upbringing. Here's one of the True Light Beavers explaining the origin of this recipe:

"While in Mexico, we frequently went into restaurants for authentic Mexican food. One of the great surprises to me was the color of the food. Accustomed to California-Mexican cooking, I associated it all with red sauce—from tomatoes or red chili. In southern Mexico, the sauces were either green or black. The green sauce is from green tomatoes or green chilies, and the black is from red chili and chocolate. The chocolate sauce is called mole and is delicious."

Ingredients:

1 green chili

1 Tablespoon sesame seeds

2 cloves garlic

1 slice dry toast

¼ cup almonds

¼ teaspoon cinnamon

1 Tablespoon chili powder

¼ teaspoon pepper

1 square unsweetened chocolate

Pinch each powdered cloves and cumin powder

2 cups chicken stock (can substitute with vegetarian chicken stock if using mole on something besides chicken)

1 chicken

Preparation:

To prepare the chicken, either brown in olive oil in a frying pan or boil in water till tender. Set aside. (An easy, modern shortcut is to skip making the chicken and use a rotisserie bird from a local supermarket. Even Whole Foods and local organic stores sell them.)

Steps:

1. Preheat oven to 350°F.

2. In a blender, place all ingredients and puree.

3. Pour blended mixture into a large saucepan. Add chicken stock.

4. Cook over medium heat while stirring until mole is smooth. Remove from heat and set aside.

5. Remove meat from chicken and place into casserole dish. Pour mole over chicken.

6. Place cover on casserole dish and place into oven. Bake for 15 minutes.

7. Remove from oven and serve with rice and tortillas.

TRUE LIGHT BEAVER SWEET AND SOUR BEEF STEW

(Serves at least 12 . . . according to the Beavers.)

Tools: Paper grocery bag, Dutch oven

Tasting note from the True Light Beavers: "Serve on a cold winter day with fresh baked bread. It is deelicious."

Ingredients:

1 cup flour

1 teaspoon salt

⅛ teaspoon pepper

½ teaspoon garlic powder

6 pounds chuck steak or roast, cut in 1-inch cubes

A few Tablespoons vegetable or sunflower oil

1 large head cabbage, cut into eighths

2 bottles ginger ale

2 bottles chili sauce

3 pounds sliced carrots

1 teaspoon ginger, or little more, to taste

Steps:

1. In paper bag, pour and mix flour, salt, pepper, and garlic salt. (Shake to mix.)

2. Cut beef into 1-inch cubes. Add the cubed beef to paper bag and shake until pieces are coated.

3. In a large frying pan, add oil. Brown coated beef cubes under medium-high heat. Drain off excess oil. Place beef into Dutch oven.

4. Clean and cut cabbage into eighths. (Can cut smaller if cabbage is extra large.) Add to Dutch oven.

5. Peel and slice carrots into ½-inch coins. Add to Dutch oven.

6. Add ginger ale, chili sauce, and ginger to the pot.

7. Cook over low heat for 2 hours. Remove from heat.

Serve with boiled or mashed potatoes.

EGGS WOODSTOCK

(Vegetarian. Serves 4.)

Tools: Large skillet or frying pan

Ingredients:

2 Tablespoons butter or oil

1 large onion, sliced into rounds

¼ pound mushrooms, sliced

1 cup sour cream

4 eggs

1 Tablespoon fresh snipped dill or 1
    teaspoon dried dill weed

½ teaspoon paprika

½ teaspoon salt

⅛ teaspoon black pepper

¼ pound cheddar cheese, sliced

Steps:

1. Peel and slice onions. Sauté onions
   in butter or oil in a saucepan for
   5 minutes over medium heat.

2. Add mushrooms and sauté
   another 5 minutes.

3. Add sour cream and lower
   heat. Simmer 5 minutes.

4. Make 4 depressions in the sour
   cream with the back of a spoon.
   Break an egg into each depression. Do not stir; the eggs should sit on top of the sour cream.
   Sprinkle with dill, paprika, salt, and black pepper. Cover pan and allow to steam for 5 minutes.

5. Remove lid and cover with cheese slices. Recover, and let heat of pan melt cheese.

Serve with fresh or toasted bread.

Front cover of 1972 edition of *Feast: A Tribal Cookbook*. Author's collection.

HEAVEN'S GATE

Years active: 1974–1997

Affiliation: UFO/New Age

Founders / Leaders: Marshall Applewhite (Do) and Bonnie Nettles (Ti)

TOMATO VINAIGRETTE SALAD DRESSING

(Serves 4.)

Tools: Large bowl, whisk

Ingredients:

2 Tablespoons minced garlic

1 cup condensed tomato soup

¾ cup distilled white vinegar or cider vinegar

2 teaspoons salt

½ teaspoon ground paprika

½ teaspoon ground black pepper

¼ cup sugar

2 Tablespoons Worcestershire sauce

1½ teaspoons dry mustard

1½ cups vegetable or olive oil

sprinkle of onion powder

Steps:

1. Peel and mince garlic. Place into bowl.

2. Add remaining ingredients.
   Vigorously whisk together.

3. Serve over mixed greens of your choice.

To store, cover and refrigerate.

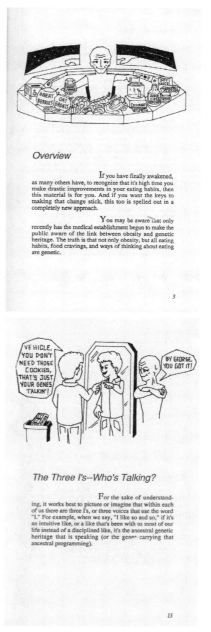

Overview

If you have finally awakened, as many others have, to recognize that it's high time you make drastic improvements in your eating habits, then this material is for you. And if you want the keys to making that change stick, this too is spelled out in a completely new approach.

You may be aware that only recently has the medical establishment begun to make the public aware of the link between obesity and genetic heritage. The truth is that not only obesity, but all eating habits, food cravings, and ways of thinking about eating are genetic.

3

The Three I's--Who's Talking?

For the sake of understanding, it works best to picture or imagine that within each of us there are three I's, or three voices that use the word "I." For example, when we say, "I like so and so," if it's an intuitive like, or a like that's been with us most of our life instead of a disciplined like, it's the ancestral genetic heritage that is speaking (or the genes carrying that ancestral programming).

13

Illustrations from *Transfiguration Diet*.

PASTAFARIAN

Years active: 2005 to present day
Affiliation: Atheist
Founder / Leader: Bobby Henderson

FLYING SPAGHETTI MONSTER HOLY NOODLES/HOLY PASTA RECIPE
(Vegetarian, unless meat sauce is added. Makes a single large batch of pasta.)
Tools: Mixing bowls, stockpot

A note from the Pastafarians: "It is required to serve this dish with meatballs and sauce and this dish can only be made on Fridays, so you don't piss the Flying Spaghetti Monster off. For good luck next week wear an eye patch while eating this dish."

Ingredients:
"Thy holy ingredients"
3 Tablespoons milk
2 cups semolina flour
1 cup white flour
3 eggs
3 teaspoons salt
4 Tablespoons malt powder
1 Tablespoon olive oil
1 teaspoon baking soda/powder
For cooking noodles:
32 ounces light beer
32 ounces of water
2 Tablespoons olive oil
Steps:
1. In a medium-sized bowl, add flours, malt, and 2 eggs. Mix until thoroughly blended.
2. In a separate medium bowl add the salt, 1 egg, baking powder, and milk. Mix until blended.
3. Pour 1 bowl into the other and mix (by hand if necessary) until mixture is thick.
4. Separate dough into smaller dough balls. On a floured surface, roll dough until ¼ inch thick. OR use pasta machine to make long, rectangular pieces.
5. Hand-cut into "noodles" (linguine width of approximately ⅛ inch).

Holy Food

6. Hang noodles on drying rack OR lay on lightly floured cotton towel to air-dry until surface of noodles feels dry. (Note ambient humidity will affect how quickly noodles will dry.)

7. Repeat steps 4 through 6 until all dough is used.

8. While dough is drying, add beer and water into a stockpot.

9. Bring beer mixture to boil under high heat. When liquid is at full, rolling boil, add noodles. Add olive oil.

10. Reduce heat slightly to steady boil and cook noodles for approximately 5 minutes. Stir to prevent noodles from sticking.

11. Drain and serve immediately with sauce of your choice.

Official portrait of the Flying Spaghetti Monster.

THE SATANIC TEMPLE

Years active: 2012 to present day
Affiliation: Atheism
Founder / Leader: Lucien Greaves

PANISSE A.K.A. CHICKPEA FRIES

(Vegetarian. Makes 4 servings.)
Tools: Blender, large saucepan, large frying pan, plastic wrap, Bible

Note: Chef Adam, who teaches cooking at the Satanic Temple, provided this recipe. No changes or edits have been made to his very detailed instructions. The style provides insights into how members of the Satanic Temple successfully use a combination of humor and absurdity to advocate for their belief in individual rights for everyone.

Ingredients:
2 cups onion, diced
¼ cup garlic, minced
1 quart + 1 cup of milk (can substitute soy or unflavored nut milk)
24 ounces sifted chickpea flour
1 Tablespoon ground fennel seed
1 Tablespoon ground cumin seed
¼ teaspoon of fennel pollen
¼ teaspoon of maras pepper (a dried and ground Turkish red pepper)
1 cup ground cooked chickpeas
¼ cup chopped parsley, cilantro, and thyme
2 Tablespoons butter
salt to taste
vegetable oil, for frying
1 Bible page

Steps:
1. In order to make this super satanic Saturday night main event dish, you are going to have to head to your grocery store and purchase the above ingredients.
2. When you come home and are ready to start, take a page from a bible and light it on fire. Hopefully, this dish will summon up magical Goetia demons. Or you could just make a super awesome dish, fry them, mix some chipotle in with some mayo and sit on the couch eating these like a slob. That's what I would do.

3. Take your store-bought or freshly cooked chickpeas in a blender and blend till smooth.
4. Melt your butter in a saucepan.
5. Add your onions, garlic, and dry herbs. Cook all the ingredients until the onions are translucent. Next, slowly pour your milk into this fine witches' brew and let it come to a simmer.
6. Place in your cauldron the chickpea flour using a thick-toothed whisk and slowly incorporate it into the mixture. Once that is done, using a wooden spoon churn the pot.
7. You must cook the chickpea flour in the milk for several minutes without scorching the bottom of your pan. I would recommend doing this on a lower setting. Chickpea flour if it is not cooked thoroughly can taste bitter. The batter should be thick and easy to put into a dish. At the end once you have shut off the heat add your herbs, salt, and place into the preferred method to complete this ritual.
8. Take plastic wrap and cover the bottom of a small shallow baking dish. Spray the plastic wrap with nonstick panspray evenly all around. Pour your batter inside. The baking dish should be small enough that you have at least ½ an inch of batter on the bottom. Cool it in a fridge for several hours till it is firm and most of the moisture has released from the panisse.
9. Cut into small squares and put them aside.
10. Bring some cooking oil to a temperature of 350°F, fry your panisse till it is golden brown and crispy. Depending on how many small squares your recipe yields you can use the extras as a delicious treat or even serve at parties with a dipping sauce of your choice.

Probably something really cool to serve with a vegetarian soup or an alternative to proteins in a salad! Shemhamforash!

A Devil's Dinner, 2018. Courtesy of The Satanic Temple.

Marijuana leaf found by author in pages of used copy of *Golden Temple Cookbook*.

Holy Food

SELECTED BIBLIOGRAPHY

Ardell, Donald B. *High Level Wellness: An Alternative to Doctors, Drugs, and Disease*. Emmaus: Rodale Press, 1977

Bainbridge, William Sims. *The Sociology of Religious Movements*. New York and London: Routledge, 1997

Bauer, Cheryl, and Rob Portman. *Wisdom's Paradise: The Forgotten Shakers of Union Village*. Wilmington, OH: Orange Frazer Press, 2004

Belasco, Warren J. *Appetite for Change: How the Counterculture Took on the Food Industry*. Ithaca and London: Cornell University Press, 2007

Bell, Rudolph M. *Holy Anorexia*. Chicago: University of Chicago Press, 1987

Burton, Tara Isabella. *Strange Rites: New Religions for a Godless World*. New York: Public Affairs, 2020

Bynum, Caroline Walker. *Holy Feast and Holy Fast: The Religious Significance of Food to Medieval Women*. Berkeley: University of California Press, 1987

Cargill, Kima, ed. *Food Cults: How Fads, Dogma, and Doctrine Influence Diet*. Lanham: Rowman & Littlefield, 2017

Chireau, Yvonne P. *Black Magic: Religion and the African American Conjuring Tradition*. Berkeley and Los Angeles: University of California Press, 2006

Cope, Suzanne. *Power Hungry: Women of the Black Panther Party and Freedom Summer and Their Fight to Feed a Movement*. Chicago: Lawrence Hill Books, 2021

Cox, Harvey. *The Feast of Fools*. Cambridge: Harvard University Press, 1972

Dorman, Jacob S. *Chosen People: The Rise of American Black Israelite Religions*. Oxford: Oxford University Press, 2016

Dorman, Jacob S. *The Princess and the Prophet: The Secret History of Magic, Race, and Black Muslims in America*. Boston: Beacon Press, 2020

Ehret, Arnold. *Rational Fasting: A Scientific Method of Fasting Your Way to Health*. New York: Benedict Lust Publications, 1971

Elmen, Paul. *Wheat Flour Messiah: Eric Jansson of Bishop Hill*. Carbondale and Edwardsville: Southern Illinois University Press, 1976

Fieldhouse, Paul. *Food, Feasts, and Faith: An Encyclopedia of Food Cultures in World Religions*, Volumes 1 and 2. Santa Barbara, CA: ABC-CLIO, 2017

Finley, Stephen C., Editor, Margarita Simon Guillory, Jr., and Hugh R. Page. *Esotericism in African American Religious Experience: There Is a Mystery*. Leiden, Netherlands: Brill Academic Publishers, 2014

Finley, Stephen C. *In & Out of This World: Material and Extraterrestrial Bodies in the Nation of Islam*. Durham & London: Duke University Press, 2022

Fogarty, Robert S. *Dictionary of American Communal and Utopian History*, Westport: Greenwood Press, 1980

Friedenreich, David M. *Foreigners and Their Food: Constructing Otherness in Jewish, Christian, and Islamic Law*. Berkeley and Los Angeles: University of California Press, 2011

Friedman, Benjamin M. *Religion and the Rise of Capitalism*. New York: Knopf Publishing, 2022

Hanh, Thich Nhat. *How to Eat*. Berkeley: Parallax Press, 2014

Hine, Robert V. *California's Utopian Colonies*. Berkeley and Los Angeles: University of California Press, 1983

Ingram, Matthew. *Retreat: How the Counterculture Invented Wellness*. London: Repeater Books, 2020

Jackson, Holly. *American Radicals: How Nineteenth-Century Protest Shaped the Nation*. New York: Crown, 2019

Kauffman, Jonathan. *Hippie Food: How Back-to-the-Landers, Longhairs, and Revolutionaries Changed the Way We Eat*. New York: HarperCollins Publishers, 2018

Kennedy, Gordon. *Children of the Sun*. Mecca, CA: Nivaria Press, 1998

Madden, Etta M., Martha L. Finch, eds. *Eating in Eden: Food and American Utopias*. Lincoln and London: University of Nebraska Press, 2006

Martin, Walter. *The Kingdom of the Cults*. Bloomington, MN: Bethany House Publishers, 2019

Mikul, Chris. *The Cult Files: True Stories from the Extreme Religious Belief*. New York: Metro Books, 2009

Miller, Timothy. *The 60s Communes: Hippies and Beyond*. Syracuse: Syracuse University Press, 1999

Millner, Lyn. *The Allure of Immortality: An American Cult, a Florida Swamp, and a Renegade Prophet*. Gainesville, FL: The University of Florida Press, 2015

Morris, Adam. *American Messiahs: False Prophets of a Damned Nation*. New York: Liveright Publishing Corporation, 2019

Perez, Elizabeth. *Religion in the Kitchen: Cooking, Talking, and the Making of Black Atlantic Traditions*. New York and London: New York University Press, 2016

Seeman, Erik R. *Speaking with the Dead in Early America*. Philadelphia: University of Pennsylvania Press, 2019

Seldes, Gilbert. *The Stammering Century*. New York: New York Review of Books Classics, 2012

Smith, Timothy L. *Revivalism & Social Reform: American Protestantism on the Eve of the Civil War*. Baltimore and London: Johns Hopkins University Press, 1980

Stevens, Errol Wayne. *In Pursuit of Utopia: Los Angeles in the Great Depression*. Norman, OK: Oklahoma University Press, 2021

Subin, Anna Della. *Accidental Gods: On Men Unwittingly Turned Divine*. New York: Metropolitan Books, 2021

Sutton, Matthew Avery. *American Apocalypse: A History of Modern Evangelicalism*. Cambridge: Belknap Press, an imprint of Harvard University Press, 2017

Sutton, Robert P. *Heartland Utopias*. Dekalb, IL: Northern Illinois University Press, 2009

Veit, Helen Zoe. *Modern Food, Moral Food: Self-Control, Science, and the Rise of Modern American Eating in the Early Twentieth Century*. Chapel Hill: University of North Carolina Press, 2013

Watt, Jill God. *Harlem U.S.A.: The Father Divine Story*. Berkeley and Los Angeles: University of California Press, 1992

Weisenfeld, Judith. *New World A-Coming: Black Religion and Racial Identity during the Great Migration*. New York: New York University Press, 2016

Whalen, William J. *Minority Religions in America*. Staten Island: Alba House (A Division of the Society of St. Paul), 1972

Wirzba, Norman. *Food and Faith: A Theology of Eating* (2nd edition). Cambridge, UK: Cambridge University Press, 2019

Zafar, Rafia. *Recipes for Respect: African American Meals and Meaning*. Athens: University of Georgia Press, 2019

Zeller, Benjamin E., Marie W. Dallam, Reid L. Neilson, Nora L. Rubel, eds. *Religion, Food, & Eating in North America*. New York: Columbia University Press, 2014

COOKBOOKS AND TEXTS FROM CULTS, COMMUNES, AND RELIGIOUS MOVEMENTS

Acciardo, Marcia Madhuri. *Light Eating for Survival*. Fairfield, IA: 21st Century Publications, 1978

Ali, Delores, and Sharon Ali. *Cooking with Sister Delores Ali: Basic Cooking Manual, Volume 1*, self-published, 2019

Anderberg, Kirsten. *Liberation and Other Source Family Teachings*, self-published, 2013

Bates, Albert. *The Post-Petroleum Survival Guide and* Cookbook. Gabriola Island, BC: New Society Publishers, 2006

Ben Moshe, Arron (C. Edward Miller). *The Diet of Black Hebrew Israelites in the Americas*, self-published, 2019

Bhajan, Yogi. *The Golden Temple Vegetarian Cookbook*. New York: Hawthorn Books, 1978

Bloodroot Collective (The). *The Second Seasonal Political Palate: A Feminist Vegetarian Cookbook.* Bridgeport, CT: Sanguinaria Publishing, 1984

Brown, Edward Espe. *Tassajara Cooking*. Berkeley: Shambhala Publications, Inc., 1973

Calkins, Fern. *It's Your World Vegetarian Cookbook*. Washington, D.C.: Review and Herald Publishing Association, 1973

Carr, Sister Frances A. *Shaker Your Plate: Of Shaker Cooks and Cooking.* Sabbathday Lake, ME: United Society of Shakers, 1985

Clymer, R. Swinburne *Diet: A Key to Health, The Selection and Combination of Foods for the Prevention or Cure of Disease*. Quakertown, PA: Humanitarian Publishing Company, 1930 and 1983 (revised edition)

Crumb, Dana, and Sherry Cohen. *Eat It: A Cookbook*. San Francisco: Bellerophon Books, 1972

Dasi, Krsna Devi, and Sama Devi Dasi. *The Hare Krsna Cook Book: Recipes for the Satisfaction of the Supreme Personality of the Godhead*. New York: The Bhaktivedanta Book Trust, 1973

Devi, Yamuna. *Lord Krishna's Cuisine: The Art of Indian Vegetarian Cooking*. Boulder: Bala Books and New York: Dutton Books, 1987

Drutakarma dasa, Goswami, Mukunda, Bhutatama dasa, Bhadra dasa, Nirakula dasa, eds. *The Higher Taste: A Guide to Gourmet Vegetarian Cooking and a Karma-Free Diet,* Los Angeles: The Bhaktivedanta Book Trust, 1983 edition and 2002 edition

Duquette, Susan. *Sunburst Farm Family Cookbook: Good Home Cookin' the Natural Way*. Santa Barbara, CA: Woodbridge Press Publishing Company, 1978

Fraternitas Rosae Crucis. *Cookbook*. Quakertown, PA: Philosophical Publishing Company, year unknown

Gentle World. *The Cookbook for People Who Love Animals*. Umatilla, FL: 1989, fifth edition

Hagler, Louise, ed. *The Farm Vegetarian Cookbook with an Introduction by Stephen*. Summertown: The Book Publishing Company, 1975

Ha'nish, Otoman Zar-Adusht (Otto Haenisch). *Mazdaznan Science of Dietetics*. London: The British Mazdaznan Association, 1950

Hannaford, Kathryn. *One World Family: Cosmic Cookery*. Stockton, CA: Starmast Publications, 1974

Horton, Lucy. *Country Commune Cooking*. New York: Coward, McCann & Geoghegan, Inc., 1972

Hurd, Frank J., and Rosalie. *A Good Cook...Ten Talents*. Chisholm, MN: self-published, 1968

Jardine, Winnifred C. *Mormon Country Cooking*. Salt Lake City: Bookcraft, 1983

Ladies Auxiliary of the Homestead Welfare Club (The). *A Collection of Traditional Amana Colony Recipes: Family-size Recipes of the Foods Prepared and Served in the Amana Villages for Over a Century.* Homestead, IA: Homestead Welfare Club, 1948

Levitt, Jo Ann, Linda Smith, and Christine Warren. *Kripalu Kitchen: A Natural Foods Cookbook & Nutritional Guide*. Lenox, MA: Kripalu Yoga Retreat Publications, 1980

Littlegreen Inc.'s Think Tank, *Transfiguration Diet*. Mesa, AZ: Littlegreen, 1986

Muhammad, Elijah. *How to Eat to Live: Book One*. Phoenix: Secretarius MEMPS Ministries, 1997 edition

Muhammad, Rasheed. *The Original Muslim Cookbook, Vol. 1: A Return to Life and Health*, self-published, 2015

Murphet, Howard. *Sai Baba Avatar: A New Journey into Power and Glory*. San Diego: Birth Day Publishing Company, 1977

Rosen, Steven. *Diet for Transcendence*. Badger, CA: Torchlight Publishing, 1997

Rosicrucian Fellowship (The). *New Age Cookbook*. Oceanside, CA: The Rosicrucian Fellowship, 1968

Samraj, Adi Da (Adi Da). *The Yoga of Right Diet: An Intelligent Approach to Dietary Practice That Supports Communion with the Living Divine Reality*. Middletown, CA: The Dawn Horse Press, 2006

Samraj, Ruchira Avatar Adi Da (Adi Da). *Green Gorilla: The Searchless Raw Diet*. Middletown, CA: The Dawn Horse Press, 2008

Shurtleff, William, and Akiko Aoyagi. *History of Seventh-Day Advent Work with Soyfoods, Vegetarianism, Meat Alternatives, Wheat Gluten, Dietary Fiber and Peanut Butter (1863–2013)*. Lafayette, CA: The Soyinfo Center, 2014

Swami Premdharma, Ma Dhyan Yogini, eds. *Zorba the Buddha: Rajneesh Cookbook*. Rajneeshpuram, OR: Rajneesh Neo-Sannyas International Commune, 1984

Telesco, Patricia, ed. *Cakes and Ale for the Pagan Soul: Spells, Recipes, and Reflections from Neopagan Elders and Teachers*. Berkeley: The Crossing Press, 2005

True Light Beavers (The). *Feast: A Tribal Cookbook*. Garden City and New York: Doubleday & Company, Inc., 1972

Understanding, Supreme, and Patra Afrika. *A Taste of Life: 1,000 Vegetarian Recipes from Around the World*. Atlanta: Supreme Design Publishing, 2011

Willett, Mo. *Vegetarian Gothic*. Harrisburg, PA: Stackpole Books, 1975

PAPERS

Andrews, Pamela M. "Ain't No Spook God: Religiosity in the Nations of Gods and Earths," Master's thesis presented to Memorial University of Newfoundland, 2013

Barnes, Roma Penelope. "Blessings Flowing Free: The Father Divine Peace Mission Movement in Harlem, New York City, 1932–1941," Dissertation submitted to the University of York, Department of History, for the Degree of Doctor of Philosophy, January 1979

Barstow, Geoffrey Francis. "Food of Sinful Demons: A History of Vegetarianism in Tibet," Dissertation presented to the Graduate Faculty of the University of Virginia in Candidacy for the Degree of Doctor of Philosophy, 2013

Dick, Jennifer. "Tea and the Hidden History of Islam," Master's thesis presented to the University of Florida, 2010

Easterling, Paul H.L. "The Moorish Science Temple of America: A Study Exploring the Foundations of African American Islamic Thought and Culture," Doctoral thesis presented to Rice University, 2012

Finke, Roger, and Rodney Stark. "Turning Pews Into People: Estimating 19th Century Church Membership," *Journal for the Scientific Study of Religion*, 1986

Krug, Howard P. "Charles Finney and Willam Miller: Revivalists, Reformers, and Millennialists Looking Downward and Upward," Master's thesis presented to The College at Brockport, 2008

Morley, Gabriel Patrick. "Tripping With Stephen Gaskin: An Exploration of a Hippy Adult Educator," Dissertation presented to the University of Southern Mississippi, 2012

ARTICLES

Bowman, Patrick D. "Abdul Hamid Suleiman and the Origins of the Moorish Science Temple," *Journal of Race, Ethnicity, and Religion*, Volume 2, Issue 13, 2011

Cusack, Carole. "Apocalypse in Early UFO and Alien-Based Religions: Christian and Theosophical Themes," unpublished chapter of future work, January 2015

Finley, Lana. "Paschal Beverly Randolph in the African American Community," *Esotericism in African American Religious Experience: There Is a Mystery ...*, Leiden, Netherlands: Brill, 2014.

Friedenwald, Julius, and Samuel Morrison. "The History of the Enema with some Notes on Related Procedures (Part 1)," *Bulletin of the History of Medicine*, Vol. 8, No. 1 (January, 1940), pp. 68–114, The Johns Hopkins University Press

Harper, Lillian, and Arna Bontemps. "Early Studies in Black Nationalism, Cults and Churches in Chicago," Works Progress Administration, 1941

Hartman, Stephanie. "The Political Palate: Reading Commune Cookbooks," *Gastronomica*, Vol. 3, No. 2 (Spring 2003), pp. 29–40, University of California Press

Johnson, Matthew W. "Consciousness, Religion, and Gurus: Pitfalls of Psychedelic Medicine," *ACS Pharmacology & Translational Science*, 2021, 4, pp. 578–581

Jordan, Ryan P. "Race and Religion in the United States," *Oxford Research Encyclopedia of Religion*, 2016

Key, Andre E. "Toward a Typology of Black Hebrew Thought and Practice," *Journal of Africana Religions*, Volume 2, Number 1, 2014, pp. 31–66

Winiarski, Douglas L. "Seized by the Jerks: Shakers, Spirit Possession, and the Great Revival," *The William and Mary Quarterly*, Vol. 76, No. 1 (January 2019), pp. 111–150

NARRATIVE INDEX

Holy Food

RECIPE INDEX

ACKNOWLEDGEMENTS

Recipe Testers

Special thanks to all who volunteered to test recipes. Our testing procedure ensured that each recipe was attempted by experienced food industry professionals and home-cooks with less experience. Thank you! Jana Braam, Kiersten M. Cira, Erica Hernandez, Leica Jacobs, Jen B. Larson, Desiree Pointer Mace, Petra Orlowski, Jessica Parfrey, Ellie Piper, Jenny Plevin, Cameryne Roberts, Jolene Siana, and Monica Thomas.

Personal Thanks

Numerous people have knowingly—and unknowingly—provided help and support during the five years it has taken to bring *Holy Food* from obsession to the book you hold in your hands. These are the kind people to whom I am indebted.

To my Feral House family, thanks is never enough. Jessica Parfrey who generously supports my work with love and patience. Laura Smith is more than a copy editor; she is a collaborator. (Any errors within are because I didn't take her advice.) Ron Kretsch also exceeds his title of book designer. His aesthetic and skills are equally matched by his good humor and arcane knowledge. And everyone should have the opportunity to experience pep talks from Martin Olson.

Thank you to Dr. Christopher Stewart, archivist for Father Divine's Peace Mission for answering many questions and providing access to the Mission's archives. Thank you to Amy Waldman for walking me through the Jewish holy books. Thank you to Mike Cartmell and Mike Touchette for speaking to me at length about their respective experiences with Jim Jones and the Peoples Temple. Thank you to Peter Simon for his valuable insights into Prabhupada's thoughts about food and the theological importance of food and food preparation within the ISKCON community. Thank you to Lucy Horton, author of *Country Commune Cooking.* Her 1972 book was an important catalyst for my research. So too was Jonathan Kauffman's *Hippie Food,* and Jonathan himself who encouraged me to pursue this project. Thank you, Jonathan. Thank you to Adam Chandler and Dr. Julia Skinner for their kind words and endorsement.

My dear friend Tod Davies provided developmental editorial guidance at a critical juncture. She asked all the right questions and gave me the unvarnished framework I needed to get out of my head. Desiree Pointer Mace slogged through early drafts giving important feedback wrapped in gentle support. I'm eternally grateful to Martin Billheimer for numerous late-night conversations about theories and convergences in American politics, socio-economics, and religion. My most important insights came out of those conversations. A no-less-special thanks to Sally Timms for putting up with our often nonsensical rambling.

None of my work would be possible without the support of my husband Dan Niedziejko. I could fill pages with evidence of his assistance but will spare readers. Instead help me thank him by listening to his band Sleepersound. (Find them on Bandcamp.)

It's common for an author to forget to thank someone. I know I've forgotten who mentioned their sister was in a commune or that they grew up in a cult (more folks than you might think)—please consider yourself thanked!